THE U

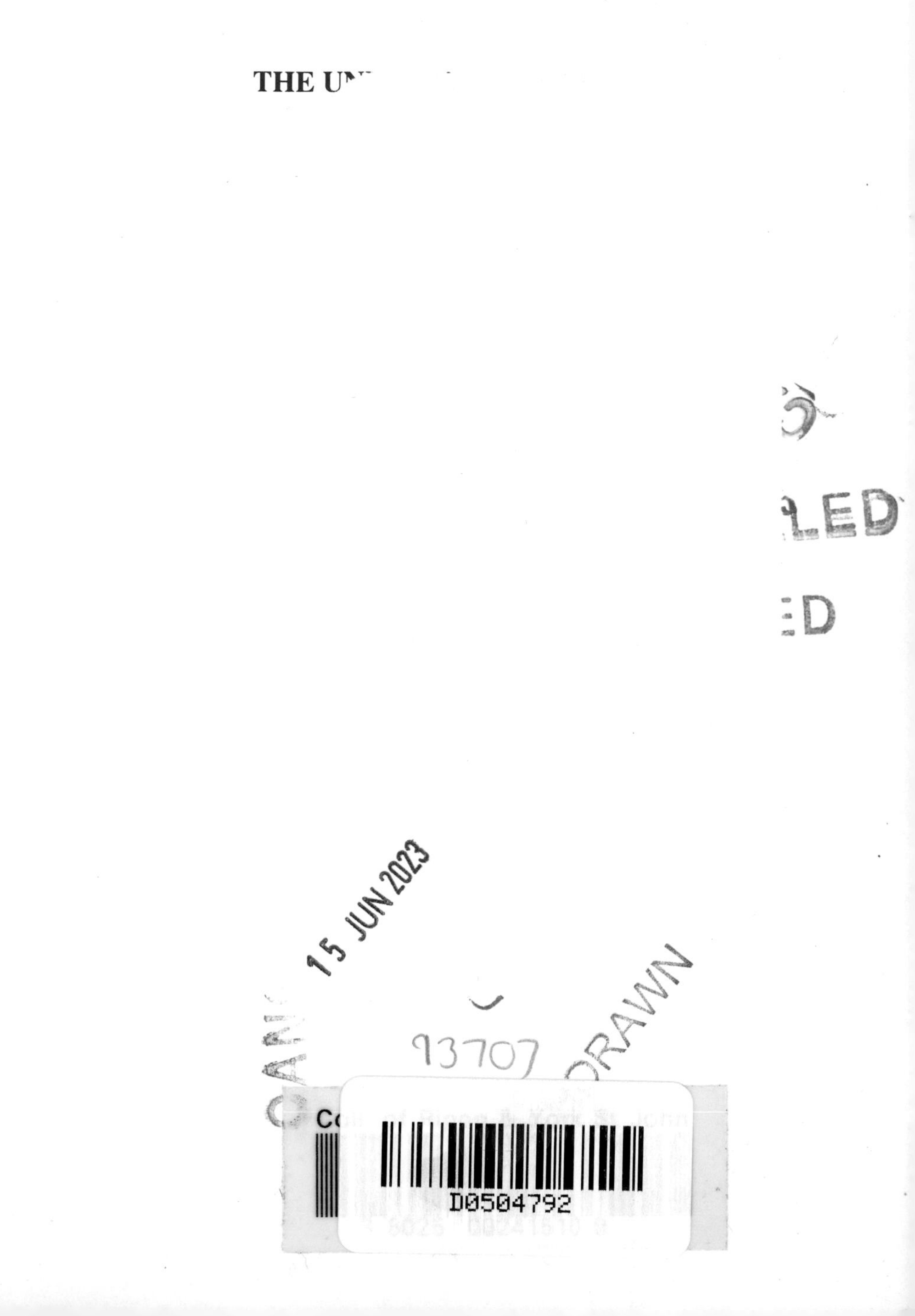

A History of the Jews in Britain since 1858

V.D. Lipman

Leicester University Press
(a division of Pinter Publishers Ltd)
Leicester, London

First published in Great Britain in 1990 by Leicester University Press
(a division of Pinter Publishers Ltd)

Editorial offices
Fielding Johnson Building, University of Leicester,
University Road, Leicester, LE1 7RH

Trade and other enquiries
25 Floral Street, London, WC2E 9DS

British Library Cataloguing in Publication Data
A CIP cataloguing record for this book is available
from the British Library
ISBN 0-7185-1336-3 hardcovers
ISBN 0-7185-1339-8 paperback

Typeset by GCS, Leighton Buzzard, Beds.
Printed and bound in Great Britain by Biddles Ltd.

Contents

In Memory of
Sonia
Partner in
Life and Work

Preface

Cecil Roth's *History of the Jews in England* remains a classic achievement in comprehensiveness and style, although there has been considerable research published since the last edition appeared in 1964. But the book, in effect, stops at 1858, with the granting to Jews of the right to sit in the House of Commons, which he regarded as the coping-stone of Jewish civic emancipation. There is no book which carries the story through into the twentieth century on the same scale as Roth's work. Yet such a book is urgently needed for at least three reasons. First, there is an increasing interest among non-Jews about the Jewish community in Britain and how it came to take the form it has today. Second, there have been numerous books, articles and conference papers on Anglo-Jewry since 1858, particularly on the period between 1881 and 1914 when the size of the community was quadrupled by immigration from Eastern Europe. The time has come when the results of these studies should be combined into a single work, covering the period from 1858 to at least the outbreak of war in 1939. This - a development which would have greatly pleased Cecil Roth - the history of the Jews in England has in recent years become a course of study undertaken by undergraduates, both as internal students and as part-time students working for the new degree in Jewish History of London University; and there is a growing interest among other adult students in Anglo-Jewish history as in other aspects of modern Jewish history. For all such students, Roth's *History*, with updating in study and lectures, can still provide a basic textbook; but they need a readily accessible work to help them study the very important period after 1858.

This book is intended to meet these three needs. It is not a simple continuation of Roth's work, although it is a sequel to it. The scale of the community has become so much greater since 1858, and its character so much more complex, that it requires different treatment, at least in a book of moderate length. Nor is it possible, or perhaps necessary, to provide a catalogue of how British Jews have contributed to British life and society in its various aspects. This book is planned as a study of the development of the Jewish community and of groups within the community, rather than of the careers of individuals. There is therefore little biographical detail in the main text and individuals are mentioned only if they are of key significance in influencing the development of events or as examples of a general trend. However, to meet the need for some background on individuals mentioned in the text, there is a biographical appendix which gives basic details about some of them. This is limited to members of the Anglo-Jewish community and therefore excludes British Jews who were converted (eg Disraeli) or Jews who were not normally resident in this country or were world figures (eg Herzl, Weizmann). Dates of birth and death are given in the text for a number of Jewish individuals not included in the Biographical Appendix.

The three needs previously mentioned have been borne in mind in writing this book. First it is aimed at the intelligent and interested general reader, as well as at students. The Jewish background to Anglo-Jewish developments is therefore explained, in what some may regard as elementary form, and, in addition to a glossary, Hebrew or Yiddish terms are generally explained in the text when they first appear.

Second, an attempt has been made to use recent writing on Anglo-Jewish history although, as several important works have appeared in 1988 or since, it has been possible to use these only to a limited extent.

Third, the book has been kept to a manageable length by concentrating on the period from 1858 to 1939. Two chapters, however, go beyond these limits. Chapter 1 gives a brief introduction to bring the reader up to 1858 and to explain why that date was important for Anglo-Jewry. Chapter 10 gives a prospect from 1939 of the next fifty years. The object is to compare the situation of Anglo-Jewry as it appeared in 1939 with what seemed to be the situation in 1989 and to suggest possible reasons for the changes.

In order not to overload the book with lengthy references, I have kept references in the notes so far as possible to works which themselves give sources and further references. I have normally limited the citation of archival sources to cases where I have consulted those sources for this book and the sources are not given in books or articles already published by myself or others. Again, with the object of helping students and others to follow up further reading, I have substituted for the usual undifferentiated list of all works cited a bibliographical note which discusses the main relevant works under a number of headings.

Because of the difference of character of chapters 1 and 10 from the rest of the book, I have not provided these with detailed reference notes but have appended to each chapter a note on relevant sources.

It is unfortunately impossible for me to thank everyone from whom I have learned or who has helped me in the preparation of this book because this would include all those who have contributed to my writing on Anglo-Jewish history over the past nearly forty years (my first paper was given in 1951), and because so much of this book is the result of earlier research. But I must express my gratitude to Dr David Latchman and to Mr Aumie and Mr Michael Shapiro for their very generous help in providing the majority of the illustrations. I have indicated some other debts for help in the reference notes. Quotations from Crown-copyright records in the Public Record

Office appear by permission of the Controller of Her Majesty's Stationery Office. I am grateful to my friend, Professor Aubrey Newman, himself a professional historian of distinction in both English and Jewish history, for introducing me to Leicester University Press, and all associated with that Press for courtesy and help - notably, in order of my meeting them, Dr Iain Stevenson, Alec McAulay, the Publisher, Patrick Armstrong and Sara Wilbourne.

I cannot close this preface without mentioning one who urged me to write this book and had begun, as so often in the past, to add to my knowledge and clarify my style. It has been a poignant experience in assembling the text to find the corrections in her handwriting on the early chapters and to reflect how much better a book it would have been had she been spared to complete it with me.

V D Lipman
1 January 1990.

Explanatory Notes

References

Full details of author, title, date of publication or volume number in the case of periodicals are given the first time a book or article is mentioned in a chapter; thereafter in that chapter only an abbreviated name of author and title are used.

The place of publication of books, unless otherwise stated, is London.

Abbreviations

CZA	Central Zionist Archives, Jerusalem
DNB	*Dictionary of National Biography*
EJ	*Encyclopaedia Judaica* (1972, Jerusalem)
JC	*Jewish Chronicle*
JE	*Jewish Encyclopaedia* (New York, 1902–6)
JJS	*Jewish Journal of Sociology*
JSS	*Jewish Social Studies*
MJHSE	*Miscellanies* of the Jewish Historical Society of England
PRO	Public Record Office, London
TJHSE	*Transactions* of the Jewish Historical Society of England

Biographical Appendix

Names of persons included in the Appendix are marked by an asterisk the first time the name occurs in each chapter.

Bibliographical Notes

This summary covers sources for the main period of the book, 1858–1939. Notes on sources for the period up to 1858 and from 1939 to 1989 are appended to chapters 1 and 10 respectively.

General Works

V.D. Lipman, *Social History of the Jews in England 1850–1950*, 1954 covers the whole period but gives only an outline after 1914. It was also written before virtually any of the recent studies, and some of the detail (eg population figures for provincial communities) now needs correction. Harold Pollins, *Economic History of the Jews in England*, London and Toronto, 1982 is a detailed survey and includes allied material eg on Jewish trade unions. Geoffrey Alderman, *The Jewish Community in British Politics*, Oxford, 1983 contains much important material, although the author's views on the existence of a Jewish vote are controversial.

The 1881–1914 Immigration

Lloyd P. Gartner, *The Jewish Immigrant in England 1870–1914*, 2nd edn, 1976 remains the major comprehensive work, covering social, religious and economic aspects. It has an introduction which lists relevant studies published between the first edition (1960) and 1976. John A. Garrard, *The English and Immigration 1880–1910*, 1971 deals with the origins of the 1905 Aliens Act and its repercussions, with special attention to the political left. Bernard Gainer, *The Alien Invasion: Origins of the Aliens Act of 1905*, 1972 covers similar ground and examines the passage of the legislation in depth; it analyses tensions between the immigrants and other residents of the East End of London, identifying these as being concerned more with housing and education than employment. Eugene C. Black, *The Social Politics of Anglo-Jewry 1880–1920*, Oxford, 1988 begins by examining the leading personalities and institutions of the older Anglo-Jewry responsible for settling communal policies in relation to the immigrants and shows how these were applied in fields like welfare, education, religion movements of self-help and 'self-assertion' (friendly societies, trade unions, Zionism); and concludes with the clash of policies during the 1914–18 war and its aftermath. It is a very detailed study but because of the date of its publication could not be taken into account in the present book as much as I should have wished.

Perhaps the best analysis of the numbers and nature of the migration from Eastern Europe to the West is Simon Kuznets, 'Immigration of Russian Jews to the United States: Background and Structure' in *Perspectives in American History*, IX, Harvard, Cambridge, Mass., 1975, pp. 35–120. For the causes of the emigration, see Leonard Schapiro, 'The Russian Background of the Anglo-Jewish Immigration', *TJHSE*, XX, pp. 25–31.

London

There is no adequate history of the Jewish community of London, although much of the writing about the Jews of England tends to concentrate on London, which has had about two-thirds of the Anglo-Jewish population. The Charles Booth survey of the *Life and Labour of the People in London* produced its first volume on East London in 1889 and the final and revised form in 17 volumes in 1902. Volume I contains several chapters dealing in whole or in part with the Jews of East London, who also feature in the later series on economic life and religious and social influences. The Booth material, including much unpublished, in the British Library of Political and Economic Science is analysed in V.D. Lipman, 'The Booth and New London Surveys as source material' in Aubrey Newman (ed.), *The Jewish East End 1840–1939*, 1980. This neostyled volume, proceedings of a conference on 22 October 1980, contains many other essays, including otherwise unavailable material and bibliography. W.J. Fishman, *East End Jewish Radicals 1875–1914*, 1975 is particularly detailed on the anarchists but begins with a vivid description of the process of migration. One aspect of housing, the tenement block, is the subject of Jerry White, *Rothschild Buildings*, 1980. C. Russell and H.S. Lewis, *The Jew in London*, 1900 is by now itself a historic document. Among other studies of Jewish trade unions, Anne J. Kershen, 'Trade Unionism among the Jewish Tailoring Workers of London 1872–1915', London Museum of Jewish Life Research Papers no.1 n.d. and 'Trade Unionism amongst the Jewish Tailoring Workers of London and Leeds 1872–1915' in David Cesarani (ed.), *The Making of Modern Anglo-Jewry*, Oxford, 1990. V.D. Lipman, 'The Rise of Jewish Suburbia', *TJHSE*, XXI, pp. 78–103, examines the origin and character of Jewish life in the suburbs up to 1914.

The Provinces and Scotland

The outstanding work, for content and technique, is Bill Williams, *The Making of Manchester Jewry 1740–1875*, Manchester 1976, and this is continued in outline in the same author's *Manchester Jewry: A Pictorial History 1788–1988*, Manchester, 1988. For Birmingham, there are the studies in Zoe Josephs (ed.), *Birmingham Jewry 1749–1914*, 1980 and *1740–1930*, 1984 (both published in Birmingham). Lloyd P. Gartner, 'Urban History and the Pattern of Provincial Jewish Settlement in Victorian England', *JJS*, XXIII 1981, pp. 37–56 is based on a paper which appeared in A. Newman (ed.), *Provincial Jewry in Victorian Britain*, 1975, a neostyled collection of varied and often important conference papers, which merit republication in permanent, accessible form. L. Olsover, *Jewish Communities of North East England*, Newcastle 1981; Arnold Levy, *History of the Sunderland Jewish Community*, 1956; Ernest Krausz, *Leeds Jewry*, 1964; and Daphne and Leon Gerlis, *The Story of the Grimsby Jewish Community*, Hull, 1986 (a model study of a small community, maximum population 450, 1899–1918) are examples of local history from the north east alone. Kenneth Collins (ed.), *Aspects of Scottish Jewry*, Glasgow, 1987 includes a three page bibliography of Scottish Jewry.

Institutions

There is an array of generally adequate, occasionally excellent, histories of communal institutions, especially religious: A.M. Hyamson, *The Sephardim of England*, 1951 covers the Spanish and Portuguese Congregation and its offshoots; Cecil Roth, *History of the Great Synagogue 1690–1940*, 1950, covers the history of the Ashkenazim in the eighteenth century and much else; Aubrey N. Newman, *History of the United Synagogue 1870–1970*; 1976, includes social development and relations with the Chief Rabbinate; S.S. Levin (ed.), *A Century of Jewish Life*, 1971 includes essays on the spiritual and lay leadership of the United Synagogue, its architecture and the development of London Jewry; Geoffrey Alderman, *The Federation of Synagogues, 1887–1987*; B. Homa, *A Fortress in Anglo-Jewry*, 1953 deals with the origins of the Machzke Hadath, with copies of original documents, and his *Orthodoxy in Anglo-Jewry 1880–1940*, 1969 includes material on other right-wing orthodox movements, Albert M. Hyamson, *Jews' College, London 1855–1955*, 1955;

V.D. Lipman, *A Century of Social Service: A History of the Board of Guardians, 1859-1959* sets the story of that institution against changes in the Jewish welfare situation and of British welfare provision. There is no full-length history of the Board of Deputies, although Charles H.L. Emanuel, *A Century and a Half of Jewish History*, 1910 gives extracts from the minute books up to 1910; nor of the reform and liberal movements, although Steven Bayme, 'Claude Montefiore, Lily Montagu and the Origins of the Jewish Religious Union', *TJHSE*, XXVII, pp. 61-71 discusses reform as well as liberal Judaism. Religious life between 1870 and 1914 is treated in articles by Steven Sharot in *JJS*, 1973, pp. 57-78, 167-188, 1974, pp. 39-50 and in his 'Reform and Liberal Judaism in London 1840-1940', *JSS*, 1979, pp. 211-228.

Biographies

A short list of biographies and autobiographies of Anglo-Jews of the nineteenth century, published up to about 1960, is included in V.D. Lipman (ed.), *Three Centuries of Anglo-Jewish History*, Cambridge, 1961, p. 95; and in the full list up to 1970 in Ruth Lehmann, *Anglo-Jewish Bibliography*, 1973, pp. 244-283. Important works published more recently include Richard Davis, *The English Rothschilds*, Chapel Hill, 1983; Stanley Jackson, *The Sassoons*, 1968; Miriam Rothschild, *Dear Lord Rothschild*, 1983 (which is important for the first Lord as well as the second); Selig Brodetsky, *Memoirs*, 1960; Robert Henriques, *Sir Robert Waley Cohen*, 1966. Sonia and V.D. Lipman, *The Century of Moses Montefiore*, Oxford, 1984, includes essays on various aspects of Montefiore's activities, that by Israel Finestein, pp. 45-70, discussing him as communal leader.

Zionism to 1918

The works on the history of Zionism are innumerable. Two helpful for the background to Anglo-Jewish Zionism are David Vital, *The History of Zionism*, 3 Vols., Oxford, 1975-82, and Jehuda Reinharz, *Chaim Weizmann*, I (up to 1914), New York, 1986, the only volume so far available. Stuart Cohen, *English Zionists and British Jews, 1895-1920*, Princeton, 1982, has revolutionized the study of Anglo-Jewish domestic politics by its methodology and use of archival sources. Leonard Stein, *The Balfour Declaration*, 1961 is comprehensive and a stylistic masterpiece but was written before the author could cite the relevant papers in the Public Record Office; Isaiah Friedman, *The Question of Palestine*, 1973 is the first full study of the origins of the Declaration which can cite all official papers. For a fresh insight into the role of the recipient of the Declaration, see Miriam Rothschild, *Dear Lord Rothschild,* 1983.

1918–39

Relatively little has been published on this period. David Cesarani (ed.), *The Making of Modern Anglo-Jewry,* Oxford, 1990, in which five essays deal with this period, unfortunately appeared too late in the production of this book to allow me to make adequate use of it but will serve as a major source for this period. Anti-Semitism is covered in Colin Holmes, *Anti-Semitism in British Society 1876–1939,* 1979 and Gisela Lebzelter, *Political Anti-Semitism in England 1918–1939,* 1978.

So far as I know, the only full length study of Zionism in this period is the as yet unpublished Oxford D. Phil thesis by Dr David Cesarani, on Zionism in Anglo-Jewry 1918 to 1939, 1986. But there are important articles on Zionism in the 1930s by Gideon Shimoni, 'From Anti-Zionism to Non-Zionism in Anglo-Jewry, 1917–1937', *JJS,* XXVIII, pp. 19–47, 'The Non-Zionist in Anglo-Jewry 1937–48', *JJS,* XXVIII, pp. 89–115, and 'Selig Brodetsky and the Ascendancy of Zionism in Anglo-Jewry', *JJS,* XXII, pp. 125–61. The question of admission of Central European refugees in the 1930s is dealt with in A.J. Sherman, *Island Refuge 1933–1939,* 1973; evidence on how refugees were received in local Jewish communities can be found in R. Kölmel, 'German Jewish Refugees in Scotland' in Kenneth Collins (ed.), *Aspects of Scottish Jewry,* Glasgow, 1987 and Zoe Josephs, *Survivors: Jewish Refugees in Birmingham 1933–45,* Birmingham, 1988.

Statistics and Demography after 1900

There are two important inter-war studies: H.L. Trachtenberg, 'Estimate of the Jewish Population of London in 1929' and M. Kantorowitsch, 'Estimate of the Jewish Population of London 1929–1933'; both are published in the *Journal of the Royal Statistical Society,* XCVI, pp. 87–98 and XCIX, pp. 372–379 respectively. The *New Survey of London Life and Labour,* Vol. VI contains a detailed chapter on the Jews by Henrietta (Nettie) Adler (1869–1950), daughter of the Chief Rabbi, Dr Hermann Adler, and herself an active voluntary social worker. The statistical material for 1929/30 is based on survey data, much of it unpublished, in the British Library of Political and Economic Science. This is discussed in V.D. Lipman, 'The Booth and New London Surveys as source material for East London Jewry' in A. Newman (ed.), *The Jewish East End,* 1980, pp.

41–50. Two of the many papers on Anglo-Jewish demography and statistics by S.J. Prais and M. Schmool include the pre-1939 period: 'Statistics on Jewish Marriages in Great Britain 1901–65', *JJS*, IX, pp. 149–174 and 'Synagogue Statistics and the Jewish population of Great Britain 1900–1970', *JJS*, XIV, pp. 215–228. Finally, B.A. Kosmin, 'Nuptiality and Fertility Patterns of British Jewry 1850–1980: An Immigrant Transition?' in D.A. Coleman (ed.), *Demography of Immigrants and Minority Groups*, 1982, pp. 245–261 is a pioneering and illuminating paper.

Bibliography

Cecil Roth, *Magna Bibliotheca Anglo-Judaica* Pt. I, 1937 lists secondary material in Part I, published up to 1937. Ruth Lehmann, *Anglo-Jewish Bibliography*, 1973 includes material from 1937 to 1970. Lloyd P. Gartner, 'A Quarter Century of Anglo-Jewish Historiography', *JSS*, XLVIII, pp. 105–126 gives an annotated list of books and articles published between 1960 and 1985. The archives of the Board of Deputies are listed in a catalogue available in the National Register of Archives. Other collections in Anglo-Jewish Archives are due to be transferred to the James Parkes Library at Southampton University. Important archival sources are discussed in Stuart A. Cohen, 'Sources in Israel for Study of Anglo-Jewish History, *TJHSE*, XXVII, pp. 129–147.

Chapter 1

Before 1858

Jews lived in England from after the Norman Conquest in 1066 until their expulsion in 1290 but there was no continuity between the medieval community and that of later times.

There were a few Jewish visitors to Britain in the fourteenth and fifteenth centuries but the events which eventually brought the resettlement of the Jews as a community in Britain took place in Spain and Portugal at the end of the fifteenth century. In 1492 the Jews of Spain, who had formed a prosperous and cultured community - the largest in Europe - were expelled from that country. Many of them crossed the border into Portugal where in 1497 the king ordered their forcible conversion to Christianity, together with the native Portuguese community. In addition, many Jews had already converted in Spain, rather than leave the country. From the end of the fifteenth century, therefore, there were two kinds of Spanish and Portuguese Jews. First, there were professing Jews who had gone into exile from Spain or escaped from Portugal. These settled in North Africa, Italy and the Ottoman empire, particularly in the Balkans, Salonika, Constantinople, Anatolia, Syria and the Holy Land. Wherever they went the Spanish and Portuguese Jews maintained their Iberian identity and culture; and often their religious traditions prevailed over those of the native Jews in the places in which they settled. Collectively, the Spanish and Portuguese Jews were known as *Sephardim*, from *Sepharad*, the Hebrew term used to denote Spain.

Second, there remained in Spain and Portugal the converted Jews and their descendants, who were known as New Christians, *conversos* or (a derogatory term originally) *Marranos*. Among them Judaism persisted as a secret faith, even if in attenuated form, in some cases for up to five centuries. They spread throughout the Spanish and Portuguese empires, in Europe (including the Low Countries), Central and South America and Portuguese India. They often referred to themselves as the 'Portuguese Nation' or 'the Nation', and indeed for non-Jews outside the Iberian peninsula in the sixteenth and seventeenth centuries the term 'Portuguese' often seemed synonymous with the secret profession of Judaism. In Spain and Portugal and their empires the New Christians became a powerful caste in commerce, the bureaucracy, the professions and the church. But they were increasingly the object of suspicion for secret adherence to Judaism and the target of the Inquisition (which was not concerned with professing Jews but with heretical or disloyal Christians). Many New Christians suffered imprisonment, torture or burning at the stake, although it is not clear whether all these were genuine secret Jews or victims of envy and greed for the confiscation of their property. New Christians tended, when they wanted to leave Spain or Portugal for other lands, to go first to other possessions of Spain or Portugal, such as the Netherlands, or to south-west France, or Italy. In Catholic countries, they continued, if they were secret Jews, to live as such. When they settled in the Ottoman empire or in the seventeenth century in Holland they could openly return to Judaism, and many did so.

It is within the framework of this Marrano diaspora that we must put the secret Jewish settlements in England from 1492 to 1656. While there may have been some Marrano merchants in England immediately after the 1492 expulsion from Spain, the first Marrano community seems to date from 1531, when it was part of a great Marrano mercantile network. Inquisitional records from the evidence of informers portray communities in London and Bristol following Jewish rites. This community seems to have lasted until the mid-1550s, although at least one family, the Anes or Ames, continued into the next community under Elizabeth I, which included Dr Roderigo Lopes, the queen's physician, who was executed in 1594 on a charge of trying to poison her. Individuals survived to form part of a third community under James I, which may have been broken up in 1609, although there are references to Marranos in England until 1618. Called Portuguese and outwardly practising Catholics, these settlers were known to be Jews. Mostly they lived as a group in the parish of St Olave, Hart Street in the City of London, buried their dead in part of Stepney churchyard and were, apart from physicians, merchants trading with the Spanish and Portuguese empires.

The next Marrano settlement was that which gave rise to what has been termed the Resettlement in 1656, although in fact the Jews concerned were mainly living in England already: what happened in 1656 was that they were able to live openly as Jews. The events of 1656 need some attention because they were to determine the character and status of the future Anglo-Jewish community. The settlement began in the 1630s, probably as a result of the breakup of a Marrano group in Rouen in 1632: the most notable member of the settlement was Antonio Fernandes Carvajal, a merchant and shipowner, who came from the Canary Islands and later supplied intelligence to Cromwell. Others in the group also had connections with the Canaries; some came from Amsterdam, where there was now an open Jewish community, or from Brazil or the West Indies. Two factors brought the community into the open in 1656. First, Menasseh ben Israel, an

Amsterdam rabbi born in Madeira, whose writings in Latin had made him known to Christian scholars, was concerned to hasten the Messianic redemption and to find a haven for his persecuted brethren, especially refugees from Brazil (which had returned from Dutch to Portuguese rule) and from Eastern Europe, where massacres had taken place in 1648 and 1649. Menasseh believed that a necessary precondition for the coming of the Messiah was the presence of Jews in every corner of the earth. Having heard that a lost tribe of Jews had been found in South America, England was the last 'corner' without Jews. In October 1655, he came to England with a petition to the Lord Protector, Oliver Cromwell, that the laws against Jews be repealed and they be readmitted under special arrangements for supervision.

The religious climate in England was not unfavourable for a readmission. The Puritans had a devotion to the Old Testament; the toleration of a variety of sects under the Commonwealth suggested that this might be extended even to the Jews; and there was a certain amount of philo-semitism, although this looked mainly to the conversion of the Jews. Equally, in government circles there was an appreciation of the economic advantage of Jewish mercantile contacts, although the prospect of competition aroused hostility in the City of London. Possibly the utility of Jewish links with the West Indies commended itself to Cromwell, who was planning the capture of Jamaica and had benefited from Jewish 'intelligencers'.

Cromwell referred Menasseh's petition to a conference of lawyers, clergy and merchants which met at Whitehall in December 1655. The two leading judges advised there was no legal bar to the Jews' readmission, because the expulsion had been an act of the royal prerogative and there was no statute to repeal. But there was opposition to readmission from clergy and merchants at the conference, and Cromwell dissolved it at the end of December 1655 without a decision.

Then the second factor appeared. England had been at war with Spain since autumn 1655 and two ships and cargoes of one of the London Marranos, Antonio Rodrigues Robles, were seized as enemy merchandise. In March 1656 Robles petitioned the Lord Protector on the ground that he was not a Spaniard but a Portuguese 'and of the Hebrew nation': ten fellow-Marranos testified that he was a Jew and several, in doing so, admitted their own Judaism. Also on 24 March Menasseh submitted a second petition, signed by the leaders of the Marrano group as well as himself: this asked only for permission to meet privately for prayer, and for a burial ground.

Robles' petition was granted in May 1656 but no answer to Menasseh's petition has yet been found. However, the London Marranos decided to bring a religious leader from Hamburg, were sent a scroll of the law from Amsterdam, and began negotiations for a burial ground and for a place to worship in Creechurch Lane, near their homes on the eastern side of the City. Yet in November 1656 the scroll was returned to Amsterdam, to which

Menasseh also returned, apparently disappointed. There was no proclamation of a resettlement, yet somehow the Marranos, who had declared themselves openly as Jews, knew it was safe to make this declaration and in fact obtained what the second petition had asked for, a place of worship and a burial ground.

The lack of formality in the permission was to the Jews' lasting benefit. When Charles II was restored in 1660 there was no Act of the Protectorate to rescind. Even more important, whereas everywhere on the continent, Jews, if tolerated, had to conform to prescribed conditions, there was nothing of the kind in Britain and no special status. Jews, if foreign-born, were generally subject to the same conditions as any other alien; if British-born, they generally suffered only from such absence of rights as applied to any other Englishmen who were not members of the Church of England. The new community grew from some 150 souls in 1660 to around 600 by the end of the seventeenth century. Sephardi newcomers came from Holland, the West Indies and the Iberian peninsula. They were merchants engaged in overseas trade, especially with the Americas and the West Indies, Spain, Portugal and Italy; dealers in bullion, diamonds and dyestuffs; a few were army contractors, supplying military stores and provisions, a characteristic of Jewish entrepreneurship in seventeenth- and eighteenth-century Europe; and, of course, there were Jewish physicians. The community was tightly controlled and built a fine new synagogue in Bevis Marks on the east side of the City of London in 1701, which was the centre for a range of educational and welfare institutions. Spanish remained the cultural language of the London Sephardim, although they also retained, in addition to English, a knowledge of Portuguese as a vernacular.

They were soon joined by a new element, the *Ashkenazim* or Jews from Central and Eastern Europe. There were about 300 of them in London by 1700, mainly from Holland or Hamburg, although a few came from further east. They differed from the Sephardim in pronunciation of Hebrew, to some extent in their form of prayers and in their use of Yiddish (Judaeo-German) as a vernacular and by the 1690s they opened their own synagogue in Duke's Place, near Bevis Marks. This soon became known as the Great Synagogue, partly because of the increase in numbers of the Ashkenazim, and partly because – unlike the Sephardim – the Ashkenazim split to form lesser congregations in the eighteenth century.

Sephardim continued to come to England in the eighteenth century. The recrudescence of the Inquisition in Portugal, where there was still an appreciable Marrano population, produced an immigration of over 1,000 up to 1735; and Jews born in the peninsula continued to come to England up to the end of the eighteenth century. Immigrants continued to come from Holland and from Italy, from which came the grandfathers of both Benjamin Disraeli and Sir Moses Montefiore. Others came from North Africa, especially Morocco, and later from Gibraltar. But at the end of the eighteenth century there were only about 2,000 Sephardim in London: in view of the amount of immigration, it must be deduced that many of the Sephardim had assimilated into the non-Jewish population. The increase in the number of Ashkenazim was much more marked, they had reached about 20,000 by the end of the century. On average, the Ashkenazim were much poorer than the Sephardim. They earned a precarious living as hawkers in towns and pedlars in the countryside, familiar figures from contemporary caricatures and even small pieces of pottery. Disturbances in Eastern Europe and severe restrictions on Jewish life in Central Europe resulted in a continuing westward movement of poor Jews. This was facilitated by the free passages across the North Sea and Channel available on the postal sailing packets until the 1770s. This influx from Holland and small towns in Germany led, in the middle of the eighteenth century, to the formation of a score of small Jewish communities in the provinces. The settlers were mainly former pedlars who set up as shopkeepers, often as watchmakers, jewellers, silversmiths and other craftsmen. In the ports Jews who began supplying clothing and other items to sailors became their agents for the receipt of pay and prize money; by the end of the Napoleonic Wars, one-third of the 400 navy agents were Jews. But the sheer number of Ashkenazim and the difficulties of making a living caused some to turn to crime; a case of murder in the course of robbery at Chelsea in 1771 caused an outbreak of anti-Jewish feeling, and the end of free passages on the postal packets.

Jews suffered from some disabilities beyond those to which Roman Catholics and dissenters were subject. Until 1832 they were not admitted to the freedom of the City of London and therefore could not engage in retail trade in the City. They were, in practice, excluded from the Chartered Companies and, when admitted to the Levant Company, could not use Jewish factors in the Levant. There were doubts about the ability of Jews to own land freehold, although this was satisfactorily resolved. If born abroad, Jews could be endenizened but could not take the oath for full naturalization. An Act was passed in 1753 to enable Jews after three years' residence to be naturalized by private Act of Parliament – a very expensive process. This very limited measure met increasing opposition, especially in the City of London; and it gave rise to a fantastic, xenophobic agitation, expressing fears of Jewish domination and the subjection of Christianity. In six months the government, which had introduced the measure, brought in a repeal; and in the following year's general election lost Oxfordshire partly on the issue. But soon later the agitation disappeared and the issue was forgotten.

While Jews could not hold political office, a succession of gifted individuals acquired great wealth and exercised considerable influence. Sampson Gideon in the middle of the eighteenth century organized the provision of loans for the government, played a key part in steadying public confidence during the Jacobite rising in 1745, and was the confidential adviser to ministers on public finance; his son, baptised at birth, was created a baronet while a schoolboy, at his father's request. In the 1760s Joseph Salvador played a similar role. During the Napoleonic Wars the brothers Benjamin and Abraham Goldsmid were contractors for government loans and founded what was in effect the first London discount house. Nathan Mayer Rothschild, who came to England to import cotton textiles from Manchester, found means of transmitting money for the British forces in Spain during the Peninsular War and, developing his relationship with government, laid the foundations of his increasingly powerful family banking house. That the first two financiers were Sephardim and the latter were Ashkenazim illustrates the ascent to wealth and position of a number of Ashkenazi families.

From the mid-eighteenth century Anglo-Jewry showed a tendency to centralize its institutions. Until 1840 the Sephardim retained their single, severely disciplined community. The Ashkenazim, on the other hand. developed two breakaway congregations in the City of London: the Hambro' Synagogue, founded in 1707 and the New Synagogue founded in 1761, as well as a Western or Westminster Synagogue in the West End of London (which itself had an offshoot in Maiden Lane, Covent Garden in 1815). But the Rabbi of the Great Synagogue in Duke's Place became recognized as the rabbi of the other Ashkenazi congregations, first in the City of London, then elsewhere in Britain and later in the British colonies. In 1844 the Ashkenazi congregations of London and the rest of Britain, Ireland and the Channel Isles sent electors who chose *Dr Nathan Marcus Adler as their Chief Rabbi. The City synagogues were also from 1808 joined by 'treaty' for various common purposes and from 1804 had joined with the Spanish and Portuguese congregation in a joint Shechita Board for the provision of meat slaughtered for food according to Jewish law. In 1760 an address of loyalty on the accession of George III was jointly presented by the Spanish and Portuguese and the Ashkenazi synagogues of London. From this developed the London Committee (later known as a Board) of Deputies of British Jews. Before 1835 they met very irregularly but with the election in 1836 of *Moses (in 1837 he became Sir Moses) Montefiore as president they adopted a constitution and set out to provide a standing body to represent British Jews and monitor legislation and other matters in the field of government which might affect Jews. The following year, 1837, the government used the board as the certifying authority for marriage secretaries of synagogues, who were empowered to register Jewish marriages under the new Marriage and Registration Acts. By the middle of the nineteenth century British Jewry had developed, by voluntary action, a measure of centralization in religious leadership and political representation.

The almost half a century from the end of the Napoleonic Wars in 1815 to the full achievement of political rights in 1858 saw developments in several spheres for the Jewish community – social and economic, religious and political. Socially, the community, which continued to grow by immigration, was now much more British-born. This was because of the virtual stoppage of immigration during the quarter of a century covered by the French Revolutionary and Napoleonic Wars. The community also began to reflect the new economic and social pattern of Britain after the Industrial Revolution. The old county town communities began to decline in size and importance; new communities grew in the new industrial areas of the North and the Midlands; a social framework dictated by peddling in the countryside and market towns served by horse transport began to conform to a new pattern set by the development of railways. While there continued to be hawkers in large towns, the community made strenuous efforts to apprentice youths to trades; and the competition of Irish immigrants reduced the scope for selling goods in the streets. The proportion of the middle classes in the community grew as Jews took to shopkeeping, commerce, manufacture and even, in a few cases, the professions.

This increasingly anglicized and middle-class community was open to external influences both in the Jewish world and in its British environment: the first produced a movement for religious reform, the second led British Jews both to come to the aid of their oppressed coreligionists abroad and to seek full political rights for themselves. Until the end of the eighteenth century Jewish religious life in Europe had remained traditional but with the onset of political emancipation following the French Revolution there were pressures to modernize religious services, to fit them for emancipated citizens of western society. In Germany in the 1840s radical religious changes were introduced in some, although far from all, congregations. By comparison, the reform congregation formed in London in 1840 was far more restrained, but its theological implications temporarily produced an atmosphere of schism. The new congregation was excommunicated by the Spanish and Portuguese authorities for setting up a rival synagogue to Bevis Marks; and the aged Ashkenazi Chief Rabbi, *Solomon Hirschell, issued a solemn 'caution', forbidding 'any communion with us Israelites... in any religious rite or sacred act'.

Intervention on behalf of oppressed Jews abroad was largely due to the personal initiative of Sir Moses Montefiore. In 1840 Jews were imprisoned and tortured in Damascus on a charge of murdering a friar and his servant. Damascus was then under Egyptian rule and Montefiore went to Egypt with the French Jewish leader, Adolphe Crémieux, to intercede on their behalf. Subsequently, after Syria had reverted to Ottomon rule, Montefiore went to Constantinople and received a firman from the Sultan, promising equal rights for the Christian and Jewish subjects of the Porte. Montefiore's initiative coincided with the interests of a forward British foreign policy, and he received royal recognition for his efforts. While Montefiore was untiring in trying to secure human rights for Jews abroad, in Britain he considered Jews had by 1830 full social and economic freedom and, although he had served in 1837 as one of the two sheriffs of the City of London, he was not prepared to see full political rights for Jews if this meant any compromise of their traditional religion.

The age was one of liberalization and Jews had already benefited from a number of minor changes which removed most of the remaining differences between them and other British citizens. In 1826 the need to take the sacrament according to the rites of the Church of England before naturalization was abolished, thus accomplishing at a stroke what had caused such a furore when it was attempted in 1753. In 1832 the City of London allowed Jews to become freemen; in 1833 *Francis Goldsmid became the first Jew to be called to the Bar and Jews had already been admitted as solicitors. Jews were able to vote at parliamentary elections if not challenged by the returning officer to take the oath of abjuration (which ended 'on the true faith of a Christian'), and even this requirement was completely abolished in 1835.

All that remained was the exclusion of Jews from municipal corporations and parliament, although there was no bar to their serving as parish officers, then responsible for much of the routine work of local government. In 1828 the political disabilities of dissenters were removed and in 1829 those of Roman Catholics. The discrimination against Jews thus became more evident, especially as in 1828 the words 'on the true faith of a Christian' were inserted in the declaration necessary before taking municipal office or a seat in parliament.

This exclusion from political life was resented by the now growing group of British-born Jews who had achieved, or were achieving, prominence in the City of London. There was also a much larger class of respectable middle-class shopkeepers and businessmen who felt they should be able to take part in the government of their own towns and cities. There was support for political rights for Jews from several quarters. There was a philo-semitic movement among the evangelicals and liberal churchmen, partly but not exclusively motivated by hopes of converting the Jews.

In 1832 the Great Reform Act widened the parliamentary franchise and in 1835 the municipal corporations (except the City of London) were reformed and councillors were to be elected by the ratepayers. Modernization and the abolition of privileges in politics was part of government policy in the 1830s.

The campaign for Jewish political emancipation began with comprehensive attempts to remove all the disabilities. The first Bill introduced in 1830 by Sir Francis Grant failed in the unreformed House of Commons. Grant tried again in 1833 in the reformed House and succeeded, but the Bill was defeated in the Lords; and this happened again in 1836. The strategy then changed. The advice of the Whig notable, Lord Holland, to Jews was to so conduct themselves as to show that their exclusion was a practical grievance .... Make yourselves beloved by, and useful to your fellow countrymen in your counties and cities, and when they shall elect you to be their representatives and magistrates and the law will not allow you to take office, it will be a practical grievance on them as well as on you, and must be amended.

This strategy was enthusiastically adopted by *David Salomons, who began his long campaign in the City of London.

The change in the City of London was remarkable: from opposing the admission of Jews to the freedom of the City, companies began to admit Jews as liverymen and in 1835 Salomons was elected sheriff, necessitating legislation to enable him to take office. In the same year he was also elected alderman but was refused admission by the Court of Aldermen; and this happened again in 1844. In 1845 the declaration for municipal office was amended; Salomons became an alderman in 1847 and Lord Mayor of London in 1855. Even before 1845, Jews were elected as councillors at Portsmouth, Birmingham and Southampton and apparently were able to take office without opposition. Montefiore had become the second Jew to serve as city sheriff of London in 1837 and Jews had also served as county sheriffs before 1845, as these did not have to make the declaration 'on the true faith of a Christian'.

In 1847, after Jews had thus proved their electability, three Jews stood for the House of Commons and one, *Baron Lionel de Rothschild, was elected for the City of London. He could not take his seat without the oath ending 'on the true faith of a Christian'; and, although the House of Commons was willing to change the form of the oath, the House of Lords refused. In 1851 the more combative Salomons was elected for Greenwich and actually took the oath without the concluding words, took his seat, spoke and voted before he was excluded. Eventually, in 1858, after Lionel de Rothschild had been elected by the City of London five times and there had been eight votes by the Commons to alter the oath - all frustrated by the Lords - a compromise was arrived at. It was agreed each House should resolve to determine the form of the oath for its own membership. Baron Lionel de Rothschild was able to take his seat as the first Jewish MP. This was widely regarded as the completion of Jewish political emancipation and Jews entered a new era on the same basis of citizenship as anyone else in Britain.

Note on Sources for the Introduction

Cecil Roth, *A History of the Jews in England,* Oxford 1964 (3rd edn; the latest reprint, London, 1988) is still the main authority. This is now supplemented by, among many others, Todd Endelman, *Jews of Georgian England,* Philadelphia, 1979; H. Pollins, *Economic History of the Jews in*

England, London and Toronto, 1982; V.D. Lipman, *Social History of the Jews in England*, 1954; and M.C.N. Salbstein, *The Emancipation of the Jews in Britain*, London and Toronto, 1982 (from which, on p. 124, the quotation above from Lord Holland is taken).

Chapter 2

From Emancipation to Mass Immigration 1858-81

When Lionel de Rothschild took his seat in the Commons on 26 July 1858 he did so by virtue of a resolution of the House which applied only to him and to that session of parliament. Two years later, however, in 1860 a standing order was passed to allow the omission of the words 'on the true faith of a Christian' from the oath and in 1866 the Parliamentary Oaths Act provided for the oath taken by all members to end instead with 'so help me God'. Only one significant political disability remained in 1866: a Jew could not be appointed Lord Chancellor, but this was removed by the Promissory Oaths Act in 1871.

Why was the House of Commons so set in the 1850s on admitting Jews to parliament? The answer may be found in the five reasons which the Commons gave in May 1858 for persisting with the Bill to admit Jews when the Lords wished to reject it. These reasons were first that the formula 'on the true faith of a Christian' had not been introduced in 1829 to exclude Jews but to find a formula acceptable to Roman Catholics; second, freedom of conscience was now recognized as a principle of the constitution; third, no charge of lack of patriotism could be imputed to the Jews; fourth, they had shown their fitness for executive and legislative office; and finally, since Christians who were not members of the established church now enjoyed full political liberty, to exclude Jews alone was admission of discrimination amounting to persecution.[1] These were contemporary Liberal political principles; and in 1858, subject to exceptions on both sides, Liberals supported and Conservatives opposed Jewish political emancipation.[2] Between 1858 and 1881 ten Jews were elected as Liberal MPs and in 1871 *Sir George Jessel, as solicitor-general in a Liberal administration, became the first Jew to hold British ministerial office. But it was perhaps even more significant, as a sign of the normalization of the position of Jews in British political life, that a Jew *Saul Isaac, should be elected in 1874 as a Conservative MP, to be followed in 1880 by *Baron Henry de Worms, who became a junior minister.[3]

There was, however, an underlying issue which featured prominently in the earlier debate on political emancipation and which remained to divide Jews in Britain over the next century: were Jews members not merely of a religion but also of a separate people or nation? The Conservative leader in 1857, the Earl of Derby, evidently thought they were when he said: 'though among us, they are not with us... they retain their laws... their political customs... they do not generally associate freely with their fellow-subjects... they have interests wholly apart'.[4] Derby was opposing the political emancipation of the Jews but he was not urging an anti-Semitic programme on racial grounds; he was, after all, the loyal colleague of Disraeli. The achievement of political emancipation meant that there was no longer an objection to non-Christians participating in the government of a country that was officially Christian but it still left unresolved - not least for British Jews themselves - a question of identity: religious community or membership of a people or nation?

Numbers and Immigration

In 1858 there were about 36,000 Jews in Britain; in 1881 a little over 60,000. Between the two dates their proportion of the total population increased from 0.15 per cent to 0.2 per cent, which meant they were still numerically a trivial minority.[5] The normal census in Britain has never asked questions about religious affiliation. Accordingly, figures of Jewish population can be based only on contemporary estimates and a very limited range of demographic information. These suggest that at this period Jews had a relatively high rate of marriage, a low death rate and a moderate birth rate in relation to the rates in the general British population. The birth rate may have been lower than the British average - it was certainly lower than the East European Jewish birth rate - because westernized Jewish communities had a low birth rate at this date; the lower death rate has been attributed to higher standards of hygiene.[6] Even taking these factors into account, the increase of the Jewish population from 36,000 to over 60,000 in just over twenty years must have been due to the amount of Jewish immigration in these years. The amount can only be conjectured but was probably of the order of 15,000, with annual numbers of migrants rising from 500 to 1,000 over the years 1858 to 1881.

In the first half of the nineteenth century Jewish immigrants to Britain had come predominantly from Central Europe (including Holland) with smaller numbers from North Africa, Gibraltar, Italy and the Levant; after 1850, while immigrants continued to come from those areas, immigration was increasingly from Eastern Europe. Writing in 1883, the historian and folklorist, Joseph Jacobs, estimated that since 1860 there had been about 12,000 immigrants from Russia and Poland, and 7,000 from Germany and

Holland. The total figure of 19,000 exceeds the 15,000 immigrants mentioned above because it includes the first of the mass immigration from Eastern Europe which began in 1881.[7] Jews had been coming to Britain from Eastern Europe from about the 1840s, at least. Jews then had an incentive to leave the Russian Empire because of Nicholas I's persecution (which included conscripting Jewish children for long terms of military service, restrictions on Jewish economic activities, measures against traditional Judaism and the removal of Jews from frontier areas). They also now had the means to travel to the West because of the opening of railways from Russia to the adjacent areas of Germany. Jews from Prussian Poland, although not subject to the same persecution, also began to move westwards. The direction of migration was to Central and Western Europe - including Britain - and to America. By the late 1840s and 1850s there was a recognized route for Jewish migrants from Eastern Europe to America. This involved travelling by train to Hamburg, then by ship to Hull, by rail through Leeds, Manchester and Liverpool, and then by ship to America.[8] The Jewish community of Hull was affected because they had to cope with the problems on landing of several hundreds, even thousands, of immigrants a year. But the impact on the Jewish community of Manchester was even greater. It was the largest town on the route through northern England and therefore offered the greatest opportunities for those who found they did not wish to, or could not, continue across the Atlantic. In consequence of Russian and Polish Jews settling in Manchester, the proportion of the Manchester Jewish community born in Russia or Poland increased from 19 per cent in 1861 to 35 per cent in 1871.[9] In Birmingham, which was off the main route of migration to America, the corresponding figures were 14 per cent in 1861 and 17 per cent in 1871.[10] The figures for both Manchester and Birmingham exclude Jews from the Prussian (Posen) and Austro-Hungarian (Galicia) parts of Poland. Other factors which increased the movement of Jews from Eastern Europe to Britain, even before the mass immigration began in 1881, were the Crimean War, which brought Russo-Jewish prisoners of war;[11] the cholera epidemic in western Russia in 1868; the Lithuanian famine of 1868-9, which affected Kovno, Suwalk and Mariempol in particular; the Odessa pogrom of 1871; the Russo-Turkish War of 1876-7; and some influx of political refugees after Jews began to join Russian revolutionary movements in the 1870s. The Russo-Jewish immigrants of the 1858-81 period were predominantly young men in their twenties who, after settling in Britain, generally married or sent back for wives and children to join them. Many began as pedlars or hawkers, or as tailoring employees; but by 1881 many had established their own businesses. By 1881 at least a quarter, if not more, of British Jews were of Russo-Polish origin.[12]

Jewish immigrants to Britain from Central Europe in the nineteenth century numbered only a few thousands but they included a high proportion of men who achieved business and professional status, including some who rose to national prominence. They came mainly from north Germany – those from Germany south of Frankfurt-on-Main generally went direct to America[13] – or other German-speaking lands such as Austria. They settled in the main commercial and industrial centres in Britain: thus in Manchester in 1851 over 10 per cent of the Jewish community was born in Germany, and about the same percentage in 1871.[14] In Birmingham in 1851 German-born Jews were nearly 20 per cent of the community, although just above 10 per cent in 1871.[15] In Bradford, however, at this period, German Jews predominated in the Jewish community.[16] In the mid-nineteenth century there was also a continuing, although numerically small, inflow of Jews from North Africa, Turkey and the Levant.[17]

In spite of the immigration, however, a high proportion of the Jews in Britain between 1858 and 1881 were British-born. To give exact figures means laborious examination of census forms but this has been done for Manchester, showing that nearly half of Manchester's Jews between 1851 and 1871 were British-born, and this in a city on a main immigration route;[18] the comparable figure for Birmingham, which was off the main immigration route, was three-quarters.[19] For the much larger community of London, only fragmentary material has so far been published from the census returns, but in 1841 three samples showed that 90 per cent of the Jewish population were British-born.[20]

Distribution

In 1858 about two-thirds of the Jewish population lived in London; the remainder lived mainly in a limited number of large towns. Within the towns the Jewish population tended voluntarily to concentrate in identifiable areas. In London until about 1825 nearly the whole Jewish community lived in the City and the streets immediately to the east, with detached groups in the Pall Mall and Covent Garden areas, in Southwark and in what were then residential villages like Hampstead and Highgate. From about 1825 the very wealthiest still living in the City or east London moved to the West End; the upper-middle class followed, with a substantial settlement first in Bloomsbury, moving west in the 1860s to Bayswater and in the 1870s further along the northern side of Hyde Park and Kensington Gardens. The majority of the middle class moved first north to Islington and Canonbury. The less affluent moved in the 1870s from east London to Dalston and Hackney. Finally, by the 1870s Jews had begun to move into north-west London, which then meant St John's Wood and Maida Vale. In 1881 probably about two-thirds of the over 40,000 Jews in London still lived in the area of the City, and the remaining third in west, north and north-west London.[21]

As immigrants arrived they tended to settle in the original Jewish quarter; but older Jewish residents tended to move out to the suburbs when their economic status improved and their social aspirations increased. The reasons for this continuing process of concentration and dispersal were partly specific to Jews as a largely immigrant community, but also partly that Jews were influenced by trends experienced by British society generally in the period. Like most immigrant communities Jews tended to cluster, at least initially, in particular neighbourhoods. But Jews were also affected by a special consideration. Traditional religious practice forbids riding on sabbaths and festivals; Jews therefore tended to settle within walking distance of a synagogue.

The reasons for Jews originally settling on the eastern side of the City of London go back to the mid-seventeenth century;[22] but, once the original settlement took place, later arrivals naturally came to live in the same area, and the community gradually spread eastward from its original nucleus. On the other hand, in the nineteenth century Jews tended to move out of east London for the same reasons as other Londoners did at the same time: the growth of London, the development of urban transport, and the desire of the middle class to move from congested areas to more spacious and healthier residential areas further out from the centre. However, when moving to the suburbs, London Jews followed a distinctive pattern. First, their tendency to cluster in particular neighbourhoods continued. Second, as they moved outwards from the centre, they followed a limited number of lines of dispersal. By 1881 it is possible to identify three main lines: a westward axis, mainly for the wealthier middle class, from Bloomsbury, through the Marble Arch area to Bayswater and beyond, always keeping to the north of the central royal parks.

A second axis ran north from Dalston and Hackney and into Islington, Canonbury and Highbury; a third had begun to move into the north-west, from St John's Wood into Hampstead. Finally there was an extension of the main Jewish quarter itself, mainly by the older, more comfortably off and anglicized residents, into Stepney and Bow. This distinctive pattern of residential settlement can be confirmed by negative evidence: in 1881, there were relatively few Jews in London living south of the Thames.

Outside London, the years between 1858 and 1881 came at the end of a period of transition in the pattern of Jewish settlement. From the mid-eighteenth century to about 1840, some forty Jewish communities had developed in the provinces, Wales and Scotland. For economic reasons they were mainly in county towns, seaports and resort towns (like Bath and Brighton). This distribution reflected the occupations of Jews outside London: from peddling in the countryside to shopkeeping by jewellers, silversmiths, clock and watchmakers and repairers, and quasi-professionals such as opticians or dentists; in the ports, they were navy agents and in other occupations associated with ships and seamen; and in the commercial centres there was a small number of merchants. Between 1840 and 1880, however, the coming of the railways, the development of industry in the Midlands and North, and changes in the methods of retail distribution transformed the pattern of Jewish communities outside London. Bath, Bedford, Canterbury, Cheltenham, Falmouth, Gloucester, Ipswich, King's Lynn, Penzance, Sheerness and Yarmouth all ceased to have organized Jewish communities in this period. On the other hand, new communities were founded in the industrial areas of South Wales, the Midlands and the North-East.[23] The communities which had been formed in the eighteenth century in Manchester, Liverpool and Birmingham became the largest Jewish communities outside London. The Manchester community grew from 15 families in 1815 to 1,100 persons in 1851 and over 3,000 in 1871 as the original nucleus of small shopkeepers was swelled first by an influx of about 30 merchants from Germany, Holland and London in the 1830s and 1840s - men already in the textile trade and attracted by the opportunities afforded by Manchester as a cotton manufacturing centre; then by the migration of former hawkers and small tradesmen, who by the 1840s had become prosperous retailers or manufacturers; and finally by poorer immigrants, increasingly from Eastern Europe, who provided the labour for the small workshops or tried to make a living by urban street trades, for example as glaziers. Leeds, which had about 70 Jews in 1850, had 2,250 in 1877.[24] The rapid development of the Leeds community during this period was due both to the growth of Leeds itself as an industrial and commercial centre and to the arrival of Eastern European immigrants.

These changes were due first to a general movement to take advantage of economic opportunities in the growing industrial areas, including relocation from the towns which, once a number of Jews had left, were no longer viable as organized communities.[25] Second, while London was obviously the principal magnet for immigrants, the trans-Pennine route of migration from Eastern Europe to Liverpool and America produced a spin-off effect of settlement in towns on, or accessible from, the migrants' route. The increasing movement from Eastern Europe after about 1865 resulted in immigrants from Polish Prussia, Lithuania and the adjacent areas of the Russian Empire going by steamer from Hamburg, Danzig and Memel to other north-eastern ports besides Hull: Newcastle, Hartlepool and Middlesbrough; and to immigrants settling there.[26]

Third, there were local factors which might attract Jewish settlers to form a community which did not necessarily survive: e.g. the army base at Aldershot, watchmaking in Coventry, wholesale clothing in Stroud.[27]

The provincial communities of any size developed a residential pattern analogous to that of London. First there was a concentration near the centre, followed by a movement to the suburbs, normally along one axis, as in Birmingham towards Edgbaston, although in Manchester both northwards along Cheetham Hill and southwards. It is noticeable that even as early as the 1830s the wealthiest followed their non-Jewish peers to villas in Higher Broughton, going beyond the ordinary middle-class inner suburb of Cheetham Hill, which filled up later with middle-class Jewish settlers. The move to south Manchester was also impelled by social considerations.[28]

Social Classes

In trying to define the class structure of British Jews in this period, one cannot identify a class corresponding to the landed aristocracy – there was no Jewish peer till 1885 and only four professing Jews had been created baronets before 1870[29] – but there was an upper-middle class of some 200 families, largely linked by marriage, which took the lead within the community.[30] Some had acquired landed estates and could be regarded as part of the landed gentry; by occupation they were financiers, merchants, manufacturers and a few professional men. Families like the Rothschilds, Goldsmids, Cohens, Montefiores, Salomons, Mocattas, Henriques, Josephs, Moses (Mertons), later joined by the Franklins, Samuels and Montagus, lived near one another in London and even their country homes tended to be in the same area: the Rothschilds had houses near one another in the Vale of Aylesbury and there were several Jewish-owned country houses in Kent.[31]

While these families mixed socially in non-Jewish circles, they assumed leadership in the complex of voluntary bodies (synagogal, representative, educational, philanthropic) within the Jewish community. Most maintained at least a formal outward adherence to Jewish religious tradition and some were careful in their observance. There were divisions of opinion between them – for instance over the foundation of the reform congregation and over policy on the struggle for political emancipation – but socially they formed a homogeneous group. Their attitudes both to acculturation to British society and to religious tradition were shared by a much wider Jewish middle-class group, who to some extent lived in the same residential areas. From 1840 to 1880 there was a successful campaign, which in some ways mirrored the struggle for Jewish emancipation and the contemporary widening of the parliamentary franchise, for opening up control over Jewish communal institutions from a small oligarchy of leading families in each community to at least a broadly middle-class electorate.

Before 1840 the synagogues, whose management was lay rather than ecclesiastical, had been oligarchically controlled in at least two respects. First, control was in the hands of small, self-perpetuating group in each congregation, composed of those who had held honorary posts and who selected their successors in those posts; in many respects this form of constitution resembled that of the eighteenth-century 'close' or select vestries in the parishes in which the Jews lived. Second, synagogue membership was divided between 'privileged members' and those who merely rented seats in the synagogue. Admission to privileged membership was in the hands of, and at an entrance fee set by, the governing group. The 'privileged members' were eligible for synagogal office and honours but as a group had no real say in the government of the congregation, while the seat-holders, who had to pay their share of the costs of the congregation, could not even be elected to office.[32] Between 1840 and 1880 the congregations underwent a process of reform which first introduced election to office, instead of selection by a small group, and then abolished differences between 'privileged members' and seat-holders. This occurred, with variations, in both London and the provinces. It reflected not only a feeling of resentment against the monopoly of control by a few families but the wish of more recent settlers, especially if they had built up successful businesses, to participate on equal terms with the older-established residents.

Mr Bill Williams attributes the formation of the New Congregation in Manchester in 1844, not to any doctrinal difference, but to the resentment of a group of newly prosperous and more recent arrivals at being excluded from communal power. Having founded their own congregation on the principle of 'equality' of all members, they rejoined the original synagogue in 1851 and in turn joined in trying to exclude a new generation of *nouveaux riches*. However, at a national level, leadership remained in the hands of the Anglicized upper-middle class until well into the twentieth century.[33]

Occupations

In their occupation, British Jews, while still tending to be concentrated within limited economic fields, showed an increasing trend towards diversity. In finance, they were still mainly merchant bankers and stockbrokers, such as the Rothschilds and more recent firms, such as those of *Samuel Montagu and his brother-in-law, Ellis Abraham Franklin (1822–1909), which was founded in the 1850s. Perhaps ten out of the fifty British firms engaged in the issue of foreign government loans were Jewish family merchant banking firms. On the other hand, Jewish participation in the joint-stock banks was virtually limited to *Sir David Salomons' directorship in the Westminster Bank and *Sir Moses Montefiore's in the Provincial Bank of Ireland. On the Stock Exchange, however, it was estimated that about 1880 there were 138 Jewish stockbrokers, 5 per cent of the total.[34] By 1880 these branches of finance accounted for about 10 per cent of British Jews in the upper and middle class in gainful occupations. Diversification of occupations was shown by increasing Jewish participation in the professions. From a very few barristers, and a handful of doctors, solicitors and architects about 1850, Joseph Jacobs estimated that in London in the early 1880s there were 27 barristers, 47 solicitors, 23 doctors,

19 dentists and 12 architects (in a total Jewish population of just over 40,000.[35] On the other hand in Manchester in 1871, in a Jewish population of 3,000, there were four Jewish solicitors, two doctors, four dentists and two architects, and in the provinces generally there may have been proportionately fewer solicitors and doctors than in London.[36]

Manufacturing represented about 22 per cent, merchants 21 per cent, and retailers nearly 40 per cent of the Jewish middle-class occupations in 1880,[37] and in the provinces the traditional connection of Jews with overseas trade was maintained by merchants, especially in the textile trade: in Manchester and Bradford there was an appreciable number of immigrant Jewish traders among the many immigrants there from Central Europe; and Jews from North Africa, Turkey and elsewhere in the eastern Mediterranean (e.g. Corfu) settled in Manchester and formed their own congregation in 1872.[38] In domestic retailing, the Jewish middle class ranged from the major entrepreneurs of ready-made clothing (E. Moses and Son of London and Hyam of Manchester) who had developed their empires by mass production and pioneer advertising methods in the 1830s and 1840s, to the traditional provincial callings of jewellers, watchmakers and silversmiths which were a survival from the economic pattern of the previous century.

As manufacturers, the Jewish middle class was largely occupied with objects traditionally associated with Jews: textiles, clothing and footwear, with local adaptation such as cotton manufacture in Manchester, woollen goods in Bradford, lace-making in Nottingham, linen manufacture in Belfast and chemicals in Cheshire. Special mention should be made of tobacco manufacture, particularly cigar-making: while Jewish manufacturers were not significant in relation to total British output in the tobacco trades (except in east London cigar-making), the tobacco manufacturers were numerically important within the Jewish community.[39]

It is difficult to draw a line between the middle and working classes in British Jewry between 1858 and 1881. The smaller shopkeepers and craftsmen who sold their own products were on the margin of the two classes. Estimates in the 1850s put half of London's Jews, or fewer, in the middle class, over half in the working class and 'poor'.[40] *Joseph Jacobs, in his study published in 1883 of the 46,000 London Jews, put 14.6 per cent in the upper or upper-middle classes with family incomes over £1,000 a year; 42.3 per cent in the middle class with family incomes between £200 and £1,000 a year; and 19.6 per cent with family incomes around £100 a year, together with 23.6 per cent in receipt of at least occasional relief, with incomes of between £10 and £50 a year. These estimates are based only in part on hard facts but they confirm the perception of mid-Victorian Jewry as having a substantially greater middle-class element than the general population, and that the middle-class element was on the increase. In the provinces, where census data has been analysed by occupation, it is possible to say that the middle class was between a third and a quarter of Manchester Jewry in 1871.[41]

There was now a contrast between the developing suburban settlements of the Jewish middle class, and the majority of the Jewish community still living in the traditional Jewish quarter or area of first settlement. In London this area still had in 1880 about two-thirds of London's Jewish population. In 1850 there were about 12-15,000 Jews, about a third middle class, in the area on the east of the City; by 1880, this had increased to about 30,000, of whom the great majority had incomes around or below £100 a year. In the 1870s this area saw the development of a sizeable Jewish industrial proletariat. Previously a considerable part of the Jewish poor had been hawkers, pedlars or street sellers. By 1880 these had become the occupations of a minority. This was due to a number of reasons - communal efforts to apprentice children to trades, competition from Irish immigrants, and the entrepreneurial initiative of individuals, who were helped by small loans from Jewish charities to set up their own businesses.[42]

In London in 1880 about 25 per cent of the Jews in the lower income groups were tailors, 10 per cent in boot and shoemaking, and 10 per cent in cigar and cigarette-making. There was however a very wide variety of trades among the remaining 55 per cent. There were 31 trades among the 1,105 members of the Jewish Working Men's Club in east London in 1875, and Joseph Jacobs found a similar diversity in 1883 among members of the Jewish Lads' Institute. There was a similar development of an industrial proletariat in Manchester. By 1871, the Red Bank area, which had a third of Manchester's Jewish population, was a Jewish proletarian urban quarter; and the trades of tailoring, cap-making, shoe and slipper-making and glazing, which were trades largely followed by recent immigrants, accounted for half Manchester's Jewish employed population.[43]

The growth of an industrial proletariat led to attempts to organize Jewish workers, and an industrial dispute involving collective action by the east London Jewish cigar-makers occurred in 1856.[44] In 1874 there was a short-lived organization of Lithuanian Jewish tailors in east London and two years later there were formed both the first Jewish socialist workers' organization, the Hebrew Socialist Union, and a Jewish trade union of up to 300 members. These developments were due to the presence in London of the pioneer Jewish socialist and Hebrew writer, *Aaron Liebermann, who was then working as writer and typesetter on the Russian socialist periodical *Vperiod*. Although the conditions experienced by Jewish workers favoured such organizations, and the numbers to support them were available, suitable leadership was lacking; and with Liebermann's departure in 1876 (though he was in London again in 1879-80) these attempts to organize Jewish workers on socialist, or even specifically Jewish, trade union lines were unsuccessful until the mid-1880s.[45]

Religious Organization

The religious condition of British Jewry during this period was related to the background of both the religious situation in the wider Jewish world and the religious climate of Victorian Britain. The most dramatic event - the formation of a reform synagogue, the West London Synagogue of British Jews - had already taken place in the early 1840s, and the effects of the reform schism had been moderated by 1858. In the mid-nineteenth century Jewish religious life in Eastern Europe was mainly traditional, with the masses respecting the norms of the rabbinic codes or following the various charismatic, usually hereditary, leaders of the sects of Hasidic pietism. While there was a movement in Eastern Europe towards modernization - the *Haskalah* or enlightenment - it was grounded in traditional Hebraic culture. It was also bound to remain in a minority so long as external society limited the opportunities for social acculturation of any but a privileged few of the Jewish population.

In Central Europe, on the other hand, a movement had begun earlier in the century to reform the content and conduct of Jewish religious services. This was inspired both by a desire for modernization and because it was thought these were necessary changes that would be expected of Jews if they wanted to become emancipated citizens of a western state. There followed changes in theology, partly inspired by the beginnings of biblical criticism and a new 'Science of Judaism', which aimed at unravelling the historical development of Jewish religious literature and practice. By mid-century those favouring reform had introduced drastic changes in the religious life of many Jewish communities in Germany, and rabbinical conferences had been held there in which fundamental theological issues had been exhaustively, if inconclusively, discussed. Among the more advanced proposals were the elimination from prayers of references to the Temple sacrifices, to the ultimate restoration of the Temple, and to the return of the Jewish nation to the Holy Land in Messianic times. Restrictions on sabbath activities were to be reduced as inappropriate to modern conditions, and some even urged the transfer of the sabbath from Saturday to Sunday. There was no doubt some element of political expediency, in that such changes were regarded as likely to facilitate the acceptance of Jews as equal citizens of their countries of residence. This argument logically involved the abandonment of the idea of a future restoration of a Jewish state, and the redefinition of Jews, in contemporary terms, as a religious denomination and no longer a nation or people. This was justified theologically by the theory of a Jewish mission to spread the Old Testament's ethical ideals among the peoples of the world: this made the dispersion or Diaspora which had always been regarded as an evil, not merely perpetual but divinely intended to be so.

While such ideas found only limited acceptance even in Germany, they evoked a reaction, loosely termed orthodoxy, with a variant, neo-orthodoxy (for those who combined strict adherence to traditional religious belief and practice with a measure of acceptance of western secular culture).

Orthodoxy was a term first used in 1795 when the overwhelming majority of religious Jews were traditional, and included those who opposed any change, even in custom or costume, let alone the particular minutiae of religious observance, which they had inherited.

British Jewry in the mid-nineteenth century fitted neatly into none of these continental categories of orthodoxy or reform. Even its reform movement was insular and influenced by local, and even possibly personal, factors. The twenty-four prominent and prosperous members of the Spanish and Portuguese and Ashkenazi congregations (many of them linked by family ties) who founded the West London Synagogue of neither Ashkenazi nor Sephardi but 'British' Jews were motivated not only by the desire for a shorter, more decorous service but by a wish to have a place of worship within sabbatical walking distance of their central or west London homes, instead of in the City of London. This latter desire was prohibited by the first article of the Spanish and Portuguese Synagogue's constitution (Ascama No. 1) against founding another congregation within six miles of the Bevis Marks Synagogue, under pain of excommunication. So far from founding a new congregation based on biblical criticism of the Pentateuch, they insisted on its validity to the extent of rejecting the binding authority of the Oral Law, the rabbinical corps of tradition of interpretation and deduction from the Written Law, going back to divine communication to Moses. Accordingly, they issued a prayer book providing for the omission of the observance of the second days of festivals, a rabbinic institution for the Diaspora. It was the denial of the validity of the Oral Law that led the ageing Chief Rabbi, *Solomon Hirschell, to issue in 1841 the 'caution' that 'any person or persons declaring that he or they reject and do not believe in the authority of the Oral Law cannot be permitted to have any communion with us Israelites in any religious rite or sacred act'.[46] This was not an excommunication: the latter, issued by the Spanish and Portuguese Congregation against the seceders, was for establishing a separate synagogue, and was withdrawn in 1849. Indeed the Spanish and Portuguese themselves opened a branch congregation in the West End in the same year.

By 1858, the social and, to some extent, the religious and political impact of the schism had abated. British Jews have seldom been deeply moved by theological issues and the external features of worship at the reform synagogue were not greatly changed. The service was still largely in Hebrew; prayers for the restoration to the Holy Land were retained; and male worshippers – in contrast to those in the spreading congregations of the Reform movement in the USA in the 1860s – kept their heads covered.[47] On the other hand, the mainstream congregations, while maintaining their basic orthodox position, improved the decorum of their services, introduced English sermons, and even omitted some supplementary hymns (*piyyutim*) or slightly modified the arrangement of sabbath morning services to make them shorter or more convenient for family attendance.[48] It was probably only the traditionalist opposition of Sir Moses Montefiore and the dominance he exercised over the Board of Deputies as president that prevented the admission of the reformers to that representative body: the election of four members of the reform congregation as representatives of other congregations was prevented in 1853 by his casting vote.[49] Further, under the relevant legislation, Jewish marriages could be officially recognized only if registered by a marriage secretary, who had to be certified by the president of the Board of Deputies as secretary of a synagogue of 'persons professing the Jewish religion'.[50] The ecclesiastical authorities whom, by its constitution, the board had to recognize were those of the established orthodox congregations, and Sir Moses, as president, refused to certify marriages carried out under reform Jewish auspices as being within these provisions. The reform congregation therefore had to secure the inclusion in the 1856 Dissenters' Marriage Act of a provision enabling them to appoint their own secretary to register marriages.

In the 1850s Montefiore did try, perhaps in a characteristic reversion to the eighteenth century principle of communal separation, to get Jewish marriage and divorce recognized by English law; but he failed. The pressure to assimilate Jewish practice to that of the state was too strong.[51]

The reform movement did not spread widely in Britain in the nineteenth century, establishing congregations only in Manchester and Bradford, both communities with an important German-Jewish immigrant element. While desire for aesthetic improvement in the services and to fit Victorian Jewry for emancipation played some role in Manchester, it is significant that two-thirds of the founders of the reform congregation were German immigrants, including the committed advocate of reform, Professor Tobias Theodores (1808–86). Even though the theological changes were more limited even than in London – initially the second days of festivals were retained – the influence of German reform is probable.[52] In Bradford, where German Jews formed, as in Manchester, part of a wider contemporary German mercantile immigration, the first German Jewish immigrants seemed uninterested in founding a congregation at all; and when a 'Jewish Association' was formed in 1872–3, its minister was nominated by the Chief Rabbi of Stuttgart and it affiliated itself to the London reform congregation.[53]

Thus, apart from three exceptions (two influenced by German reform Judaism), the synagogues of Britain in this period remained governed by traditional norms, whatever the degree of observance or personal belief of individual congregants. The explanation for the religious uniformity of mid-Victorian Jewry can be found in a man and an institution: the Chief Rabbinate and its occupant between 1845 and 1879 (when he delegated his duties to his son), *Nathan Marcus Adler. The much smaller Spanish and Portuguese congregation maintained its own rabbinate under their Haham (when there was one in office) but there was no theological difference with the Ashkenazi Chief Rabbinate. This had developed in the eighteenth century from the recognition accorded to the Rabbi of the Great Synagogue in London, first by the Ashkenazi synagogue in the City, then by the provincial congregations which looked to him for decisions on matters of Jewish law, and then by Jewish communities in the British colonies.[54] This process was reinforced by the need of the three City Ashkenazi synagogues to co-operate under a 'presiding' or 'chief rabbi' for the supply of ritually killed and supervised meat, for the burial of the poor, and for other religious purposes; and it was given definitive form in 1844 when the vacancy caused by Hirschel's death was filled by an election in which not only five London, but nineteen provincial congregations participated, and agreed to contribute to the costs of the Chief Rabbinate.[55] Nathan Marcus Adler combined rabbinic scholarship with a German university doctorate and set himself, by imposing and reinforcing central control of Jewish religious life in Britain, to unify religious practice in accordance with traditional orthodox tenets while adapting to the needs of a community living in Victorian society. He also determined to provide a new kind of religious leadership through training ministers, to provide Jewish popular education, and to ensure the founding of synagogal and welfare institutions where needed.[56]

Adler began in 1845 by calling for statistical and other factual information about synagogues and Jewish education.[57] He followed this in 1847 by issuing a code of Laws and Regulations which made quite explicit the supremacy of the Chief Rabbi in matters of ritual and religious practice. He enforced his authority by intervention in local communal disputes and pastoral visits, preventing the possible development of independence in a local rabbinate in Manchester in 1851–3.[58] Next, Adler tried to provide for the new type of religious leader, or 'minister', which he envisaged for the needs and capacities of British Jews. This concept accorded with the general desire among the larger middle-class mid-Victorian congregations to have, in addition to cantors or readers to lead the prayers, ministers who would preach in English, act as pastors for the families of the congregation, and be men of general culture who could mix as gentlemen with the clergy of other faiths.[59] In the 1850s there was a handful of English-born synagogal preachers, with others born abroad who spoke in English,[60] but there was no seminary on the lines of those founded in the previous thirty years in western and Central Europe; nor were the minute institutions of higher Jewish learning in England then capable of producing rabbis of the traditional type, so that Britain had to draw its rabbis, like Adler himself, from abroad. Adler's original plan for a 'Jews' College' was to found a Jewish secondary school for middle-class boys between the ages of 9 and 15, offering a Hebrew and secular education; candidates for the Jewish ministry would then go on to study for degrees at University College London while receiving at Jews' College 'the requisite theological and scholastic education and the necessary preparation for their future sacred offices.'[61]

Between 1855 and 1879, the college had forty to eighty schoolboys but never more than ten or eleven student ministers at a time. Although originally conceived as an institution of higher Jewish learning whose graduates would not necessarily become professional Jewish ministers, it became specifically vocational in 1879. Its objects were defined as 'the training of ministers, preachers, readers and teachers of religion for Jewish congregations whose vernacular is English'.

In the same year, the school was closed. There had been some opposition to it – for instance from *Sir David Salomons – as leading to segregation of Jewish boys from their English peers; but the main reason for its failure, apart from Jewish families moving from the Bloomsbury area in which it was situated, was that there were now a number of good independent schools to which Jewish parents could send their sons without the need to attend Christian prayers and instruction. The college itself, whose principal from 1865 to 1907 was the noted scholar, *Michael Friedlander, produced a small but steady output of graduates who came to occupy most of the pulpits of major British congregations in the Victorian era. Some of them later achieved scholarly and rabbinic distinction, but it was not the college's objective to produce rabbis with the profound knowledge of the Talmud, rabbinic commentaries, and the successive codes of Jewish Law acquired by study in the *Yeshivoth* or institutions of rabbinic learning of Eastern Europe (which were intended in any case for the education of men of learning and not as purely vocational institutions). Nor did Jews' College equal the academic levels in this period of the 'Jewish science' imparted in the Central European seminaries, which also conferred the rabbinical title on their graduates. Jews' College did not for its first forty years seek to produce rabbis and its goals were expressed in a leading article in the *Jewish Chronicle* in 1855: 'The future ministers of the Anglo-Jewish congregations will be men of thorough English feelings and views, as conversant with the classics of their own language as with those of the sacred tongue'.[62]

The United Synagogue was another unifying factor in religious life, whose influence extended beyond London and the Ashkenazi congregations of which it was composed. If, as traditionally said, it was inspired by a remark of Adler, it owed its form to the efforts and concepts of its first president, *Lionel Louis Cohen, and secretary, Dr Asher (1837–89). They faced certain practical problems which had arisen in the relationships of the three City Ashkenazi congregations, and of their two daughter congregations in central and west London: in particular, how to provide for the needs of members who moved into areas distant from their synagogues without overlapping, competition and secession.[63] They found a solution by founding what became a permanent institution. The essence of this solution lay in a strict pooling of financial resources by the uniting congregations, thus enabling the new organization to assist – albeit on prudent financial conditions – the formation of new congregations as the Jewish population of London moved into new residential areas. This meant that the new congregations came within the ambit of the United Synagogue, which was significant because of its religious posture.

Because of the need to deal with problems involved in the merging of charitable trusts, the United Synagogue was created by private Act of Parliament in 1870, thus giving it an added flavour of the establishment. The Deed of Trust annexed to the Act of Parliament provided for the form of worship and all religious observances to be under the supervision and control of the Chief Rabbi, and these had to be in accordance with 'the Polish or German ritual' (i.e. Ashkenazi orthodox); no marriage could be solemnized and no person could conduct a religious service within the United Synagogue without his consent.[64] But the Chief Rabbi, although thus the unquestioned authority for the United Synagogue, could act only within the Polish or German ritual.[65] The Chief Rabbi, in the early years of the United Synagogue, tended to be the only rabbi. The earlier graduates of Jews' College, unless they obtained the rabbinical ordination abroad, were not rabbis; and such rabbis as were employed by the United Synagogue - for instance the *dayyanim* or judges of the ecclesiastical court (*Beth Din*) - were not encouraged by Dr Adler to describe themselves as rabbis but merely as 'the Reverend'.

The United Synagogue Act used the phrase 'places of worship for persons of the Jewish religion who conform to the Polish or German ritual': no test was demanded other than that the members should be Jewish and prepared to accept the orthodox ritual in its German or Polish form (i.e. Ashkenazi, not Sephardi). Thus the degree of personal observance or commitment of individuals could vary widely but the institution - certainly as manifested in its form of worship - was to be orthodox. Hence the United Synagogue, the embodiment of mainstream Judaism in Britain by its numerical predominance in London and its example to the provincial communities, set a pattern different from that of Eastern European communities, which were orthodox and observant. It differed also from Central Europe, where many communities were mildly reform, with or without separate provision for the orthodox, and separatist communities were set up by the orthodox, notably in Berlin and Frankfurt. Finally, it differed from the United States, where geographical dispersion, lack of central authority and local factors led to the spread of reform Judaism, which was regarded as an indication of achievement of higher economic and social status.

In addition to the United Synagogue and similar synagogues in the provinces, there was a growing number of 'minor' synagogues or *hebroth*. These developed from small prayer groups (*minyanim*), often meeting in private houses, and whose members might also belong to larger congregations; if so, their group was usually formed for some religious purpose, such as study. But there was also often a motive of mutual help. This is explicit in the purposes for which in 1853 about fifty Jewish workers of Dutch origin, in or near Spitalfields, formed a friendly society; the contributions of 2d. (nearly 1p) a week would provide a benefit of 10/- (50p) for the week of confined mourning for close relatives (when the members could not work), a quorum of ten adult males at the mourner's house for prayers during the week of mourning (*Shiva*), and the services of a rabbi to speak at the mourner's home and during sabbaths in the first thirty days of mourning. The members then began to meet regularly to hear their preacher deliver a Talmudic discourse between sabbath afternoon and Saturday evening services. Next, by 1867 they leased a former French chapel, off Artillery Lane, Bishopsgate, and by 1870 had a regular synagogue with 500 members (the Parliament Court Synagogue, later changed to Sandys Row, because of the relocation of the entrance). Although the members of this congregation were mainly of Dutch origin, this combination of synagogue with benefit society was adopted by the increasing number of Eastern European immigrants from the 1860s on. Such institutions were normal in their countries of origin and by 1870 there were in East London alone at least 20 of these small congregations with over 2,500 members and at least 15 in Manchester in 1876. They also met the need for cheaper membership dues, collected at short intervals; a more informal, less anglicized service; and a democratic milieu, where members could continue to speak Yiddish and individuals so inclined could aspire to leadership which they could not in the larger congregations. They developed a variety of services and benefits, including arrangements for sick visiting and burial.

Already in the 1870s there was controversy over the spread of these small congregations. Opponents condemned their accommodation as unhealthy, and their proceedings as disorderly; their very existence was regarded as a threat to established congregations whose membership was declining as members moved out of the area but which still had to bear the financial burden of general communal services to which the members of the small congregations did not contribute. Their defenders, who included some establishment figures such as the architect, social worker and amateur theologian *N.S. Joseph, and later *Samuel Montagu, argued that they met a proven need, especially for the provision of benefits; they maintained orthodoxy; and they provided an environment in which recent immigrants, or the poor generally, need not feel second-class citizens.

These controversies, which perhaps first crystallized in 1870 with the attempts of the Sandys Row congregation to raise funds to enlarge their building, were to increase as more immigrants came from Eastern Europe and naturally joined or formed such small congregations. But because there was no fundamental difference in religious doctrine or ritual between these conventicles and the larger congregations (other than the few Reform synagogues), members of the small congregations tended later to join the large, established congregations when they rose economically and socially, especially if they moved outward to a residential suburb. In the United

States the analogous process at the same period would have led them to join a reform congregation.[66]

Since traditional Judaism places great stress on religious observance in all aspects of daily life, how observant were British Jews in this period? By Eastern European standards, they would not have been rated very high. For instance, the statistical returns collected by the chief rabbi in 1845 showed that only half the congregations had provision for a ritual bath (*mikveh*), required for strict observance of the laws of conjugal life according to the rabbinic codes.[67] Observers such as Mayhew refer to the reasonable observance among the Jewish proletariat of the sabbath and dietary laws, but that Jews attended synagogue even on sabbath, let alone weekdays, less than Christians attended church on Sundays. The 1851 Census of worship showed Jews having a lower weekly attendance in relation to accommodation available (24 per cent) than any other denomination except Quakers. About 10 per cent of the Jewish population attended services on the census sabbath in 1851, suggesting that the majority attended only on the main festivals and that the provision for 8,000 sittings in Jewish places of worship would not have sufficed for the Jewish population if most of them had been regular attendants at daily and sabbath services. This would apply even allowing for unrecorded small congregations and special temporary accommodation for the Jewish population on the high holydays.[68] On the other hand, in the suburban congregations of the 1870s the rate of attendance seems to have approximated to that of churchgoing in areas of Victorian middle-class respectability, and the increasing Eastern European immigration may have improved attendance proportionately by 1881. The memoirs and literature of the period suggest that in the upper-middle-class families religious practice and instruction was often perfunctory.[69]

There was a dichotomy between public and private standards of observance. Communal leaders and others insisted that public functions should be strictly Kasher and that salaried employees of the congregations be punctilious in their observance of all the requirements of the *Shulhan Arukh* (the normative code). But, apart from a traditionalist minority, the individuals making up the community were far less observant and, where they did generally observe the requirements, they tended to ignore details which were inconvenient or difficult to maintain.

Education

Jewish instruction was given both in part-time classes, akin to Sunday schools - though there was some more intensive instruction among the East European immigrants - and in day schools, which provided both secular and Jewish studies. The latter were influenced by the school systems developed by the Church of England and the Free Churches; in London at least the Jewish day schools were provided or expanded as a counter to missionary schools for the Jewish poor. The largest was the Jews' Free School, developed from a much smaller congregational school but which had nearly 3,000 pupils in its buildings in Bell Lane, Spitalfields by 1881. Similar schools were already in existence in 1858 in the west central area of London, and to cater for Sephardi children, and for infants, similar schools were opened in the 1840s in Birmingham, Liverpool and Manchester. The opening of these three schools, within a few months of each other in 1841 and 1842, was motivated by the desire to educate the Jewish poor, raise their 'intellectual character', and help them to acquire 'the means of self-dependence', as much as by the wish to give Jewish instruction. As London's Jewish population spread, new day schools were opened in the 1860s in Stepney, Bayswater and the Borough. The number of pupils in Jewish day schools rose from about 2,000 in the early 1850s to 5,687 in London and 2,127 in the provinces in the early 1880s.[70]

The Jewish day schools which submitted themselves to government inspection eventually succeeded in obtaining grants on the same basis as other denominational schools. But with the provision of free non-denominational education by the school boards after 1870, communal policy changed and it was considered appropriate not to open any more Jewish voluntary day schools but to use the school board system. This was facilitated by the practice which developed in London after 1876 of providing some Jewish instruction on school premises after school hours. This was supervised by the Jewish Association for the Diffusion of Religious Knowledge, which was founded in 1860 to distribute Jewish educational literature, and later renamed the Jewish Religious Education Board. The first school at which this combination of public secular and Jewish religious education was provided was Old Castle Street in east London, with 95 per cent Jewish pupils on the roll of over 1,200, and with a Jewish headteacher, Abraham Levy, appointed because the Jewish parents in the area had previously mistrusted the school.[71]

The Jewish curriculum did not go beyond Hebrew reading and writing, translation of prayer book and Pentateuch, and sometimes of other parts of the Old Testament. Apparently no biblical commentaries or Talmud (not even Mishnah extracts) were studied except in some special classes, like the advanced class (the survival of the original Talmud Torah) of the Jews' Free School. The curricula of the Jewish schools outside London are detailed in the returns made to the Chief Rabbi's questionnaire in 1845 and there seems to have been little change up to 1881.

Probably the most influential figure in Jewish education in this period was Moses Angel (1819-98), headmaster for fifty-one years of the Jews' Free School; a rigid disciplinarian, he was determined to anglicize the children of the immigrants, even if it meant that their religious education was rudimentary, and he had a negative attitude to the traditions of the increasing immigrant population from Eastern Europe. His emphasis on anglicization was probably shared by most of those concerned with the provision of schools for the Jewish working class and the poor. His headmastership was so long, his personality so forceful and his school so large that many of the early generation of Jewish preachers, and even more of the teachers, were his pupils; and his attitudes thus had a pervasive influence on Jewish opinion in the second half of the nineteenth century.[72] The Jewish middle class had educated their children first at Jewish fee-paying schools. The most famous was that originally opened in Highgate by *Hyman Hurwitz, first professor of Hebrew at University College London and which was then run at Kew between 1842 and 1875 by *Leopold Neumegen: it was said in 1875 that there was scarcely a family of any position in the Jewish community whose members had not received part at least of their education there, including *Sir B.S. Phillips, Lord Mayor, *Sir George Jessel, Master of the Rolls, *Professor Jacob Waley, the mathematician *J.J. Sylvester and the chemist and naturalist, *Raphael Meldola.[73] Other boarding schools were kept by *H.N. Solomon at Edmonton, Raphael Isaac Cohen at Dover, and by Montefiore's associate, *Louis Loewe, at Brighton and later Broadstairs. The West Metropolitan Jewish School, originally founded in Bloomsbury by the reform congregation but soon attended by a wide range of pupils, was turned into a 'Jewish middle-class school' in 1874, but without lasting success.[74] From the 1870s middle-class Jewish parents increasingly sent their children to schools like St. Paul's, City of London, University College School or Manchester Grammar School. In 1878 a Jewish house for ten boarders was opened at Clifton, so that upper-middle-class families could secure an appropriate education for their sons while allowing for provision of Jewish instruction, facilities for sabbath observance and Jewish dietary requirements.[75]

For further education, the community in this period looked primarily to University College London. Before 1871, Jews could matriculate at Cambridge but not proceed to degrees; at Oxford professing Jews could not even matriculate until after the University Tests Act of 1871. The pressure for the removal of these tests at Oxford and Cambridge, which required subscription to a Christological declaration, was intensified by the case of Numa Hartog (1846–1871) who in January 1869 was senior wrangler but could not take his degree or take up a college fellowship. University College London had been founded with the help of *Isaac Lyon Goldsmid; it had a Goldsmid Chair of Hebrew, filled after Hurwitz by *David Woolf Marks, minister of the West London Synagogue; Jacob Waley was professor of political economy there, and Jessel chairman of the College Committee. *Dr Hermann Adler, delegate Chief Rabbi and later Chief Rabbi, was a graduate.

There were sporadic attempts to organize Jewish cultural activity, such as a Society for Hebrew Literature in the 1870s. But these efforts only took permanent root among native-born Jews in the next decade. Perhaps the most effective means of disseminating information about Jewish literature and history was through the Anglo-Jewish press, which had developed since the 1840s. *The Jewish Chronicle,* founded in 1841 and, after an interval of two years, restarted in 1844, had been acquired by 1854 by *Abraham Benisch, who edited it (apart from 1869 to 1875, when Michael Henry was editor) till his death in 1878. A scholar, who was a forerunner of Zionism and a founder of the Anglo-Jewish Association, Benisch changed the paper from 'a parish magazine into a newspaper' and set it on a firm financial basis.[76] It became the leading and almost universally read weekly newspaper among British Jews, a forum for the discussion of issues affecting them and, through its publication of learned articles, a potential means of instruction for the community. This role was, among its competitors, also taken up by the *Jewish World* founded in 1873 and noted for its scholarly contributors.[77] But British Jews in this period relied for such scholarship as they had mainly on immigrants from Europe: *Zedner and *Deutsch of the British Museum from Silesia, whence came also Louis Loewe; Benisch himself from Bohemia; *Albert Löwy from Moravia; *Leopold Dukes, *Adolf Neubauer and *Solomon Schiller-Szinessy from Hungary; *B.H. Ascher from Poland and Hersch Filipowski (1816-72) from Russia.[78]

Welfare

What British Jewry did excel at in this period was the organization of philanthropy, both domestically and on behalf of oppressed Jews abroad. Each of these activities was, at least in part, a reflection of the community's contemporary environment. The Victorians were great organizers of charity and Britain's position in the world gave prestige abroad to Britain's Jews, especially if they were able to enlist the support of their government. In the Victorian age, when voluntary social organizations proliferated, British Jews equalled or surpassed their neighbours in the number and variety of their voluntary bodies for charitable purposes. In addition to the influence of the British environment, this activity was rooted in the Jewish religious concept of charity as a positive obligation. It reflected the practical need of a minority to provide for their own, particularly religious, requirements. There was also a vaguely formulated assumption by the Jews themselves that it was an unwritten condition of their resettlement that they should look after their own poor, who should not become a charge on public funds. Hence, by the mid-nineteenth century, there were charities for 'orphans, widows, invalids. lying-in women, the aged, and burials, as well as ones distributing food and fuels in winter and at festivals, and others sponsoring education. The needy could be provided for from virtually "the cradle to the grave"'.[79] There were separate organizations for Sephardim and Ashkenazim; and the structure of the organizations ranged from those which were purely eleemosynary to those based on mutual self-help, with some combining elements of both. This number of organizations provided opportunities for the exercise of charitable inclinations, and also for those who wanted to devote their energies to administering bodies for which they would have had limited scope in the wider society.

But this provision of charity had demonstrable disadvantages. There was overlapping between organizations; some cases, on the other hand, were unprovided for, because they fell between the spheres of different bodies; there could be no proper investigation of needs, assessment of the appropriate help and assurance that it would be provided; nor, assuming that the problems of any individual applicant were capable of long-term solution, was there any strategy for attaining it. These problems, inherent in a system of small voluntary bodies operating without professional help, were found by the British upper and middle classes generally in grappling with the problems of mid-Victorian charity, outside the ambit of the new Poor Law. This had been introduced on a national scale in 1834, due to the fear that unrestricted relief, especially out-relief, would bankrupt the ratepayers. It was therefore initially a system for dealing with 'destitution', trying to deter applicants by making relief dependent on entry to the workhouse, which would be 'less eligible' than any other option. Although out-relief had in fact to continue, the character of the Poor Law after 1834 was such as to encourage ample competition from voluntary agencies, whether of charity or self-help (friendly societies).

The problems of organizing charity on planned lines were apparent to British society, as shown by the formation in 1869 of the Charity Organization Society (later the Family Welfare Society).[80] However, the Jewish community seems to have done it first. Jewish Boards of Guardians (using the names of the Poor Law authorities) were formed in London in 1859, in Manchester in 1867 and in other provincial communities. The object was first to remove relief from the scope of the individual synagogue congregations, because they were too restricted as units of organization, and to transfer it to the local Jewish community as a whole, defined as widely as possible: in Manchester it facilitated the co-operation of the orthodox and reform congregations.[81] The larger unit also made possible the employment of paid staff, who could help the voluntary workers to carry out a thorough investigation of the circumstances and needs of each applicant.

The London Jewish Board of Guardians, founded by *Ephraim Alex, the honorary 'overseer of the poor' of the Great Synagogue, was originally limited to the 'strange poor' i.e. immigrants who had not yet established any association with one of the three main City Ashkenazi congregations that originally formed the board. But, aided by the young stockbroker Lionel Louis Cohen, who was first honorary secretary and succeeded Alex as president in 1869, Alex and the board planned from the first to expand their activities across the whole range of Jewish charity. Between 1869 and 1882 the board dealt on average with over 2,000 cases a year representing families totalling 7-8,000 persons, about 20-25 per cent of the London Jewish population (25-30 per cent of whom were in receipt of at least occasional relief from some Jewish source).[82]

Within twenty years the board had taken over all the former synagogal responsibilities for poor and medical relief, for the payment of pensions on the synagogues' charitable lists, and the investigation of applications for other charities. It had also developed new services in sanitary inspection to stimulate local authorities into statutory action against landlords who did not keep the homes of the Jewish poor in repair; and sought to attack what were seen as the causes of poverty by loans to set up applicants in self-supporting businesses and to help towards the purchase of sewing machines. The boards of guardians and similar bodies in the provincial communities developed along similar lines.

The policies of the Jewish boards of guardians were detemined partly by traditional religious norms, for example the need to help the poor in ways which maintained their self-respect by helping them to become self-supporting (although the applicants whose means were investigated by committees did not always see things in the same light); partly by current theories of philanthropy; and partly by local and temporal factors. For instance, the effect of the American Civil War on Lancashire's cotton-based economy produced a crisis for Manchester Jewish charity organizations; all Jewish charities found the demand for relief much higher in winter because of the reduction in economic activity; and the impact of the trade cycle can be discerned in the figures of relief given.[83] But the basic problem was that these organizations were trying to cope with a steady, but in this period manageable, flow of immigrants. Attempts were made to head them off by demonstrative refusals of any appreciable relief to newly arrived immigrants (although as the London refusal rate was about 5 per cent this could not have had much effect in keeping expenditure down). Several hundreds a year were encouraged, by small payments, to emigrate: most of them to Europe, and most of these emigrants had been in Britain less than seven years. In dealing with the majority of the immigrants who remained, the Jewish authorities' strategy was influenced by the fact that in the Eastern European immigrant of the 1870s they could see what has been termed 'perhaps the only working example of the principles of *laissez-faire* and individual self-help ... industrious ... thrifty ... very sober, very law-abiding .... He was intensely competitive and his great ambition, and frequently his crowning achievement in life was to become a small master.'[84] Hence came the policy of trying to make the immigrant self-supporting by setting him up as a small businessman. This seemed a credible way of curing poverty: it also contributed to the growth of the small workshop economy of the next generation in the crowded Jewish quarters in the great cities.

The Jewish upper and middle classes financed the Jewish welfare bodies either directly by subscription, gifts and legacies, or indirectly by subventions from synagogues; and they expected them to have an anglicizing influence on the immigrant poor: in Manchester, for instance, attendance at the Jews' (day) school by the recipients' children was a condition of relief.[85] But while the Jewish contributors did not want, for a variety of reasons, to turn the responsibility for relief on to the Poor Law, they now felt sufficiently secure in their capacity as taxpayers and ratepayers to insist on the right, in appropriate cases, of Jews to receive poor relief without infringement of their religious requirements. The threat of the workhouse might also serve as a deterrent to undesirable immigrants, such as those who tried unreasonably to avoid the responsibility of maintaining their families. Little however was achieved in practice. In 1866, the East London Union, as an emergency measure, provided accommodation and Jewish food in their workhouse for Jewish families who had fled the Polish famine, and did not even make a charge for their special food. The Certified Schools Act, 1862, empowered Poor Law unions to send workhouse children to schools of their own denomination, at the cost of the union, and the orphan department of the Jews' Hospital and the Jews' Orphan Asylum (amalgamated in 1876 as the Jewish Orphanage, Norwood) were certified for the reception of such Jewish children, as was the Jewish Deaf and Dumb Home in 1874. Sir David Salomons, MP, secured the insertion in the 1869 Poor Law Amendment Act of section 17, enabling the poor of any one religious denomination to be put together in a particular workhouse. Subsequently, the London and Manchester Jewish Boards of Guardians, with the help of the Jewish Board of Deputies and the sympathy of the central government department concerned, negotiated with the Poor Law authorities in East London and Manchester on the practicability of providing to some extent for Jewish dietary requirements in selected workhouses, and for exempting Jewish inmates from work on the sabbath. Action to implement these concessions seem to have been more successful in Manchester than in London, where it was allowed to lapse in favour of attempts to put more Jews on to out-relief. This would have been of great help to the Jewish organizations who were paying inevitably inadequate pensions to the aged. These efforts however failed because they ran counter to central government policy in the 1870s to reduce out-relief in the east London unions.[86]

Politics

Leadership in these Jewish voluntary bodies was almost exclusively in the hands of laymen. In London, they were mainly merchants and members of the Stock Exchange (most notably Lionel Louis Cohen and his family), with a few doctors, solicitors and architects (especially *N.S. Joseph). By comparison with analogous Christian organizations, clergymen were absent from the leadership, although they played an active role in visiting and providing ideas. For instance, the *Revd A.L. Green, by persuading Baroness Lionel de Rothschild in 1861 to donate ten sewing machines, started a process of equipping small would-be entrepreneurs in the clothing industry (by 1874, 412 machines had been issued by the London Board of Guardians). The absence of clergy from leadership no doubt reflected the longstanding dominance of British synagogal administration by laymen and the relatively late development of a class of Jewish pastoral clergy. The notable exception was the Revd Samuel Landeshut (1825–77), who was reader (not rabbi) of the Manchester Old Congregation and founded the Manchester Jewish Board of Guardians. He was so effective in the negotiations with the Poor Law authorities at national level that he was invited to become full-time secretary of the London Jewish Board of Guardians, a post which he occupied as a successful administrator, with a passion for collecting statistics, until his early death in 1877.[87]

Relations with the government and action in support of Jews abroad was the responsibility of the Board of Deputies.[88] It is not perhaps remarkable that a community so compact, geographically and socially (compared, for instance, with American Jewry) should have developed a representative body. Continental Jewries had such bodies, but they were the result generally of some kind of initiative by, or response to, government action, not voluntary agreement as in Britain.

The constitutencies of the Board were synagogue congregations, and as their constitutions became more responsive to the particiption of the middle class around the middle of the century, the elections to the board reflected this. By 1835 it had adopted a constitution and instituted regular meetings, probably due to the initiative of its then new president, Moses Montefiore, who was president, with brief intervals, from 1835 to 1874. Elections were triennial and at the 1853 elections there were thirty-two deputies from the provinces, compared with twenty-six representing London congregations (although two-thirds of the representatives of provincial congregations were London residents).[89]

Because of the opposition of Montefiore, members of reform congregations were not eligible as deputies until 1874 and deputies from the West London Synagogue of British Jews did not join the board until 1886 (the year after Montefiore died). In 1860, six London and only nine provincial congregations were represented on the board, the numbers increasing to fourteen and thirteen respectively by 1879.[90]

The board played only a limited part in the struggle for political emancipation. After 1858 its main domestic concerns were the examination of new legislation to safeguard the interests of members of the Jewish community (e.g. the effect of legislation restricting Sunday trading on Jews closing their shops on Saturdays and wishing to trade on Sundays), education (grants for Jewish voluntary schools or arrangements for Jewish pupils who would otherwise have to take examination on sabbaths or festivals), the possibilities for observant Jews of receiving relief under the Poor Law, and the board's statutory functions and other concerns about marriage law.

The board's concern with Jews abroad was integrally linked with the devotion to this cause of Sir Moses Montefiore; he was succeeded as president by his nephew, Joseph Mayer Montefiore and then in 1880 by another nephew,* Arthur Cohen. There was a precedent for intervention on behalf of Jews abroad in 1745, when there was an appeal to George II in connection with the expulsion of the Jews from Prague.[91] British Jewry's role began effectively in 1840 with the mission undertaken by Montefiore (together with Adolphe Crémieux of France) on behalf of the Jews imprisoned in Damascus on a charge of murdering a friar and his servant. Sir Moses went as president of the board but it is fair to say that he arranged his own despatch by the board, as he did in 1859 to Rome to try to reclaim Edgardo Mortara, who had been baptized and removed from his parents. Montefiore went to Morocco in 1862-3 to intercede for imprisoned Jews and to secure 'a favourable edict from the Sultan'; to Rumania in 1867; and to Russia in 1846 and 1872.[92] There was thus a combination of Sir Moses' 'unceasing exertions on behalf of his injured and persecuted brethren in the East and the Jewish nation at large',[93] and the leadership of a representative body of British Jewry which, in its nineteenth-century form, was largely his creation and very much under his control. Yet the role of the board as champion of oppressed Jews abroad, although it led to many appeals for intervention, was not without rival. In 1860 the Alliance Israelite Universelle (the Alliance) had been founded, partly as a reaction to the Mortara Affair, as a French-based but international organization of Jews enjoying emancipation to work for the emancipation and moral progress of other Jews, and to help Jews suffering from anti-Semitism and discrimination. Its methods included diplomatic action, assistance for emigration and the founding of schools to give a modern Jewish education; these were based on French language and culture.[94] Branches of the Alliance were formed in 1867 in Birmingham and in 1868 in Liverpool but the defeat of France in the Franco-Prussian War stimulated the movement for a British version of the Alliance.

In 1871 the Anglo-Jewish Association (AJA) was founded by about 200 leading British Jews, with the lawyer, Jacob Waley as president, to promote 'the moral, social and intellectual advancement of the Jewish people', which included a concern for persecuted Jews abroad. Abraham Benisch, editor of the *Jewish Chronicle*, advocated the formation of the AJA to work with representative Jewish bodies in other countries. It was felt that the Board of Deputies was underfinanced, unduly rigid in its procedure, and given so much to the passing of formal resolutions that it was known as the 'Board of Congratulations and Condolence'. It was therefore considered insufficiently flexible in its response to foreign emergencies.[95] Opposition to the board was also expressed by Sir David Salomons, who had earlier regarded its efforts to secure political emancipation as too lukewarm; and some considered even the idea of a Jewish representative body, expressing a collective communal view, as derogating from the status of British Jews as ordinary British citizens, whose views, now they had political emancipation, should be expressed through Jewish MPs.[96]

At first the board rejected the overtures for collaboration put forward by the AJA, which it regarded, by comparison with itself, as a self-appointed, unrepresentative body. But in 1874 it began to refer matters concerning the education of Jews abroad to the AJA; and in 1878 it agreed to give up its monopoly of approach to government on foreign affairs to a Conjoint Foreign Committee (the Conjoint), on which each body was to have seven representatives. Neither body was to approach the government without a meeting of the committee; if the representatives of the two bodies on the Conjoint could not agree, the matter should be referred to the parent bodies, which would then be free to act independently. In fact, the Conjoint developed into the nearest approach British Jewry could make in the next forty years to an executive for foreign policy.[97]

Before about 1870 the objectives in foreign policy of British Jewry's representatives generally marched with those of the British government and the growth of British power and prestige carried with it British Jewry's influence both on the fate of Jews abroad and in world Jewish affairs. Further, Montefiore's efforts to secure British protection for the Jews of the Holy Land coincided with the wish of the British government to extend its influence in the Ottoman empire: if the French were the protectors of the Latin Catholics, and the Russian of the Greek Orthodox, there were hardly enough native Protestants for Britain to protect, and the Jews might therefore be appropriate protégés for British government protection.[98] Even in Greece Palmerston was willing to use the threat of British force on behalf of Don Pacifico, on the ground that he was a British subject born in Gibraltar.[99] By the 1870s, however, interests were beginning to diverge. While Disraeli and the Conservatives supported Turkey against Russian expansion, Gladstone and the Liberals were more influenced by Turkish ill-treatment of their Christian minorities. Generally speaking, the Jews of the Ottoman empire looked to their Turkish rulers for protection against their Arab and Christian neighbours; and the fate of the Jews in the nascent Balkan states, Rumania above all, was unhappy.

In the 1870s therefore British official and Anglo-Jewish aims in foreign policy were in danger of divergence. Disraeli was even accused of being influenced by his Jewish origin in siding with Turkey against Russia and in insisting at the Congress of Berlin in 1878 on human rights for Jews as a condition for recognizing Rumania as a new sovereign state. Gladstone referred in 1876 to Disraeli's 'Judaic sympathies' as influencing his political judgement; and anti-Turkish, pro-Russian writers – E.A. Freeman,

T.P. O'Connor, J.A. Froude, Goldwin Smith, even a writer in the *Church Times* - referred to him in terms of anti-Semitic virulence. The cause of oppressed Jews abroad was presented in parliament by Jewish MPs, notably *Sir Francis Goldsmid and then *Sir John Simon, who, although a loyal Liberal, warned Gladstone publicly in 1879 that his championing of Eastern European Christians while ignoring Jewish persecution risked alienating the three-quarters of Jewish voters who then voted Liberal.

At this stage, the main effect within British Jewry may have been to confirm in their decision those Jews who had decided for other reasons to be Conservatives, even though the Liberals had been the party, on the whole, who had supported Jewish emancipation.[100] But the expressions of anti-Semitism in Britain were a very limited parallel to the rise in Central and Western Europe of a new wave, almost a new brand, of anti-Semitism (a term coined in 1879 by Wilhelm Marr). The reappearance in Britain, France, Germany and Austria-Hungary of anti-Jewish feeling had different causes and different degrees of intensity; but the coincidence of these phenomena in the 1870s was no doubt a reminder to British Jews that political emancipation had not solved all problems in their relations with the rest of British society. The events in Eastern Europe which came to a head in 1881 were to provide an even greater challenge.

Notes

1. M.C.N. Salbstein, *The Emancipation of the Jews in Britain*, London and Toronto, 1982, p. 232.
2. Dr. Geoffrey Alderman (*The Jewish Community in British Politics*, Oxford, 1983, p. 23) has suggested that the Liberals were aiming to gain the not inconsiderable vote in the politically sensitive City of London constituency.
3. See Alderman, *Jewish Community*, pp. 31 and 44.
4. Cited by Israel Finestein, *Post-Emancipation Jewry: The Anglo-Jewish Experience*, Oxford Centre for Postgraduate Hebrew Studies Sacks Lecture, 1980, p. 9.
5. V.D. Lipman, *Social History of the Jews in England*, 1954, p. 65. In the light of the detailed studies of census material on provincial Jewish communities such as Birmingham and Manchester published since 1954, I think the estimate of 35,000 I gave then for the Jewish population too high for 1850 but that it might well be about right for 1858.
6. This analysis is based on Barry A. Kosmin, 'Nuptiality and fertility patterns of British Jewry 1850-1980: an immigrant transition?', in D.A. Coleman (ed.) *Demography of Immigrants and Minority Groups in the United Kingdom*, London, 1982, pp. 248-52.
7. Lipman, *Social History*, p. 66.
8. The early Russo-Polish emigrants to America mostly came via England. See A.R. Rollin, 'Russo-Jewish immigrants in England before 1881', *TJHSE* **XXI** 206.

9. Bill Williams, *The Making of Manchester Jewry 1740-1875*, Manchester, 1976, pp. 143-4, 170-2, 269.
10. Birmingham Jewish Research Group, *Birmingham Jewry 1789-1914*, I, 1980, pp. 8, 27.
11. Rabbi Dr. B.,Susser has kindly shown me his unpublished Ph.D. thesis (Exeter) in which he describes how Russian Jewish prisoners from the Crimea in Dartmoor were visited by members of the Jewish community of Plymouth where a number of them settled after the end of the war.
12. Rollin, 'Russo-Jewish immigrants' p. 211, suggests 20,000 or nearly a third, but includes Rumanians, Galicians and transmigrants. The standard work on Eastern European immigration, L.P. Gartner, *The Jewish Immigrant in England 1870-1914*, 2nd edn, 1973, deals with this period; see especially pp. 38-40.
13. C.C. Aronsfeld, 'German Jews in Victorian England', *Leo Baeck Yearbook* VII, especially pp. 12-13.
14. Williams, *Manchester*, pp. 169, 372 (census figures for those born in 'Germany' and 'Prussia').
15. *Birmingham Jewry*, pp. 8, 27.
16. M.R. Heilbron, 'Bradford', in Aubrey Newman (ed)., *Provincial Jewry in Victorian Britain*, 1975.
17. A.M. Hyamson, *The Sephardim of England*, 1951, p. 359.
18. Williams, *Manchester*, p. 372.
19. *Birmingham Jewry*, p. 36.
20. V.D. Lipman, 'Social structure of London Jewry in the mid-nineteenth century', in H.J. Zimmels *et al.* (eds) *Essays presented to Chief Rabbi Brodie*, 1967, p. 273.
21. V.D. Lipman, 'The rise of Jewish suburbia', *TJHSE* XXI, pp. 78-102.
22. V.D. Lipman, 'The development of London Jewry', in S.S. Levin (ed.) *A Century of Anglo-Jewish Life*, n.d. (1971), pp. 43-4.
23. See the various papers in Aubrey Newman (ed). *Provincial Jewry in Victorian Britain*, 1975, and Lewis Olsover, *The Jewish Communities of North-East*
24. A.S. Diamond, 'A sketch of Leeds Jewry in the 19th century', in Aubrey Newman (ed.) *Provincial Jewry*.
25. Williams, *Manchester*, p. 362: of 3,444 Jews in Manchester and Salford in 1871, almost 300 were born in other parts of provincial England.
26. Olsover, *North-East England*, e.g. pp. 266, 303, 310. See also Lloyd P. Gartner, 'Jewish settlement in Victorian England', *JJS* June 1981, 41.
27. L.P. Gartner, 'Urban History and the Pattern of Provincial Jewish Settlement in Victorian England', *JJS*, XXIII, p. 39.
28. *Birmingham Jewry*, maps on pp. 28-30; Williams, *Manchester* maps on pp. 366-9.
29. Sir Isaac Lyon Goldsmid, created 1841; Sir Moses Montefiore, 1846; Sir Anthony de Rothschild, 1846; Sir David Salomons, 1869.
30. Lipman, 'Structure of London Jewry', pp. 235 ff.
31. See, for instance, the genealogical details in Arthur Ellis Franklin, *The Records of the Franklin Family*, 1935 and R.J. D'Arcy Hart, *The Samuel Family*, 1958; also C. Bermant, *The Cousinhood*, 1971.
32. For these congregational constitutions and their parochial and municipal

parallels, see V.D. Lipman, 'Synagogal organization in Anglo-Jewry', *JJS* I, 1960, 80-6.

33. This analysis is developed for Manchester in Williams, *Manchester,* especially Ch. 6. on the formation of a separate congregation. For the process of democratization, see Lipman, 'Synagogal organization', 86-8.
34. Harold Pollins, *Economic History of the Jews in England,* London and Toronto, 1982, pp. 108-11; for the calculation by Joseph Jacobs about the number of Jews on the Stock Exchange, see Lipman, *Social History,* p. 79.
35. Lipman, *Social History,* p. 79.
36. Williams, *Manchester,* p. 379.
37. Lipman, *Social History,* pp. 79-80.
38. Williams, *Manchester,* pp. 320-2; A.R. Rollin, 'The Jewish contribution to the British textile industry: builders of Bradford', *TJHSE* XVII, pp. 45-51.
39. Pollins, *Economic History,* pp. 93-101; pp. 91-3 discuss the marginal involvement of Jews in coalmining, shipbuilding and railways during this period.
40. Lipman, *Social History,* p. 27.
41. Ibid. pp. 76-7; Pollins, *Economic History,* p. 90 (based on Williams, *Manchester,* pp. 358-60).
42. V.D. Lipman, 'Trends in Anglo-Jewish occupations', *JJS* II, 1960, pp. 202-5; see also Pollins, *Economic History,* pp. 126-7 for evidence drawn from comparison of the occupations of Sephardi bridegrooms in the 1870s with those of the 1840s, and of their fathers' occupations.
43. Williams, *Manchester,* pp. 270, 274.
44. Pollins, *Economic History,* pp. 123-5.
45. Peter Elman, 'The beginning of the Jewish trade union movement in England', *TJHSE* XV, pp. 53-62; William J. Fishman, *East End Jewish Radicals 1875-1914,* 1975, pp. 97-134; Leonard Prager, 'The beginnings of Yiddish fiction in England', in Dov Noy and I. Ben-Ami (eds) *Studies in the Cultural Life of the Jews in England,* (Jerusalem), 1975.
46. Text in James Picciotto, *Sketches of Anglo-Jewish History,* 1875, p. 319.
47. Steven Bayme, 'Claude Montefiore, Lily Montagu and the origins of the Jewish Religious Union', *TJHSE* XXVII, p. 61; see also Jakob Petuchowski, *Prayerbook Reform in Judaism,* New York, 1968.
48. C. Roth, *A History of the Jews in England,* Oxford 3rd edn, 1964, p. 257; Lipman, *Social History,* p. 45.
49. I. Finestein, 'The Anglo-Jewish revolt of 1853', *Jewish Quarterly* 26, 1975, gives a full account of the affair and its implications.
50. H.S.Q. Henriques, *Jewish Marriages and the English Law,* 1909, pp. 26-40.
51. C.H.L. Emanuel, *A Century and a Half of Jewish History,* 1910, pp. 69, 71; 'The Uneasy Victorian', in Sonia and V.D. Lipman (eds.), *The Century of Moses Montefiore,* Oxford, 1985, p. 47.
52. Williams, *Manchester,* pp. 194-5, 240-67.
53. Heilbron, 'Bradford' in *Provincial Jewry in Victorian Britain.*
54. C. Roth, 'The Chief Rabbinate of England', in I. Epstein and E. Levine (eds) *Essays Presented to J.H. Hertz,* 1942.
55. Lipman, *Social History,* pp. 39-40.
56. Raymond Apple, 'Religious founders and leaders', in S.S. Levin (ed.) *A Century of Anglo-Jewish Life,* 1970, pp. 14-15.

57. See B. Susser, 'The Questionnaire of 1845', in Aubrey Newman (ed.) *Provincial Jewry in Victorian Britain,* a valuable study which amplifies and corrects V.D. Lipman, 'A Survey of Anglo-Jewry', *TJHSE* XVII, p. 172.
58. Williams, *Manchester,* Ch. 8.
59. Michael Goulston, 'The status of the Anglo-Jewish Rabbinate 1840-1914', *JJS* X, 1968, p. 55-65.
60. For names and biographical details, see V.D. Lipman (ed.) *Three Centuries of Anglo-Jewish History,* 1965, pp. 85, 101.
61. A.M. Hyamson, *Jews' College,* 1951, p. 19.
62. *Jewish Chronicle,* 23 November 1855.
63. The events leading up to the formation of the United Synagogue are given in Lipman, *Social History,* pp. 58-64 and Aubrey Newman, *The United Synagogue 1870-1970,* 1977, pp. 1-14.
64. Clause 3, Deed of Foundation and Trust; Clause 158, By-laws of the United Synagogue, 1881.
65. By-laws 161, 1891, 190 of the 1881 edition. The intention is made clear in the recommendations of the delegates of 13 December 1867 'that all ecclesiastical matters shall, as heretofore, be under the control of the Chief Rabbi for the time being, who shall regulate the order of service and the forms of prayer, according to *Minhag Polin* [i.e. the eastern or 'Polish' form of the Ashkenazi or German and Polish rite] as established, and all religious observances in the several congregations of the United Synagogue'.
66. For the London *hebroth* of the 1850-80 period, see Lipman, *Social History,* pp. 71-5. The larger provincial communities showed a similar picture; see e.g. Williams, *Manchester,* pp. 183, 202, 271-3, 333.
67. Susser, 'Questionnaire of 1845', in Aubrey Newman (ed.) *Provincial Jewry.*
68. Lipman, *Social History,* pp. 35-6.
69. For a short list of biographies and autobiographies of British Jews of the 1815-80 period see Lipman, *Three Centuries,* p. 95.
70. See Aubrey Newman (ed.) *Provincial Jewry* especially C. Hershon and Sharon Rothstein on the Liverpool and Birmingham Jewish schools respectively; Lipman, *Social History,* p. 76; Gartner, *Jewish Immigrant,* p. 224.
71. Lipman, *Social History,* p. 152; Gartner, *Jewish Immigrant,* p. 227.
72. Gartner, *Jewish Immigrant,* pp. 222-4.
73. *Jewish Chronicle,* 16 April, 1875.
74. Curtis Cassel, 'The West Metropolitan Jewish School 1845-97', *TJHSE* XIX, 115-28.
75. For Clifton, see Robert Henriques, *Sir Robert Waley Cohen,* 1966, pp. 39ff. The story is that the house originated in the headmaster's friendship with Lionel Louis Cohen, who as an MP helped Clifton to get a Royal Charter in 1877, the year before the Jewish house was opened: the odd point is that Cohen did not become an MP till 1885.
76. J.M. Shaftesley, 'Abraham Benisch as newspaper editor', *TJHSE* XXI, 214-31.
77. For the Jewish press in England in this period, see Lipman, *Three Centuries,* pp. 89-90.
78. For Deutsch, see B.Z. Abrahams, 'Emanuel Deutsch', *TJHSE* XXIII, 53-63; for Schiller-Szinessy, see Raphael Loewe, 'Solomon Marcus Schiller-Szinessy',

TJHSE XXI, 148-89; Tobias Theodores in Williams, *Manchester*, especially Ch. 8. See also articles in *Encyclopaedia Judaica* and *Jewish Encyclopaedia.*

79. Miriam Steiner, 'Jewish philanthropy', in Aubrey Newman (ed.) *Provincial Jewry*, summarizing the information relating to London Jewish charities in Lipman, *Social History*, pp. 49-56.
80. For the general situation of charity and Poor Law in the 1850s, see V.D. Lipman, *A Century of Social Service: The History of the Jewish Board of Guardians*, 1959, Ch. 1.
81. Williams, *Manchester*, p. 284.
82. Lipman, *Social Service*, p. 34.
83. For London, see ibid., Ch. 2; for Manchester, see Williams, *Manchester*, pp. 273-97.
84. J.A. Garrard, *The English and Immigration*, 1971, pp. 96-7. This point is brought out by Miriam Steiner in her paper in Aubrey Newman (ed.) *Provincial Jewry*.
85. Williams, *Manchester*, pp. 285-6.
86. On the relations between the Jewish charities and the Poor Law, see Lipman, *Social Service*, pp. 50-3; Williams, *Manchester*, pp. 287-9; Edward S. Conway, 'The origins of the Jewish orphanage', *TJHSE* XXII, 58-62.
87. For A.L. Green and the sewing machines, see Lipman, *Social Service*, pp. 67-8; for Landeshut, see Williams, *Manchester*, pp. 281-90; Lipman, *Social Service*, pp. 41-3, 56-8, 71, 104.
88. For the origins of the Board in the 18th Century, see Roth, *History of the Jews in England*, pp. 224-5.
89. Finestein, 'Anglo-Jewish Revolt.
90. C.H.L. Emanuel, *A Century and a Half of Jewish Life*, 1910, pp. 76, 110.
91. Aubrey Newman, 'The expulsion of the Jews from Prague in 1745', *TJHSE* XXII, 30-41.
92. See e.g. L. Loewe (ed.) *Diaries of Sir Moses and Lady Montefiore*, 1890 (reprinted in facsimile with index by W.M. Schwab, 1983).
93. Quoted from the royal grant of supporters to the arms of Sir Moses, Loewe, *Diaries*, I, p. 300.
94. *Encyclopaedia Judaica*, 1970, I, pp. 648-54.
95. Shaftesley, 'Abraham Benisch', pp. 220-2.
96. I. Finestein, *A Short History of Anglo-Jewry*, 1957, p. 96.
97. Emanuel, *A Century and a Half*, pp. 95, 98, 103, 107-8.
98. Roth, *England*, p. 259.
99. A.M. Hyamson, 'Don Pacifico', *TJHSE* XVIII, 1-40.
100. Robert Blake, *Disraeli*, 1966, pp. 604-7; Alderman, *Jewish Community in British Politics*, 1983, pp. 36, 40.

Chapter 3

The East European Immigration 1881-1914

Causes of Emigration

On 13 March (1 March in the Russian calendar) 1881, Czar Alexander II was assassinated. Although only one of the five conspirators was Jewish, the Jewish population of Russia suffered a series of pogroms,[1] beginning in Yelzavetgrad in the Ukraine on 27 April and spreading through the south and east Ukraine, the most serious being in Kiev. Pogroms continued sporadically into 1884. Apart from an outbreak in Warsaw on Christmas Day, 1881, the pogroms of the 1880s were confined to southern Russia: in Lithuania and White Russia the authorities took firm action to prevent pogroms and any disturbances were confined to outbreaks of fire in which Jewish property was destroyed. The extent to which these pogroms were officially inspired is uncertain, and the attitudes of the local authorities varied.[2] But governmental measures added to the pressures towards Jewish emigration. In 1882 the 'May Laws' - the 'Temporary Orders concerning the Jews' which lasted till 1917 - removed the possibility of some broadening of the narrow economic base of Jewish life that had seemed possible under Alexander II. They forbade the Jews to settle or own land outside the towns or other urban areas, or to engage in any business on Sundays or Christian holidays. The Jews were generally restricted to the Pale of Settlement. This was an area on the western edge of the Russian Empire of fifteen 'governments' in European Russia and ten 'governments' in the Russian part of the former Poland - 'Congress Poland', in which less than a third of Russian empire's population lived. Even within the Pale, Jews were confined to towns or villages where they were already living, being forbidden in 1887 to move from one village to another. In 1891 Jews who could not prove a right of residence were expelled from Moscow, followed by similar administrative measures in other cities. Administrative action, which often meant the discretion of the local police, multiplied the possibilities for discrimination: there were restrictions on admission of Jews to the professions, high schools and universities; and they were virtually excluded from any civil or military offices, while disproportionately subject to conscription as private soldiers. In 1903 there began at Kishinev in Bessarabia a series of pogroms, in loss of life even worse than those of the 1880s; the worst was at Odessa in 1905, where 300 were killed and thousands wounded. The pogroms continued until 1906; of about 700 outbreaks, nearly all were in the Ukraine or Bessarabia, few in White Russia and none in Lithuania.[3]

Immigration to Britain came mainly from Lithuania and White Russia, areas hardly affected except indirectly, by pogroms. But there were underlying economic and demographic factors which contributed to the movement of some 2.75 million Jews from Eastern Europe to the West between 1881 and 1914, of whom over two million went to the United States. This mass movement was part of a great upheaval which took over 60 million Europeans - Irish, Italians, Germans, Austro-Hungarians, Poles - overseas in the century before 1914.[4] Thus the movement of Jews from Eastern Europe to Britain was only a small part of a much greater migration, of which the causes were poverty, lack of economic opportunity and - for the Jews at least - persecution in their native lands.

But this movement could not have taken place on this scale had there not become available the means of transport by railway and steamship, and the prospects of free entry to lands of wider opportunity. For the Jews of the Russian empire, the pogroms and restrictions which followed the death of Alexander II intensified a movement which had already brought 250,000 Jews from Eastern Europe since 1800. Underlying this movement was pressure of population with diminishing economic prospects. The number of Russian Jews increased from about 1.6 million in 1825 to about 4 million in 1880, a growth of about 1.8 per cent per year by natural increase, compared with just over 1 per cent for the population of the Russian empire as a whole. The Jewish birth rate was lower than that of the general Russian population but the death rate (including infant mortality) was also lower: more of the Jewish babies survived and, when they grew up, they lived longer. But 94 per cent of the Jewish population was confined to the 'Pale of Settlement'. Within the Pale, the Jews were in general confined to incorporated cities and urban villages. In 1897 the Jews were 11.5 per cent of the population of the Pale but over 40 per cent of its urban population.[5]

This growth of a population, restricted in area of residence and in its changes of earning a living, took place within a wider society subject to the dislocation of small-scale production and crafts caused by industrialization and economic modernization.[6] In such circumstances - quite apart from persecution - an outflow of migrants was to be expected in the last decades of the nineteenth century. But it was persecution which varied the flow of emigration of Jews between 1881 and 1914. This can be measured from the statistics of migration to the United States, which received about 75 to 80 per cent of the emigrants. Taking the annual rate of Jewish migration from Russia to the United States in the 1870s as a base, the level of migration in 1881-9 was ten times; this reflected the impact of the 1880s progroms and the May Laws. But the level went up to twenty times the 1870s base in 1890-8, reflecting the administrative expulsions; twenty-six times in 1899-1902; and sixty-four times in 1903-7, showing the effect of the second series of pogroms, the Russo-Japanese War of 1904-5 and the 1905 Revolution; in 1908-10 there was a relative reduction to forty-one times the 1870s level and to fifty-four times in 1911-14.[7]

The Volume of Migration

In so far as the rise and fall of Eastern European immigration to Britain can be accurately measured, it showed an exactly parallel curve, although the increase in numbers was less dramatic compared with the level of the 1870s when there was already an appreciable immigration to Britain. There was a peak in 1881-2, with a decrease in the later 1880s. A sharp increase followed in 1891, rising to a new peak in 1891, followed by a decline and then another peak in 1896; a decline again till 1899 was followed by a steady rise to an unprecedented high in 1903-6; after this, the Aliens Act caused a check, with a decline to 1911, after which the figures rose again till the outbreak of the First World War. There was a parallel with the United States, where the stiffening of immigration restrictions caused a check, which was then followed by a rise in immigration.[8]

How many Jewish immigrants settled in Britain between 1881 and 1914 it is impossible to determine with certainty. First, many of the aliens arriving in Britain were en route to America, even if they did not hold 'through tickets'. Figures from the Poor Jews Temporary Shelter in London, which received some 95 per cent of the Jewish immigrants arriving in London, suggest that between 1889 and 1902 over 60 per cent went on, mainly to the USA. Second, although from 1890 the Board of Trade collected figures of aliens who landed and from 1890 of all 'non-through' steerage passengers, the Royal Commission on Alien Immigration in 1903 found it impossible to distinguish Jews from non-Jews or 'through' from 'non-through' passengers and regarded the 1901 census figure of 95,425 Jews in Britain as a less unreliable guide. Probably the number of Russo-Jewish immigrants actually settling in Britain between 1881 and 1905 was about 100,000, with 8,000 in the peak year 1905. Up to another 50,000 arrived from 1906 to 1914. Again one cannot be certain, because while the Aliens Act inspectorate published annual figures, these included only steerage passengers, and some of the Russians and Poles counted as not being transmigrants in fact moved on after a short stay. There were also from Eastern Europe a few thousand immigrants from Galicia (although most of those who left Galicia could settle more easily elsewhere in the Austro-Hungarian empire) and over 1,000 Jews from Rumania.[9]

These figures, an annual range of 3-8,000 immigrants settling, with an average of 5,000, seem small by comparison with the United States. On the other hand, if nearly three times this number actually disembarked, even if only for a short time on their way to America or elsewhere, the Eastern European immigrants were quite noticeable as an alien feature in the limited number of areas to which they came. Further, if the East European immigrants of the 1870s are also taken into account, within just over a generation East European Jews and their children outnumbered the pre-1881 British Jews and their children by nearly 3 to 1. Hence the East European immigration had a profound effect on both the internal life of the Anglo-Jewish community and on their relations with their neighbours.

Jewish emigrants from Russia to the United States, initially at least, came disproportionately from the northern provinces (Lithuania and White Russia), as distinct from Poland, the south-west and southern provinces. They came from areas with a high ratio of Jewish to total urban population, high proportions of crafts and manufacturing and low proportions of commerce within the Jewish labour force and without the greater employment opportunities of the rapidly growing Polish factories. This would suggest economic pressure rather than direct experience of pogroms as an incentive to migration. There may have been a change after 1903 when the even more severe pogroms of the 1900s increased emigration from south and south-west Russia.[10] There is no comparable statistical evidence for migrants to Britain but it is possible they conformed to the same pattern.

Routes of Migration

The first emigrants of 1881-2 were however refugees from the south Russian pogroms and they streamed in whole familes across the nearest frontier to concentrate outside the Austrian border town of Brody in Galicia, where within a year about 23,000 Jews encamped in a sort of no man's land, without the money or even knowledge to take themselves further. The Alliance sent Charles Netter to relieve their immediate needs and move them on to points of embarkation. Other organizations in Britain (the Mansion House Fund was inaugurated by the Lord Mayor of London at a public meeting on 1 February 1882), Germany, Austria and Belgium joined in; and Brody was eventually cleared of refugees. But Jewish organizations outside Russia at this period were frightened to organize the flow of migrants systematically, lest they encourage immigration to their own countries with which they feared they would be unable to cope. They used all means, including advertisements in the Russo-Jewish press, to convince would-be migrants that western cities offered little prospect of employment; and they urged rabbinical authorities in the east to warn their flocks about the religious dangers of life in the west. Migration in the later 1880s and the 1890s became again a matter of individual initiative, with one or two members of a family (usually the husband or father) going first to establish a base and then normally - but not always - sending back for the rest of the family.[11]

The main route from the northern provinces of the Russian empire involved crossing the east Prussian frontier at Eydtkeuhnen or Werblow; from central, or even southern, Russia the crossing point was opposite Thorn; from Ukraine or Bessarabia the crossing was into Austrian Poland or via Rumania. The journey to the frontier was usually by train, though sometimes by wagon or boat (especially down the Dvina to the Baltic). Crossing the frontier officially required a passport, which was bureaucratically complicated for Jews and expensive, since 15 roubles for a passport compared with 50 for crossing the Atlantic steerage. Many crossings of the frontier were therefore illicit, with local guides, especially on a Saturday night when the Russian officers on the frontier were more agreeably employed and their unsupervised subordinates could be more readily bribed if necessary.[12]

Emigrants from Lithuania and the Baltic provinces could embark at Libau, Memel or Riga. But most travelled across Germany by train, usually changing at Berlin, to Bremen, Hamburg or Rotterdam. The continental shipping companies established their own medical inspection and transit stations at the German or Austro-Hungarian frontiers and provided accommodation for the emigrants awaiting embarkation.[13] There was fierce competition between the shipping companies for the Atlantic emigrant traffic, since ships which made the eastward journey across the Atlantic filled with grain found emigrants the easiest and most economic cargo for their holds on the westward journey. The British lines competed with the continental companies and between 1902 and 1904 it was cheaper to travel from Europe to England and then from Liverpool to America, than from Europe direct.[14] Fares to England were low: at one time the journey from Hamburg to London cost only 15/- (75p) though by 1903 it was 24/- (£1.20).[15]

The complex arrangements for emigration were made by ticket agents inside Russia or along the route, who bought space in the ships and sold individual tickets to migrants, often taking advantage of the latter's ignorance of language and conditions outside their home area; there are many stories of ticket agents cheating migrants by selling them tickets for England when the fare had been paid to America. Eventually, the practices of the ticket agents, the danger from white slave traffickers to unaccompanied females and - above all - the increased flow of refugees at the time of the pogroms of the 1900s forced the Jewish communal bodies in the West to put aside their earlier reluctance to organize migration. An international conference of Jewish relief organizations at Frankfurt in 1904 led to the establishment of immigrant aid committees in twenty-four centres across Europe, the stationing of welfare representatives and interpreters at the border posts and on the trans-European trains, and the provision of clothing, medical aid and *Kasher* food for migrants.[16]

While there were sailings direct to the east coast ports and many transmigrants with through tickets went from Hull via Liverpool to America, London was the main port of arrival for those intending either to settle or to wait before travelling on. Weekly during the 1890s and early 1900s there were at least four weekly steamers from Hamburg, three each from Rotterdam and Bremen and one from Libau - all for London. The conditions for steerage passengers on these boats were bad and, though the German boats were improved after 1895, conditions on the Libau boats remained poor. As a result emigrants who probably had no chance to change their clothes since leaving home arrived in a condition that aroused adverse comment. On the boat the steerage passengers subsisted on food brought with them, such as potatoes and herring.[17]

Arrival of the Immigrants

Before disembarkation, officials checked the health and other details of those arriving, including the money they had with them. Their health was found to be fairly good, and cases of infectious disease not numerous. Of those arriving between 1894 and 1902, 22 per cent said they had no money and 15 per cent less than 10/- (50p).

Contemporary observers described the immigrants seated on the ship's deck, looking strange and bewildered, with their scanty baggage in baskets and bundles. Beatrice Webb noted the contrast between the 'greeners' or new arrivals dressed in Eastern European clothes and the relatives who came to meet them and were dressed in British style. Before 1885 many of the immigrants had been defrauded and robbed by Yiddish-speaking touts who promised to find accommodation and provide tickets for onward travel. In 1884, a Jewish baker, against the wishes of the Jewish Board of Guardians (who thought it would encourage immigration), set up a Jews' Temporary Shelter. He succeeded, in spite of attempts to have the accommodation closed as inadequate and insanitary. Gaining the backing of communal leaders, the shelter was financially aided by the communal bodies, the Rothschilds and the shipping companies. Its representatives boarded the ships, interviewed the migrants, provided accommodation for up to fourteen days for single men and helped families to find lodgings.[18]

To deal with the problem of women travelling alone, Lady Battersea (daughter of *Sir Anthony de Rothschild), aided by *Claude G. Montefiore and *Simeon Singer, founded a Jewish Ladies Society for Protection and Rescue Work. This employed an agent to meet all boats and boat trains likely to be carrying girls or women without friends to meet them; and it also set up a hostel for rescue cases and unmarried mothers. It subsequently took the lead among Jewish and general organizations for combating the white slave traffic, with a central bureau for exchanging information, and inspectors in Liverpool, Buenos Aires, Rio de Janeiro and Montevideo.[19]

Demographic Aspects

The addition of a generation of 150,00 Eastern European immigrants to a community of 65,000 produced marked, if temporary, changes in the demographic profile of British Jewry. To judge by information about immigrants arriving in 1891-2, about 54-5 per cent were men, 25-6 per cent women and 17-20 per cent children. For the males, an age classification for 1888-93 showed 26 per cent under 20, 63 per cent between 21 and 40, 10 per cent between 41 and 60, and only 0.5 per cent over 60.[20] The effect of immigration from a society with high rate of marriage, early age of marriage and high number of children per marriage was to increase the birth rate for London Jewry from an estimated 30.3 per 1,000 in 1856-9 to 45 in 1903, the marriage rate from 8.2 to 9.6, and to reduce the death rate from 17.6 to 14.7. After 1905, with an initial check to immigration and then its continuance at a rather lower rate, the immigrants began to merge with the native-born Jewish population; in particular, there seems to have been a marked tendency for native-born Jewish women to marry immigrants. The immigrant Jewish population began to resemble the native-born in birth, death and marriage patterns: smaller families, say three children rather than six, and later age of marriage.[21] In estimating the total size of the Jewish population in Britain in 1914, account has to be taken of the convergence of these two patterns. Contemporary estimates put the population of British Jewry at about 250,000 in 1914, this estimate seems to be on the low side and the real figure was possibly nearer to 300,000, of whom 180,000 were in London.[22]

Geographical Distribution of the Immigrants

The effect of immigration on the geographical distribution of British Jewry was twofold. First, it reinforced the previous tendency to concentrate in industrial centres, particularly in the north, and to the decline of the small communities in the southern seaports and market towns. By 1914 the once flourishing communities in Canterbury, Sheerness, Penzance, Cheltenham, Falmouth, Yarmouth and Ipswich had disappeared.[23] Other communities like Bristol[24] were relatively little affected by the immigration. On the other hand, some small communities were founded or reinforced: in Reading a settlement of about 200 immigrants, mainly tailors, was sponsored by a communal agency, the Jewish Dispersal Committee, founded by *Samuel Montagu to relieve pressure of immigration on the main centres.[25] In Blackburn, a prosperous regional centre, a market centre and a recently expanded industrial town, the presence of a middle-class clientele fostered a community of tailors and market traders. The community grew from a handful of families in 1881 to over 250 souls in 1904, possibly by decentralization from the Manchester community, as Reading was by dispersal from London.[26] But the outstanding example of a community's growth through immigration is that of Leeds, which rose from about 2,500 in 1881 to 6,000 in 1888, 10,000 in 1897, 15,000 in 1904 and 20,000 in 1907.[27] Similar dramatic rises were found, although with much smaller absolute numbers, in the small communities in the north-east and in south Wales.[28] These communities almost all owed their growth to the attraction of developing commercial and industrial environments - such as the diverse growth of industries in Leeds or the metal and mining industries in the north-east and south Wales. Occasionally, as at Reading, there is evidence of planned dispersion by the communal authorities. But generally economic forces worked without outside stimulus. While London, with 180,000 Jews in 1914, retained about two-thirds of British Jewry, an increasing proportion of the 120,000 Jews outside London in 1914 were in a relatively few centres. Of the 100,000 in England outside London, about half were in the two communities of Manchester (30,000) and Leeds (20,000). If Liverpool (about 8,000) and Birmingham (6,000) are added, two-thirds of the English Jews outside London lived in four communities. Of the 10,000 Jews in Scotland, at least three-quarters were in Glasgow. Of the 4,500 in Wales, nearly half were in Cardiff and nearly a quarter in Swansea, although the remainder were scattered in a dozen small communities, mainly in the mining villages and largely recruited from fairly recent immigrants.[29] Yet the scatter of the Jewish population was such that, in relation to the local population of the metropolitan area or town, it was insignificant. Generally, as in south Wales, it was around 1 per cent or less of the total population; in Greater London, Jews formed under 3 per cent of a population of over 7 million; only in Leeds did they reach 5 per cent of the total population of the area.

The Jewish Quarter

Within more limited localities, however, the immigration produced a noticeable intensification of a phenomenon that had already appeared in many cities - the development of a Jewish quarter with a sizeable Jewish population, which formed the overwhelming majority within a definable area. Just as the traditional Jewish quarters in the inner areas adjoining the central business districts in London, Manchester, Leeds, Liverpool and Glasgow were beginning to empty as their residents moved outwards, even if only to an adjoining area (as from Whitechapel to Dalston), the immigration brought in new residents to make the original Jewish quarter more densely populated and, to extend it, and to intensify its specifically Jewish character. These areas probably reached their maximum Jewish population in the first decade of the twentieth century. Then the Jewish East End of London spread beyond its original area in Whitechapel into Spitalfields, St George's in the east, Mile End, Stepney and Bethnal Green. At its peak, this quarter had a Jewish population of some 125,000 in an area of 1.5 square miles. By 1914 this population may have declined to around 100,000, as even some of the immigrant population had moved outwards.[30] There were external barriers to expansion: the Irish dockers prevented the Jewish immigrants from spreading south of Cable Street and a tough, inward-looking community retained its hold around St Matthew's Church, Bethnal Green (the 'Old Nichol' of Arthur Morrison's *Child of the Jago*), although the slum clearance in south-west Bethnal Green in the 1890s brought in many Jews as tenants of the new blocks of flats.[31]

The concept of a Jewish immigrant quarter was familiar in the literature and public discussion in Europe and America in the late nineteenth century.[32] Such a concentration of immigrants and their immediate descendants was perceived to be marked by limitation of occupation, the retention of the customs, language and external habits of the country of origin, and by a distinctive economic, social and cultural life. Topographically, the area was adjacent to the central business district and typically in the inner ring of the city where property had deteriorated and conditions of life were affected by the encroachment of industry, warehousing and transportation (such as the construction of railway lines and stations), leading to overcrowding. Apart from the fact that it was usually where their predecessors had settled, such an area attracted immigrants because it was close to the docks or rail termini where they arrived, there was suitable employment available, and accommodation which was open to them.[33] The immigrant quarter has also been defined as an area of 'first settlement' for immigrants 'just off the boat', from where they or their children moved to an area of 'second settlement' in the process of improving their economic and social position, and then to an area of 'third settlement' in the suburbs, in which residence symbolized the attainment of full middle-class status.[34]

The Pattern of Jewish Settlement in London

As an example of the coexistence of these areas of settlement at the end of the nineteenth century, the Chief Rabbi, *Dr Hermann Adler, described in

1897 to an interviewer for Charles Booth's survey eleven geographical groups of the Jews of London:

(1) Whitechapel and Commercial Road (St George's in the East): working class, artisans, pedlars, hawkers and small shopkeepers; (2) Stepney and Bethnal Green: small shopkeepers and the better class of cabinetmakers; (3) East Central London: small traders in and around Houndsditch; a large number of Jewish teachers in Goodman's Fields; (4) Highbury, Canonbury and Dalston: middle-class employers, large shopkeepers, some professional men; (5) West Central (Bloomsbury): middle-class: merchants, manufacturers, professional men; (6) West (Hyde Park, Kensington Gardens, Maida Vale): rich merchants, bankers, stock exchange and professional men – the less wealthy in Maida Vale; (7) South West (Belgravia): a very few, very rich merchants etc. (e.g. Sassoons, Rothschilds): no synagogue; (8) North West (St John's Wood): middle-class – merchants and a few professional men; (9) North West (Hampstead): as (8), except that the younger people are moving to this area; (10) West (Hammersmith) artisans, tradesmen (active and retired) and fairly well-to-do merchants; (11) South East (The Borough): artisans, small employers, and shopkeepers.[35]

This account, based on personal knowledge (Dr Adler had, for instance, previously been minister of the congregation in Bayswater and Maida Vale) can be supported by the objective evidence collected in Charles Booth's survey, the *Life and Labour of the People in London,* of the same period. On the basis of the school attendance officers' reports, the third series of the Booth survey – 'Social and Religious Influences' – classifies every street in London according to social and economic class, with appropriate colours on maps. Although for east London the information was collected in the 1880s, this was updated to match the information of the rest of London in the 1890s.[36] In addition, Charles Russell and *Harry S. Lewis used similar material, which indicated the religion of the families, to compile the map attached to their book, *The Jew in London,* showing the percentage of Jewish population in each street in east London in 1899.[37] At the 1901 census, 31.8 per cent of the population of Whitechapel were born abroad, and in St George's in the East, 28.8 per cent. In an area of about three-quarters of a square mile in Whitechapel and St George's, Russell and Lewis showed nearly all the streets in 1899 as having at least half the population Jewish and in about a quarter of the streets 95 per cent of the population was Jewish. This was the core of the London Jewish quarter, the area of first settlement. If Russell and Lewis' map is compared with that in the second (Inner Ring North) of the third series of Booth, those streets with at least 75 per cent Jewish population are, in the Booth classification, mainly 'higher class labour mixed with poverty' (£1.50 to £2 per week family income) or 'working class comfort' (£2–2.50), with areas of 'very poor' or 'poor' below the £1.50 per week 'poverty line' as defined by Booth; on the other hand, there are some 'well-to-do' (middle-class with one or two servants) along the main thoroughfares, where the main shops were, who were presumably shopkeepers, or the teachers mentioned by Dr Adler in his group (3), and merchants, ministers of religion and other middle class still in the East End. There is also confirmatory evidence about the distribution of social classes from information on synagogue membership. On the eastern fringe of the main Jewish quarter – an example of group (2) in Dr Adler's classification – the East London Synagogue, founded in 1877, near Stepney Green, provided for the pre-1881 Jewish residents of the area and for some of the better-off immigrants; the latitudinarian tendencies of the minister, the Revd J.F. Stern (1865–1934) led to the foundation nearby of the Stepney Orthodox Synagogue by more traditionally minded immigrants.[38] Stern himself described his congregation as mainly working class but slightly better off than those who attended the immigrant *hebroth* and as being 30 per cent foreign-born.[39] Analysis of the addresses of a sample of the members of the East London Synagogue shows 20 per cent as living in streets of 'working-class comfort mixed with poverty' (£1.05–£1.50 per week), 60 per cent in streets of 'working-class comfort' (£1.50–£2.50) and 20 per cent in middle-class streets;[40] this accords with an average annual membership contribution to the synagogue of around £3.[41]

If the Stepney Green area thus typified the better-off working class among London Jews around 1900, north London represented the middle class, (4) in Dr Adler's grouping. Charles Booth wrote that the 'northern part of the district from Islington to Stamford Hill and from Holloway to Ball's Pond and Canonbury provides the best example of London middle-class life and of the religious and social influences to which it is subject'.[42] Within this area there were social differences between Dalston 'villadom' with its 'dingy perspectives'; the 'genteel suburb' of Highbury; and Hackney, which was drab compared with Highbury but provided *petit bourgeois* comforts compared with the East End.[43] The membership of the North London Synagogue, which was itself in Barnsbury ('comfortable working-class' with some middle-class streets, in Booth's classification) but drew also on Highbury and Canonbury for its membership, reflected this social mix. In 1898 only 9 per cent of its membership was in 'wealthy' streets, 50 per cent in middle-class streets, 39 per cent in streets of 'middle-class comfort' with a large proportion of the lower-middle-class or small tradesmen, and only 2 per cent in streets where working-class comfort was mixed with poverty.[44]

The Bayswater synagogue, the majority of whose members by 1900 lived in Maida Vale or nearby, represented part of Dr Adler's western group (6). This was a very important suburban area in London Jewry before 1914. Forty-seven per cent of its members were in 'wealthy streets' (with three or more servants per household), 45 per cent in middle-class streets (one or two servants), 7 per cent in streets of lower middle-class or working-class comfort, and 0.3 per cent in streets where working-class comfort was mixed with poverty.[45] Even so, at this time the Bayswater congregation was less affluent than the New West End Synagogue, which had been founded in

1879 as a neighbourhood synagogue for Jews in the wealthy area north of Kensington Gardens and Hyde Park. Even in 1913, two-thirds of the members lived in this area which Booth (who wrote in 1899 that 'Bayswater is known for its rich Jews') defined almost entirely as 'wealthy', with households having at least three servants. This area held the wealthiest Jewish community in London – as Dr Adler noted, the families who lived south of the park had no synagogue – and before 1914 the male members of the New West End Synagogue paid the highest average annual contributions in the United Synagogue, up to about £15 a year, five times those of the East London Synagogue.[46]

Housing Conditions

In the area of first settlement, however, as in similar areas of Victorian cities, living conditions, which were already bad, were worsened by overcrowding caused by demolition and the failure to provide rehousing at rents they could afford, even for families displaced under the early slum clearance schemes. In 1885 the Royal Commission on the Housing of the Working Classes found 'a mass of evidence... that the pulling down of buildings inhabited by the very poor, whether undertaken for philanthropic, sanitary or commercial purposes, causing overcrowding into the neighbouring slums with the further consequence of keeping up high rents'.[47] Although these findings coincided with only the beginning of the mass Jewish immigration, the latter was highlighted in March 1884 by a *Lancet* report on working-class Jewish immigration into Leeds.[48] This was among the first of a series of attacks on the immigrants as responsible for overcrowding, insanitary conditions, increases in rents and the demand for premiums, or 'key money', as a condition for the granting of tenancies. In fact, the evidence suggests that these problems were largely those of the areas into which the immigrants came, and from which they suffered, rather than problems caused merely by immigration.[49]

The Jewish community intensified the efforts they had already made to secure sanitary inspections and to get repairs and improvements carried out by landlords of accommodation occupied by the Jewish poor.[50] Immigrants were themselves among the landlords who acquired property occupied by other immigrants. One method of improvement was the building of blocks of tenements, but where these buildings were inadequate for family accommodation the effect was to aggravate the problem: some commercially erected blocks (such as Booth Street Buildings) were so defective and let at such high rents that, combined with other profiteering by private landlords, they caused immigrant tenant resistance in the 1890s.[51] *Lord Rothschild, Samuel Montagu, the architect *N.S. Joseph and other communal leaders associated with the United Synagogue and the

London Jewish Board of Guardians joined to establish the Four per cent Industrial Dwellings Company in 1885. This had two principles. First, it offered a return of 4 per cent to investors, which meant a rent of 5/- (25p) a week for a flat of two rooms and a scullery; the previous 5 per cent 'philanthropic' or 7 per cent return on commercial blocks meant rents that the poor could not afford. Second, it aimed to provide apartments large enough at least to avoid whole families sharing a single room, although even communal bathrooms were not provided until 1896 in Stepney Green for tenants who could afford higher rents (6/6 - 32.5p for two rooms, 9/6 - 47.5p - for three).[52] The problem of overcrowding and rent levels eased in the years before 1914 partly as a result of the general improvement in London after 1903, when hundreds of apartments in east London were empty, and partly as a result of the 'Four per Cent' and similar enterprises. The 'Four per Cent' housed 4,303 individuals by 1899 and the death rate in their blocks was a third of the Whitechapel average, while that of the Booth Street Buildings was above it.[53]

Further, one cannot regard the Jewish quarter as merely a static pool of immigrants. Immigrants were always arriving but, like the earlier Jewish inhabitants, they were also leaving for the outer areas. To a limited extent this was due to efforts made by the communal authorities to encourage dispersal[54], but it was increasingly due to socially and economically motivated movement by the immigrants themselves. For instance, by 1914, there was a colony of about 3,000 Eastern European Jews in the Soho area.[55] The move of factories from east London up the Lea Valley to Tottenham and Walthamstow provided employment for thousands of Jewish workers in making furniture, boots and shoes and office equipment. Previously there had been some Jewish settlement in this area but Jews had commuted to industrial employment in east London on the Great Eastern and Great Northern Railways, assisted by workmen's fares. But from 1900 the prospect of industrial employment in the Lea Valley attracted thousands of recent arrivals, including young transmigrants on their way to America, since there seems to have been a considerable turnover in Jewish employees in these factories up to 1910.[56]

Generally, however, there was a trend for the immigrants to move out of the Jewish area of first settlement as soon as they could acquire enough money to do so. In London they moved either eastwards to Stepney Green and Bow, or along one of the three axes of Jewish settlement in north, north-west or west London which had developed in the previous generation. As a result, by 1914 while there were perhaps 100,000 Jews in east London, compared with 125,000 a decade earlier, there were 50,000 outside east London: 25-30,000 in north, up to 10,000 in north-west and over 10,000 in west London. The outermost communities had reached Kew and Brentford in the west and Brondesbury, even Golders Green, in the north-west.[57]

Communities outside London

An analogous pattern of immigrant Jewish quarter and suburban community, with one gradually spilling over into the other, was found in the main centres outside London. In Leeds, there was already by 1889 a settlement of about 5,000 recent immigrants in the Leylands, an area about half a mile square, adjacent to the Belgrave Street area, the location of the existing synagogue and Jewish community.[58] On the other hand, in Glasgow the first post-1880 Eastern European immigrants did not settle in the west end of the city where the established Jewish community was located but south of the river in the Gorbals, where there developed a working-class, Yiddish-speaking community, orthodox in religious practice, and separate from the middle-class, acculturated Jewish community of the west end.[59] In Manchester, the immigrants who increased the community from about 10,000 in 1881 to around 30,000 in 1914, moved first into Red Bank, the area of the earlier Jewish working-class settlement, and then spread north into Strangeways. Meanwhile, in addition to the suburban middle-class Jews in south Manchester, there was an increasing suburban middle-class community in Cheetham Hill, which steadily spread north.[60] As *Lord Sieff, who grew up in this milieu before 1914, wrote: 'The social ascent could almost be equated topographically - almost by yards north-west up the Bury New Road'.[61] Newcastle can be taken as an example of the medium-sized Jewish community. Here the original settlers of the early nineteenth century had come to settle between the river and the area west of the central railway station, west of the city centre, and the post-1880 immigrants came to the same area, although by 1880 a new large synagogue had been opened further north in Leazes Park and by the early 1900s the wealthier, older families had moved out to the suburb of Jesmond.[62]

Occupation

The social and residential differences between the immigrants and the older-established elements in the community were reflected in their occupations. For a period, the immigrants constituted what was almost a separate economy in which they were predominantly engaged and which was distinguishable from the general economy of the area. This phenomenon was intensified by the concentration of the immigrants in limited areas of the great cities. To some extent the occupations of the immigrants reflected those in Eastern Europe. Of the gainfully occupied Jews in Russia in 1897, 27.7 per cent were in manufacturing or mechanical skilled occupations, 31.4 per cent in commerce (including trade), 18.6 per cent were labourers and only 5 per cent were in the professions. Among the

Russo-Jewish immigrants to the United States 1899–1914, the corresponding percentages were 62.7, 7.2, 23.3 and 1, showing a disproportionate tendency of the industrial workers and the unskilled to emigrate – at least after 1899 – while those in commerce or the professions were more likely to remain in Russia.

Within the industrial sector, the proportion of Russo-Jewish industrial workers engaged in clothing manufacture was 47.2 per cent, and among immigrants to the United States (1899–1914) 52.2 per cent. From this one might assume that roughly a third of those who emigrated were in the clothing and footwear manufacturing trades; and about 10 per cent were in the various forms of woodworking associated with the furniture or building industries, or craftsmen like glaziers.[63] Of those who came to Britain, the Jews' Temporary Shelter collected information between 1895 and 1908 from a sample of some 9,000. Of these some 29 per cent said they were previously in clothing manufacture (excluding footwear), 11 per cent were boot and shoemakers, 23 per cent were in trade or commerce, and 8 per cent were carpenters.[64] The 1901 census gave the occupations of those in London born in Russia or Poland (24,164 males and 5,358 females). Of the males 40 per cent, of the females 50 per cent, were in tailoring; 12.5 per cent of the men were in the boot, shoe and slipper trades, and 10 per cent in furniture-making.[65]

Thus of the gainfully employed male immigrants in London in 1901, almost two-thirds were in these three trades, but with tailoring predominant. There is a reasonable correlation with the occupations of immigrants to America and with the occupations of Jews in Eastern Europe, although possibly due to the dislocation among small artisans caused by industrialization in Russia and the limitations placed by the government on the economic opportunities of Russian Jews, there was a marked tendency to emigrate among artisans.[66]

There was also a strong local influence in Britain attracting Jewish immigrants into these occupations. For instance, Leeds, which after about 1865 became a world centre for the wholesale manufacture of clothing, attracted immigrants as garment workers: in 1891 about two-thirds of the employed males of Russo-Polish origin in Leeds were tailors, compared with 13 per cent in footwear manufacture; and of the employed females nearly 70 per cent were tailoresses.[67]

These three trades of tailoring, footwear and furniture-making were also those in which Jews already in Britain, not least those who had arrived a few years earlier, were engaged. The 1881–1914 Eastern European immigrant could therefore find employment with people of his own area of origin, religion and customs, or at least with whom he could speak Yiddish. Since the tailoring and footwear trades involved a number of repetitive operations – at least in the form in which they were practised in the workshops – they were relatively easy to learn for those without skills, although there were a number of skilled tasks. All three trades could be operated on a small scale in improvised premises (houses, cellars, sheds or disused buildings) by a small number of operatives. Hours could be adjusted to the exigencies of demand or of the Jewish religious calendar. They could be operated with a minimum of capital: an immigrant could set himself up as an employer and conversely could easily fail and revert to the status of an employee.

These factors, while they explain why these trades attracted so high a proportion of the immigrants, produced most unattractive conditions. Workshops were cramped, unhygienic, lacking in sanitary facilities, and sometimes dangerous. In London there were probably over 1,000 workshops, most employing a handful of workers.[68] In Leeds, where there were some larger workshops before 1900, there were about 100 small tailoring workshops.[69] In Manchester, in addition to the small tailoring workshops, larger workshops or factories made first waterproofed garments (cloth treated with rubber) and then rainproofs.[70]

The immigrant sector of the tailoring industry, using the Singer sewing machine introduced in the late 1850s, made ready-to-wear garments under contract to merchants and wholesale clothiers or, as in Leeds, to provide additional output for large factories at times of high demand, thus enabling the factories to operate at optimum economic size. The specialization of the immigrant workshops in certain types of garments or certain types of operation and their dependence on those for whom they contracted meant that the work was both seasonal and concentrated within a few days of the week to meet the delivery times: the workshops might work only three or four days a week but during those days working hours between 12 and even 18 were not uncommon.[71] The whole condition of the immigrant manufacturing trades, with contract work in small workshops undertaken by a subdivision into repetitive processes, and irregular but long hours of work for poor pay, attached the name of 'sweating' to the Jewish immigrant trades, even though these conditions and patterns of employment antedated the Jewish immigration of the period.[72]

At a time when Charles Booth put the 'poverty line' in London at the equivalent of £1.50 a week, the learner or 'greener' in the immigrant trades, after a few months at a nominal wage, would for the rest of the first year make only a few shillings a week subsisting on the proverbial herring and coffee and even sleeping on the floor of the workroom. After about a year's work, the operative's wages varied with skill, from 75p to £1 for the 'general hands', £1 to 1.50 for the middle grades to £2 or even £2.50 a week for the most skilled worker. Earnings in the footwear industry, particularly in slipper-making and ladies' shoes, which became more or less limited, so far as the small workshops were concerned, to the Jewish immigrants, were generally lower than in tailoring. It was a declining form of the trade, vainly trying to compete with the increasingly mechanized factory production, and one in which price-cutting led to impossibly long hours for diminishing returns.[73] Earnings in cabinetmaking, in which before

1914 the absolute number of immigrants was not large, were better than in the other two immigrant trades.[74]

Earnings of the masters in the immigrant workshops, even allowing for the return on their own labour, were not much more than those of the workers, perhaps not exceeding around £3 a week; their conditions were virtually as bad as their employees', and they had usually to pledge something to find the initial capital. Although there were many success stories, there were many, usually untold, failures.[75]

While tailoring, footwear and furniture-making were the three distinctively immigrant trades of the period, there was considerable fluidity of employment between them, and between these trades and occupations such as hawking and market trading. The glaziers, with large panes of glass on their backs, were familiar figures in the Jewish areas of large cities.[76] Many recent immigrants of the 1881–1914 period began life, as their predecessors had done, by hawking wares or selling on credit, especially in the rural areas.[77] This was characteristic, as was small shopkeeping and market trading, of the smaller communities. For instance, Hartfield's *Commercial Directory of the Jews of Great Britain* of 1894 gives ninety-eight entries for the small communities on Tyne, Wear and Tees (excluding Newcastle and Sunderland). As the total Jewish population of these communities (Gateshead, North and South Shields, Durham, Hartlepool, Stockton, Darlington and Middlesbrough) was less than 1,000 at this time, these must represent a substantial part of these small communities which had developed mainly from the recent immigration. Over 25 per cent were pawnbrokers (usually associated with another trade such as clothing or jewellery), 13 per cent of the entries were clothiers and tailors, 10 per cent drapers, 9 per cent financial agents, 6 per cent watchmakers, jewellers and silversmiths, 6 per cent picture-frame makers and/or sellers, 5 per cent house furnishers, 5 per cent general dealers, 4 per cent boot and shoe dealers, two tobacconists, two slipper-makers, two coal merchants, two ministers of religion and the remainder one each picture dealer, wallpaper seller, optician, auctioneer, physician and shipbroker.[78] The prominence of shopkeeping and small trading, with emphasis on pawnbroking and moneylending, was probably representative of the small immigrant communities, where there was not a strong manufacturing element. For instance, in Blackburn, tailoring in small workshops was the main Jewish occupation; this was followed by market trading and general shopkeeping (in optical supplies, cheap jewellery and fancy goods, footwear, lacework, textile piece goods, leathers and sponges); there were a few cabinetmakers, glaziers and picture framers. The relatively few moneylenders, with the more successful master tailors, picture framers and shopkeepers, formed the most prosperous group in what was, socially and residentially, a lower-middle-class and working-class community.[79]

A medium-sized community – Newcastle, which increased from 750 in 1875 to 2,000 in 1900 – would in 1894 have retained much more of the pattern of the pre-1881 provincial Jewish community. In that year Hartfield's *Directory* had eighty-four entries: fifteen jewellers and watchmakers (seven wholesalers); fifteen general drapers and furnishers (four wholesalers); thirteen slipper manufacturers and merchants; seven tailors; five cabinetmakers; five pawnbrokers; four picture framers and gilders; three synagogue officials; two financial offices; one shipbroker; one engraver and dye-stamper; one baker; and three others. A number of these concerns were manufacturers, and it is estimated that about a third of Newcastle Jewry around 1900 were working-class operatives in manufacture, mainly tailors and slipper-makers.[80]

The occupational distribution of an Anglo-Jewish group not materially affected by the 1881-1914 Eastern European immigration can be seen in the London Spanish and Portuguese congregations. This was about 3,000 strong, with a reasonably representative geographical spread across London and it recorded the occupation of its bridegrooms (41.4 per cent of whom in 1881-90 and 52.9 per cent in 1891-1900 lived outside east London - over 20 per cent in the west, north-west or west central areas). The largest single occupation was that of cigar-maker but this had declined to 17.1 per cent in 1891-90 (from 22.5 per cent in 1851-60). Tailoring and clothing had around 10 per cent, the boot and shoe trades 6-10 per cent. About 7 per cent were merchants, 4 per cent commercial travellers, 3 per cent Stock Exchange and 2 per cent clerks. But the predominant group was that of 'other occupations' - 32 per cent of the bridegrooms in 1881-90, 38.6 per cent in 1901. These figures show how far diversification of occupations had gone in the pre-1881 community. In addition to traditional occupations like jewellers and watchmakers, there were physicians and surgeons, glass and china dealers, a music teacher, leather merchants and dressers, printers and lithographers, cabinetmakers, commission agents and cabdrivers; in 1891-1900 the diversity of occupations is particularly marked.[81]

As the native-born Jews diversified into lower middle-class occupations an increasing number became clerks and commercial travellers. But the continuing pressure of the Victorian Jew towards middle-class status continued unabated and included a number of small-scale manufacturers; these were not only in the traditional Jewish trades like clothing or tobacco but in metal-using industries; they also developed large-scale retailing especially in clothing, furniture and food. A number of major industrial undertakings were founded by Jews (Mond in chemicals, Siegfried Bettman in engineering, Hugo Hirst in the electrical industry, Sigmund Gestetner in office machines) but these were examples of individual enterprise rather than characteristic Jewish occupations. The higher economic echelons for Jews remained finance (particularly raising loans for foreign governments), the Stock Exchange and foreign trade, although this now included new developments, such as the building up by Marcus Samuel and his brother of the Shell Oil Company.[82]

Of the just under fifty Jews dying between 1881 and 1919, who left over half a million pounds and whose source of wealth is identified, thirty-one were bankers, six stockbrokers, six merchants, two in diamonds, and one each in chemical and machinery manufacture, one a newspaper proprietor and one an art dealer.[83] Occupations connected with finance still predominated as the sources by which British Jews acquired exceptional wealth. For instance, of the three Jewish peers of the 1890s - Rothschild, *Pirbright (de Worms) and *Wandsworth (Stern) - all were bankers and incidentally of families originating in Frankfurt.[84] Before 1914 the great majority of the wealthy among British Jews were still of Central European origin, although the Eastern European immigrants were beginning to contribute major entrepreneurs: Michael Marks, whose firm had thirty-six stores by 1900, had come to Britain in 1882 from Russian Poland and Sir Montagu Burton (1885-1952), born in Russia in 1885, opened his factory to supply his retail shops in 1910.[85] Finally, the children of these immigrants, some of them born in Eastern Europe, began to follow the established community into the professions. Whereas earlier in the nineteenth century, Jews had been underrepresented in the professions, the established community produced an increasing number of barristers, solicitors, physicians, architects and engineers, and some civil servants, a few of whom achieved senior rank.[86] With Oxford and Cambridge fully open to Jews from 1871, a number studied at the universities and a few became academic teachers (in addition to those in the field of Hebrew and rabbinics). By 1914 there were probably up to twenty-five undergraduates and a few fellows of colleges at both Oxford and Cambridge, in addition to those at other universities.[87] It had become not unusual for the sons, and occasionally the daughters, of the anglicized upper-middle class to go to university. But it was significant that the children of the immigrants, some born abroad, joined in the process so soon. The outstanding example was the placing as senior wrangler in 1908 of *Selig Brodetsky (as great a landmark as the achievement of Numa Hartog had been in 1869 which influenced the repeal of the University Tests). Brodetsky, born in Olviopol in 1888 and educated at the Jews' Free School in East London, was to become a leader of the Jewish community and a distinguished professor of a British university: it was a portent of the integration of the new immigrants in Anglo-Jewry and British society.[88]

Notes

1. A Russian word defined by the *Encyclopaedia Judaica* (XIII, p. 694) as an attack, involving destruction and looting of property, murder and rape, perpetrated by one section of the population against another.
2. Leonard Schapiro, 'The Russian background of the Anglo-American Jewish

Immigration', *TJHSE* XV, 220-3.
3. *Encyclopaedia Judaica* XV, pp. 697-8.
4. See e.g. *Chambers' Encyclopaedia*, 1959, IX, p. 397.
5. Simon Kuznets, 'Immigration of Russian Jews to the United States', *Perspectives in American History* IX (1975), pp. 68-72.
6. Kuznets, 'Immigration', p. 84.
7. Ibid., p. 43, Table II, col. 4.
8. V.D. Lipman, *Social History of the Jews in England*, 1954, pp. 85-7, 142-3; *A Century of Social Service: The History of the Jewish Board of Guardians*, 1959, pp. 79-80 (for figures based on applications to the London Jewish Board of Guardians); L.P. Gartner, *The Jewish Immigrant in England, 1870-1914*, 2nd edn, 1973, pp. 41-9.
9. Gartner, *Jewish Immigrant*, p. 49 estimates the total of East European Jewish immigrants in Britain in 1911 at 120,000; the total of arrivals would have been higher since some would have arrived and died in Britain before 1911. The estimates are discussed in Lipman, *Social History*, pp. 85-90.
10. Kuznets, 'Immigration', pp. 116-19.
11. Gartner, *Jewish Immigrant*, pp. 44-6.
12. Selig Brodetsky, *Memoirs*, 1960, p. 15; W.J. Fishman, *East End Jewish Radicals*, 1975, pp. 34-6.
13. Gartner, *Jewish Immigrant*, pp. 31-6.
14. Lamar Cecil, *Albert Ballin*, 1967, pp. 8-13, 40-3.
15. *Royal Commission on Alien Immigration* (1902-3). At this time £1 a week was about a minimum wage in London. Q.16,286.
16. Howard M. Sachar, *The Course of Modern Jewish History*, 1958, pp. 310-11.
17. Lipman, *Social History*, pp. 90-1.
18. Ibid., pp. 92-3; Gartner, *Jewish Immigrant*, pp. 52-4; Royal Commission, Q.19,002 for statistics of aliens dealt with by Shelter, 1901-2.
19. The name was changed in 1887 to the Jewish Association for the Protection of Girls and Women; it was absorbed into the Board of Guardians in 1945. See Lipman, *Social Service*, pp. 247-59. For the white slave traffic and Jewish action to combat it see Edward J. Bristow, *Prostitution and Prejudice: The Jewish Fight against White Slavery 1870-1939*, 1982; Lloyd P. Gartner, 'Anglo-Jewry and the Jewish international traffic in prostitution, 1885-1914', *Association for Jewish Studies (AJS) Review* VII-VIII, 1982-3, pp. 129-78.
20. Lipman, *Social History*, p. 93. Figures for Russian immigrants to the USA 1889-1914 show 56 per cent male, 45.6 per cent female; the number of children under 14 as a percentage of total Jewish immigrants was 24.4, persons aged 14-44, 69.8 per cent; 45 and over, 5.8 per cent (Kuznets, 'Immigration', pp. 94-9). The London figures generally agree with these except that they have fewer children, but stress the predominance of immigrants of working age.
21. Kosmin, 'Nuptiality and fertility among British Jews', pp. 263-4, 267.
22. Lipman, *Social History*, p. 160. 300,000 for British Jewry and 180,000 for London in 1914 are the figures arrived at by B.A. Kosmin, S. Waterman and N. Grizzard in their study 'The Jewish dead of the Great War as an indicator of the location, size and structure of the Jewish community in Britain'; I am grateful to Dr Kosmin and the Board of Deputies of British Jews for allowing me to read this valuable study in draft before its appearance in *Immigrants*

and Minorities, 5 (1986).
23. Lipman, *Social History,* p. 161.
24. Alex Schlesinger, 'Victorian Jewry in Bristol', in, Aubrey Newman (ed.) *Provincial Jewry in Victorian Britain,* 1975.
25. Lipman, *Social History,* p. 100; Gartner, *Jewish Immigrant,* p. 149; see 'Reading', in *Provincial Jewry* (article prepared by Aubrey Newman).
26. Edward Conway, 'Blackburn', *Provincial Jewry* is an excellently rounded vignette of a small provincial Jewish community in its environment in the late nineteenth century.
27. A.S. Diamond, 'Leeds', in *Provincial Jewry.*
28. Lewis Olsover, *The Jewish Communities of North-East England,* 1981; Geoffrey Alderman, 'South Wales Jewry before 1914', in *Provincial Jewry,* and in *TJHSE* XXVI pp. 62-70.
29. These figures are based on Kosmin and Grizzard's paper on the addresses of Jewish war dead in the First World War (which itself takes account of Lipman, *Social History*), the estimates appearing annually in the *Jewish Year Book,* and figures quoted in *Provincial Jewry in Victorian Britain*; the figures for Leeds, Liverpool and Glasgow are especially approximate. For Leeds, see also Joe Buckman, *Immigrants and the Class Struggle: The Jewish Immigrant in Leeds, 1880-1914,* Manchester, 1983, who gives 25,000 for 1908 and 5.6 per cent of recruits in 1917-18.
30. Lipman, *Social History,* pp. 94-7; and the two papers by R. Kalman and V.D. Lipman in Aubrey Newman (ed.) *The Jewish East End 1840-1939,* 1980, pp. 1-40. The figure of 100,000 is independently arrived at by V.D. Lipman, 'Rise of Jewish Suburbia', in *TJHSE* XXI, and Kosmin, Waterman and Grizzard, 'Jewish dead of the Great War'.
31. Millicent Rose, *East End of London,* 1951, Ch. 17, esp. p. 266.
32. The word 'ghetto' has been avoided because historically this term, taken from the precedent of Venice, implies an area in which Jews were compelled to live. In the Jewish quarter of modern great cities they lived without governmental compulsion. While *Zangwill used the term 'ghetto' for London's Jewish quarter in the late nineteenth century in *The Children of the Ghetto* (1892), the sociological analysis of an immigrant quarter was developed by Louis Wirth in *The Ghetto.* First published in 1928, this was based on the Jewish immigrant quarter of Chicago and sought to explain other immigrant quarters of other national and cultural groups in America by analogy from American Jewish experience.
33. Wirth, *The Ghetto,* 1956 edn., p. 198 quotes low rents and absentee landlords willing to accept foreigners as features of immigrant quarters in America; but in Britain such areas were usually already short of residential accommodation due to conversion of housing to other uses. The consequent high rents and demands for premiums would have been a deterrent, were it not for other factors, e.g. the presence of earlier Jewish settlement.
34. Marshall Sklare, *Conservative Judaism: an American Religious Movement,* 1953, pp. 47 ff., which applies this conceptual framework, also originally based on Chicago, to American Jewish social, economic and religious life.
35. British Library of Political and Economic Science (BLPES), Booth Papers, B.197, p. 8.
36. The Booth survey was published between 1889 and 1902; the final edition in

1902 comprised seventeen volumes. The Booth classification, shown by colours on maps included in the *Life and Labour of the People in London* was based on the notebooks of the London School Board visitors employed to enforce school attendance. It was as follows:

(i) 'lowest' (black), earnings less than 18-21/- per week [90p-£1.05];
(ii) 'very poor' (dark blue), with either intermittent or very small regular earnings averaging 18-21/- [90p-£1.05] over the year;
(iii) 'moderate poverty' (light blue): regular earnings of 22-30/- [£1.10-50] per week;

All below this were below the 'poverty line' of 30/- (1.50) per week.

(iv) 'poverty and comfort mixed' (purple): streets which included 'higher class labour' at over 30/- [£1.50] as well as those with 18/- - 30/- [90p - £1.50]
(v) 'fairly comfortable' (pink): over 30/- up to 50/-[£1.50-£2.50] a week;
(vi) 'well-to-do' or 'middle-class' (red): keeping one or two servants;
(vii) 'wealthy' (yellow): keeping three or more servants.

See also V.D. Lipman, 'The Booth and New London surveys as source material', in Newman, *Jewish East End* pp. 41-5.

37. Lipman, *Social History*, p. 95. C. Russell and H.S. Lewis, *The Jew in London*, 1900, pp. xxxiii-xlv.
38. I. Finestein, 'J.F. Stern', in Newman, *Jewish East End*, p. 97, n.7.
39. In an interview with a representative of Charles Booth, BLPES Booth Papers, B.197, p. 89.
40. S.A. Sharot, 'Religious change in native orthodoxy in London 1870-1914', *JJS* XV(1), 1973, p. 61.
41. Lipman's 'Suburbia', p. 97.
42. Booth *Life and Labour*, series III, vol. I, p. 119.
43. The descriptions are those of Israel Zangwill in 'Transitional' and 'They that walk in darkness', in *Ghetto Tragedies*, 1893.
44. Sharot, 'Religious change', p. 62.
45. Ibid., p. 63.
46. Ephraim Levine, *The New West End Synagogue 1879-1929*, 1926; S.L. and V.D. Lipman 'Back from the Precipice' in *JC* 18 May 1979 p. 21; *TJHSE* XXI, p. 84. The area south of the central royal parks, though it contained some even wealthier Jewish families had, as Dr Adler noted in the interview quoted above, no synagogue.
47. Report, pp. 19-21.
48. *The Lancet*, 5 March 1884; Gartner, *Jewish Immigrant*, pp. 42-62.
49. Lipman, *Social History*, pp. 104-6, 134-40.
50. Lipman, *Social Service*, pp. 124-9.
51. Jerry White, 'Jewish landlords, Jewish tenants: an aspect of class struggle within the Jewish East End' in Newman, *The Jewish East End*, pp. 205-16.
52. Accounts from different standpoints are K.D. Rubens, 'The 4% Industrial Dwellings Company Ltd: 1885-1901', in Newman, *The Jewish East End*, and Jerry White *Rothschild Buildings*, 1980.
53. Bernard Gainer, *The Alien Invasion: the Origins of the Aliens Act of 1905*, 1972, pp. 39 ff.
54. Lipman, *Social History*, pp. 100, 105; Gartner, *Jewish Immigrant*, p. 149.
55. Lipman, *Social History*, pp. 101, 159-60.

56. Jeffrey and Barbara Baum, in 'The Jews of Tottenham before the Great War', *Heritage* 1 (published by the Jewish Research Group of the Edmonton Hundred Historical Society, 1982) suggest a possible dichtomy between a smaller, religiously affiliated settlement of Jewish families, who were either English or determined to settle in England and a larger, foreign transient population of young immigrants, mainly non-religious, liable to be charged with minor offences and interested mainly in moving on to America.
57. Kosmin and Grizzard, 'Jewish dead of the Great War'; Lipman, *Social History*, pp. 157-60, and 'Suburbia', especially pp. 91-2.
58. E. Krausz, *Leeds Jewry*, 1964, pp. 5-6.
59. Tova Benski, 'Glasgow', in A. Newman (ed.) *Provincial Jewry*.
60. Gartner, *Jewish Immigrant*, pp. 142, 145.
61. Israel Sieff, *Memoirs*, 1970, p. 17.
62. Olsover, *North-East England*, pp. 45, 173.
63. Kuznets, 'Immigration', pp. 100-12, especially Tables X and XLL.
64. Gartner, *Jewish Immigrant*, pp. 57-8.
65. Lipman, *Social History*, p. 107.
66. Kuznets, 'Immigration', pp. 87, 106-11.
67. Diamond, 'Leeds' in A. Newman (ed.) *Provincial Jewry*, especially n.4; and in same volume Rosalind O'Brien, 'The Jewish minority in Leeds 1860-1901'.
68. For instance, in 1888 a survey of tailoring workshops in the 'coat trade' in an area of less than a square mile in and around Whitechapel showed that only 15 had over 25 workers, 201 between 10 and 25 and 355 under 10 (Lipman, *Social History*, pp. 108-9).
69. In Leeds, small Jewish tailoring workshops increased from 165 in 1903 to 240 in 1914.
70. Gartner, *Jewish Immigrant*, pp. 90-1.
71. Ibid., p. 99.
72. Lipman, *Social History*, pp. 111, 135-6.
73. Ibid., pp. 110-12; Buckman, *Immigrants and Class Struggle*, Ch. 5.
74. Lipman, *Social History*, p. 112.
75. Ibid., p. 111; Gartner, *Jewish Immigrant*, pp. 66-72.
76. The number of glaziers receiving relief from the London Jewish Board of Guardians was 132 in 1882 but gradually declined to 5 in 1912. See V.D. Lipman 'Trends in Anglo-Jewish occupations', *JJS* II, 1960, pp. 207, 211.
77. Ibid., p. 203.
78. This population estimate is based on material in Olsover, *North-East England* under the communities mentioned, adjusted for 1894. The figures for occupations are taken from pp. 331-40.
79. Conway, 'Blackburn' in Aubrey Newman (ed.) *Provincial Jewry*.
80. Olsover, *North-East England*, pp. 165-6, 170, 176.
81. Geoffrey Whitehill, *Bevis Marks Records* III, 1973, especially pp. 10, 12-14. Occupations are recorded for a very few of the brides, whose average age was 24-5.
82. Robert Henriques, *Marcus Samuel*, 1960.
83. W.D. Rubinstein, 'Jews among top British wealth holders', *JSS* XXXIV, 1972, pp. 73 ff.
84. Harold Pollins, *Economic History of the Jews in England*, London and Toronto, 1982, p. 168.

85. Goronwy Rees, *St. Michael: A History of Marks and Spencer*, 1969; Krausz, *Leeds Jewry*, p. 29.
86. Pollins, *Economic History*, pp. 180-2. The public servants included Sir Barrow Ellis (1823-87) and *Sir Lionel Abrahams at the India Office and the Nathan brothers (Sir Nathaniel (1843-1916), acting chief justice of Trinidad, and his half-brothers, Sir Frederick (1861-1933), president of the Institute of Chemical Engineers, Sir Matthew (1862-1939), permanent secretary and colonial governor, and Sir Robert (1866-1921), Indian civil servant).
87. R. Loewe, 'Jewish Students... in Oxford and Cambridge', in D. Noy and I. Ben-Ami (eds) *Studies in the Cultural Life of the Jews of England*, 1975, p. 169.
88. Brodetsky, *Memoirs*, gives an account of his early life. For Numa Hartog, see Chap. 2 above.

Chapter 4

Aliens and Citizens 1881–1914

The first reactions of British public opinion to the persecution of the Jews in Russia was sympathetic. The Lord Mayor of London convened a great meeting of protest at the Mansion House on 1 February 1882. The way had been prepared by two articles in *The Times* by *Joseph Jacobs on 9 and 11 January 1882 and the meeting was supported by, among others, the Archbishop of Canterbury, Cardinal Manning, Charles Darwin, Matthew Arnold and the Poet Laureate, Lord Tennyson. The principal resolution was moved by Lord Shaftesbury, and a Mansion House Fund inaugurated to help the victims raised £108,000. A second meeting was held at Guildhall on 10 December 1890. A further £100,000 was raised and, in the name of the citizens of London, a resolution was sent to the Czar, deploring the sufferings of Russian Jewry, asserting that every Christian country should recognize religious liberty as a natural human right, and praying him to grant the Jews of Russia political and social equality with his other subjects. Alexander III refused to accept the resolution and ordered it to be returned through the British Foreign Office.

The Alien Question

But the Russo-Polish Jews who actually reached Britain received a less sympathetic reception. From 1884 until the passing of the Aliens Act of 1905, the 'alien question' was intermittently an issue in British politics and in the local politics of at least east London. Everyone knew that 'aliens' meant Eastern European Jews, who indeed were two-thirds of all the foreign-born who settled in Britain between 1891 and 1901. The difficulty of distinguishing the immigrants who actually stayed from the much greater figure of those who passed through gave rise to exaggerated estimates and this was compounded by the concentration of the newcomers in a limited area.[1] At the 1901 census 18.2 per cent of the population of the metropolitan borough of Stepney was foreign-born and this was the area on which interest in contemporary social conditions, from General Booth to Charles Booth, had been focused for over a generation. In 1884 the *Lancet* published articles on Jewish aliens in London, Liverpool, Manchester and Leeds,[2] and Arnold White began the investigations into the conditions of the East End which he published in 1886 as *Problems of a Great City*.[3] From 1884 to 1905 there were several strands to the campaign against aliens and for restrictions on their immigration. First, there was the protest against the absence of any effective statutory control over immigration, and of any power to deport, even where those concerned were known criminals or genuinely suspected of terrorism. There was a wide measure of agreement that some provision of this kind was necessary, though not at the expense of the traditional British policy of offering political asylum, or if it meant excluding all aliens. Second was the argument that the immigrants, because of their poverty and eagerness to work, accepted wages and conditions which resulted in unfair price-cuting and competition, causing unemployment and reduction of living standards among British native workers. This – the 'sweating' argument – was given plausibility because the peaks of immigration happened to coincide with troughs in the trade cycle in Britain. It was a familiar theme in the late 1880s and 1890s and was enunciated in the reports in 1887 to the Board of Trade of its first labour correspondent, the former trade union official, John Burnett. It led to the appointment in 1888 of the House of Lords Committee on the Sweating System, under the former Conservative junior minister, Lord Dunraven, and of the House of Commons Select Committee on Immigration in the same year. Neither of these produced recommendations for action against immigration, although with the Lords committee this was due to the replacement of the chairman by the veteran *laissez-faire* Liberal, Lord Thring. The committee's report, as distinct from Dunraven's unaccepted draft, concluded: 'Undue stress has been laid on the injurious effect on wages caused by foreign immigration, inasmuch as we find that the evils complained of obtain in trades which do not appear to be affected by foreign immigration.' The Commons Select Committee on Emigration and Immigration (Foreigners) included *Samuel Montagu and Ferdinand de Rothschild (1839 – 1898) as members. The committee found the immigration statistics useless and recommended the collection of figures of 'non-through steerage passengers in an effort to obtain the number of entrants who actually settled. But neither committee saw need for immediate action to restrict immigration.[4]

There was a close logical and political connection between anti-alienism and protectionism ('fair trade'): if it were accepted that immigrants competed unfairly with native firms and labour, unfair competition had thus been imported into Britain in the person of the immigrant; and, if it were correct to institute tariffs against unfair competiton from abroad, it was illogical to allow it to be imported into Britain. It is true that a number of official inquiries found that, generally speaking, immigrants did not compete with existing British industry and introduced new lines of output into Britain. Nevertheless a number of protagonists of protection, led first by Sir Howard Vincent and then by Joseph Chamberlain, eventually followed by the Conservative Party in their 1895 general election campaign, took up the case for restriction of alien immigration. It is arguable that anti-alienism was due to an attempt by the Conservatives in the 1890s partly to attract Labour voters and partly to capitalize on local opposition to immigrants in the East End of London.[5]

The Trades Union Congress passed resolutions against alien immigration in 1892 and 1894, which indicated the feeling prevalent at that time among organized labour against the immigrants on grounds of price-cutting. Leading figures in 1894 were Charles Freake, president, and William Inskip, secretary of the National Union of Boot and Shoe Operatives (NUBSO), who were no doubt influenced by the special circumstances of Jewish slipper-makers, especially in Leeds.[6] Advocates of protection could hope that workers, who were anxious about the traditional implications on tariffs of food prices, would welcome the logically associated case for the restriction of the import of alien workers. The local dimension – that this was pre-eminently an east London issue, though not exclusively so – is suggested by the leading role taken first from 1886 by J.C.R. (later Sir John) Colomb, who was MP for Bow and Bromley. While Sir Howard Vincent (a Sheffield MP) then took the lead in parliament, he was followed in 1900 by Captain (later Sir) William Evans-Gordon, MP for Stepney, who directed the campaign that resulted in the Aliens Act of 1905. The British Brothers League, which he founded in 1901 to combat immigration, was virtually confined to east London, where in 1902 it collected 45,000 signatures (10 per cent of the population of Tower Hamlets); essentially it seems to have been a support group for Evans-Gordon and other Conservative MPs in east London constituencies between 1901 and 1905.[7]

Possibly the focus of anti-alienism changed from the arguments about price-cutting and unfair competition, which were advanced in the late 1880s and early 1890s but found little support in official investigations, to other issues associated with housing in the later 1890s and 1900s: increase in rents and key money, overcrowding, insanitary conditions, immigrants depriving local shopkeepers of business. Papers circulated to the Cabinet indicate such changes in the perception of the aliens problem within government. In 1891 Sir Henry Calcraft, permanent secretary of the Board of Trade, identified 'a feeling that wages are being reduced by the newcomers' as the main cause of a 'marked dissatisfaction' in the areas where the immigrants settled, while accepting that the extent of the immigration did not yet appear formidable in relation to the size of the population, especially taking into account movement out of the country.[8] Another paper by Dr (later Sir) Robert Giffen, then head of the Board of Trade Commercial, Statistical and Labour Department also recognized that the size of the influx was exaggerated and that the immigrants, while strange in their new surroundings, were 'not a bad lot'. Giffen, a believer in free trade and an economist of national standing in his own right, advised the government that there was 'no evidence that the influx of these foreigners does in fact depress wages by taking the bread out of the mouths of English people' and that tailoring for export, in which they were largely engaged, 'might not have existed at all if they had not come'.[9]

Nevertheless the lack of any control over the admission of aliens and the political advantages of advocating restriction of immigration, at least in certain political areas, led to a rather half-hearted attempt at a restriction Bill by Lord Salisbury, then leading the Opposition in the Lords, in 1894, and to further Bills introduced by Sir Howard Vincent in 1897 and 1898, and by Lord Hardwicke, also in 1898. These last were unsuccessful, even though the Conservatives were now in government. By 1902 the increase in immigration led to a decision by government that a full-scale inquiry into the aliens question could no longer be avoided. In arguing the case to his Cabinet colleagues in January 1902, the responsible minister, Gerald Balfour (President of the Board of Trade) accepted that the earlier allegations about crime, pauperism and competition leading to lower wages and unemployment had never been substantiated and 'such evidence as exists points the other way'. But he identified as 'real evils... insanitation [sic], overcrowding, high rents, extrusion of considerable numbers of the native population from particular areas and loss of custom of English shopkeepers'. Even so, Gerald Balfour was doubtful that immigration control would make a difference, since the United States had restrictive tests on health and poverty, and still less than 1 per cent of the immigrants were excluded. He was, however, worried about the expected stiffening of American restrictions, which might have the effect of diverting to Britain the 'full stream of low class continental immigration' – the document makes clear he had southern Italian immigration in mind – and Britain would have to react against that 'in self-defence'.[10] Accordingly, on 21 March 1902, a Royal Commission was appointed

to inquire into and report on:
(1) The character and extent of the evils which are attributed to the unrestricted immigration of aliens, especially in the metropolis;
(2) The measures which have been adopted for the restriction and control of alien immigration in foreign countries and British colonies; and to advise what remedial or precautionary measures it is desirable to adopt in this country, having regard to the above matters and to the absence of any statutory powers to exclude or expel any individual alien or aliens from its borders.

The chairman was Lord James of Hereford and the members included *Lord Rothschild and Major Evans-Gordon. In the year before the commission reported on 10 August 1903 it took a mass of evidence, including over 23,000 questions and answers in oral evidence. Among the Jewish witnesses were *Leonard L. Cohen, president of the Board Sir Samuel Montagu, both as MP for Whitechapel and as acting president of the Federation of Synagogues (Lord Rothschild was nominal president as well as of the London United Synagogue); *Herman Landau and Joseph Somper for the Jews' Temporary Shelter; B.A. Fersht on the Jewish friendly societies; C.H.L. Emanuel for the Board of Deputies; Theodor Herzl, 'president of the Zionist Congress', who argued that a Jewish homeland was the only solution to the alien immigration problem in Britain, and *L.J. Greenberg of the English Zionist Federation; *N.S. Joseph for the Russo-Jewish Committee, the principal relief organization for recent arrivals; *Harry S. Lewis and H.H. Gordon (1873–1939), Jewish social workers resident in east London, who showed that pressure on housing there was due to demolition rather than immigration; and others including Joseph Prag (St. Pancras), Israel Ehrenburg (Reading, a community virtually created to remove immigrants from the congested areas of London) and Maurice Wigram (Sheffield).

The commission was unanimous in its view that there was no case for the total exclusion of alien immigrants from Britain or for throwing any unnecessary difficulties in the way of foreigners generally in the country. But five of the seven members thought it necessary to regulate the entry of certain classes of immigrant, especially those from Eastern Europe; to control their residence in particular localities to avoid overcrowding; and to take power to repatriate aliens found to be 'undesirable'. They accordingly recommended the establishment of an Immigration Department with officers at the ports empowered to enquire whether immigrants were 'undesirable' (i.e. criminals, prostitutes, idiots, persons of notoriously bad character and those likely to become a charge on public funds). Immigrants who within two years of arrival were ascertained, or reasonably supposed, to be members of these undesirable classes should be liable to be ordered by a court of summary jurisdiction to leave the country; and the owner of the vessel which had brought them might be ordered to take them back to their port of embarkation.

As regards overcrowding, the majority of the commission recommended that, if immigration of aliens were found to have contributed substantially to this in any area, it might be declared a 'prohibited area'. Aliens would then be required to give notice of their residence within it and if, within two years after an area being so declared, an alien who had arrived in the country after the declaration were found resident within it, he should be removed and be guilty of an offence. In a minority report, Sir Kenelm Digby, who was permanent under-secretary of the Home Office which would have had to implement the recommendations on prohibited areas, argued that they were both impracticable and undesirable. (A similar line had been taken by the assistant secretary of the Local Government Board, responsible for environmental health and housing: the answer was to use the existing statutory powers against overcrowding more effectively.) Digby also criticized the proposals to exclude undesirable aliens because criminals and persons of bad character could not be detected at the port and European criminals did not come in with the Eastern European immigrants: the remedy was deportation after an offence was committed. Immigrants who were mentally or physically ill could be detected at the ports, but the evidence showed there was very little illness among the immigrants: they had not been found to introduce infectious or contagious diseases, and their health was shown to be better after arrival than that of the native population. On the other hand, mere want of means should not be reason for exclusion: Digby was a Liberal, as well as a civil servant.[11]

Lord Rothschild concurred with Digby's minority report and added that he was 'opposed to the adoption of restrictive measures because, even if they were directly aimed at the so-called undesirables, they would certainly affect deserving and hard-working men, whose impecunious position on their arrival would be no criterion of their incapacity to attain independence'.[12]

Aliens Legislation

In 1904 the government, now headed by Arthur Balfour who took a personal interest in the aliens question,[13] introduced an Aliens Bill which implemented the majority report's recommendations in their full rigour, including power to immigration inspectors to exclude aliens on the ground of poverty. This Bill was referred to a Grand Committee of the House of Commons, even though such a committee could deal only with the non-contentious parts of a Bill and afforded unlimited opportunities for the delay. The Liberal Opposition, led on the Bill by Winston Churchill, whose constituency, north-west Manchester, had a significant Jewish middle-class element, took full advantage of this;[14] and after the committee had devoted seven sittings to only three lines of an eleven-clause Bill, the government withdrew the Bill.

Early the next year, 1905, a by-election in the east London constituency of Mile End focused on the aliens issue. The Conservative majority in accordance with a national trend was greatly reduced; their candidate, Harry S. Lawson (who was of Jewish descent) favoured the 1904 Bill, and the Liberal, B.S. Straus (1870–1933) – a Jew – opposed it. The Aliens Bill introduced in 1905 omitted any provision for prohibited areas; and, while giving immigration inspectors power to exclude immigrants for want of means, provided that this should not apply to any one who proved he was seeking admission 'solely to avoid persecution or punishment on religious or political grounds or for an offence of a political character . . .'[15]. There was also an appeal to an immigration tribunal of three members, among whom it was intended to include persons recommended by Jewish organizations like the Board of Guardians.[16] This was a concession but also an admission that the Bill, although avowedly general in scope, was aimed at Jewish immigration. The Board of Deputies campaigned against it, organizing a canvass of MPs to secure at least a number of amendments. This was largely unsuccessful but the Bill was to come into force as an Act in January 1906, just after the Liberals replaced the Conservatives after a landslide electoral victory. Whether the aliens legislation helped the Conservatives by lessening their electoral defeat is doubtful: in east London the anti-Conservative swing was below the national average but the party still lost six of its eight seats there.[17]

There was a marked decline in the number of Eastern European immigrants after 1906, although factors other than the Aliens Act may have been responsible. Even so, the reduction was not excessive and after a low point in 1909 immigration increased again to reach 5,000 a year – the 1881–1905 average – by 1914. The new Act was administered by Home Secretaries of the party who had opposed it. As Lord Rothschild wrote to his French cousins in 1911:

> The Alien Acts [sic]... was brought in by a Conservative Government, and it certainly is a novel feature of English legislation; as the Act is drawn and as it stands, it was bound to be very defective and very difficult of administration. Although pretended that the object of the Act was to keep out undesirables, it probably was meant to exclude, and has to a certain extent excluded, a large immigration of foreigners who either swelled the pauper classes or helped to lower wages. Liberal Home Secretaries have interpreted the Act in a different way from their predecessors and have always given those who asserted they were political refugees the benefit of every doubt.[18]

The Liberal government did as much as it could to reduce the impact of the aliens legislation, although it did not repeal it. In this it was no doubt aided by the perceived reduction in both overcrowding and sweating in the East End of London.[19] Originally, due to faulty interpretation of immigrants' statements, misreading of the Act and failure by immigrants to state facts that would have secured them entry, many immigrants were rejected and sent back on the ships that had brought them. The newly founded Liberal daily, *Tribune*, published accounts of the maladministration of the Act and, joined by the *Daily Chronicle* in one specific case, brought the problem to the attention of the Home Secretary, Herbert Gladstone, who issued a circular to the tribunals encouraging them to give the benefit of any doubt to the immigrants 'who allege that they are flying from religious or potential persecution'.[20] The Houndsditch murders and the Sidney Street siege in 1911 involved a gang of Russian criminals – apparently Letts who seem to have passed themselves off as Jews for camouflage – but these events again led to identification in the public mind of immigrants with terrorists. This led to a private member's Bill to register all aliens and a government Bill, introduced by Churchill as Home Secretary, to prevent crime by aliens and facilitate their expulsion if convicted. Both Bills foundered in committee - parliament had wider constitutional issues in hand - and it was the outbreak of war in 1914 which led to registration of aliens and powers of deportation in circumstances which had little to do with the earlier arguments for control of immigration.

Anglo-Jewish Reactions to Immigration

How to react to the mass immigration and the campaign for restriction provided a dilemma for the communal leadership of Britain's Jews. As regards the persecution itself, the Board of Deputies in 1881 asked the Foreign Secretary to make representations to the Russian government, which Lord Granville declined to do on the grounds that it would be interference in the domestic affairs of a foreign power, unacceptable in international usage, and liable to have an adverse effect, although he promised to mention the matter unofficially to the Russian ambassador.[21] An attempt in 1882 by *Baron Henry de Worms MP to get representations from the British to the Russian government did not gain the support even of the president of the Board of Deputies, *Arthur Cohen MP.[22] A similar suggestion was made in 1891 within government by the permanent secretary of the Board of Trade, on the ground that this might reduce the flow of immigration, but this was rejected by the Foreign Office.[23]

However there was a campaign to mobilize public opinion against pogroms and persecution, of which the high points were the Mansion House and Guildhall meetings of 1882 and 1891 respectively. Earlier in the nineteenth century protests against the persecution of Jews abroad generally marched with British interests and Russia was perceived, especially by the Conservatives, as hostile to British interests, notably in India. But after 1900 first Lansdowne, as Foreign Secretary (1900-5), and then the 1906 Liberal government were working towards a rapprochement with Russia as the ally of France, with whom Britain was associated from 1904 in the *Entente Cordiale*. Even Anglo-Jewish protests against Russia, the classic country of governmental anti-Semitism before 1914, came up against the general public desire to associate with Russia as an ally against expanding German imperialism. There was thus a potential conflict of interest between the foreign policy of the government and that of the Anglo-Jewish community as articulated by the Conjoint Foreign Commitee of the Deputies and the Anglo-Jewish Association (led by David Lindo Alexander KC (1842-1922), *Claude G. Montefiore and *Leopold de Rothschild, with *Lucien Wolf as secretary). In so far as communal leaders were trying to influence public opinion against Russia in the years before the First World War, they were increasingly against the national tide and ran the risk of being accused of pro-German links or even pacifism.[24] In relation to Russia the position of the first Lord Rothschild was sensitive. He was the leading Jewish lay leader in Britain but also head of the banking house to which the Russian government looked primarily for loans. Unlike German or French Jewish bankers, he deliberately raised the issue of Jewish persecution when the Russian government sought to borrow. His attitude was not that if the Russian government behaved decently to their Jewish subjects, it would get a loan but rather that if the Russian Jews had liberty and equal rights, Russia's financial position would improve and she would not be in such desperate need of loans; and that the policy pursued by the Russian government would drive Russian Jews into revolution (a prospect to which Lord Rothschild was naturally sensitive). His brothers and partners were equally concerned: in January 1899 Alfred de Rothschild was against lending money to Russia on any account; in June 1908 Leopold de Rothschild, in the Royal Enclosure, asked Edward VII, about to visit the Czar, to intercede with him to bring about 'an amelioration in our co-religionists' fate'. Lord Rothschild however did not consider it prudent to refuse all Russian applications for loans point-blank. If that were done, the prospect of exerting any leverage on Russian policy would be lost, and the Russians might even discover they could raise money elsewhere.[25] There is no doubt that Lord Rothschild's commitment to Russian Jewry was genuine. He signed the minority report of the Royal Commission against any restrictions on immigration, even though as his private letter of 1911 quoted above shows, he had some reservations about the immigrants. In the 1905 Mile End by-election, between the two Aliens Bills, he supported the anti-restrictionist Liberal candidate against his party loyalties - he was a Liberal Unionist - because the Conservative favoured restriction.[26]

Rothschild and Samuel Montagu, MP for Whitechapel and founder of the Federation of Synagogues (largely for immigrants), gave leadership to a community initially divided on the question of the immigrants. There was anti-immigrant feeling among the Jewish working class in East London, who feared that the immigrants, whose appearance and ways were foreign, might imperil their own position; and they reacted much as did the non-Jewish majority in the area.[27] Among the leaders of the communal welfare organizations there was concern that the machinery of relief would be unable to cope with the influx as the Alliance had been nearly overwhelmed at Brody in 1882. N.S. Joseph, active in the London Jewish Board of Guardians and honorary secretary of the Russo-Jewish Committee which administered the Mansion House and Guildhall Funds, wrote in 1892 of the lifeboat which was full and would capsize with the present passengers if more tried to climb on board. In order to discourage immigration, the Board of Guardians refused relief to immigrants in their first six months in the country; but they collaborated with the Russo-

Jewish Committee through a Conjoint Committee working from the board's offices; this made comprehensive arrangements for helping victims of Russian persecution and persons from areas in which persecution had taken place, to assist them on arrival and settle them in Britain. The Board of Guardians itself, ostensibly dealing with Eastern European immigrants who were not refugees, paid for sending back some 17,500 'cases' - about 54,000 individuals - between 1880 and 1914. In 1905 the board stopped this practice and resumed it in 1906 only at the direct request of the applicants.[28]

Another attitude was that of the philanthropist *F.D. Mocatta that

> it is not for us as Englishmen to try to close the entrance into our country to any of our fellow-creatures, especially such as are opressed. It is not for us as Jews to try and bar our gates against other Jews who are persecuted solely for professing the same religion as ourselves.[29]

After 1905 experience of the pogroms showed that any hopes that the Czarist regime might adopt a milder policy were ill-founded, and with the Aliens Act on the statute book, the principle of control of immigration was no longer an issue. Henceforth the community's main concern in this field was to ease the administration of the immigration regulations[30] and to integrate the immigrants into British life.

Jews in Politics

The earlier divisions of opinion among British Jews had been shown by the fact that of the twelve Jewish MPs in 1905, four voted for the Aliens Bill, four against it and four abstained.[31] This indicates also the extent to which Jews in British politics voted in accordance with their party affiliations as British citizens rather than as members of a single community; or, if they did take account of their interests as British Jews, how different were their perceptions of what those interests were. Of the twelve MPs, eight were Conservatives or Liberal Unionists and four Liberals. These figures suggest how far Jewish MPs had diverged from the pre-1880 pattern, where if a Jew was other than a Liberal, he was regarded as an exception to a natural rule. While one cannot be sure what proportions of Jewish voters were Liberal or Conservative - although I should guess that Liberals were in the majority - the allegiances of MPs, party activists and prominent individuals are known. It is clear that, in spite of the fact that the Conservatives introduced control of immigration and that the Liberals generally opposed it, Jews were active Conservatives and that in the 1880, 1892, 1895 and 1900 elections more Jews were returned as Conservatives or Liberal Unionists than as Liberals.[32] The reasons for this change can be sought first in the close association of the Rothschilds, whose family provided a substantial proportion of the first Jewish MPs, with Disraeli; the unsympathetic stance of Gladstone towards Jewish rights in Rumania; the growing identity of interest between the financial and mercantile class, of which Jews formed part, with the Conservatives; and the emergence of the Liberal Unionists over the Irish question. This meant that former Liberals, like Nathaniel (the first Lord) Rothschild made the transition more easily from Liberal via Liberal-Unionist to Conservative. Perhaps there was an underlying feeling expressed as early as 1865 by the then young communal leader, Lionel Louis Cohen, later a Conservative MP, that it was neither natural nor advantageous for emancipated British Jews to be exclusively identified with any one party in the state;[33] and circumstances in Britain did not virtually close the right-wing parties to them, as in many continental countries, because these parties were based on religion or xenophobic nationalism.

Jews in parliament, notably Henry de Worms and Arthur Cohen, naturally spoke on issues of interest to Jews, such as Rumania, the pogroms, alien immigration, Jewish denominational schools and the right of Jews to have animals slaughtered for food in accord with their own religious requirements (*shechita*). But they were not in parliament mainly as representatives of the Jewish community; indeed the majority sat for constituencies in which Jewish voters were negligible. In so far as Jewish MPs attained prominence, they did do because of their contribution to the general work of the House: *Sir Julian Goldsmid as deputy chairman of Committees, Lionel Louis Cohen because of his expert knowledge of banking and currency, Baron de Worms (later Lord Pirbright) as parliamentary secretary to the Board of Trade and the still young *Herbert Samuel as Chancellor of the Duchy of Lancaster (the first Jew in a British Cabinet). Another cabinet minister was *Rufus Isaacs, previously solicitor-general and then attorney-general. Even Samuel Montagu, one of the most influential leaders of the Jewish community and representative of the constituency with probably the most significant Jewish vote, made his contribution to the continuing policy of Britain not only as an authority on finance and an advocate of decimalization and metrication, but also in 1894 by his amendment of the Finance Act to exempt from death duties nationally important works of art and gifts to universities, museums and galleries (a measure of lasting importance for the preservation of the British national heritage).

Jews in Upper-Class Society

This participation in British political life reflected an increasing social identification of British Jews with the analogous groups of the wider society. The wealthiest of the Jewish community continued to acquire country estates, even if only for weekend and holiday residence, and their members aspired to play a part in county society. In Buckinghamshire, where Lord Rothschild was lord-lieutenant, the family, with five estates in or adjoining the county, exercised considerable influence in local Conservative politics.[34] Elsewhere the entry of Jews may have been less accepted but their presence was a fact: the short stories of 'Saki' (H.H. Munro) testify to the entry of Jews, identifiable by their Teutonic names, into Edwardian country house society, although their accepted liberality did not always evoke a sympathetic response.[35] The Jewish middle class were more self-contained in their social life; but while creating their own voluntary social enclaves, reproduced the patterns of Victorian middle-class society by moving into characteristically middle-class suburbs and imitating in their synagogues some at least of the externals of non-Jewish religious life around them. The Jewish novelists of the late nineteenth century, Amy Levy (1862-89) and Julia Frankau ('Frank Danby') (1864-1910) perhaps unfairly exaggerated the tendency of these Jewish middle-class milieux to materialism, lack of culture and denominational isolationism – 'educated at Jewish schools, fed on Jewish food, brought up on Jewish traditions'. On the other hand, other observers perceived the cultural tastes of many of the Jewish upper-middle class as cosmopolitan in their patronage of music and the theatre, not only in London but in provincial cities like Manchester and Bradford. As Bernard Shaw wrote in the preface to *Three Plays for Puritans* (1900): 'The stalls cannot be fully understood without taking into account the absence of the rich evangelical English merchant and his family and the presence of the rich Jewish merchant and his'.[36]

Jews in Literature and Art

Apart from writers of Jewish origin (like Pinero), there was an increasing number of professing Jewish novelists, playwrights and other writers who made their contribution to general literature, in addition to those like Amy Levy whose writing was especially on Jewish themes. The Shakespearean scholars Sir Israel Gollancz (1863–1930), a founder and first secretary of the British Academy, and Sir Sidney Lee (1856–1926), editor of the *Dictionary of National Biography*, also wrote on Jewish subjects, although the latter in later life was not associated with the community. Alfred Sutro (1863–1933) was one of the most popular Edwardian playwrights, Leonard Merrick (1864–1939) was appreciated by leading literary figures of the age as a novelist and short story writer, and Ada Leverson, an Edwardian novelist, had attracted to her salon in the 1890s artistic and literary figures including Beardsley, Sickert and Wilde (to whom she almost alone remained a loyal friend in his time of trials). Rachel Beer (1858–1922), a

Sassoon who married the owner of the *Observer*, in 1893 bought its rival the *Sunday Times* and until 1904 edited both papers. But the outstanding Anglo-Jewish writer of this period was *Israel Zangwill. His works on Jewish themes - notably *Children of the Ghetto* (1892) and *The King of Schnorrers* (1894) - approached genius; but he longed also for recognition as a writer and playwright on general themes, with much less success, although the title of his play on America, *The Melting Pot*, (1909) has passed into cliché. He sought to combine advocacy of Jewish causes, such as first Zionism and then territorialism (a Jewish homeland not necessarily in the Holy Land), with involvement in issues like women's rights, and to pontificate on Jewish religious issues while marrying outside the Jewish faith. The son of an immigrant from Eastern Europe of an earlier generation, he depicted the life of the immigrants of his own for the wider English-reading public, with unrivalled depth of knowledge and sympathy.[37]

The immigrants themselves were initially Yiddish-speaking but they aspired generally to middle-class status and integration in British society if not for themselves at least for their children. Such a process was bound to take time but in one sphere at least the immigrant generation was able to make a contribution speedily to British culture - the visual arts. There had been Anglo-Jewish artists since the seventeenth century. In the nineteenth century S.A. Hart RA (1806-85), though his subjects were generally Jewish, was not untypical of mid-Victorian painting. Of the two brothers Solomon, Abraham (1824-62) was a genre painter, while Simeon (1834-1905) and their sister Rebecca (1832-86) were pre-Raphaelites and 'succumbed to fashionable decadence'.[38] In their way they fitted into the English artistic society as readily as the fasionable portrait painter and academician, Solomon J. Solomon (1860-1921),[39] and his sister, the impressionist Lily Delissa Joseph (1863-1940), who was imprisoned in 1912 as a suffragette and later was a pioneer woman motorist and pilot, fitted into their respective milieux. Solomon J. Solomon, a committed Jew and the first president of the Maccabeans, a dining club for Jewish professional men and intellectuals, did not usually paint Jewish subjects; whereas Sir William Rothenstein (1872-1945), who cut loose from his German-Jewish origins in Bradford, as a young man painted Jewish religious scenes among the immigrants in east London and was a friend and patron to the young Jewish artists of the immigrant generation.

It was these artists, born in Eastern Europe or in recent immigrant environments, who introduced a new form of creative experience into British art. They drew on Jewish experience of life in Eastern Europe, where the number and concentration of Jews, and the influence of developments in Russian art, combined with a heritage of Jewish folk art, produced what internationally became known as *l'école juif*. Artists of this immigrant generation in Britain began with Alfred Wolmark (1877-1961); the towering figure of Sir Jacob Epstein, born in New York in 1880 but settled in London from 1905; David Bomberg (1890-1957); Mark Gertler (1891-1939); Bernard Meninsky (1891-1956); Jacob Kramer (1892-1962); and the poet Isaac Rosenberg (1890-1918). The last five were all students at the Slade School around 1910, where they both learned from and influenced their non-Jewish environment. They were all products of the immigrant quarter, took advantage of the facilities available in London for free education and cultural experience (such as the Whitechapel Art Gallery) and were helped by the established Anglo-Jewish community, particularly through the Educational Aid Society.

Wolmark had startled Edwardian galleries by his use of colour, becoming known as 'the colour king'. Bomberg, Gertler and Kramer sought for a time to develop in England a Jewish style that would represent the Jewish culture of their origins, but were more restricted and more sober in their colour than the analogous Russo-Jewish painters of their generation in Paris and elsewhere - possibly because of the sobering influence of the English environment, in which they immersed themselves. The relationship which developed, for instance, between Gertler and the Bloomsbury Group symbolized a new form of association of the Jewish immigrant with British society: his personal and artistic contribution was perceived as distinctively Jewish yet there was an attempt to merge beyond the measure of acculturation which was practised by the conventional Jewish middle class (who retained traditional Jewish practices and a separate social life while adopting the external culture of the environment).[40]

Anti-Semitism

A quite different relationship was that which resulted in the continental or even oriental flavour brought into Victorian society through the Jewish members of the entourage of the Prince of Wales, later Edward VII. Lord Rothschild and his brothers had made the acquaintance of the Prince when undergraduates at Cambridge in the early 1860s and when the Prince took over the leadership of London society, the 'Marlborough House set' showed its reaction against the austere court of the widowed Queen by including persons who were not members of the traditional British aristocracy or courtiers but were qualified by wealth, intellect, charm and, in the case of the ladies, good looks. In addition to the Rothschilds, the circle included the brothers Reuben (1835-1905), Arthur (1840-1912) and Albert (1818-96) Sassoon, the bankers Sir Ernest Cassel (1852-1921) and *Baron de Hirsch, Sir Felix Semon (1849-1921), the physician and Sir George Lewis (1833-1911) the most fashionable solicitor of the day and perhaps the recipient of the most confidences. The Prince would stay at the homes of some of his Jewish friends and, where occasionally the matter arose, accommodate himself to their religious obligations. The Prince's apparent taste for the company of Jewish friends, and even for Jewish humour, aroused considerable comment and may well have contributed to the building up of social anti-Semitism in Edwardian Britain.[41] Anti-Semitism was a recurring preoccupation of Lord Rothschild, as emancipation had been of his father, from about 1880 onwards. This was due not merely to the effects of the aliens issue on public opinion, which was, broadly speaking, prejudice against poor East European Jews. But Britain also experienced, albeit in modified and limited form, part of the resurgence of anti-Jewish feeling which developed in central and western Europe from the mid-1870s. This was, again broadly speaking, a prejudice against rich Jews, especially those whose wealth or position was thought to give them political, economic or cultural influence. Here the acquisition of wealth, admission to public office or recognition in literature or the arts could be perceived as a danger, as well as an achievement.

It was, however, perhaps significant that anti-alienism before 1905 almost always disclaimed anti-Semitism as a motive, protesting - however insincerely - that it was not anti-Jewish as such: before about 1900 the new continental anti-Semitism was not politically or intellectually respectable in Britain.[42]

The Dreyfus case had attracted immense interest and, on the whole, sympathy with the victim, to judge by the articles in the popular and illustrated press. This may have been influenced by antipathy to what was perceived as a characteristic expression of French militarist and clerical chauvinism in the period of the 1898 Fashoda incident.[43] But analogous influences developed in Britain from about the time of the Boer War. The first new strand in the web of anti-Semitism was the identification by anti-imperialist and capitalist writers like J.A. Hobson of Jews with British imperialist expansion in South Africa and even with responsibility for the Boer War to further the alleged interests of prominent Jewish financiers such as Alfred Beit or Barney Barnato.[44] A direct link with French clerical anti-Semitism was supplied by Hilaire Belloc - born in France, educated there and, after service in the French army, naturalized as a British subject at the age of 33 - for whom British-born Jews were always an alien element in British society. His views and those of the brothers Cecil and G.K. Chesterton were expressed in the magazine *Eye-Witness* founded in June 1911 (refounded as the *New Witness* in 1912 after the bankruptcy of its financial sponsor). A further strand was the nationalist, Conservative opposition to German expansion which identified Jews, of whom many prominent at that period in British life were of German origin, with German and anti-Russian interests: this tendency was characteristic of the *National Review*, edited by L.J. Maxse.

The Marconi Affair

These strands came together in 1912–13 almost simultaneously in the Marconi affair and the less prominent Indian silver case. Both affected the position of British Jews because in each a group of Jews in prominent position in the state was involved. These, while no doubt guilty of acting unwisely or even with some impropriety, were accused through a campaign of rumour and misstatement of deliberate corruption in which attention was deliberately drawn to their Jewishness.[45] In the Marconi case, Herbert Samuel as Postmaster-General was the minister responsible for arranging with the (English) Marconi Company for building an empire-wide chain of wireless stations, vital for communications in the event of war. Marconi was the only possible option, since the alternative contractors were inexperienced, less technically proven or German. The English Marconi Company's managing director, Godfrey Isaacs, had undertaken to help the American Marconi Company by personally undertaking responsibility for taking up half a million of their shares issued to enable them to acquire the rival United Wireless Telegraph Company of America. Some of these shares were passed on by Godfrey Isaacs (1867–1925) to his brother Harry and by him to the third brother, Rufus. Sir Rufus Isaacs had been appointed Solicitor-General in March 1910 and attorney-general later that year; in June 1912 he was given a seat in the Cabinet. Through Rufus Isaacs, American Marconi shares were also taken up by Lloyd George, then Chancellor of the Exchequer and by the Master of (later Lord) Elibank, then Liberal Chief Whip, investing, as it later appeared, Liberal Party funds. The Marconi tender had been agreed in March 1912 and the contract tabled in the House of Commons in July 1912. Meanwhile rumours about the contract circulated, shares in both the English and American companies fluctuated widely, and criticism concentrated on two points: that the postmaster-general had given unreasonably favourable terms to a company whose managing director was a brother of a member of the government and that ministers had used their official knowledge to speculate profitably in Marconi shares.

While anti-Semitism was clearly a driving force behind the most damaging accusations, the period was one of high political tension between the main parties over Irish Home Rule, taxation and national insurance, and the 1911 Parliament Act for overcoming Conservative opposition to the implementation of these Liberal policies. Any political issue which involved personalities was therefore likely to be pursued with acrimony, with each side defending or attacking without restraint. The government had to concede a Select Committee of Inquiry into the contract and in the debate on 11 October 1912 into the appointment of the committee, Rufus Isaacs and Lloyd George denied any ownership of shares in 'that company' (i.e. the English Marconi Company) but kept silent about their holdings of American Marconi shares. In the course of hearings before the Select Committee, which was composed and acted along party lines, Leo Maxse (whose *National Review* had published articles by W.R. Lawson alleging corruption by ministers) managed to provoke the disclosure of ministers' holdings in the American company. The Select Committee produced majority and minority reports along party lines. But both accepted that ministers had not been influenced in their official decisions by personal considerations or used privileged knowledge to speculate in Marconi shares; the majority insisted that their Liberal colleagues' conduct was flawless while the minority considered their opponents were guilty of impropriety in purchasing shares (even if they made a loss) on information from a government contractor and that such conduct, if condoned, could open the door to corruption in future. Cecil Chesterton, who was prosecuted for criminal libel on Godfrey Isaacs, was fined £100 and costs: a verdict which was regarded by him and his friends inaccurately as a vindication.[46] The ill-founded rumours about the correctness of the choice of the Marconi company by Herbert Samuel led to delays as a result of which the imperial chain of wireless stations was incomplete when war broke out in 1914.

The Indian Silver Case

Herbert Samuel's elder brother, *Sir Stuart Samuel, who had succeeded his cousin Samuel Montagu as MP for Whitechapel in 1900, was a central though unwitting, figure in the Indian silver case. He was also a partner in the family firm of Samuel Montagu, bankers and bullion brokers. The government of India required large amounts of silver. Another relative and partner in the firm, Ernest Franklin, suggested to Sir Felix Schuster (1854-1936; of German-Jewish origin although not identified with the Anglo-Jewish community), who was chairman of the finance committee of the Council of India, the advisory body to the Secretary of State, that £5m of silver could be acquired without the price being forced up by so large a purchase if it were secretly acquired for the government by Samuel Montagu, the only firm capable of so large a purchase. The proposal was made confidentially so that neither Sir Stuart Samuel nor *Edwin Montagu, parliamentary under-secretary for India and Samuel Montagu's son, were aware of it. The proposal was accepted but became public knowledge. Not only the readers of Belloc and Chesterton but Conservative MPs and the *Pall Mall Gazette* suggested a plot to enrich the firm of Samuel Montagu at public expense through a family conspiracy: coincidentally, the assistant under-secretary of state, the senior civil servant involved, was *L.B. (later Sir Lionel) Abrahams. A Select Committee chaired by the Prime Minister, Asquith, referred the matter to the Judicial Committee of the Privy Council which found that Sir Stuart Samuel, although unaware of the contract, had technically disqualified himself from speaking and voting as an MP through being a partner in a firm with a government contract, and had incurred a penalty of £500 a day. At a by-election, he was returned with a reduced majority. A Bill to relieve him of the financial penalties was blocked by the Conservatives – apparently because the firm of Samuel Montagu as bankers had refused to open their books to inspection – and he also had to pay £13,000 to a common informer who successfully prosecuted him.[47]

The Marconi and Indian silver affairs coming together saw the expression of a virulent anti-Semitism, albeit in a limited number of papers, which drew attention to the Jewishness of those attacked, to the prominence of their positions in public life and to alleged attempts to stifle criticism through Jewish influence over the press.[48]

While the circulation of papers like *Eye-Witness* was small, the charges received wide publicity and were taken up: Rudyard Kipling, who closely followed the Marconi case, wrote 'Gehazi', a virulently anti-Semitic poem, on the advancement of Rufus Isaacs to the position of Lord Chief Justice, which was then customary for an attorney-general on the vacancy of a senior judicial post, in 1913.

There were even allegations that Jews prominent in public life were part of some conspiracy, internationally inspired, although the *Protocols* of *The Elders of Zion* did not gain currency in Britain until after 1918 (see Chapter 7 below).

Thus the three-quarters of a century which had begun with emancipation and brought Jews to almost the highest offices in the state had shown that this did not necessarily mean universal acceptance and an end to prejudice against Jews but that prominence had its own risks. British Jews reacted to this experience and to possible solutions differently according to their view of Jewish history and current trends. As Sir Henry d'Avigdor Goldsmid commented of two Jewish ministers whose characters had been impugned and who had emerged with honour, Herbert Samuel became the first advocate within government of Zionism and Edwin Montagu its most violent opponent.[49]

Notes

1. Bernard Gainer, *The Alien Invasion: the Origins of the Aliens Act of 1905*, 1972, p. 3; he also quotes (p. 11) an estimate published in the *East London Press* in 1901 of 836,280 aliens already settled, which at the same alleged rate of arrival would have produced 1.6m in 20 years; and another estimate that 708,000 aliens had arrived by October 1902, which would have meant 7m in 10 years.
2. The *Lancet*, 14 and 21 April; 3 May; 9 and 16 June 1884.

3. Whatever others dissembled. Arnold White was an avowed anti-Semite on racial grounds, although paradoxically he also condemned Jews for their reluctance to integrate with the general population (Gainer, *Alien Invasion,* pp. 123–5).
4. Report of Select Committee of the House of Commons on Immigration and Emigration (Foreigners), P.P. 1888; XI; 1889, X; Report of Select Committee of the House of Lords on the Sweating System, P.P. 1888, XX, XXI; 1889, XIII, XIV, Pts I and II; 1890, XVII; Reports . . . on the Sweating System in Leeds, P.P. 1887, LXXXVI; . . . in the East End of London, LXXXIX. Sweating could be defined in two ways: as the subcontracting by a small master, often on a 'labour only' basis, of work from a merchant or larger contractor and carrying it out in his own workshop or home; or as the subdivision of labour between operatives, in accordance with skill. In either case the implication was that hours of labour were long, pay low and premises below acceptable standards. See V.D. Lipman, *A Century of Social Service: The History of the Jewish Board of Guardians,* 1959, pp. 90–1.
5. Israel Finestein, 'Jewish immigration in British party politics', in A. Newman (ed.) *Migration and Settlement,* 1971, pp. 128–44.
6. J. Buckman, *Immigrants and the Class Struggle,* Manchester, 1983, pp. 132–3.
7. Gainer, *Alien Invasion,* pp. 67–73. See also J.H. Robb, *Working-Class Anti-Semite,* 1954; Colin Holmes, *Anti-Semitism in British Society,* 1979 especially Ch. 6.
8. PRO Cab.37/30 No. 30.
9. Ibid., No. 31.
10. Ibid., Cab. 37/59 No. 146. Circulated to Cabinet, 7 January 1902.
11. Gainer, *Alien Invasion,* p. 184.
12. For the Royal Commission generally, see V.D. Lipman, *Social History of the Jews in England,* 1954, pp. 138–41. The report was published as Cd.1741; Minutes of Evidence, Cd.1742 with appendices in Cd.1741 and an index in Cd.1743.
13. Gainer, *Alien Invasion,* p. 281, n. 91.
14. O.K. Rabinowicz, *Winston Churchill and Jewish Problems,* 1956, pp. 54–63.
15. Lipman, *Social History,* p. 142.
16. A. Akers Douglas, Home Secretary in *Parliamentary Debates, House of Commons,* 14 April 1905, cols 460–8.
17. John A. Garrard, *The English and Immigration,* 1971, p. 72; Gainer, *Alien Invasion,* p. 197; C.T. Husbands, 'East End racism 1900–80', *London Journal* VIII (1), 1982, 9.
18. Rothschild Archive RAL XI/130 A/5, 11 June 1911. I am grateful to the Rothschild Archive for permission to quote this passage.
19. Garrard, *English and Imigration,* p. 109. London County Council returns of housing in Stepney and the Factory Inspectorate testified to improvement of conditions in and after 1907.
20. For the circular and Gladstone's administration of the Act, see Gainer, *Alien Invasion,* pp. 202–5. Israel Cohen stated in his memoirs (*A Jewish Pilgrimage: The Autobiography of Israel Cohen,* 1956), that, as a journalist on the *Tribune,* he gained admission to the London tribunal as 'assistant' to A. Mundy of the Jews' Temporary Shelter and published details of cases of injustice; that the David Rabinovitz case was publicized by H.W. Nevinson of the *Tribune* and N.H. Brailsford of the *Chronicle* and, through Ramsay MacDonald, then a

newly elected Labour MP, that it was brought to the attention of Herbert Gladstone, who issued the circular (pp. 59-61).

21. C.H.L. Emanuel, *A Century and a Half of Jewish History*, 1910, pp. 113-14.
22. Israel Finestein, *Short History of Anglo-Jewry*, 1957, p. 141.
23. PRO Cab.37/30 No. 30.
24. E. Halevy, *History of the English People, 1905-14*, 1952 edn. pp. 409-10. Lucien Wolf, as a journalist specialising in foreign affairs, campaigned against the Anglo-Russian entente of 1907, and was attacked as pro-German. See Max Beloff, 'Lucien Wolf and the Anglo-Russian Entente 1907-1914', Lucien Wolf Memorial Lecture, 1951 (reprinted in Lord Beloff, *The Intellectual in Politics*, 1970).
25. Richard Davis, *The English Rothschilds*, 1983, pp. 230-2.
26. Gainer, *Alien Invasion*, p. 148; C.C. Aronsfeld, 'Jewish bankers and the Tsar', *JSS* XXV, 1973.
27. For evidence of anti-alien sentiment among working-class East End Jews, see Dr Geoffrey Alderman, *The Jewish Community in British Politics*, Oxford, 1983, pp. 95-6.
28. Lipman, *Social Service*, pp. 79, 92-6.
29. Letter from Mocatta to J.F. Stern, 13 May 1894, quoted in *F.D. Mocatta: A Memoir* (collected by Ada Mocatta, 1911).
30. Emanuel, *A Century and a Half*, pp. 16, 8-9, 173, 174-6, 183.
31. Alderman, *Jewish Community in British Politics*, pp. 73, 186-7 n. 34.
32. Ibid., pp. 174-5.
33. *JC*, 11 August 1865.
34. Davis, *English Rothschilds*, p. 120.
35. For instance, the practical jokes played on them in Saki's 'The Unrest-Cure', in *Chronicles of Clovis*, 1911, and 'The Gift'.
36. See further V.D. Lipman, 'Anglo-Jewish community in Victorian Society', in I. Ben-Ami and D. Noy (eds) *Studies in the Cultural Life of the Jews of England*, Jerusalem 1975, pp. 157-9.
37. For personalities mentioned, see *Encyclopaedia Judaica* s.v. For a discussion of Zangwill's ambivalent attitude to Judaism and assimilation, see introduction by V. D. Lipman to I. Zangwill *The Children of the Ghetto*, Leicester University Press Victorian Library, 1977.
38. Charles Spencer, 'Anglo-Jewish artists', *Jewish Quarterly* XXX (4), 47; Lionel Lambourne, 'Abraham ... and Simeon Solomon', *TJHSE* XXI, 274-86.
39. Of whom *Punch* wrote, when he was exhibiting at the Academy but not yet an Academician, 'Solomon in all his glory was not RA'd as one of these'.
40. For an analysis of the older Anglo-Jewish artists and those of the immigrant generation, see Charles Spencer in the *Jewish Quarterly*, spring/summer 1983, and his catalogue of the exhibition; 'The Immigrant Generations: Jewish Artists in Britain 1900-45', The Jewish Museum, New York, 1983. For Rosenberg, see Jean Liddiard, *Isaac Rosenberg*, 1975.
41. Cecil Roth, 'The court Jews of Edwardian England', in *Essays and Portraits in Anglo-Jewish History*, 1962.
42. Davis, *English Rothschilds*, p. 227. In addition to minor clashes on the fringes of immigrant areas (e.g. the resistance of the Irish in the Cable Street area of East London to the spread of the Jewish quarter), there were a few cases of popular violence against Jews. Perhaps the most serious was from

30 August to 1 September 1911 in the western valley of south Wales, where an outbreak of rioting and looting of Jewish property began at Tredegar and spread to Ebbw Vale, Rhymney and Brynmawr; the small Jewish communities there ranged in size from about 80 to 160 people. The reasons for the violence were apparently complex, but probably included the general stress caused by the Cambrian Railway strike and the consequent unemployment in mines and blast furnaces. While there was resentment against Jewish landlords and credit traders, these do not seem to have been singled out for attack. The fullest modern account of the background and incidents is in G. Alderman, 'Jews in south Wales before 1914', *TJHSE* XXVII, pp. 62–70. These incidents may be compared with the attacks and subsequent two-year boycott against the not dissimilar small (120 souls) Jewish community of traders in Limerick: this was however clearly attributable to the preaching of the Redemptorist parish priest, Father John Creagh (Louis Hyman, *The Jews of Ireland,* 1972, pp. 210–17).

43. The coverage of the *Illustrated London News, Sphere, Graphic,* and *Strand Magazine* was generally sympathetic and the *National Review,* whose editor L.J. Maxse was later to attack the 'Marconi ministers' and to identify Jews with German interests, published in June 1899 Sir Godfrey Lushington's exposé of 'The Conspiracy against Captain Dreyfus'.
44. Colin Holmes, 'J.A. Hobson and the Jews', in Colin Holmes (ed.) *Immigrants and Minorities in British Society,* 1978.
45. For a wide-ranging and detailed analysis, see Colin Holmes, *Anti-Semitism in British Society 1876–1939,* 1979, Part I.
46. Frances Donaldson, *The Marconi Scandal,* 1962.
47. Sir Henry d'Avigdor-Goldsmid, 'The little Marconi case', *History Today,* April 1964, 283–6.
48. Holmes, *Anti-Semitism,* pp. 85–6, 259–60.
49. D'Avigdor-Goldsmid, 'Marconi case', p. 286.

Chapter 5

The Welding of a New Community: 1881–1914

Religious Movements

Between 1881 and 1914 the religious life of British Jews showed divergent patterns in both organization and ideals between the older-established community and the successive groups of immigrants from Eastern Europe. Yet towards the end of the period a tendency towards convergence was already discernible.

In 1891* Dr Hermann Adler, who had acted from 1879 onwards as delegate for his father, succeeded him as Chief Rabbi. Born in Germany, Hermann Adler had come to Britain at the age of 6 and was educated at University College School and University College London, as well as pursuing rabbinical studies in Prague and gaining a German doctorate. His attitude was more latitudinarian than that of his father. His writings were apologetic - defending traditional Judaism against modernist criticism - and pastoral, rather than purely scholarly like his father's study of the Targum. He was at home in the world of the court. Edward VII, who appointed him a commander of the Royal Victorian Order (conferred for personal services to the sovereign or members of the royal family) is said to have referred to him as 'my Chief Rabbi'.[1]

Adler was also subject to some pressures for change from influential elements within his own flock. Already in 1879, a conference of lay leaders of synagogues within the United Synagogue, whose spokesman was *Lionel Louis Cohen, founder and then vice-president of the United Synagogue, asked for modifications of the service; some of these were sanctioned by *Nathan Marcus Adler and Hermann as delegate Chief Rabbi, and some refused - the decisions being accepted by the conference. A more forceful movement in 1892 involved both proposals to modify the service and broader theological issues. It centred around Hampstead, where the expanding Jewish suburban settlement assembled an intellectually inclined middle-class community, who were members of the United Synagogue, the Reform Synagogue and the Spanish and Portuguese Congregation. An attempt to organize a congregation combining change with tradition failed when the introduction of the organ – the playing of which on sabbaths and festivals would be contrary to Jewish law – was proposed and rejected on the chairman's casting vote. The majority applied to join the United Synagogue as the Hampstead Synagogue; the supporters of the organ began their own services on sabbath afternoons aimed at attracting those previously uninterested in the traditional service; these services, which continued to 1893, were conducted by the Revd Morris Joseph (1848–1930), who had officiated in north London and Liverpool, and *Israel Abrahams, a scholar in rabbinics who then taught English and mathematics at Jews' College. The new Hampstead United Synagogue joined with other congregations in requesting certain modifications in the ritual from the newly appointed Chief Rabbi, some of which were, after negotiations, accepted. But he refused consent to the appointment as minister at Hampstead of the Revd Morris Joseph. Apart from Joseph's participation in services with an organ, Joseph disclaimed belief in the messianic restoration of sacrifices and felt that 'progress, with its attendant salvation for English Judaism, is impossible within the confines of the synagogue as by Rabbinical Law established'. The Chief Rabbi found this incompatible with traditional Judaism and in 1893 Morris Joseph departed to succeed *Professor David Woolf Marks as minister of the Reform Synagogue.[2]

Modifications were however made with the consent of Dr Hermann Adler in the service of individual constituents of the United Synagogue, but always stopping short of the introduction of the organ or the abolition of the Diaspora second days of festivals. But among some of the prosperous suburban sections of the anglicized middle class there was dissatisfaction with the traditional form of service and even with accepted beliefs: it was felt by these that traditional Judaism must adapt to changing intellectual attitudes or the synagogues would be empty.

Whereas in the 1840s the proponents of reform Judaism had appealed to the text of the Written Law, the Bible, against its interpretation in the Talmud and rabbinic tradition, in 1892 the wealthy young scholar-theologian, *Claude G. Montefiore argued in his Hibbert Lectures that the Old Testament was not acceptable except in the light of modern biblical criticism. Judaism had to be interpreted against its historical background and what was valid for one age was not necessarily so for another; and he praised as superior the moral insight of the ethical teachings of the New Testament. This went too far for his teacher, the Rumanian-born scholar, *Solomon Schechter, Reader in Rabbinic at Cambridge. But while Schechter condemned spiritual assimilation, he also emphasized the increase in ignorance 'among our better situated classes. Very few are capable of reading their prayers and less are able to understand what they read.' A primary cause of this failing was, in his diagnosis, the Anglo-Jewish religious establishment's demand that its spiritual leaders divide their time

> between the offices of cantor, prayer, preacher, bookkeeper, debt-collector, almoner and social agitator. No leisure is left to him to increase his scanty stock of Hebrew knowledge acquired in his undergraduate days. Occasionally rumour spreads anent some minister that he neglects his duty to his congregation through his being secretly addicted to Jewish learning. But such rumours often turn out to be sheer malice....[3]

Schechter left England for America in 1902 to become president of the Jewish Theological Seminary. While Schechter condemned tests on belief, such as that which had excluded Morris Joseph from the pulpit of the Hampstead Synagogue, he insisted on learning and scholarship and more knowledge of the traditional sources of Judaism – Bible, Talmud and the later rabbis. Modern Jews had to adapt to Judaism rather than Judaism be adapted to modern Jews.

In 1902 the influence of Claude Montefiore led to the foundation of the Jewish Religious Union.[4] This had features and personalities associated with the sabbath afternoon services held in Hampstead a decade earlier. The union was a movement aimed at stemming a perceived trend among the wealthier English Jews towards religious indifference or even Christianity. The idea was to hold services, including prayers in English, and to adjust the practice and theology of Judaism to the findings of modern biblical and historical scholarship; if certain practices which seemed to distinguish Jews from other citizens could be attributed to current superstition or medieval custom, then their abolition was held to be acceptable. At first the movement stood outside the established synagogal organizations and included members from all, including Morris Joseph, now minister of the West London Reform Synagogue, and A.A. Green (1860–1933), minister of the Hampstead United Synagogue, as well as Israel Abrahams, who had succeeded Schechter at Cambridge, and Samuel Montagu's daughter, Lily, a dedicated social worker, who parted from her father's views on the ability of orthodoxy to prevent religious indifference even among the recent immigrants.[5] The Jewish Religious Union was thus at first a movement seeking to transcend the institutional framework of the community, but the radical attitude of Claude Montefiore (notably his advocacy that Judaism should follow Christianity in universalizing its ethics and even include parts of the New Testament in its scriptures) and of Lily Montagu led to the withdrawal of the orthodox and more traditional supporters; the union refused the offer of the use of the West London Reform Synagogue for services and formed its own Liberal Jewish Synagogue in St. John's Wood as a separate institution of Liberal Judaism.[6]

The movement towards Liberal Judaism was no doubt stimulated by the fact that the reform Judaism in Britain had become very little more radical since its inception over half a century before. There was very little English in the service; prayers were still said for the restoration of Jews to the Holy Land and (until the 1890s) for the restoration of sacrifices, and men and women were seated separately.[7]

On the other hand, the United Synagogue services, and those of analogous congregations in the provinces, while they underwent some reduction in content, were strictly controlled by the Chief Rabbi and did not deviate from the minimum requirements of orthodox worship: no organ or instrumental music was permitted on sabbaths and festivals, though the admission of female voices into the choir – at first forbidden but later permitted by Dr Hermann Adler – did contravene rabbinic codes.[8] But if the content of the service in the United Synagogue and elsewhere remained traditional, there was a subtle acculturation to the standards of the Victorian middle-class churchgoer. There was an emphasis on decorum; in some synagogues the reading desk was moved from its traditional central position to the eastern end and joined with the entrance to the ark and pulpit, the whole providing a theatrical focus. This was reinforced by choral singing, which tended to restrict the worshipper to being a member of an audience, sung and read to and preached at, rather than one of a congregation actively participating in the service.

The trend towards uniformity within the established community was enhanced by the publication in 1890 by the *Revd Simeon Singer of the New West End Synagogue of an Ashkenazi prayerbook, authorized by the Chief Rabbi. Singer's translation was intended to serve not only for personal use, thus facilitating the continued use of Hebrew by those able to read but not readily to translate it, but also for classroom use, to train children to translate the prayers. Thanks to a subsidy[9], the book was sold at a shilling and was spread widely enough to standardize the Anglo-Jewish *minhag* or ritual, which was set out in rubrics clearly specifying the occasions on which specific prayers should or should not be said. Over 130,000 copies were printed between 1890 and 1914 and spread the rite of the United Synagogue, as authorized by the Chief Rabbi, across the Anglo-Jewish community, through the use of what became known as 'Singer's prayerbook' in synagogue, school and religion class.

The United Synagogue increased further between 1870 and 1914 from the original five to twenty-one synagogues, four of which were associate synagogues in what were then outlying areas whose members were adjudged unable to bear the full financial burdens; male membership rose from under 1,400 to well over 5,000.[10] The central organization for finance made it possible for new settlements of Jews in the suburbs of London to obtain from the United Synagogue loans for building synagogues. These were advanced on strict security, including the vesting of the synagogue buildings in the United Synagogue; and the financial viability of the new congregation had generally to be assured before it could be admitted as a constituent of the United Synagogue. Even so, the existence of the organization meant that the new congregations in the London suburbs had an incentive to join the United Synagogue - with what that implied in the maintenance of the Chief Rabbi's control over religious practice. Once in the United Synagogue as a constituent synagogue it was impracticable to leave because of the ownership of the buildings, although one or two of the poorer, less closely integrated non-constituent synagogues, like Sandys Row, did so. But the United Synagogue quoted the original statutory limitation to the metropolis as a reason for rejecting applications from provincial congregations for admission or help.[11]

In the provinces the numbers of the established community in each place were insufficient in this period to produce anything like the United Synagogue (apart from a nominal exception for a few years in Glasgow), but in each of the more populous communities outside London there developed at least one major congregation, broadly similar to a constituent of the United Synagogue, accepting the Chief Rabbi's jurisdiction and worshipping from the Singer's prayerbook authorized by his predecessor. Such a congregation would move its building to the suburbs as the Jewish community of the city grew in wealth and settled in more favoured residential areas, but retained the general pattern of ritual; apart from the reform congregations in Manchester and Bradford founded before 1881, no reform synagogues were found outside London - or indeed outside the original congregation in West London before 1914, apart from a short-lived congregation in south London in the 1870s.[12] This was very different from the situation in the United States, where the movement to a higher-status neighbourhood generally involved joining a Conservative or reform congregation, swelling the 'ranks of Reform Judaism, not only because of its principles, but because of the natural human tendency to associate with a relatively high status group'.[13]

The standard of religious observance among the membership of the United Synagogue and analogous provincial congregations varied from a fairly meticulous observance to an almost nominal adherence, limited to marriage, burial and attendance perhaps only on high holydays (Atonement and New Year) and for family celebrations. In the anglicized suburban communities of London and other cities, the patterns of membership and attendance resembled those of the surrounding Victorian middle-class environment. Synagogue membership in the suburbs was high - possibly as much as 90 per cent of the Jewish population in north, north-west, west and south-west London in 1890[14] - but sabbath attendance, to judge from the figures of a census of attendants at all places of worship in the *British Weekly* in 1886 were, outside the City and East London, between one-third and two-thirds of the number of male seat-holders. Bearing in mind that the number attending presumably included women and children, the proportion of the potential congregation actually attending on that sabbath was perhaps in the range of 10–25 per cent, with higher scores in areas north of the central parks or St John's Wood and lower in areas like south London.[15] On the other hand, on festivals a similar census in 1902 by the *Daily News*, which happened to coincide with the first day of Passover, and which distinguished between men, women and children, showed that male attendants exceeded the number of seat-holders in the Bayswater and New West End Synagogues; and in north London (Highbury and Canonbury) were about four-fifths of male seat-holders; in Hampstead and St John's Wood, about the same proportion.[16] In addition in these areas about as many women as men attended on the first day of Passover. One can infer from this that on the high holydays synagogue attendance in these areas was virtually the whole membership.[17]

The Right-wing Orthodox

The United Synagogue and its provincial analogues were thus, within the established and anglicized sector of the community, examples of what may be termed inclusive orthodoxy: that is to say, provided that members were prepared to accept the orthodox standards of ritual, and the orthodox tests for admission (whether by birth, or occasionally, conversion), no tests of personal observance were imposed. But in 1886 there was a group, largely of German origin, in suburban north London, inspired by the strict, yet westernized, orthodoxy of Frankfurt-on-the-Main, which established a Beth Hamedrash (house of study which functioned also as a synagogue) in Newington Green Road. This was transferred to Ferntower Road in 1892 and to 125 Green Lanes in 1905. The aim was to form a self-contained and independent, strictly orthodox community, with its own institutions, on the model of the German *Austrittsgemeinden* (which had left their parent communities because they included non-orthodox majorities). In 1905 Rabbi Victor Schonfeld (1880–1930), born in Hungary, was called from Vienna to be rabbi of this congregation, which in 1911 became the Adath Yisroel community.[18] This might be termed 'exclusive' orthodoxy, because it excluded those whose religious observance fell below the standard of the congregation, as distinct from the United Synagogue, which admitted any prepared to accept the religious standards of the organization.

The north London orthodox were also associated until 1905 with a group of recent, strictly observant East European immigrants in east London. Some of the latter had formed in 1891 a synagogue in Booth Street for strict sabbath observers (*Shomrei Shabbat*). A *Machzike Hadath* (roughly equivalent to 'upholders of the faith') Society was formed in 1891 to reinforce orthodox observance, concentrating its criticism on the communal arrangements for ritual slaughter of meat (*shechita*) and the supervision of its sale in butcher shops. They protested unsuccessfully to

Dr Hermann Adler, the new Chief Rabbi, in 1891: he was thus being assailed simultaneously after his appointment by those wanting radical reform at Hampstead, those in the United Synagogue seeking modifications of the existing service, and those urging much stricter application of religious standards. The Machzike Hadath appointed their own *shochet* ritually to kill meat for their members; the Chief Rabbi refused to recognize him and declared the meat *trefah* (religiously unfit for Jewish consumption). There followed appeals to rabbinical authorities in Eastern and Central Europe. Dr Adler secured the support of the great rabbi of Kovno, Isaac Elhanan Spector, and of Rabbi Samuel Mohilewer, then rabbi of Bialystok and a founder of religious Zionism. The Machzike Hadath secured letters of support both from Central European rabbis like Dr Breuer of Frankfurt and Rabbi Solomon Spitzer of Vienna, and from Eastern Europe, including the normative authority, Rabbi Meir Hacohen Poupko, known from the title of one of his writings as the *Hafez Hayyim*. The issues became complex because there was dispute over the adequacy of the ritual arrangements of the Chief Rabbi - Rabbi Mohilewer had been in London and declared himself satisfied - but also over the right of a separate group to question the propriety of the arrangements of the recognized rabbinical authority of the place. In the mean time the Machzike Hadath had taken advantage of the presence in London on a private visit of Rabbi A.A. Werner (1837-1912) from Helsingfors to ask him to be their rabbinical authority and to found a Machzike Hadath community for *shechita* and other communal functions, covering both the Machzike Hadath congregation and the north London orthodox. The former, who had increased in numbers from immigration, acquired in 1898 the building in Spitalfields erected in 1743 as the Huguenot Neuve Eglise. They added to it a religious school of Talmud Torah for 600 children. The rift over the question of *shechita* continued until 1905.[19]

Religion in East London

While the mass of Eastern European immigrants were not so strict as the Machzike Hadath, they nevertheless differed very much in the patterns of their religious observance and the climate of their worship, although not in essential tenets of doctrine, from the United Synagogue and the analogous provincial congregations which accepted the jurisdiction of the Chief Rabbi. They continued the tradition of previous recent immigrants from Eastern Europe in forming small *hebroth*, worshipping in makeshift, sometimes unhygienic, premises; they prayed with an informality and enthusiasm, unlike the more formal services of the established community, which aimed at decorum and dignity. The *hebroth* were often associated with friendly societies or with the provision of friendly society benefits and in a few cases with Jewish trade unions; and they tended to group those coming from a particular town or area in Eastern Europe.[20]

Since there was no basic difference in doctrine, increasing numbers of immigrants, as they became more settled in the country, tended to join the United Synagogue and similar synagogues in the provinces. Towards the majority, however, the leadership of the established community had two distinct attitudes, each expressing a different form of paternalism. One attitude was exemplified by the attempt of the United Synagogue from 1885 to 1898 to found an East End Scheme, which would include a large synagogue in the immigrant area, with friendly society benefits, a meeting hall and arrangements for district visiting by the clergy, which were based on Christian parochial experience. A *dayyan* (ecclesiastical judge) and preacher would be appointed who 'while studying the necessities of the poor will elevate their social condition by inculcating lessons of morality, health and cleanliness, and will at the same time minister to their spiritual wants in time of distress and affliction'.[21]

The underlying policy was anglicization by direct methods. In the end, the East End Scheme was dropped through opposition, not least from *Samuel Montagu, who was active within the United Synagogue and the founder of its most fashionable synagogue, the New West End. But, as MP for Whitechapel, he saw himself as the leader of the immigrants and adapted a more indirect approach to their anglicization. In 1887 he formed sixteen *hebroth* (including eight which antedated 1881) into a Federation of Minor Synagogues – the word 'minor' was soon dropped from the title.[22] As distinct from the complete union and pooling of funds of the United Synagogue, this was a federation for strictly defined objects: to secure representation on communal bodies collectively, which the synagogues were too small to expect individually; to secure joint provision for burial at inexpensive rates (although this was not initially an objective); and to provide a spiritual leader. Montagu was keen to promote the interests of his religious and immigrant constituents, while hoping that by strengthening the cause of religion among them he would hold at bay the socialists whom he regarded as both unrepresentative and dangerous. He continued through his lifetime and by his will to contribute materially to the resources of the Federation; indeed it may be doubted if it could have operated in its initial years without his financial support.[23]

Montagu respected the desire for independence and the religious faith of the members of the *hebroth* but he had certain objects in view. 'The chief object was to get rid of the insanitary places of worship and to amalgamate two or three small ones together and have a suitable building'.[24] This was achieved by refusing admission to congregations of less than fifty members or which did not conform to standard building requirements, until the defects were remedied; and 'model' new synagogues were opened in East London. To maintain a formal unity in the London Jewish community, *Lord Rothschild, as president of the United Synagogue, was elected president of the Federation, with Montagu as acting president. But this was a formality and there was friction between the two organizations because the United Synagogue feared that the Federation was poaching on its preserves by admitting synagogues outside east London or otherwise drawing in members who might otherwise have joined the United Synagogue.[25] Montagu aimed to make the Federation an indirect method of anglicization, while still retaining the religious loyalty and traditions of the *hebroth*. One way was the appointment of a Minister, whose salary was met by Montagu, and who would not only be a Talmudical scholar and able to speak Yiddish to the immigrants but could also preach in English and work under the religious jurisdiction of the Chief Rabbi. A considerable personality, Dr M. Lerner (1856-1930) of Wurzheim (Alsace) was appointed in 1891 but after initiating developments, particularly in education, he left in 1894 to be Chief Rabbi of Altona and Schlesvig-Holstein.

In 1894 the celebrated religious orator, known as the *Maggid* or preacher of Kaminetz, Chaim Zundel Maccoby (1859-1916), who was already in London, was appointed as Preacher of the Federation, but not its Minister or religious authority. A saintly character and vegetarian, and a champion of the proto-Zionist Hovevei Zion movement, Maccoby became a widely respected figure in London Jewish religious life and remained as Preacher of the Federation till his death in 1916. In the meanwhile Montagu, to celebrate his elevation to the peerage in 1911 as Lord Swaythling, provided £5,000 to pay for a Chief Minister for ten years if a candidate he considered suitable could be found. He wanted a man with 'a great reputation for orthodoxy, a doctor of the theology, and a good orator, also a gentleman of refined manners, about 40 years old, and able to take a prominent position among Jewish clerics'. There was in this case no reference to the incumbent being under the authority of the Chief Rabbi and thus began an ambivalent relationship between the ministry of the Federation and the Chief Rabbi. Such a paragon as Montagu prescribed was found in Dr Maier Jung (1859-1921), rabbi of Ungarisch Brod in Moravia, but the appointment could not be made until after Lord Swaythling's death. His son, *the second Lord Swaythling, succeeded him as president of the Federation.[26]

The Federation thus became a distinct force in Anglo-Jewry, with a membership which rivalled in numbers that of the United Synagogue, and combining the traditional rites and customs of Eastern European Jewry, with – at least in the initial years – acceptance of the authority of the Chief Rabbi.[27] It thus was able to provide the communal authorities with a solution for the problem of the Machzike Hadath. The cost of acquiring and adapting their building in Fournier Street put them in financial difficulties and they looked for help, applying to join the Federation of Synagogues in 1901. The communal establishment was also disposed to a settlement as the Liverpool Shechita Board had lost a case for libel brought by unlicensed butchers whose meat the board had declared *trefa* and the

Admiralty Committee on Humane Slaughtering had included conclusions critical of the Jewish method of slaughtering animals. It was a time for closing ranks. Lord Rothschild and Samuel Montagu lent £1,000 to clear immediately the pressing liabilities of the Machzike Hadath. The latter joined the Federation of Synagogues in 1905; they accepted in this way the authority of the Chief Rabbi, while retaining their own *shochetim* and butcher shops under the supervision of their own rabbi but under the administrative control of the London Board of Shechita; all future appointments were to be subject to the approval of the Chief Rabbi, provided he acted in accordance with the *Shulhan Arukh* (the normative code of Judaism).

It is perhaps significant that this compromise was welcomed by the Eastern European immigrants of the Machzike Hadath, who felt they had obtained recognition of their own standards and might hope to influence standards in the London Jewish community generally. But the Central European group in north London refused to recognize the Chief Rabbi, seceded from the Machzike Hadath community and a few years later set up their own separate community. This is probably indicative of a difference of attitude between orthodox Jews of Eastern European origin (especially those from Lithuania) who at this time did not include any of the Hasidic sects and were prepared to join the inclusive orthodoxy of the Anglo-Jewish establishment, and on the other hand those of German or Hungarian origin, whose tradition was that the strictly orthodox should set up exclusive orthodox communities of their own.[28]

The Provincial Congregations

In the provincial communities the immigrants formed their own *hebroth* on the same pattern as in London, and often a community of moderate size, say of a couple of thousand, might have an immigrant congregation (often styled *Beth Hamedrash* or House of Study, to mark the devotion to regular Talmud study) to match the established 'Hebrew', or colloquially 'English', congregation. The provinces had their religious luminaries from Eastern Europe who to the Anglo-Jewish 'reverends' were often merely 'immigrant rabbis'.[29] For instance, in Sunderland, the 'English' congregation (which had absorbed some smaller *hebroth*[30]) was faced by a secession of the more recent East European immigrants, largely from Krottingen, near Memel, whose dissatisfaction with the standards and attitudes of the older congregation was combined with a desire to possess their own place of worship and study. This led to the formation first of a regular *shiur* or study group, then by 1891 to a Beth Hamedrash;[31] by 1899 they consecrated a building accommodating 270 worshippers.[32] As in London, financial pressures helped towards the formation of a united organization for *shechita*. Newcastle's Beth Hamedrash was also formed in 1891,[33] but this, although intended for the use of the newcomers, was founded on the initiative of the established congregation to which it remained affiliated, although a separate synagogue was formed in 1904.

In the larger communities outside London, small immigrant congregations proliferated. Some developed into larger synagogues with their own purpose-built or adapted premises. For instance, in Glasgow there were a number of small *minyanim* or prayer groups, formed on the basis of district of origin (Minsk, Odessa etc) and to some extent on occupation (tailors, travelling salesmen). In Glasgow, the established congregations – the equivalent of the United Synagogue – after approaches by the immigrants in the Gorbals, south of the river, formed a United Synagogue from 1898 to 1906, in which the *minyanim* joined, although this was in reality only a loose association, the individual congregations retaining financial responsibility and independence.[34] In Birmingham, the main synagogue (consecrated in Singer's Hill in 1856) seems to have been preoccupied with decorum, the dignity and robing of the clergy and keeping the services running to time. The latter included curtailments that aroused the opposition of the Beth Hamedrash founded in 1894. The main congregation claimed, as had the Spanish and Portuguese Congregation in London in the eighteenth century, the right to ban any other services in the area. The leaders of the Beth Hamedrash included members of Singer's Hill, who wanted more traditional services, and they accepted the primacy of the main congregation. After protracted negotiations – conducted by Singer's Hill in a spirit of *de haut en bas* – it was agreed in 1902 that the members of the Beth Hamedrash should pay a small annual contribution to Singer's Hill which would pay £100 a year to the Beth Hamedrash. But every year until 1921 the latter had formally to apply for permission to hold services. The Beth Hamedrash later became the Central Synagogue; when they moved to new premises in 1901, the old premises were occupied by a small *minyan* (which eventually became the New Synagogue).[35]

In Manchester, by far the largest immigrant centre outside London, there were many more *hebroth*. There was a 'mushrooming of new "bedroom chevras" ', as they were slightingly called in the Anglo-Jewish press and the evolution of major neighbourhood synagogues, often out of the *hebroth* of an earlier generation: this was often due to the enterprise and support of immigrants who had made good as workshop owners or shopkeepers and this helped the *hebra* to acquire premises, attract a rabbi and build a larger congregation.[36]

If even the most fervent upholders of orthodoxy among the East European immigrants ultimately accepted at least the nominal supremacy of the pre-1881 establishment, the provincial communities, in spite of eminent rabbis who came to Britain in their early middle age, did not present any major threat to the Chief Rabbinate. Among the arrivals were Rabbi I.H. Daiches (1850–1937), who was invited to Leeds by a group largely composed of immigrants. He was a noted scholar, as were Rabbi I.J. Yoffey (d. 1934) of Manchester and Rabbi H. Hurwitz first of Sunderland (where he worked harmoniously with Rabbi Salis Daiches (1880–1945), then minister of the 'English' synagogue), later Rabbi of the Leeds Federation of Synagogues,[37] Rabbi S.J. Rabbinowitz of Liverpool and Rabbi S.I. Hillman of Glasgow, who became a member of the Chief Rabbi's ecclesiastical court in London.[38] Meetings of rabbis from Eastern Europe which took place in Manchester in 1903 and Leeds in 1911 produced unanimity on measures to strengthen Judaism in England but these were largely aimed at reproducing the institutions, such as *Yeshivoth*, or customs (such as the shaving of the hair and wearing of wigs by married women) which were the marks of orthodoxy in Eastern Europe. These conferences did not result in a united revolt against the Chief Rabbi – Dr Adler was reported to have wished the meeting well – nor did they produce a counter-reformation against the Anglo-Jewish establishment or the setting up of independent strongly orthodox communities on German lines.[39]

It would be incorrect to equate the immigrants in total with religious orthodoxy or observance. Apart from the minority who were already unobservant in Eastern Europe, many were forced by economic circumstances – for instances to meet deadlines even in Jewish-owned workshops – to work on sabbaths. That about only half were sabbath observers seems to have been the position in East London;[40] and the figures of attendance at places of worship in 1903 suggests that on the first day of Passover in the East End male attendance at synagogues and *hebroth* was about the same as in the middle-class suburban congregations as a percentage of potential attenders. It was not customary in Eastern Europe for women to attend on most festival days, especially after the pre-Passover preparations. On the other hand, there was a general impression that attendance on the high holydays, especially the Day of Atonement, was widespread, and special mass services were arranged to cater for the worshippers who could not be accommodated in synagogues.[41]

Left-wing Movements

There were powerful ideological trends besides religion – indeed sometimes in conflict with it – which operated among Jews in Britain in this period: trends often, but not exclusively, brought by immigrants from Eastern Europe and influential especially among the immigrants. The traumatic experience of the resurgence of anti-Semitism in Central Europe from the 1870s, the intensification of Russian anti-Jewish policies in the 1880s, and the Dreyfus affair in France in the 1890s all contributed to a widespread perception of the failure of emancipation and of the optimistic liberal assumption of progress towards complete acceptance of Jews in European society. On this view, Jews could not rely on the benevolence of the parties of the ruling establishment. This led to three main ideological lines of solution. First, as part of an international revolutionary movement, which aimed to emancipate Jews with other citizens, through a form of socialism or anarchism. Second, Jewish nationalism identified with the physical establishment of a Jewish polity in its own territory, generally envisaged as the Holy Land (Zionism) but possibly elsewhere (territorialism). Third, some form of minority status for Jews in their countries of residence, especially those with a number of ethnic minority groups: this was advanced after about 1901 especially by the Russian Jewish socialist party known as the Bund ('Union': short for General Jewish Workers Union of Lithuania, Poland and Russia). This had been formed in 1897, on earlier foundations but, although members of the Bund played an active part in the American Jewish labour movement, Bundists seem to have had little impact on Jewish socialism in Britain. This was possibly because in the years when Bundists left for the West after the failure of the 1905 Russian revolution, there was a decline in immigration to Britain because of the 1905 Aliens Act, and emigrants tended to go direct to America. In contrast, in the 1880-1900 period, Jewish radicals - socialists and anarchists, who were in general not nationally oriented but regarded the fight for betterment of the Jewish proletariat as part of the struggle for the working class as a whole - often came to Britain as young men before moving on to the United States.[42]

The intellectual leadership of the Jewish left-wing movement in Britain was, broadly speaking, social-democrat in the 1880s under the inspiration of the pioneer Jewish socialist, Morris Vinchevsky (1856-1932), who arrived in London in 1879.[43] Between 1890 and 1894 several of the socialist leaders left for the United States and the main intellectual influence on the Jewish left until 1914 was that of the anarchists. This was reflected in the ideological orientation of the Yiddish press. The leading Yiddish journal in London, with an influence probably much beyond its nominal circulation of a few hundred, was founded in 1884 by Vinchevsky and Joel Elijah Rabbinowitz as the *Polishe Yidel* (little Polish Jew) - the first Socialist paper in Yiddish. In October 1884 it became *Die Zukunft* (*The Future*) but this soon took a more flexible line as Rabbinowitz wanted to adjust to religious, Jewish national and even bourgeois attitudes. Vinchevsky left *Zukunft* (which continued until 1889) and founded the *Arbeter Fraint* (*Workers' Friend*) which remained the main left-wing Yiddish periodical in what became a variety of Yiddish papers in Britain. When Vinchevsky left for America in the 1890s it changed its line to anarchism. It is perhaps symbolic of the transfer of ideological leadership of the left-wing movements from Britain to America from about 1894 to 1914 that even the anarchists, who seem to have been the principal force in Jewish left-wing thinking in that period, were led by a non-Jew, Rudolf Rocker. Rocker, who had come to England from Germany in 1895, settled in east London in

1898, learned Yiddish and immersed himself in Jewish affairs as editor of the *Arbeter Fraint* and leader of the Jewish anarchists. Under his leadership the anarchists, although not numerically a large group, took over in 1892 the club at 40 Berner Street, which had been founded in 1884 as a socialist centre; and the anarchists exercised an influence on the strikes of London Jewish tailors in 1889 and 1906.[44]

Trade Unions

Jewish socialism and anarchism in Britain between 1870 and 1914 was closely linked with specifically Jewish trade unionism. The Jewish socialists and anarchists sought to awaken the Jewish working class to the possibilities of ameliorating their position either by industrial action against their employers, who were generally Jewish, or by agitation against the Jewish communal establishment, or as part of a wider movement for revolutionary change. To enable the Jewish immigrants, many of whom had little knowledge of western circumstances, to appreciate the possibilities of change in a western environment, education in western culture was an allied objective, although there was also a desire to preserve Yiddish culture against attempts to anglicize the immigrants. Yiddish was identified as the language of a Jewish proletariat: a natural means of communication through newspapers and pamphlets with those whose mother tongue it was and also as embodying a folk culture without the religious and national associations of Hebrew. This was not, of course exclusive: the socialist pioneer Aaron Lieberman, who founded the first Jewish socialist society in London in 1876 was a committed Hebraist, and Yiddish was the normal vernacular of the orthodox immigrants, especially as many of them regarded Hebrew as a sacred language inappropriate for secular use.

That there should be specifically Jewish unions at all arose from the circumstances of the recent East European immigrants - including language difficulties, differences of background and custom, anti-alien prejudice - and made sense only because for a time the concentration of immigrants within a number of limited areas produced what was in effect a separate Jewish immigrant economy of workers and employers. Indeed, the Jewish trade union movement evolved within the wider framework of the British labour movement, even though for reasons of language, and local and temporary circumstances, the Jewish movement began in the form of independent Jewish unions. There was co-operation between general union leaders and the Jewish unions, with John Burns and Ben Tillet (who were against alien immigration in principle as a threat to native workers) speaking in support of Jewish trade unionists on strike in 1889. Jewish trade unions were affiliated to local trades councils. Some general trade unions like the Amalgamated Society of Tailors formed specifically Jewish branches and eventually Jews were sufficiently adjusted to British trade unionism to join the general unions, so the Jewish unions disappeared.

The Jewish unions, at least until the 1900s, were small, numerous, and short-lived. They often grew to impressive numbers under the impulse of a strike or similar crisis. This is not necessarily a condemnation of the movement since numbers were available precisely at the times when they could most effectively be used, and the situation was similar to that of many British unions at this time. Further, not only were there difficulties in the way of Jewish unions – the smallness of the workshops in most cases (except tailoring in Leeds), opposition from employers in seasons of high unemployment, unfamiliarity of immigrants with the environment – but British trade unionism generally until just before 1914 was marked by small unions, fluid organization and membership by only a minority of the workforce.[45]

Jewish unions had a variety of bases: not only trade or subdivision of a trade but association with socialism or anarchism, provision of mutual benefits, and even religious links with *hebroth*. Ideological disputes – whether unions should be separate for Jews or part of a wider movement, what the underlying ideology should be (what form of socialism, anarchism or even Zionism), the attitude of the union to organized religion – mirror ideological conflicts in the Jewish working class in Eastern Europe and America. In the main the unions aimed at securing improvement of conditions (hours, pay and so on) but it is arguable whether they would have achieved what they did in those industrial objectives without the stimulus of organization by the ideologically committed, who saw industrial action as a way of mobilizing the proletariat for wider aims.[46]

The conditions which gave rise to strikes can be illustrated by the main demand of the London Jewish tailors in the great strike of 27 August to 2 October 1889 for a 10½ hour working day (i.e. 12 hours less 1½ hours for meals); and the fact that over a quarter of the cost to the funds of the strikers was provided by Lord Rothschild, Samuel Montagu, MP for Whitechapel and two associates. Set in the context of the developing charges against alien immigration of 'sweating' and by unfairly low-paid competition injuring the position of native workers, it was in the interest of the communal establishment, apart from any possible sympathy against exploitation, to see wages raised and conditions improved amongst the immigrant workers. But the fluctuations of trade, the intense competition between workshops for the contracts of the wholesalers and the continuing arrival of new sources of labour meant that gains achieved by strikes were difficult to maintain.

The earliest reference to Jewish workers striking against Jewish employers is in January 1858 in the London cigar manufacturing trade[47] but the first union of which details have survived is that formed in London in 1876, at least in part under the influence of *Aaron Lieberman's *Agudat HaSozialistim Haivrim* or Hebrew Socialist Society. The union broke up after a few months, when the treasurer absconded to America with its funds. But it is important because of the character of Lieberman, a committed Hebraist and nationalist from Lithuania, as well as socialist; and because issues were raised which were later widespread: between socialist and national-religious feeling (crystallized in whether to hold a union meeting on the national fast day of the Ninth of Ab), on the role of Hebrew and Yiddish, on whether Jews should organize separately or as part of a wider proletarian movement.[48] There was a lull until about 1880, and the arrival of another Lithuanian, Morris Vinchevsky, and other immigrants, although Lewis Lyons (born 1852) was a London-born activist in this period. A number of unions were formed in the mid-1880s, including one in the London furniture trade which enrolled 200 of the estimated total of 700 Jewish cabinetmakers in East London.[49] The London Tailors and Machinists Union founded in 1886 had as its objective a 12-hour day (1½ hours for meals). In Leeds, with smaller numbers and larger workshops, and even factories, union organization was less difficult, and strikes secured union recognition and a shorter working week in 1884 and 1885 respectively. But this was a temporary success. There was a general strike of tailors in Leeds, involving over 3,000 workers, for union recognition, a 58-hour week and payment for overtime, but this proved unsuccessful. This was part of a wave of strikes and industrial unrest in 1889–90, of which the best remembered is probably the great London dock strike. Among the Jewish workers, there were strikes of Manchester cigarette-makers (February 1889), the great strike of London tailors in autumn 1889, London stickmakers in 1890, London footwear workers in March 1890, Manchester tailors in April 1890, London tailors again in May 1890 (to try to confirm the settlement of the previous year's strike), Manchester cabinetmakers in May 1890, and Manchester footwear workers in autumn 1890. The 1889 London tailors' strike, supported by non-Jewish union leaders as well as by communal establishment leaders like Lord Rothschild and Samuel Montagu MP, was ended by Samuel Montagu's mediation and victory – for a time – for the strikers.[50]

But in the 1890s the membership of the unions fell, even though new unions were formed and lasted for short periods. It was a period of trade depression that affected membership of British unions generally; new immigrants added to the pool of available labour, leaders left for America and other factors reduced militancy. In Manchester and Leeds, however, single unions for the Jewish tailoring trade were built up and consolidated until they joined the main British union, then called the Amalgamated Society of Tailors, in 1906 and 1915 respectively. 1906 and 1911–12 were also years of fairly widespread industrial action – including a mass strike of tailors in London in 1906, in Leeds in 1911 and again in east London 1912: this last began as a sympathy strike with tailors in the West End but while the latter compromised the Jewish tailors held out for better terms. By 1914, when 65 per cent of the trade-union organized tailoring workers in London were Jewish, Jewish tailoring workers in London were more unionized than non-Jews.[51]

But it is clear that no permanent successes were achieved by most of the strikes, since in 1912, for instance, the East End strikers settled for the 12-hour day they should have made secure in 1889. It was the legislation on minimum wages in the Trade Boards Act of 1909, introduced by Winston Churchill as Home Secretary especially to deal with 'sweated' industries, which permanently effected a change. There was a single trade board, for instance, for wholesale tailoring, with power to fix minimum wages, and which was representative of unions and employers. To secure representation for very small unions was impracticable and Jewish workers had either to group themselves in larger Jewish unions – such as the Leeds tailors' union which had over 4,000 members – or to join the general unions. The latter course was increasingly followed, even eventually by the Leeds tailors. Separate Jewish unions, with a few exceptions, disappeared after about 1914. This was an indication also of the spreading anglicization of Jewish workers, no longer separated by language or special interest as alien immigrants from analogous non-Jewish workers. In the same way, the separate Jewish left-wing movements, first socialist and then anarchist, ceased to exist as separate secular units. The future of the Jewish left (apart from left-wing Zionists) was as part of the wider socialist and trade union movement.[52]

A perceptive analysis by Dr W.J. Fishman, the historian of the Jewish radicals, of the decline of the anarchists after 1914, offers keys to the reason for the failure to survive of the secular left-wing movements generally in Anglo-Jewry. The anarchists, although not numerous (about 200 in an immigrant community of 130,000), still played an important role in East End Jewish politics in the later 1890s and until 1914. Yet by 1920 they were 'an anachronism, shadowy ghosts of another era'. In addition to the internment at the beginning of the war in 1914 of their charismatic leader, Rocker, several more general factors can be identified. First, association with anti-religious demonstrations and militant atheism deterred many who 'returned to the security and respectability of their ancient faith'. The anarchists had been identified with demonstrations like the march to the Great Synagogue on sabbath, 16 March 1889, or the annual balls on the Day of Atonement.[53] Second, there was a number of devoted anarchists who displayed entrepreneurial tendencies, and even success in business. One might suggest that this was evidence of how widespread was a persistent desire for upward mobility among the immigrants. Third were the anglicizing influences of schools, clubs and other establishment institutions. Finally, anarchism and specifically Jewish socialism had to compete with the 'triple pulls of Zionism, orthodoxy, and communism after 1917', to which might be added the mainstream British labour movement.[54]

Education

In considering the factors which welded the immigrants first into a single community with the previously established community and then into part of the wider British population, the schools must be placed first. Communal provision of education had two objectives, inculcating Judaism and anglicization, but there seems little doubt that the latter was more effective, aided as it was by many other forces in the environment. In 1911 there were about 37,500 Jewish children of school age in London. Of these about 7,400 were in Jewish day schools - about 20 per cent compared with 63 per cent in 1886 and about 37 per cent in 1900 (though the figures are not for identical areas). The reasons for the percentage (though not absolute) decline in the numbers attending Jewish day schools were that, as mentioned in Chapter 1, it was decided not to open any more Jewish day schools after the introduction of universal secular education by the Act of 1870. A number of ordinary day schools, at least under the London School Board, became in effect Jewish schools, with an overwhelming Jewish composition of pupils, Jewish prayers and a timetable geared to the Jewish religious calendar, and with Jewish religion classes provided on school premises after ordinary school hours by the Jewish Religious Education Board. In 1902 there were sixteen such schools in east London, with over 15,000 pupils, and there were other schools, including church schools, with a substantial minority of Jewish pupils and Jewish religious instruction on school premises after school hours. Religious instruction in the ordinary schools was limited to about five hours a week and teachers were not usually trained to give it, but at least its existence reconciled the parents, who were required by law to send their children to school, to sending them to a non-Jewish school.[55]

The Jews' Free School in Bell Lane, Spitalfields was by far the largest of the London Jewish day schools, with over half of the 7,000 pupils on the rolls of Jewish day schools.[56] In addition, there were another 2,000 in Jewish voluntary day schools in Manchester (which had 1,200 pupils), Liverpool and Birmingham; there were no day schools in Leeds, with a larger Jewish population than Liverpool or Birmingham, because the Leeds community developed after 1870, when the policy of founding Jewish day schools ceased.[57] The number of pupils in the Jewish day schools remained fairly static: the increase due to immigration went into the local authority schools (from 1870 to 1902 in London, London School Board 'board schools') or even into the church schools, which were aided by the local authority.

In 1894, the Jews' Free School had 47 per cent of its pupils born abroad and 41 per cent born in England of foreign-born parents, but these percentages changed as more and more children were English-born, though of foreign parents.[58] The Board of Trade Report of 1894 referred to the far more powerful instrument for "anglicising" the foreign Jewish community: the great Jewish Free School.... As the children pass from the ABC class at the bottom, in which the energies of the teachers are mainly directed to teaching the English language and something of English notions of cleanliness, upwards through the standards to the top of the school, there is a most marked change in their appearnce and habits. They enter the school Russians and Poles and emerge from it almost indistinguishable from English children.[59]

If this was true of a specifically Jewish school, provided by the Jewish community although aided from the rates, it was so *a fortiori* of the local authority or board schools. As the non-Jewish headmaster of such a school told the Royal Commission in 1902:

Jewish boys soon become anglicised and cease to be foreigners. My first classes contain 175 boys... 67 were born abroad and practically the whole of these children are of foreign parentage. Notwithstanding this fact, the lads have become thoroughly English. They have acquired our language. They take a keen and intelligent interest in all that concerns the welfare of our country.... They enter heartily into English games... Jewish lads who pass through our schools will grow up to be intelligent, industrious, temperate and law-abiding citizens and... will add to the wealth and stability of the British Empire.[60]

This was typical of many such comments from contemporary observers.

Clubs

The anglicizing influence of the schools was continued in the clubs. This was not true of the Jewish Workingmen's Club, founded by Samuel Montagu in 1876 in Great Alie Street, London, which in the 1880s had 1,400 members and was intended for 'the anglicisation of the Jews of the East End and the provision of a place of innocent amusement': this was because the immigrants did not join it and after its membership dwindled to below 200, as English-born Jews moved from the East end, it closed in 1912.[61] But the clubs founded for boys and girls did attract the young people of immigrant background. For instance, in 1903 three-quarters of the boys at the Brady Street Boys Club (founded 1896) were of foreign parentage. The same was true of the other clubs which in London included West Central Lads Club (1898), Stepney Jewish Lads (1900), Jewish Girls Club (1886) and West Central Jewish Girls (1887). These clubs were inspired by the settlement movement, of which Toynbee Hall was the supreme example, under which young people from the more prosperous areas regarded it as their duty to serve in the areas of urban deprivation, particularly by founding and managing clubs. With these origins, it was natural that English, not Yiddish, should be the language of the club and normal English sports - cricket, football, swimming - should be routine activities. A similar role was played by the Jewish Lads' Brigade, founded 1895 and led by *Colonel Albert E.W. Goldsmid, which held its first summer annual camp in 1896. It was an adaptation to Anglo-Jewish needs of the Boys Brigade and Church Lads Brigade. The brigade was described by a non-Jewish headmaster as 'an admirable movement for developing the physique, for inculcating habits of obedience and self-restraint and for fostering a spirit of true patriotism'.[62] There were youth clubs and branches of the brigade in the main provincial communities and, unlike the London equivalent, the Manchester Jewish Workingmen's Club (founded 1886) does seem to have enrolled immigrants.[63]

Anglicization

Upward economic and social mobility also had its implications for anglicization because if immigrants set up in business, were successful and moved out of the immigrant quarter of first settlement to a more middle-class or suburban district, they tended to acculturate to the habits of the older-established Jewish, and indeed non-Jewish, residents. It is possible to see before 1914 the beginnings of what has been termed 'the rapid disintegration of the working-class community', which continued after 1914.[64] It has been argued that, if the immigrants were employed workers in Eastern Europe and their parents or grandparents had been independent traders or artisans, in Britain they were trying 'to re-establish the economic independence and security which they and their parents had lost in the Pale (of Settlement)'.[65] In other words, if they were proletarians in Britain when they arrived, this was not perceived by them to be their natural condition and they wanted to be economically independent. In any event, the structure of the immigrant Jewish economy provided many opportunities for workers either to become small employers - the capital required was, by present standards, minimal - or to become self-employed, even if only as hawkers. 'There was plenty of opportunity and plenty of temptation to escape the wage-slavery of the workshop by trying to become a master, rather than indulging in collective struggle'.[66]

There was help from the London Jewish Board of Guardians and analogous bodies in the provinces. From as early as 1861, there were arrangements under which sewing machines could be hired, with a view to purchase on easy terms, and this was extended to tools for glaziers, carpenters, cabinetmakers, shoemakers, printers and bookbinders. Loans were available to help aspiring entrepreneurs to set up small businesses. The scale of this operation by the London Board of Guardians rose from 268 loans, totalling £1,279, in 1881 to £3,079, totalling £21,648, in 1913. While some loans were for rescuing existing businesses from difficulty, they undoubtedly enabled hundreds, after 1900 thousands, annually to set up on their own; and the average loan, rising from £5 to £7 over the period, shows how little initial capital was required. In Manchester - and no doubt elsewhere - there developed a class of successful immigrant entrepreneurs, identified by Mr Bill Williams as 'immigrant parvenus'; and he has shown that they played a key role in founding synagogues and welfare institutions. They looked back to Eastern Europe for their values but also looked forward to acceptance in British society. Of course, not all small would-be entrepreneurs succeeded; many failed and became employees again, and the results of these failures were still traceable no doubt in the elderly residents of the original immigrant areas half a century later.[67] In the years before 1914 there was a fall in the total numbers of applications for relief to the London Jewish Board of Guardians, which reached a peak of 6,746 in 1905, to 3,348 in 1913 - the same level as in 1890, when the London Jewish community was half the size it was in 1913; and this suggests that, in addition to some reduction in the level of immigration, immigrants were establishing themselves economically and the majority of them did not need help from the board before 1914.[68]

Self-help

The immigrants' own agencies of self-help were also part of the process of anglicization. There was a proliferation of mutual aid societies, which from an origin as *hebra* benefit societies became registered friendly societies, paying benefits for funeral expenses, during *Shiva* (week of confined mourning), as well as the more normal sickness benefits and benefits for widows and dependants. By 1901 the societies were grouped in thirteen Jewish 'Orders', on the pattern of the existing friendly society orders; the first, *Achei Brith*, was formed in 1888. By 1901 there were over 20,000 members in 176 societies, of which 27 were outside London.[69] The language and elaborate rituals of these orders were English and 'the ebullience of the Friendly Society movement perhaps suggests the degree to which immigrants themselves sought acceptance in England and conformity to English standards almost as strongly as the élite pressed it upon them'.[70]

While the communal establishment did all it could to encourage English and discourage Yiddish - for instance, special classes in English for adults[71] - it was as much the surrounding environment and the wishes of at least the younger generation themselves which promoted this change from Yiddish to English in a generation. Observing the London East End in 1911, the Revd S. Levy, minister of the New Synagogue, wrote:

The national system of compulsory and free education under which thousands of children are brought up to speak English and to acquire English habits of thought and character . . . has inevitably a retroactive effect upon the parents in the home . . . . In spite of the normal immigration into this country, the forces of anglicisation are now far stronger than the ties which still bind some of the older generation to Yiddish . . . . If a language census was taken in the East End, it would disclose that the number of those who still can only speak and understand Yiddish is a relatively small percentage of the population.[72]

This process has been studied in Manchester by Mrs Rosalyn Livshin, who has shown that those who emigrated after marriage tended to continue to speak Yiddish. Only the exceptional parents, however, made a concerted effort to make their children speak Yiddish. Some parents made a conscious attempt to learn English; most accepted that learning English was an inevitable and necessary step for their children (in contrast with the USA where Yiddish persisted as a spoken language among the children of immigrants). 'Within one generation foreigners were turned into English Jews.'[73]

Whereas in Eastern Europe there had been a movement within Jewry to acculturate Jews to the language, dress, culture and social habits of their non-Jewish environment, this had made relatively slow progress and affected only limited sections of the Jewish population; some of those who adopted the cause of modernization assimilated out of Judaism. By contrast, in the politically liberal atmosphere of Britain, this process of acculturation was achieved by the East European immigrants in a generation and by force of circumstances, with little evidence of ideology or conscious policy, at least on the part of the immigrants. There was a widespread measure of integration within British society, which affected all sections: for instance, those politically on the left joined the British Labour, and later Communist, movements, not generally the specifically Jewish left-wing organizations as in Eastern Europe.

With so much gained at a stroke, a *Haskalah* programme to secure emancipation became outdated . . . . Once in England, East European Jews moved in the direction of anglicisation and assimilation into English culture, not towards enlightened Hebraic rationalism . . . . Not Westernisation but erosion was the problem affecting Judaism in England.[74]

It was in their attitude to this erosion that the Anglo-Jewish communal establishment differed from its counterparts in, say, the United States. For the communal establishment, orthodox Judaism as they conceived and defined it – although not what they regarded as ultra-orthodoxy – represented values which would keep the Jewish population moral, assist anglicization, and earn for Jews the respect of the non-Jewish world. They therefore 'championed vigorously its local orthodoxy, the type of religious life characteristic of the majority of English Jews'.[75] Viewed within the context of its age and place, this identified the Anglo-Jewish brand of orthodoxy with the religious attitudes of the Victorian middle-class, especially suburban, population - sober, dignified, punctilious in family attendance at place of worship - with the addition of the traditional observances of the Jewish home. The institutions of Anglo-Jewry were used to this end. The Federation of Synagogues provided a means of adjusting the *hebroth* to the physical standards required of Anglo-Jewish places of worship and associating the immigrants with the main religious institutions of the community, notably the Chief Rabbinate. The United Synagogue was increasingly able to attract the immigrants and their children, because its religious authority and outward ritual (if not the personal observances of all its members) was orthodox; and second, because when the immigrants became more prosperous and moved out of the immigrant quarter, there was no social reason why they should not join an orthodox synagogue: because of the membership of so many members of leading families in the United Synagogue, orthodoxy had at least parity of prestige with the older reform and new liberal congregations.

In pursuit of their religious objectives, the communal authorites gave some priority to religious education. Five hours a week was the ration for the Jewish Religious Education Board (JREB) classes attached to the local authority schools; two or three hours a week in the religion classes attached to the prosperous suburban congregations, although longer in the less fashionable areas of second settlement like Dalston, Notting Hill, Walthamstow and West Ham. These synagogal classes were grouped in 1907 into the Union of Hebrew and Religion Classes. The traditional one-room 'schools' or *Hedarim*, usually conducted by unqualified teachers in their cramped living quarters, were brought from Eastern Europe and in British circumstances were often ineffective, in spite of the long hours of nominal tuition. In so far as instruction was in Yiddish, the Revd S. Levy's enquiries in 1911 showed that at least 60 per cent of the children attending the *Hedarim* in east London had to learn Yiddish first if they were to understand what they were taught. To provide a traditional education but under more modern conditions and for longer hours than in the JREB classes or most of the synagogue classes, a number of Talmud Torahs were founded in east, and later north, London and in Manchester, Leeds, Glasgow and Liverpool. The first was in Great Garden Street in 1881, with English as the language of instruction; the Brick Lane Talmud Torah, attached to the Machzike Hadath in 1894, gave instruction to several hundred children in Yiddish; and Redmans Road, established in 1901, was the pioneer in England, under the Revd J.K. Goldbloom, in using Hebrew as the language of instruction. A Talmud Torah Trust was founded, inevitably with the aid of Samuel Montagu, under the auspices of the Federation of Synagogues to support the Talmud Torahs in east and north London.[76]

But even taking together Jewish day schools, classes in the local authority schools, synagogue classes and Talmud Torahs, and the *hedarim*, there were children of school age who did not receive any Jewish education. An estimate in 1911 for London showed 2,500 in synagogue classes, 2,600 in Talmud Torahs, 7,300 in classes in the local authority, 7,400 in day schools and 3,000 in *hedarim*. Even allowing 5,000 for other tuition (for example at home) this still accounts for only 27,000 out of an estimated total of 37,000 Jewish children of school age in London. Even allowing again for late entrants and early leavers, the number of children who received some Jewish education fell short of the total of the boys, and much more seriously missed the total of girls.[77]

How effective the education delivered was in preserving the practice of Judaism, the experience of the next generation was to show. There were many pressures, for instance, to break the traditional observance of the sabbath. Some stayed firm but often were tempted by leisure activities on Saturdays. Others, while observant at home and school, found they could not avoid Saturday work when they found what seemed suitable employment. Others rejected Judaism for ideological reasons: 'the philosophy of the left drew them away from religion towards the atheism of communism'. Very few, however, were 'willing to give everything up and marry out of *their* faith',[78] especially as they felt this was something that they could not do to their parents. Although there is no direct statistical evidence, it is very likely that the level of marriage outside Judaism was low among the middle and lower classses who constituted the mass of the community. One can get some idea of whether intermarriage was prevalent or not by comparing Jewish marriage rates with those of the general population. Between 1901 and 1914, the annual marriage rate in England and Wales was in the range of 7.4 to 8.0 per 1,000 (7.9 in 1913). In the same period the number of marriages annually varied between 1,888 and 2,061 (2,050 in 1913). To calculate the rate per thousand one has to know the total Jewish population – and the marriage figures are on the low side because they exclude registry office marriages subsequently confirmed by a religious ceremony, marriages which confirmed a religious ceremony abroad, and irregular religious marriages. In 1901 the Jewish marriage rate, on any assumptions about the size of the Jewish population, was well above the general marriage rate; and in 1913, even if we assume a Jewish population as High as 300,000, the Jewish rate would have been around 7 per 1,000. So it looks as if intermarriage, at any rate among the immigrants was low before 1914.[79]

Thus a community of 65,000 in 1881 had by 1914 absorbed some 150,000 East European immigrants and increased in size, because of the high marriage and birth rates of the new arrivals, to near 300,000. But, equally striking, the new arrivals were well on the way towards integration in British society and what had begun as two separate communities were in the process of being welded into one. At this stage, the religious, social and cultural patterns of the older Anglo-Jewish community were steadily influencing the new.

Notes

1. For Hermann Adler's student days, see A. Schischa, 'Hermann Adler' in J.M. Shaftesley (ed.) *Remember the Days,* London, 1966; for a general assessment, Raymond B. Apple, 'United Synagogue: religious founders and leaders', in S.S. Levin (ed.) *A Century of Jewish Life,* London, 1970, pp. 16-19.
2. Raymond B. Apple, *The Hampstead Synagogue 1892-1967,* 1967, Chs 1-3.
3. 'Four epistles to the Jews of England', reprinted in S. Schechter, *Studies in Judaism,* 2nd series, Philadelphia, 1945, especially pp. 196, 198.
4. Steven Bayme, 'Origins of the Jewish Religious Union', *TJHSE* XXVII, 62.
5. Bayme, 'Origins', pp. 63-67.
6. Montefiore, while praising the ethical teaching of Jesus, publicly avoided the question of divinity but seems to have conceded the possibility of 'some truth even in a definitively Christian doctrine eg. the Trinity': see the letter from Montefiore to Israel Mattuck, quoted by Bayme, 'Origins', p. 70, n.47. See also Edward Kessler, 'Claude Montefiore', *Christian Jewish Relations* XXI(4), 1988, 5-17 and his *An English Jew: the Life and Thought of Claude Montefiore,* 1990.
7. For the question of liturgy, J.J. Petuchowski, *Prayerbook Reforms in Judaism,* New York 1968, e.g. p. 69.
8. S.A. Sharot, 'Religious change in native orthodoxy in London 1870-1914: the synagogue service', *JJS* XV, June 1973. There were mixed choirs in the Hampstead, New West End, East London and, for a time, Brondesbury, Synagogues; at the New West End and East London (where Revd J.F. Stern overrode the lower middle class and immigrant opposition) the sexes in the choir were separated by a screen (Sharot, 'Religious Change', p. 71). At Hampstead, the minister, the Revd A.A. Green, when asked if his mixed choir sat together, replied that they did not even sing together. There was also a mixed choir at the Garnethill Synagogue, Glasgow.
9. The initial subsidy for the prayerbook's publication came from Emma Goldsmid, Mrs Nathaniel Montefiore, the mother of *Claude G. Montefiore, who himself was thanked by Singer in his 1890 preface for help in the translation. There was also an attempt to standardize an Ashkenazi Anglo-Jewish tradition for liturgical music through the publication by the United Synagogue in 1893 of the *Voice of Prayer and Praise,* based on an unofficial compilation of 1887. This centred on the compositions of J.L. Mombach (1813-80), brought over from Germany as boy singer in 1828 and choirmaster of the Great Synagogue till his death in 1880 (Roth, *Great Synagogue* 1950, 261-3). Other melodies included compositions by the Viennese cantor, Sulzer, Lewandowski and Naumburg: a western Ashkenazi or Central European, as distinct from the Eastern European and Hassidic traditions.
10. V.D. Lipman, Rise of Jewish Suburbia', *TJHSE* XXI, p. 96.
11. Aubrey Newman, *The United Synagogue,* 1977, especially Chs 3 and 6.
12. Lipman, 'Suburbia', p. 94.
13. Moshe Davis, *The Emergence of Conservative Judaism,* Philadelphia, 1963, p. 152.

14. S. Sharot, 'Synagogue service in London 1870-1914', *JJS* XV, June 1973, p. 63.
15. *British Weekly*, 5, 12 and 26 November 1886, giving figures for 23 October 1886.
16. Central Synagogue, Great Portland Street, 143:318; St. John's Wood, 247:216; Borough Synagogue, 55:167; New West End, 161:251; Bayswater, 261:351, North London, 60:205.
17. For the complete figures see Lipman, 'Suburbia', pp. 94-6, 100-1.
18. *EJ* XIV, pp. 994-5.
19. See B. Homa, *A Fortress in Anglo-Jewry*, 1953, and V.D. Lipman, *Social History of the Jews in England*, 1954, pp. 123-5 and correspondence on the latter in *Jewish Review*, 26 November, 10 December and 24 December 1954.
20. Lipman, *Social History*, pp. 119-20.
21. Report of the United Synagogue Executive Committee, 7 January 1890, quoted in A. Newman, *The United Synagogue 1870-1970*, 1977, pp. 68-70. See also for the East End Scheme, Lipman, *Social History*, pp. 127-31; S.A. Sharot in *JJS* XVI, June 1974, 47-52.
22. Geoffrey Alderman, *The Federation of Synagogues 1887-1987*, 1987, p. 20.
23. For a full description, see the official history by Geoffrey Alderman, *The Federation of Synagogues, 1887-1987*, 1987, Chs 1 and 2.
24. Royal Commission on Aliens, Minutes of Evidence, Q.16, 722-3.
25. Sharot, in *JJS* XVI, 46-7. But when the Federation initially sought burial rights from the United Synagogue, which would have meant some co-operation, the United Synagogue refused by demanding unacceptable terms (see Jeffrey and Barbara Baum, 'Cemeteries, housing and controversies', in *Heritage*, 3, 1988, Jewish Research Group of Edmonton Historical Society.
26. Lipman, *Social History*, pp. 122-3. For Jung and his initiatives to strengthen orthodoxy in London till his death in 1921, see Alderman, *Federation*, pp. 46-50.
27. Bernard Homa, *Orthodoxy in Anglo-Jewry*, 1969, p. 19.
28. Lipman, *Social History*, p. 125-6; Homa, *Orthodoxy*, p. 21; A.M. Hyamson, *The London Board of Shechita 1804-1954*, 1954, pp. 45-50; Alderman, *Federation*, p. 26.
29. For a list of eminent Lithuanian and Polish rabbis in the provinces 1880-1920, see Homa, *Orthodoxy*, pp. 13-14.
30. Lewis Olsover, *The Jewish Communities of North-East England*, 1981, p. 265.
31. Ibid., p. 267; Arnold Levy, *History of the Sunderland Jewish Community*, 1956, pp. 159-67.
32. Olsover, *North-East England*, p. 273.
33. Ibid., pp. 36-7.
34. Tova Benski, 'Glasgow', in Aubrey Newman (ed.) *Provincial Jewry in Victorian Britain*, 1975; A. Levy, *Origins of Glasgow Jewry*, 1949, pp. 50-1; see also Kenneth E. Collins, 'Growth and development of Scottish Jewry, 1880-1940', especially pp. 3-18 on Glasgow between 1880 and 1920, in K.E. Collins (ed.) *Aspects of Scottish Jewry*, Glasgow, 1987.
35. R.E. Levy in Zoe Josephs (ed.) *Birmingham Jewry: New Aspects*, Birmingham, 1984, pp.16-18, 24-7.
36. Bill Williams, *Manchester Jewry: A Pictorial History*, Manchester, 1987, p. 25.
37. Olsover, *North-East England*, pp. 269, 274.
38. *EJ* VIII, pp. 492-3.
39. L.P. Gartner, *The Jewish Immigrant in England 1870-1914*, 2nd edn 1973,

pp. 214-19, 248-50.
40. Ibid., pp. 192-6.
41. Ibid., pp. 196-7.
42. For a general discussion of Jewish ideological movements in the period, see Jonathan Frankel, *Prophecy and Politics: Socialism, Nationalism and the Russian Jews, 1862-1917* Cambridge, 1981. For the movement of political activists from Britain to the United States, Andrew S. Reutlinger, 'The Anglo-American Jewish experience: immigrants, workers and entrepreneurs in New York and London, 1870-1914', *American Jewish Historical Society Quarterly* 66, 1966-7, 473ff.
43. Benzion Novokovichi, born in Lithuania in 1856, adopted Vinchevsky as a pseudonym in London. He wrote extensively in Yiddish and English for socialist journals. In America, to which he went in 1894, he was a prominent poet, editor and educator, and was known as the 'grandfather of Yiddish socialist literature'. He died in 1932 (*EJ* XXI, pp. 153-4).
44. Gartner, *Jewish Immigrant,* pp. 100-17; W.J. Fishman, *East End Radicals,* 1975; R. Rocker, *The London Years,* 1956.
45. Harold Pollins, *Economic History of the Jews in England,* London and Toronto, 1982, pp. 159-60. For the relationship of Jewish unions to the wider British movement, Anne J. Kershen, 'Trade Unionism among the Jewish Tailoring Workers of London and Leeds, 1872-1915', in David Cesarani (ed.) *The Making of Modern Anglo-Jewry,* Oxford, 1990, pp. 34-5.
46. For names of unions and statistics of membership, see Lipman, *Social History,* pp. 116-17.
47. Pollins, *Econimic History,* p. 124.
48. Literature on Lieberman's activity in London is cited in Gartner, *Jewish Immigrant,* p. 104, n.3, to which should now be added Fishman, *East End Radicals,* pp. 98-134 and Pollins, *Economic History,* pp. 153-4.
49. Pollins, *Economic History,* p. 155. The ladies' outwear trade was conducted in larger workshops. The United Ladies' Tailors and Mantlemakers Association, founded in 1891, was led by a paid secretary and unionized the more skilled workers; its policy was reformist rather than revolutionary. It suffered competition from a union of the less skilled and younger workers, formed in 1902, who were in fact employed by the skilled workers. After small, 'impulse', strikes, they merged in 1903 with the United Ladies Tailors to form the London Mantle Makers Union. See R.S. Wechsler, 'The Jewish garment trade in East London, 1875-1914', Columbia University Ph.D thesis, 1979.
50. The number of Jewish tailors who went on strike in east London in 1890 was about 10,000 (Wechsler, 'Jewish garment trade', p. 250).
51. In the 1890s there were attempts to get both the employers (organized in the Mutual Tailors Society) and the employees to combine against the wholesalers and large retailers, who by the prices they set indirectly controlled conditions in the trade. But this failed because of undercutting by masters and disunity among the unions and by 1900 the conflict reverted to one between employers and employees. Union activity was stimulated around 1905 by the arrival of radical Jewish workers after the Kishineff pogroms. The 1906 London strike brought out 8-9,000 Jewish garment workers. It was settled by an agreement negotiated with the masters by the Amalgamated Society of Tailors (AST), the general union which many of the Jewish workers had joined. The masters went

back on the agreement about substituting day for piecework and the AST Jewish members reverted to independent Jewish unions (Wechsler, 'Jewish garment workers', pp. 267-77; Pollins, *Economic History*, pp. 161-2). For the proportions of unionized workers in London among Jewish and non-Jewish tailoring workers, see Kershen, 'Trade Unionism among Jewish tailoring workers', p. 36.

52. Pollins, *Economic History* p. 163; Gartner, *Jewish Immigrant*, pp. 139-41. However, the United Ladies Tailors and Mantlemakers, successfully led by J.L. Fine, did not merge in the National Union of Tailors and Garment Workers (the successor to the AST) until 1939 (Wechsler, 'Jewish garment workers', p. 286).
53. For anti-religious demonstrations, see Gartner, *Jewish Immigrant*, p. 135; Fishman, *East End Radicals*, p. 211.
54. Fishman, *East End Radicals*, Ch. 12. The quotations are from pp. 303, 308.
55. For sources, see Lipman, *Social History*, p. 155; Gartner, *Jewish Immigrant*, p. 278. The example of Jewish religious instruction on school premises and the observance of the Jewish religious calendar led to a move in 1893 by Athelstan Risley, an Anglican member of the London School Board, to obtain similar arrangements for Christian teaching in what was intended by statute to be a non-denominational system. In 1894 Christian teaching, but with a provision for exception for 'Jewish' schools and individual Jewish pupils in other board schools, was made compulsory; Jewish teachers had to refrain from specifically Jewish instruction during normal school hours (which was against the rules in any case). See Suzanne Kirsch Greenberg, 'Anglicization and the education of Jewish immigrant children in the East End of London', in Ada Rapaport-Albert and Steven J. Zipperstein (eds) *Jewish History: Essays in Honour of Chimen Abramsky*, 1988, pp. 111-26.
56. Lipman, *Social History*, pp. 146-7. The Jews' Infant School, with a roll of 2,000 in 1896, served as a training college for Jewish teachers and a feeder for the Jews' Free School, three-quarters of the Jews' infant pupils continuing there. See Eugene C. Black, *The Social Politics of Anglo-Jewry*, Oxford, 1988, p. 111.
57. Gartner, *Jewish Immigrant*, p. 224.
58. Ibid., p. 225.
59. *Board of Trade Report* C.7406:PP.1894, LXVIII, p. 33. During his fifty-one years of headmastership of the Jews' Free School, Moses Angel (1819-96) reorganized and developed it, but was uniformly hostile to the East European Jewish ethos. He was succeeded by Louis B. Abrahams (1839-1918), who in 1905 urged parents to bring up their children to be 'identified with everything that is English in thought and deed', and denounced Yiddish as 'that miserable jargon which is not a language at all' (Black, *Social Politics*, pp. 110-11).
60. Royal Commission on Aliens, Q.18,873 (*Minutes of Evidence*, Cd. 1742).
61. Gartner, *Jewish Immigrant*, p. 182. See the detailed study by Harold Pollins, *A History of the Jewish Working Mens' Club and Institute 1874-1912*, Oxford, 1981.
62. Lipman, *Social History*, p. 146.
63. Bill Williams, *Manchester Jewry 1788-1988*, 1988, p. 27; the Brady Street Club was in many ways a model and the club movement was used to improve conditions and prevent the 'descent into hooliganism and crime' (Black, *Social Politics*, pp. 144-5). Service as club managers and leaders, or as officers of the

Jewish Lads' Brigade, was regarded as a form of social service which the young upper-class Jews of the West End or of the more affluent suburbs owned to their less well-off coreligionists. For the youth clubs generally, see Black, *Social Politics*, pp. 132-48.
64. Jerry White, *Life in an East end Tenement Block 1887-1920: Rothschild Buildings*, History Workshop Series, 1980, p. 250.
65. Ibid., p. 252.
66. Ibid., pp. 256-7.
67. Bill Williams, 'East and West': Class and Community in Manchester Jewry, 1850-1914', in David Cesarani (ed.) *The Making of Modern Anglo-Jewry*, Oxford, 1990, pp. 15-33. For Jews in the 'inner city', see J.W. Carrier 'A Jewish proletariat', in Murray Mindlin (ed.) *Explorations*, 1967, pp. 126-40 and Nigel Grizzard and Paula Raisman, 'Inner city Jews in Leeds', *JJS* XVII, June 1980, 21-33.
68. Black, *Social Politics*, pp. 80-4, 93-4; V.D. Lipman, *A Century of Social Service: The History of the Jewish Board of Guardians*, 1959. p. 67 and Table I.
69. Lipman, *Social History*, p. 119; the number of Jews enrolled in friendly societies was not clear even at the time since not all societies were registered with the Registrar of Friendly Societies; there were Jewish lodges of non-Jewish orders (notably the Ancient Order of Foresters) and there was also multiple membership of societies. It was suggested that a maximum enrolment of 40,000 may have represented only 20,000 individuals. The problem is discussed in Black, *Social Politics*, pp. 195-200.
70. Williams, *Manchester 1788-1988*, p. 28.
71. Gartner, *Jewish Immigrant*, p. 239.
72. Lipman, *Social History*, pp. 144, 148-9. Classes in English subsidized by the Russo-Jewish Committee, which produced a Yiddish-English manual, were attended by many hundreds of adults (Black, *Social Politics*, pp. 108-9).
73. Rosalyn Livshin, 'The Acculturation of the children of immigrant Jews in Manchester 1890-1930', in David Cesarani (ed.), *The Making of Modern Anglo-Jewry*, Oxford, 1990, pp. 79-96 (the direct quotation is from p. 93).
74. Gartner, *Jewish Immigrant*, pp. 272-3.
75. Stanley Kaplan, 'The anglicization of the East European Jewish immigrant as seen by the London *Jewish Chronicle* 1870-97', *Yivo Annual of Jewish Social Science* X, New York 1955, 275; Lipman, *Social History*, p. 148.
76. Lipman, *Social History*, pp. 153-5; Gartner, *Jewish Immigrant*, pp. 234-7.
77. Lipman, *Social History*, p. 155.
78. Livshin, 'Acculturation of Immigrant Jewish Children', pp. 91-3.
79. The figures are given in S.J. Prais and Marlena Schmool, 'Statistics of Jewish marriages in the UK 1901-65', *JJS* IX, 2; and in Barry Kosmin, 'Nuptiality and fertility patterns of British Jewry 1850-1980', in D.A. Coleman (ed.) *Demography of Immigrants and Minority Groups in the UK*, London, 1982.

Chapter 6

The Rise of Zionism and the Balfour Declaration

There was a long tradition going back to at least the early nineteenth century of commitment in Britain to the interests of the Holy Land in general, and of its Jewish inhabitants in particular. In the late 1830s and 1840s there was a political interest in the potential role for Britain as the protector of the Jews in the Holy Land and the surrounding area, and there was even discussion of the possibility of some sort of autonomous Jewish settlement as a southern bulwark of Turkey against the encroachment then feared from her nominal subject state, Egypt.[1] Christian writers discussed the restoration of the Jews to the Holy Land, although this was normally conceived as a preliminary to their conversion as a necessary stage before the millennium or Second Coming.[2] Others discussed the possibility of Jewish settlement as an escape from European persecution, among them Colonel George Gawler (1845), his son, Colonel J.C. Gawler (1874), Laurence Oliphant (1878-9) and Edward Cazalet (also in 1879).[3]

Within Anglo-Jewry, *Sir Moses Montefiore identified himself as the foremost supporter of the Jews of Palestine, in terms not only of relief and welfare but of their modernization, including education and vocational training, housing improvement and the encouragement of agricultural pursuits. It is doubtful how far Montefiore can be called a Zionist in the later sense of one who advocated the establishment of a Jewish national home recognized by international law. But he did go on the record in 1863 that 'Palestine must belong to the Jews and Jerusalem is destined to be the seat of a Jewish Empire'.[4]

The first movement however in Britain that can be called Zionist or proto-Zionist was that of the Hovevei Zion, or Lovers of Zion. This movement began in Eastern Europe as a reaction to the Russian pogroms and anti-Jewish measures which began in 1881. There had already been a number of books and pamphlets calling for a return to Zion,[5] but the immediate catalyst was the publication in September 1882 by an Odessa physician, Leo Pinsker (1821-91), of a pamphlet, *Auto-Emancipation,* asserting that the Jews must be the architects of their own salvation and not rely on the goodwill of European nations to emancipate them; and that they needed a national home of their own (which Pinsker originally thought need not be Palestine). *Auto-Emancipation* was published in German, partly because of the Russian censorship but also because Pinsker wanted to appeal to the Jews of Central and Western Europe, whom he considered were, unlike those of Eastern Europe, able to provide the initiative and resources to bring about his objective.[6]

Migration from Eastern Europe from 1881 was largely directed to Central and Western Europe and America; as an alternative, *Baron Maurice de Hirsch, the millionaire developer of railways, set up in 1891 (and later endowed by his will) the Jewish Colonization Association to purchase large tracts of land in Argentina and settle Jews on them. However there had been from the early 1880s a few struggling agricultural settlements in Palestine, formed by Jewish idealists from Russia and Rumania, and societies to support this movement grew in Eastern Europe and elsewhere, although the financial survival of the settlements was ensured only by Baron Edmond de Rothschild (1845–1934) from 1882 onwards.[7] The movement as a whole was known as Hibbath Zion, or Love of Zion. Its aims can be summarized as a Jewish national renaissance, the return of Jews to the Land of Israel and the fostering of the Hebrew language. But its political implications were imprecise, both in terms of the sort of polity there would be in the Land of Israel and the effect on the status and citizenship of Jews in the Diaspora. A conference of the Hovevei Zion was held in November 1884 at Kattowitz in Prussian Poland, attended by thirty delegates from Russia, Rumania, Germany, France and England.[8]

The Hovevei Zion movement in Britain (as to a lesser extent in Germany and France) had basically little in common with the attitude of the mass of the movement in Eastern Europe. In Britain there was no desperate pressure to emigrate, or to found a national home for political reasons; and there was little, if any, consciousness of local anti-Semitism of the kind that manifested itself in Germany in the 1880s or in France in the 1890s at the time of the Dreyfus case. Many leading personalities who later expressed an aversion from 'political' Zionism showed benevolence towards the Hibbath Zion movement. The first Hovevei Zion groups in Britain were formed in Tredegar (South Wales), Leeds and Manchester in 1883 and, after a few other societies had been formed, the 'Chovevei Zion Association of England', with about 450 members held its first meeting in 1890.[9] The opening meeting was attended by *Samuel Montagu, *Lord Rothschild, *Benjamin L. Cohen MP (president of the Board of Guardians), *Dr Hermann Adler, *Dr Moses Gaster (Haham of the Spanish and Portuguese Jews), and the *Revd Simeon Singer, minister of the fashionable New West End Synagogue in London.[10]

From 1893 the organization in Britain was taken over by *Colonel Albert E.W. Goldsmid (1846–1904). A descendant of the eighteenth-century

Goldsmid family but brought up as a Christian, Goldsmid became a professional soldier in the Indian army (his father was in the Indian Civil Service). He discovered his Jewish origin in 1870 at 24, was admitted to Judaism and became an observant Jew: he married another Christian of Jewish decent, who was also converted to Judaism, and he adopted a passionate, even romantic, Jewish nationalism. 'I am Daniel Deronda' he said, quoting George Eliot's hero of her 1876 novel, who sees his destiny as the leadership of his newfound people and leaves in the end for Palestine.[11] Goldsmid had a moderately successful army career and in 1892, when he was a lieutenant-colonel on the staff, he took leave to go to Argentina to reorganize Baron de Hirsch's Jewish agricultural colonies. Returning to Britain, where he was colonel commanding the South Wales regimental district, he became president of the British Hovevei Zion, which he organized on quasi-military lines, with himself as 'chief', the executive called 'headquarters' and the branches as 'tents', like the children of Israel in the wilderness. While the leadership of the Hovevei Zion was from the Anglo-Jewish 'establishment', the strongest 'tent', with over 1,500 members in 1893, mainly immigrants, was that in the East End of London.[12]

The arrival of Theodor Herzl (1860–1904) on the Jewish scene in 1895 created Zionism as a political movement and an international force.[13] He urged diplomatic action to achieve a national home for the Jews, regarding the slow, gradual process of piecemeal agricultural settlement as ineffective and counterproductive. A German-speaking, Hungarian Jew of assimilated background, he was a distinguished journalist and editor, and a playwright of some achievement but knew little of the traditional Jewish world. Whether or not it was the Dreyfus case, whose early stages he observed in Paris as the correspondent of the Viennese *Neue Freie Presse*, which sparked off his determination to be the saviour of the Jewish people and to achieve a radical solution for their problems, it was in 1895 that he first made an impact on the Jewish scene. Even before the publication of his *The Jewish State* in February 1896 (in which he outlined his programme for the acquisition and development of an autonomous Jewish national home), he visited London for a few days in October 1895. Through the intermediacy of *Israel Zangwill he was invited to address the recently formed and prestigious dining club of Jewish professional men, the Maccabeans. He was favourably received – he was a personable, handsome, dynamic and charismatic figure – and he made useful contacts which he followed up on a second visit in July 1896. Then he addressed a mass meeting at the Jewish Workingmen's Club in east London and interviewed many notables – Samuel Montagu, *F.D. Mocatta, colonel Goldsmid, the Chief Rabbi (Hermann Adler), *Claude G. Montefiore, *Lucien Wolf. Wolf was then a journalist specializing in foreign affairs and was foreign editor of the influential *Daily Graphic*, a post he had held from 1890. At this time Wolf collaborated with Herzl, although he sought to conceal this later when he was a spokesman of anti-Zionism. Herzl again addressed the Maccabeans in 1896 but this time his audience was more critical. They had had time to recover from the brilliance of his presentation and the revolutionary character of his analysis and solution of the Jewish problem; and they had begun to appraise the implications for themselves as emancipated western Jews trying to acculturate themselves to British society.[14] Anglo-Jews like Hermann Adler and Simeon Singer, who were thoughtful and concerned about the Jewish future, were committed Hovevei Zionists, Lovers of Zion - Adler had been on pilgrimage to Palestine in the 1880s and called himself a Zionist - and were at first interested in Herzl and his ideas. Yet they turned emphatically against Zionism, or political or Herzlian Zionism as they called it. There was a clear distinction between the Hovevei Zion ideology and that of the early Zionists.

The Hovevei Zion believed in non-political colonization in Palestine, while the essence of early Zionism was the desire for a 'charter', an international recognition of Jewish rights to a home in Palestine. The Zionist argument was that Jews should conserve their energies and not indulge in 'petty colonization' until there could be a mass return as of right and with the agreement of the great powers. The issue became clear-cut after the holding of the first Zionist Congress at Basle in August 1897 and the adoption there of the Basle Programme - 'Zionism aims at the creation of a home for the Jewish people in Palestine to be secured by public law'. There was thus a radical difference of attitude between the leadership of the Hovevei Zion, however romantic their attachment to Zion, and the early political Zionists. One can perhaps see this difference in Lucien Wolf's words, written in the *Daily Graphic* on 16 August 1900. Referring to the Hovevei Zionists and those, like himself, who had a vague attachment to the ideal of a Jewish national renaissance, he wrote: 'We had become so habituated to looking at the ideal as one of those dreams which may be all the more safely indulged in because there is no chance of realizing them'. 'But Herzl', wrote a historian of the period, 'not only thought realization possible but insisted that the moment for realizing it had arrived'.[15]

After attempts to get a merger between the British Hovevei Zion and the supporters of Herzl, the Hovevei Zion foundered towards 1900. Probably the majority of the rank and file members joined the English Zionist Federation, the local constituent of the world Zionist movement. Colonel Goldsmid first held aloof from Zionism and then collaborated with Herzl before 1904, the year in which they both died. Most of the other leaders of the Hovevei Zion could not accept Herzlian Zionism and became anti-Zionist. As the *Jewish Chronicle* put it on 23 July 1897, 'While they have been playing with fireworks in the back garden, [Herzl] has gone round to the front door and tried to set the house on fire.... He holds out the real thing before their eyes and they shrink from it as from a spectre'.[16]

The English Zionist Federation (EZF) was founded on 22 July 1897. Its task was not so much to negotiate with the British government as to fulfil

Herzl's other injunction, 'to capture the communities', that is to mobilize the institutions of organized Jewry in the cause of achieving the Jewish national home. Among their leadership was Sir Francis Abraham Montefiore (1860–1935) great-nephew of Sir Moses, for whom Sir Moses' baronetcy was revived in 1886; he had social position, a famous name and, from 1904, the presidency of the Spanish and Portuguese community, but was hardly a charismatic leader. The rest of the leadership of the federation were typical of the rising new middle class of the Anglo-Jewish community. They included Herbert Bentwich (1856–1932), a copyright lawyer and editor of the *Law Journal*; Joseph Cowen (1868–1932), a clothing manufacturer, whose interest in Jewish affairs was aroused by Herzl, whose associate he became and whom he accompanied on the visit to the Sultan in 1902; and *Leopold Greenberg, originally a publisher and news agency proprietor, and then one of a group which acquired in 1907 the main Anglo-Jewish weekly, the *Jewish Chronicle*, of which Greenberg became editor-in-chief and which he turned into a propaganda asset for the Zionists.[17]

In the years to 1914 the English Zionist Federation had two main preoccupations, neither involved in Herzlian diplomacy or high politics. The first was internal feuding. There was continual dissension between Dr Gaster, the Haham (supported by Bentwich and, after his arrival in England in 1904, by *Chaim Weizmann) and Joseph Cowen, supported by Leopold Greenberg. After Bentwich was defeated for the vice-presidency of the federation in 1909, the Gaster party regrouped in the pro-Zionist friendly society, the Order of Ancient Maccabeans (founded in 1896), which obtained separate representation at the Zionist congresses. Another cause of dissension was the action of Israel Zangwill, who had earlier played a key role in introducing Herzl to Britain, in splitting off to form the Jewish Territorial Organization (JTO), which combined flamboyant nationalism with the humanitarian objective of finding an immediate home for the victims of Russian persecution – 1903 was the year of the Kishineff pogroms. This meant the home had to be somewhere other than Palestine, because there was no immediate chance of persuading the Sultan and, after Herzl's death in 1904, there was no one with the confidence to assume that Palestine could be won quickly by diplomatic action. Zangwill, since the JTO was non-Zionist and humanitarian, tried to get the support of the leading establishment figures like Lord Rothschild, Samuel Montagu and Claude G. Montefiore (who was president of the Anglo-Jewish Association and therefore a joint chairman of the Conjoint Foreign Committee, Anglo-Jewry's nearest approach to an executive for external affairs). In this he was unsuccessful but he did get the support of Lord Rothschild's brother *Leopold, of *Osmond d'Avigdor-Goldsmid, of *Sir Lionel Abrahams (a senior civil servant in the India Office), of Laurie Magnus (1872–1933), son of the educationist, *Sir Philip, and a man of letters and would-be politician, and even of Lucien Wolf. Zangwill could point both to the difficulties of Palestine and the urgent need for a humanitarian solution of the problem of Jewish refugees (which incidentally did not involve their settling in Britain). In pursuance of this, the ITO pursued a number of solutions, all hopeless, in Mesopotamia, Western Australia, British Honduras, Brazil and Angola.[18]

The second main concern of the EZF was to infiltrate the communal organizations – notably the representative body, the Board of Deputies, in the interests of Zionism. In this they had some success and individual leaders of the EZF were able to forward their communal careers. In doing so, they formed alliances, which were later to prove useful, with other elements who were dissatisfied with the management of the community – largely those who considered it insufficiently democratic – and unappreciative of their own claims to leadership; and those in the provinces who thought the Board of Deputies too London-centred. Chaim Weizmann was at this time based in Manchester and he formed around him from about 1913 a local group of young intellectuals: *Israel Sieff and his brothers-in-law *Simon Marks (both associated in the rising firm of Marks and Spencer) and Harry Sacher (1881–1971), lawyer and journalist associated with the *Manchester Guardian*, and Leonard Stein (1887–1973), a barrister. But the EZF, although there were Zionist adherents in the East End of London and the other immigrant quarters, did not make a wide conquest there: most of the recent immigrants were too busy trying to survive economically to have time for politics, and those who were politically inclined tended to follow the politics of the left. Nor did it have much impact on the religious leadership. Some rabbis – Gaster and the brothers Salis and Samuel Daiches – were active Zionists. But the rabbinate of the immigrants, although sympathetic for traditional reasons with the idea of the return to Zion, did not want to become involved in the political mechanics of achieving it. Indeed, while they looked forward to an ultimate Messianic restoration as an article of faith, many held it was impious to try to anticipate this by human manoeuvring and stressed the importance meanwhile of observing the religious precepts in the Diaspora; and the fact that many of the Zionist leadership were not personally religious did not endear them to the rabbinate.

Herzl's Zionism had proscribed 'creeping in by the back door' through step by step colonization. It was only in 1908 that the 'Practical Zionists' such as Weizmann managed to get some colonization under the auspices of the Zionist Organization. Even so, such colonization was small until 1911. But after 1911 when the 'Practical Zionists' took over the running of the movement, colonization expanded. While of the 85,000 Jews in Palestine in 1914, only 30–35,000 were immigrants of the post-1880 period, there were more immigrants in 1914 than in any previous year and work had begun on specifically Jewish institutions such as the Haifa Technion and even the planning of a Hebrew University.[19]

In so far as Zionism was now engaged in practical work in founding colonies, this could be supported by non-Zionists in Anglo-Jewry as a philanthropic gesture in the same way as Sir Moses Montefiore had aided Jewish settlement on the land in the nineteenth century. But the ideological aspect of Zionism, and its stress on a separate national identity for the Jews, aroused hostility among the Anglo-Jewish leadership. For instance in 1909 twenty-five members of prominent Anglo-Jewish families (including Leopold de Rothschild, Claude Montefiore, *Robert Waley Cohen and Osmond d'Avigdor-Goldsmid) signed a statement opposing the establishment of Zionist societies by Jewish undergraduates at British universities. This was endorsed by the Chief Rabbi, Dr Hermann Adler, who stated that Jews 'no longer constitute a nation; we are a religious community'.[20] Jews of this opinion were prepared to support Zangwill's plans for a territorial settlement on humanitarian grounds, because these did not involve the issue of Jewish nationality. But they regarded the pro-Zionism of non-Jews as a sophisticated form of anti-Semitism, for it implied that such non-Jews considered there was no equal place or acceptable future for Jews in British society. There was evidence indeed for some ambivalence of feeling in Balfour himself and in 1917 *Edwin Montagu headed his first diatribe against the proposed declaration in support of Zionism: 'The Antisemitism of the British Government'.[21]

For those who, like Lucien Wolf, fought for equal rights for Jews in Europe, especially in Russia, it seemed a betrayal to admit that Jews could no longer hope, even eventually, to have these rights and must emigrate to a new land of their own. Also those who followed reform Judaism accepted the doctrine of a mission of Israel to be a light to the nations, which could best be carried out by Jews in Diaspora setting an example to their neighbours; and they objected to the Zionists' apparent negation of the Diaspora and therefore of the validity of the mission theory. Nor were the details of the implementation of Zionism really thought through, at least by the English Zionists. Their opponents in the various groups had taken account of problems like the evidence of the hostility of the Arab majority in Palestine to Jewish mass settlement; and the religious opponents of Zionism were concerned with questions like the rebuilding of the Temple or the system of law to be applied in a Jewish state. The English Zionists tended to reply to these expressions of concern with generalizations.[22]

What changed the situation and brought Zionism into the sphere of practical politics was the entry of Turkey into the war against the Allies. On 9 November 1914, Asquith, the Prime Minister, in his speech at the Lord Mayor's banquet, announced: 'The Turkish Empire has committed suicide'.[23] Palestine, like the rest of the Turkish empire, was now the object of plans for sharing territory among the Allies, after their hoped-for victory. In January 1915, *Herbert Samuel, a member of the Cabinet, circulated a memorandum to his colleagues on the future of Palestine. In the course of drafting, he modified his advocacy of a Jewish state to admit that the time was not yet ripe for it, but he looked forward to Palestine developing, under a British protectorate, a self-governing Jewish majority.[24]

The Zionists could take advantage of the rivalry between Britain and France to stake out a claim to territory and influence in the Middle East. Once again, as in the nineteenth century, support for the Jews might give Britain an added claim to intervene in the affairs of the area. Another factor, which increased in importance as the war went on, was the desire to bring America into the war on the side of the Allies and, once America had entered the war in April 1917, to combat pro-German feeling in the United States. American Jewry was regarded as having an exaggerated influence on American opinion, and American Jewish opinion was regarded by British observers, such as the ambassador, Sir Cecil Spring Rice, as being in substantial part pro-German. The Allies had a built-in disadvantage with Jewish opinion in that they were until 1917 identified with Czarist Russia, whereas the Central Powers were fighting Russia; and in Jewish eyes Czarist Russia was the land of the pogroms from which Jews had to flee. The wealthier and more influential of American Jews were in any case mainly of Central European origin and had cultural links with Germany. In so far as Britain could identify herself with Jewish aspirations in Palestine, this would be a potent corrective to German propaganda among American Jews. After the February Revolution (March by the English date) of 1917 in Russia and until the October (November) Revolution of the Bolsheviks, the British government, again overestimating Jewish influence, thought that by favouring Zionism, which Russian Jews were said overwhelmingly to support, the Jews could be persuaded to keep Russia in the war.[25]

There were, of course, many countervailing factors to Britain championing Zionism but the knowledge that there were also these arguments in favour helped Weizmann to put the case for Zionism in the heart of British government circles – indeed Weizmann fed the material on this to the Cabinet Secretariat.[26] There were two separate and opposed groups in Anglo-Jewry fighting for the ear of the British government. On the one hand, there was the official community, represented by the Conjoint Foreign Committee of the Board of Deputies and the Anglo-Jewish Association, whose secretary from 1914 was Lucien Wolf, the leading expert on Jewish diplomacy and the fight for Jewish rights in Europe. On the other hand, there was a small group of Weizmann, some Zionist associates and sympathizers, Jewish and non-Jewish, including people in key positions within the government machine.[27] Since it was always the pride of the Anglo-Jewish establishment that they had the key to influence with the government, it proved a humilating disappointment that they were outmanoeuvred by Weizmann, a Russian Jew who had been resident for only about ten years in Britain.[28]

In 1914 the Conjoint Committee, which consisted of fourteen members from the two constituent bodies, was prepared to do anything to protect the rights of oppressed or underprivileged Jews abroad but was opposed to Zionism as a movement which threatened the emancipation of Jews as individuals in their countries of residence. In 1914 and 1915 the Conjoint Committee treated the Zionists with condescension. They noted that when the World Zionist Executive sent Yehiel Tschlenow (1863–1918) and Nahum Sokolow (1859–1936) to London, they failed even to get an audience with the Foreign Office. The Conjoint Committee was not to know that Weizmann was having regular meetings with members of the government such as Samuel, Balfour and Lloyd George, and that Samuel had circulated his memorandum on Zionism in January 1915. The Conjoint Committee saw as its principal objective the amelioration of the position of the Jews of Russia, an abiding concern of its secretary, Lucien Wolf. Russian Jewry constituted more than half of the world's Jewish population and, if the Russian government could be persuaded by its allies to give them improvements in status and opportunity, then the end of the Jewish problem would be in sight. The Conjoint Committee sought to achieve this aim by urging the Foreign Office to intervene with the Russian government. In fact, the only result was to irritate the Foreign Office without benefiting Russian Jewry. For the Conjoint Committee, Zionism would militate against improvements in the conditions of Russian Jews because, so they argued, it would enable the Russian government to claim that Jews were really aliens in Russia after all and would never become integrated in Russian life.[29]

There was an additional factor in that Claude G. Montefiore, who as president of the Anglo-Jewish Association was one of the two joint chairmen of the Conjoint Committee, was the philosopher of Liberal Judaism. For him, Judaism was a universal and non-national religion and the idea of a physical return to a Jewish state unacceptable on religious grounds.[30] However, in accord with the philanthropic tradition of the Anglo-Jewish establishment, the Conjoint Committee's attitude was not wholly negative. It was prepared to support colonization; since it supported equal rights for Jews everywhere, Jews in Palestine should have equal rights as citizens, and should have 'such municipal privileges as may be shown to be necessary'. But the Conjoint Committee was not prepared to agree that Palestine should be a national home for the Jews or that the Jews constituted a nation. Lucien Wolf submitted a memorandum to the Foreign Office asking for equal rights for the Jews of Palestine, cultural rights and municipal autonomy, with reasonable provision for immigration.[31]

In the meanwhile, Weizmann had been working on the British government to secure a declaration favourable to Zionism. He also sought support within the Anglo-Jewish establishment. It is not clear when *Walter, the second Lord Rothschild, became a Zionist but it was certainly not later than 1915, when he succeeded his father. Charles, the younger brother of Walter, also became a convinced Zionist. There is even evidence that the first Lord Rothschild, shortly before his death in 1915, was prepared to revise his views in favour of Herbert Samuel's proposal because of the changed position brought about by the war and the prospect that Zionism and British interests might well coincide.[32]

The Conjoint Committee realized early in 1917 that it was being outmanoeuvred by Weizmann and Samuel in influencing the British government at the highest level. This realization was confirmed when the Foreign Office twice hinted in May 1917 that it would deprecate any action by the Committee to engage in public controversy against Zionism. But the Conjoint Committee felt that it could not remain silent without trying to forestall the efforts of the Zionists. Against the wishes of *Dr Hertz, the Chief Rabbi, who was present by invitation at the meeting, on 17 May it approved a statement which appeared in *The Times* a week later over the signatures of the two joint chairmen, D.L. Alexander (president of the Board of Deputies) and Claude Montefiore (president of the Anglo-Jewish Association). The statement reaffirmed the previously expressed willingness of the committee to accept 'a Jewish spiritual centre for the local Jews and for such colonists as might join them'. But it rejected 'the wider Zionist theory, which regards all the Jewish communities of the world as constituting one homeless nationality, incapable of complete social and political identification with the nations among whom they dwell' and needing 'a political centre and an always available homeland in Palestine. This must have the effect, throughout the world, of stamping the Jews as strangers in their native lands and of undermining their hard won position as citizens and nationals of those lands'.[33]

This statement produced a number of rejoinders: from Lord Rothschild, who wrote that he could not understand how the establishment of a Jewish state under the protection of one of the powers could be subversive of the rights of other Jews; and from the Chief Rabbi, who wrote that the views of the Conjoint Committee did not represent the views of Anglo-Jewry. *The Times*, in commenting editorially on the controversy, summed up in favour of the Zionists.[34] The Anglo-Jewish Association discussed but did not vote on the publication of the statement by the Conjoint Committee. The Board of Deputies, however, voted by 56 votes to 51, on 17 June 1917, to express its profound disapproval of the statement and dissatisfaction at its publication, and that the Conjoint Committee had lost the confidence of the Board. The Conjoint Committee was dissolved and Alexander resigned as president of the Board.

The defeat of the anti-Zionists at the Board of Deputies was not an overwhelming one. As Professor Stuart Cohen has argued, a crucial part of the opposition to the Conjoint Committee's publication of its statement came from those who were not committed Zionists but who objected to the way the leadership ran the Board – these included deputies from the provinces; or those who objected to the issue of the statement without consultation with the parent bodies of the Conjoint Committee.[35] This point was taken by Edwin Montagu in the second memorandum he circulated to the Cabinet on 14 September 1917:

The Joint Committee in issuing [the letter] on its own responsibility exceeded its right as a mere executive committee of two parent organizations which should have been consulted before a large declaration of policy was given to the world . . . and in the discussion this point played a very large part.

And in new elections, *Sir Stuart Samuel (brother of Herbert), who was not a Zionist, was elected president; one of the two vice-presidents elected was Sir Philip Magnus, an anti-Zionist and the other, the second Lord Rothschild, it could be argued, was chosen as much because he was Lord Rothschild as because he had become president of the English Zionist Federation. The Conjoint Committee was reconstituted as the Joint Foreign Committee, with Lucien Wolf as its executive officer.[36]

The vote at the Board of Deputies on 17 June did, however, ensure that when the government came a few months later to take the final decision about issuing a declaration, it knew that the proposal would be accepted by the representative body of British Jewry. On 19 June 1917, two days after the debate, Lord Rothschild (who had spoken in favour of a national home in the debate) and Weizmann saw Balfour, and Rothschild told Balfour that the majority of British Jews were in favour of a national home. Rothschild was asked by Balfour for a draft declaration which was sent a month later on 18 July (this is why the declaration, when ultimately approved by the Cabinet, was addressed to Lord Rothschild).[37] On the same day, 18 July, Edwin Montagu, younger son of Samuel Montagu, was appointed Secretary of State for India, a minister of Cabinet rank but not a member of the very small War Cabinet (which had no departmental ministers except the Chancellor of the Exchequer, not even the Foreign Secretary, who like other ministers attended by invitation when business with which he was concerned was discussed). As a minister with responsibilities which could be affected by the proposed declaration (the effect on the Muslims of India was several times mentioned in Cabinet discussions), Montagu received on 22 August a copy of Rothschild's letter and proposed declaration of 18 July. The next day, 23 August, he circulated to his colleagues a long memorandum, 'The Antisemitism of the present Government'. In it he protested that if the declaration went beyond complete liberty of settlement on equal terms for Jews in Palestine, every country, if there was a Jewish national home in Palestine, would want its Jews to go there and it could hold only a third of them. His language was hyperbolical: as a Jewish regiment was being formed,

I am waiting to learn that my brother, who has been wounded in the Naval Division, or my nephew, who is in the Grenadier Guards, will be forced by public opinion or by Army regulations to become an officer in a regiment which will be mainly composed of people who will not understand the only language which he speaks - English.

There was no Jewish nation: there were in Britain only Jewish Britons and he would disfranchise and render illegal the Zionist Organization, which was run by men of alien, indeed enemy, descent or birth.[38]

On 3 September 1917 the War Cabinet had as item 2 of its agenda, 'The Zionist Movement' and it discussed the proposed declaration. Montagu was invited for this item, and also for item 1, the question of a Jewish regiment in the British army. Montagu's argument that the phrase, 'the home of the Jewish people', (which was then in the draft declaration) would prejudice the position of every Jew elsewhere was countered by the arguments that

the existence of a Jewish State or autonomous community in Palestine would strengthen rather than weaken the situation of Jews in countries where they were not yet in possession of equal rights, and that in countries like England, where they possessed such rights and were identified with the nation of which they were citizens, their position would be unaffected by the existence of a national Jewish community elsewhere.... While a small influential section of English Jews were opposed to the idea, large numbers were sympathetic to it, but in the interests of Jews who wished to go from countries where they were less favourably situated, rather than from any idea of wishing to go to Palestine themselves

- a realistic view of Anglo-Jewry by the War Cabinet.[39] It was decided to seek the views of President Wilson, as there was a 'very strong and enthusiastic organization' in the USA favouring Zionism, and it was desirable, in the Foreign Secretary's view, to have them on the Allied side.[40]

Montagu sent round another memorandum on 14 September. This was aimed at contradicting the view that his position was a minority one in Anglo-Jewry. The Board of Deputies was not a completely representative body; there were other factors such as discontent with the methods of the Conjoint Committee which influenced the vote; yet, even so, 'the views which I hold... were held by practically half of the only representative body which has expressed an opinion'.[41]

Montagu followed this up with a third memorandum,[42] which quoted Dr Hermann Adler in an attempt to refute the views of Dr Hertz and included a long list of 'every Jew who is prominent in public life with the exception of the present Lord Rothschild, Mr Herbert Samuel and a few others'; Montague claimed that all on his list were anti-Zionist.[43]

The War Cabinet next considered the question on 4 October 1917, when there was a not very encouraging reply from Colonel House about Wilson's views and a more favourable report through Weizmann from Brandeis. Balfour referred to the opposition by 'a number of wealthy Jews in this country', although Zionism was supported by 'a majority of Jews, at least in Russia and America, and probably in other countries'. The Cabinet decided that it should have the views of some of the representative Zionists as well as of those who held the opposite opinion, while also seeking the views of President Wilson on Milner's formula. Ormsby Gore, as assistant secretary of the Cabinet dealing with Zionist affairs, obtained four names of non-Zionists from Edwin Montagu and Sir Lionel Abrahams, Assistant under-Secretary of State at the India Office (who happened then to be president of the Jewish Historical Society of England). The names were Sir Stuart Samuel (president of the Board of Deputies), *Leonard L. Cohen (president of the Board of Guardians), Sir Philip Magnus (chairman of the Reform Synagogue) and Claude Montefiore (president of the Anglo-Jewish Association – the presidency of the United Synagogue was vacant at the time. The Zionists, nominated by Weizmann, were Lord Rothschild, Dr Hertz, Nahum Sokolow and Weizmann himself. Magnus, in a preliminary reply on 11 October, suggested the addition of Lionel Rothschild (presumably to represent the United Synagogue). Ths was rejected without a reason being given; and the *second Lord Swaythling (who had succeeded his father as president of the Federation of Synagogues) was rejected because he was Edwin Montagu's brother. However, when Rothschild suggested the addition of Herbert Samuel, this was accepted in spite of his being Stuart Samuel's brother. The object of the exercise seems to have been to placate Montagu by showing that the Cabinet had consulted communal leaders who were not Zionists, not to get a straw poll on Anglo-Jewish opinions of Zionism. Sokolow could hardly be described as a representative Anglo-Jewish leader. The inclusion of Herbert Samuel weighted the sample in favour of the Zionists still further. Stuart Samuel's reply was cautiously in favour of 'a national home for Jews in Palestine, under proper safeguards'. So Sir Maurice Hankey, the Cabinet secretary, in reporting to the Cabinet, could report the score as 6 to 3 in favour of the Zionists.[44]

The question was to come before the War Cabinet again on 23 October and, when it was postponed, Sir Ronald Graham, assistant under-secretary of state at the Foreign Office, who was in close touch with Weizmann, minuted Balfour, as Secretary of State on the 'deplorable' results of delay. It would lose the 'very valuable co-operation of the Zionist forces in Russia and America' – indeed, might antagonise them and give Germany the opportunity to issue a pro-Zionist declaration.[45]

When the Cabinet took its decision on 31 October to issue a declaration, the determining factors were not the opinions of British Jews but the supposed impact on Jews in Russia, America and elsewhere. 'If we could make a declaration favourable to such an idea, we should be able to carry on useful propaganda both in Russia and America'. Balfour did mention in general terms the objection – 'the difficulty felt with regard to the future position of the Jews in Western countries' – but rejected it; and the Secretary of State was authorized to take a suitable opportunity of making 'the following declaration of sympathy with Zionist aspirations . . .'.[46]

Once support for Zionism had become declared British government policy, those in the Anglo-Jewish leadership who had opposed it, or been neutral on the issue, had to consider their position. On 12 November Lucien Wolf wrote to Claude G. Montefiore:

> It is worse than 'nasty'. The more I study it, the more disastrous it seems to me. Henceforth, we are only temporary sojourners here, enjoying a political status which we obtained by some oversight and which will not be disturbed but which is none the less artificial. What a triumph for the anti-Semites!

The proviso about the declaration not prejudicing the rights and political status of Jews in other countries he dismissed almost 'as a mere technicality'. But he added to Montefiore: 'Very few people outside our two selves realize what a calamitous business it is'.[47]

One reaction was the formation, within a week of the issue of the declaration, of a League of British Jews by *Lionel de Rothschild, Sir Philip Magnus and *Lord Swaythling (who were president or president-designate of the United Synagogue, Reform Synagogue and Federation of Synagogues respectively). Its aims were 'to uphold the status of persons professing the Jewish religion; to resist the allegation that Jews constitute a separate political nationality; and to facilitate the settlement in Palestine of such Jews as desire to make Palestine their home'.[48] Or, as (the later Sir) Robert Waley Cohen put it in a memorandum in 1918:

> for the purpose of enabling Jews of British nationality, who are at home in this country, and who are proud of their British nationality, to voice their views independently of the Jews of foreign origin who are residing in this country but who feel no strong attachment to their British nationality'.[49]

The policy and philosophical direction of the league came from Claude G. Montefiore, as president of the Anglo-Jewish Association, and Lucien Wolf. The league acquired a mouthpiece through the foundation of the *Jewish Guardian*, as a rival to the pro-Zionist *Jewish Chronicle* and *Jewish World*, with Sir Philip Magnus' son, Laurie, a journalist, littérateur and would-be MP, as editor. The *Guardian* lasted longer than the league and had merits beyond spokesmanship for the league as it was a wide-ranging, serious periodical. But, in spite of its distinguished sponsorship within the establishment, the league never succeeded in becoming a popular force within Anglo-Jewry, and ended after a few years.

An attempt was made during 1918 by a committee headed by Sir Lionel Abrahams to effect a compromise, and thus a united front between the Zionists and the league, but this foundered on the issue of Jewish nationality: with a view to denying the existence of a Jewish nationality, the league insisted that there must be no religious criteria for entry or political rights in the Jewish national home, which the Zionists regarded as negating its Jewish character.[50] However, some measure of consensus was achieved between the Zionists and the Board of Deputies, which, in spite of the 1917 vote, was still under a leadership that was mainly non- or anti-Zionist. Such an accommodation was helped by the fact that the Balfour Declaration in its final form spoke not of the reconstitution of Palestine as '*the* national home for the Jewish people', which the original Zionist draft had proposed, but of 'the establishment *in* Palestine of *a* national home for the Jewish people.[51] Thus non-Zionists and even some anti-Zionists could reconcile the formula with the finding of a haven, on humanitarian grounds, for persecuted Jews who wanted to go there, an objective which had been generally accepted by them. Indeed, the Jewish Territorial Organization (JTO), led by Zangwill, had to decide whether to continue, in co-operation with the Zionists, or to 'dissolve and sink ourselves . . . in the Zionist body, which is now so largely gaining the adherence of all Jewry'.[52] In fact, while JTO nominally remained in existence until 1925, it ceased activity after the issue of the Balfour Declaration; and it sent one of its members, the psychoanalyst, Dr M.D. Eder, as a member of the Zionist Commission, which went to Palestine in 1918 under British government auspices.[53] Agreement within the community was also helped by the fact that it was unclear whether 'a national home in Palestine' did or did not mean a commitment to a Jewish state: the Zionists could believe it did, the non-Zionists that it did not. Balfour himself, in introducing the Declaration to the Cabinet on 31 October 1917, said:

> As to the meaning of the words "national home" to which the Zionists attach so much importance, [I understand] it to mean some form of British, American or other protectorate under which full protection would be given to the Jews to work out their own salvation and to build up by means of education, agriculture and industry a real centre of national culture and focus of national life. It did not necessarily mean the early establishment of an independent Jewish state which was a matter for gradual development in accordance with the ordinary laws of political evolution.[54]

Even Weizmann in 1918, writing to Ormsby Gore, then with the Zionist Commission in Tel Aviv, stated: 'We consider a British Palestine and a Jewish Palestine practically identical and that in working for a Jewish Palestine we will at the same time be working for a British Palestine . . . . We do not consider any other solution, such as, for instance, a Jewish state, satisfactory or possible'.[55] In such circumstances it is not surprising that by April 1919 Lucien Wolf, as secretary of the Joint Foreign Committee, could bring to the attention of the Paris Peace Conference a statement on Palestine agreed by both the Board of Deputies and the Anglo-Jewish Association, which accepted the Balfour Declaration, subject only to the proviso that it must not 'be held to imply that Jews constitute a separate political nationality all over the world, or that the Jewish citizens of countries outside Palestine owe political allegiance to the Government of that country'.[56]

This acceptance of the Declaration was accompanied by a growth of popular support for Zionism within Anglo-Jewry. The membership of the English Zionist Federation (EZF) rose from 4,000 in 1917 to over 30,000 in 1921.[57] A petition by the EZF to the Peace Conference in 1919, asking for the implementation of the Balfour Declaration 'to reconstitute Palestine as [the Jews'] national home' was signed by some 77,000 Jews in the United Kingdom,[58] out of a total Jewish population of probably less than 300,000.

Yet all this did not mean that the Zionists had 'captured the community'. The control of the Board of Deputies remained in much the same kind of hands as before the vote of 17 June 1917; the Joint Foreign Committee still made the Board of Deputies the partner of the Anglo-Jewish Association, a far from Zionist body, with Lucien Wolf still secretary of the committee and the chief executive for foreign policy of the community. Although the Declaration was accepted government policy, and this moderated controversy, there were still implacable anti-Zionists and many more Anglo-Jewish leaders who were prepared to co-operate in implementing the Declaration on a practical level but refused to commit themselves ideologically to Zionism.[59] While the Zionists now had a recognized place within the community's representative institutions, it was a far from dominant one and for a quarter of a century from the Declaration they had to fight for their aims, not always successfully. Looking at the community as a whole, the picture after the Declaration is as it was before: two groups of partisans for and against Zionism fighting for the support of a much larger mass of uncommitted, often apathetic, non-partisans.[60]

NOTES

1. A.M. Hyamson, *The British Consulate in Jerusalem*, I, 1939, especially pp. xlviii–ix; Naomi Shepherd, *The Zealous Intruders*, 1987, pp. 233–4. The Middle East Centre at St Antony's College, Oxford has, dated 1841, a 'Circular of a Project for the Erection of Palestine into an independent State'.
2. I. Finestein, 'Early and middle nineteenth century British opinion on the restoration of the Jews', pp. 72–101 and Lionel E. Kochan, 'Jewish restoration to Zion: Christian attitudes in Britain in the late 19th and early 20th centuries', in Moshe Davis (ed.) *With Eyes Towards Zion* II, New York, Westport and London, 1986, pp. 102–21.
3. Franz Kobler, *The Vision was There*, 1956.
4. Montefiore said this in Pest in May 1863, when interviewed by L(eo) H(ollander) for the *Allgemeine Zeitung des Judenthums* (2 June 1863). See V.D. Lipman, 'Sir Moses Montefiore: a reassessment', in Israel Bartal (ed.) *The Age of Moses Montefiore*, Jerusalem, 1987, ppxxii–iii. For recent studies of Montefiore in relation to Zionism and Palestine, see articles in the same volume by Israel Bartal, 'Nationalist before his time', pp. vii–x and Aryeh

Morgenstern, 'Moses Montefiore and the Yishuv', pp. xlii–iv, and in V.D. Lipman (ed.) *Sir Moses Montefiore: A Symposium*, Oxford, 1982, the paper by Tudor Parfitt, 'Sir Moses Montefiore and Palestine', pp. 29–46.

5. For Hess, Alkalay and Kalischer, see *Encyclopaedia Judaica* s. v.
6. David Vital, *The Origins of Zionism*, Oxford, 1975, Ch. 5.
7. In 1882 in Palestine there were 480 Jews in six agricultural settlements; in 1890. 2,960 in fourteen (Vital, *Origins*, p. 103).
8. One of the two English delegates was Zerah Barnett (1845–1935), a fur manufacturer and trader, born in Lithuania, who settled in London in 1864 but then travelled frequently to Palestine to advocate and advance Jewish settlement on the land; in 1890 he settled permanently in Jaffa (*EJ* 4,259). For the Kattowitz Conference, see Vital, *Origins*, Ch. 6.
9. Stuart A. Cohen, *English Zionists and British Jews*, Princeton, NJ, 1982, p. 8.
10. Ibid., p. 9.
11. Conversely it has been suggested that Goldsmid, who adopted Judaism six years before, was the model for *Daniel Deronda*. It is interesting that at the very time that Dreyfus was picked out as a traitor because he was the only Jew on the French general staff, Goldsmid, whose Jewish self-identification could hardly have been more evident, was serving as assistant adjutant-general at Aldershot and in effect chief of staff of the 1st Division (the British army did not have a general staff till 1904) at the annual manoeuvres (see picture of him with other members of the command of 1st Division in *Navy and Army Illustrated*, III, p. 237).
12. Cohen, *English Zionists*, p. 8.
13. Vital, *Origins*, p. 234.
14. Cohen, *English Zionists*, pp. 29–30. See also Joseph Fraenkel, 'Lucien Wolf and Theodor Herzl', *TJHSE* XX, 175.
15. Fraenkel, 'Lucien Wolf', p. 167.
16. Cohen, *English Zionists*, p. 38.
17. There are biographies of these figures in *EJ* s.v.
18. Cohen, *English Zionists*, pp. 85–9, 92–104.
19. See Jehuda Reinharz, *Chaim Weizmann*, New York and Oxford, 1985, Chs. 11–16.
20. Leonard Stein, *Balfour Declaration*, 1961, pp. 80–1.
21. Ibid., p. 165. The texts of Montagu's memorandum is given in V.D. Lipman, 'Anglo-Jewish leaders and the Balfour Declaration', in *Michael* X, 1986, (Diaspora Research Institute of Tel-Aviv University), pp. 158–62.
22. Cohen, *English Zionists*, pp. 215–42.
23. Paul Johnson, *The Jews*, 1987, p. 424.
24. Stein, *Balfour Declaration*, pp. 103–115.
25. Ibid., Chs 28, 29. For this whole period see Isaiah Friedman's comprehensive *The Question of Palestine*, 1973, which was able to utilize Public Record Office material only partially available to Leonard Stein when he wrote.
26. A paper, based on material from Weizmann, was circulated to the Cabinet as 'The growth of Zionism in America during the war', and was before them when they took the decision to issue the declaration on 31 October 1917 (G.164 on PRO CAB21/58).
27. Examples of sympathizers within the government machine were Sir Mark Sykes MP, adviser to the Foreign Office on Middle East affairs; Leopold Amery

and Major Ormsby-Gore (later Lord Harlech), assistant secretaries of the Cabinet; and Sir Ronald Graham, assistant under-secretary of state in the Foreign Office, responsible for the Middle East.

28. Professor Mayir Vereté has argued that, as distinct from the Zionists seeking to persuade the British government, the latter wanted - for its own reasons - to use the Zionists in order to influence American opinion; and therefore Sir Mark Sykes attended the meeting at Gaster's house in February 1917 as the seeker, not the sought (Mayir Vereté, 'The Balfour Declaration and its makers', *Middle East Studies* VI, 1970, 70ff.
29. Stein, *Balfour Declaration*, pp. 176-81; Cohen, *English Zionists*, pp. 225-31. On 3 March 1915, Claude Montefiore wrote to Samuel to try to influence him against Zionism: see the revealing correspondence in CZA Lucien Wolf papers A77/3/13.
30. Cohen, *English Zionists*, pp. 163-83.
31. Stein, *Balfour Declaration*, pp. 222-4.
32. Miriam Rothschild, *Dear Lord Rothschild*, 1983, pp. 241-5.
33. Stein, *Balfour Declaration*, p. 454.
34. The way the Conjoint Committee, or rather its two chairmen, operated can be seen from a letter Montefiore wrote to Milner after they had a discussion; enclosing a note of their talk, he wrote: 'The Conjoint Foreign Committee consists of 19 members. This précis is not for them. They will not even be told of our interview. There is an inner ring of about 6 people - all thoroughly trustworthy. These will be told of the interview and I may read to them part of, or even all, the précis. Lastly, there is my colleague President. To him only shall I tell anything really confidential. We used to have a triumvitrate, but now that Leopold de Rothschild is ill, we are an inner cabinet of two only...' Montefiore to Milner, 17 May 1917, CZA Lucien Wolf papers A77/3/1/9.
35. Cohen, *English Zionists*, pp. 243-8.
36. Ibid., pp. 287-96.
37. Rothschild, *Dear Lord Rothschild*, p. 261.
38. Cabinet Paper GT. 1868 (PRO CAB24/4). The paper is printed in full in Lipman, 'Anglo-Jewish leaders', pp. 153-80.
39. PRO WC 227(2) of 3 September 1917 (CAB 23/4). Apart from specified exceptions, views in cabinet minutes are not attributed to individuals: the lead in countering Montagu may have been taken by Milner, whose draft of the declaration was under discussion, and Lord Robert Cecil, the deputy Foreign Secretary. This is implied in Montagu's memorandum of 14 September 1917, in which he wrote that at the Cabinet meeting Cecil and Milner had both suggested his views were those of a minority (Lipman, 'Anglo-Jewish leaders', p. 163).
40. Ibid. This statement was attributed to Lord Robert Cecil, as acting Foreign Secretary, since he was the departmental minister concerned and therefore spoke with authority on a subject within his sphere of responsibility.
41. GT. 2191 (CAB 21/58), reprinted in Lipman, 'Anglo-Jewish leaders', p. 164.
42. GT. 2263 (PRO CAB 24/28). This is reprinted in Friedman, *Question of Palestine*, p. 266. Montagu stressed that 'Zionism had a foreign origin... Jews of foreign birth have played a very large part in the Zionist movement in England.... Dr Gaster, a native of Roumania, Dr Hertz, a native of Austria [actually of Slovakia, then part of Hungary] and Dr Chaim Weizmann, who is, I

believe, a native of Russia...'. Earlier, Claude Montefiore, after his interview with Milner on 16 May 1917, wrote to him: 'I would beg of you to trust your own fellow citizens, who, at all events, are Englishmen through and through... rather than foreigners who have no love for England and who, if the fortunes of war went wrong, would throw her over in a trice and hurry over to Berlin to join the majority of their colleagues...' (CZA A 77/3/1/9). In fact, Lucien Wolf, Montefiore's associate, was still suspect within the Foreign Office for his earlier alleged pro-German (because anti-Russian) sympathies.

43. The replies are given in Lipman, 'Anglo-Jewish leaders', pp. 153–80 with short biographical notes on those quoted as supporters of anti-Zionism.
44. HO45/10822/318095/584.
45. PRO FO371/3054. All these assumptions, which also influenced the Cabinet at its decisive discussion on the issue of the declaration on 31 October 1917, were wrong in varying degrees. The Bolshevik revolution was about to take place, ending any of the largely mythical power of Russian Jews to keep Russia in the war; the influence of the Jews of America was exaggerated, and not all of them were anti-ally; and Germany, as Professor Friedman has shown in his *Germany, Turkey and Zionism*, Oxford, 1977, was not about to issue its own rival declaration.
46. PRO CAB 23/4: WC 261 of 31 October 1917, para. 12. The final version of the declaration read: 'His Majesty's Government view with favour the establishment in Palestine of a national home for the Jewish people, and will use their best endeavours to facilitate the achievement of this object, it being clearly understood that nothing shall be done which may prejudice the civil and religious rights of existing non-Jewish communities in Palestine, or the rights and political status enjoyed by Jews in any other country'.
47. CZA Lucien Wolf papers A77/3/1/4.
48. Cohen, *English Zionists*, pp. 304ff.
49. CZA Lucien Wolf papers A77/3/1.
50. Cohen, *English Zionists*, pp. 305–12. For an account of Laurie Magnus, see Ruth Sebag-Montefiore, A Jewish Patchwork, 1987.
51. For a conspectus of the various formulae for the declaration, see Stein, *Balfour Declaration*, p. 664.
52. CZA Lucien Wolf papers A77/3/8: circular letters of 8 November 1918.
53. Montagu David Eder (1865–1936), who was a cousin of Zangwill and brother-in-law of Joseph Cowen of the EZF, stayed in Palestine for four years as a medical officer and became a committed Zionist, serving as a member of the Zionist executive 1921–3 and 1925–8 (*EJ* 6, 365–6).
54. PRO CAB 23/4: WC 261 of 31 October 1917, para. 12.
55. Copy of letter of 21 April 1918, Weizmann to Ormsby Gore, in CZA Lucien Wolf papers A77/3/1/7.
56. Stein, *Balfour Declaration*, p. 566.
57. Cohen, *English Zionists*, p. 282.
58. Stein, *Balfour Declaration*, p. 567.
59. Ibid., p. 567.
60. Cohen, *English Zionists*, p. 285. This analysis of the position of Zionism after the declaration is given by Professor Stuart Cohen, and the views of Leonard Stein quoted above are similar: both come from committed Zionists.

Chapter 7

The First World War and its Aftermath

The outbreak of war in 1914 caught Anglo-Jewry in an awkward position. Britain, because she was linked to France by the Entente Cordiale was thus the ally of Russia, France's partner in the Dual Alliance; and Czarist Russia was the anti-Jewish tyranny against which the community had for so long been campaigning. By contrast, Anglo-Jewry had various links with Germany. Jewish financiers and industrialists like Sir Ernest Cassel, Sir Edgar Speyer (1862-1932) and *Sir Alfred Mond were of German origin and were involved commercially or financially with the German economy.[1] Cassel, who had by this time been converted to Roman Catholicism, tried through the German Jewish shipowner, Albert Ballin, to bring about a rapprochment between Britain and Germany as a personal arrangement between the two monarchs, each magnate being able to approach his sovereign personally.[2] The first *Lord Rothschild in early 1914 floated a loan for Hungary, while Cassel and Speyer were involved with British-German financial collaboration. Lord Rothschild in late July 1914 tried to get the British government to maintain neutrality, appealing to the Chancellor of the Exchequer, Lloyd George, and the proprietor of *The Times*, Lord Northcliffe.[3] This confirmed the anti-Semitic suspicions of Wickham Steed, editor of *The Times*, who had previously been its correspondent in Vienna and had from spring 1914 been writing leading articles accusing Jews of pro-German sentiments. Steed regarded Rothschild's attempts to keep Britain out of war as a 'dirty German Jewish industrial financial attempt to bully us into adopting neutrality'.[4] In the week before the outbreak of war, the *Jewish Chronicle* condemned the idea of Britain going to war in alliance with Russia as 'an outrage and a crime'. The struggle between Germany and Russia was one in which Britain 'had no moral or conceivable concern'. The *Chronicle* considered the case for fighting to maintain the balance of power in Europe

an atrocious diplomatic superstition . . . a foul idol . . . . We Jews, just because we owe every duty of loyalty and love to this great country, have special obligations cast upon us at this critical moment in her affairs .... Let us bend our energies in any direction which will ensure that this country should take the stand firmly and determinedly upon the solid ground of neutrality, and peace, and should not be led into the madness of war.[5]

The following week the *Chronicle* had to reverse its policy. Britain was already at war and the situation was changed by the German invasion of Belgium, whose integrity both Britain and Germany were pledged by treaty to maintain. It was the invasion of Belgium which was now

an outrage and a crime ... Great Britain is engaging in a monumental struggle for life and death as a nation, a struggle that was not of her seeking and that was forced upon her .... Irrespective of whether this or that policy of this country has contributed to the position ... we are one and undivided as a nation ... England has been all she could be to the Jews. The Jews will be all they can be to England ....

This last sentiment so commended itself to the *Chronicle* that it occurs three times in the editorial and was placarded in large letters outside the newspaper office.[6]

Although compulsory military service did not become law until May 1916, the Anglo-Jewish community provided about 10,000 volunteers before then. About 41,500 Jews from Britain served in the armed forces during the First World War. Assuming an Anglo-Jewish population of 300,000 (a high estimate for 1914), that is 13.8 per cent of the population, compared with 11.5 per cent for the British population generally One can attribute this to the demographic structure of a largely recent immigrant population, with a disproportionate number of younger men and to the virtual absence of Jews from most of the occupations which provided the 2.5 million who were exempted from military service - railways, mines, agriculture, shipbuilding, munitions. Of the 10,000 who joined before conscription, 1,800 served as officers - about twice the average proportion for the population as a whole. This suggests, given the methods of officer selection at the time, a higher than average percentage of middle and upper classes in the 'native' Anglo-Jewish community, from which the bulk of the volunteers were likely to have come. On the other hand, of the 30,000 post-conscription servicemen, the number of officers was 1:19.75, which was lower than the general average of 1:16.5. This suggests a higher than average percentage of working class among the more recent immigrants conscripted, and possibly some difficulty for working-class Jews of recent immigrant origin in obtaining commissions in the armed forces, although the difference was not so great. The Royal Navy would not take foreign-born recruits, or those with parents born abroad, so only 400 Jewish naval ratings and 60 officers are recorded. About 2,000 British Jews serving in the forces were killed or died on active service: about 300 of these were officers, which was the general percentage for commissioned ranks among the casualties. But the proportion of other ranks killed was well below the national average – 0.7 per cent compared with 1.7 per cent – and was possibly due to a number of factors. Many Jews served in theatres of war, like Egypt and Palestine, which had lower casualty rates than the Western front; there were 4,900 Jews in the Labour Corps, which had lower casualty rates, as did the air force in which nearly 2,500 Jews served. Certainly Jews were awarded military honours at least on a par with others in the armed forces: for instance, they won 1 per cent (5 out of 578) of the Victoria Crosses when Jews were well below 1 per cent of the population.

The war stimulated further diversification in the occupations of the community and led to improvement of economic status. There was expansion in the mass production of uniforms by the clothing trade, including boot and shoe manufacture. At first the outbreak of war was followed by a complete dislocation of all industry in east London and similar areas, with a consequent rise in applications for relief. But this was for only a brief period. The placing of government contracts from October 1914 began to revive trade, and labour shortages resulted because of the number called up as reservists or joining the armed forces as volunteers. War contracts enabled many of the small workshop owners to expand production and become wealthy. One can see the effect on poverty in the Anglo-Jewish community generally from the figures of applications for relief to the London Jewish Board of Guardians. There were 3,438 applications in 1913; 4,508 in 1914 (reflecting the initial dislocation of trade); 3,267 in 1915; 2,942 in 1916; 2,487 in 1917; and 2,024 in 1918, less than two-thirds of the 1913 figure.[8]

Jewish success in the war industries brought charges of profiteering and consequent unpopularity. This was added to by the continuing identification by the media of Jews as people with German interests or connections. There were attacks on German-owned property in the East End and elsewhere, and people with foreign names that were thought to be German suffered; this was not directed against Jews as such but Jews suffered incidentally. Leo Maxse, whose *National Review* had attacked the Liberal ministers at the time of the Marconi case, asserted that 'victory for Germany is for some reason the desideratum of almost the entire Jewish race' – the 'almost' making a nominal allowance for the 'national Jew who is a patriot'.[9] Maxse and the Chesterton brothers and Hilaire Belloc, the last three the Catholic group who had been so active at the time of the Marconi case, were perhaps of marginal influence but *The Times* and the *Morning Post* were mainstream opinion formers; the latter had an anti-Jewish tradition and the views of Wickham Steed, editor of *The Times*, on Jews as pro-German have already been quoted.

Although prominent financiers like Cassel and Speyer were no longer members of the Jewish community, Anglo-Jewry was identified with them in the public view and this damaged the community, even though the attacks were made on them as Germans rather than as Jews. Sir George

Makgill, a Scots baronet, brought a case against Speyer and Cassel for them to show cause why they, not being natural-born British subjects, claimed to be members of the Privy Council. The case, over which *Lord Reading (Rufus Isaacs, former attorney-general at the time of the Marconi case) presided as Lord Chief Justice, lasted for five months before it failed. While Cassel was merely embittered by it, Speyer resigned all his offices and left with his family for America. In 1921 he was removed from the Privy Council and deprived of his knighthood because of charges of unlawful exchange dealings in 1915.[10]

*Lucien Wolf, because of his anti-Russian and therefore pro-German views before the war, lost his job on the *Daily Graphic* in November 1914 and had to undergo a police investigation. In January 1915 he was appointed the paid secretary of the Conjoint Foreign Committee of the Board of Deputies and the Anglo-Jewish Association.[11] The communal establishment became hypersensitive over Jews with German associations or any foreign links. In December 1915 Sir Francis Montefiore urged that 'the strictest enquiry should be made before admitting or appointing persons to the various Jewish institutions in this country' and himself resigned the honorary presidency of the English Zionist Federation on the ground that patriotic Englishmen should be concerned only with British affairs when the country was in danger;[12] and the president of the Board of Deputies decided not to look into the question of internment of Jewish enemy aliens, since this might suggest that Jews put 'racial interests before patriotism'.[13] Both the *Jewish Chronicle* and the *Jewish World* felt bitter about the description by *The Times* of all Jews as Germans and about press comments which 'incited the people, day by day, to identify the Jews with Germans'.[14]

In addition to the attacks on German property after the outbreak of war, the sinking of the *Lusitania* in 1915 caused further disturbances in Liverpool and Manchester, and there were disturbances in the Ancoats district of Manchester in 1916.[15] The riots in Leeds in June 1917, which lasted two days, were probably the most serious and were specifically directed against Jews. They seem to have begun with hooligan confrontations, for which Jewish teenagers were not without responsibility. But they developed into disturbances in which 1,500 or 2,000 people were present on 3 June and 3,000 or 4,000 on 4 June. There were attacks on Jewish property, including smashing of windows and some looting; but no personal injuries seem to have been caused. The police were slow to take control but this was due to unpreparedness and lack of strength rather than intent.[16] The causes of the trouble are not certain. Jews were unpopular because they were regarded as profiteers from war industries, or because they were regarded as running away from the inner cities to avoid air raids. But the Chief Constable of Leeds attributed the disturbances to the presence of some 1,400 Russian Jews of military age in Leeds, of whom only twenty-six had joined the forces, when British men of the same age (including, of course, British Jews) had to join up and were dying on the Western Front.[17]

This brings in a major problem of Anglo-Jewry during the last three years of the war, after the introduction of conscription in 1916: the position of Jews who were not naturalized and therefore remained Russian subjects exempt from conscription to serve in the British forces. There were about 45,000 male Russians over 18 in the country, about two-thirds in London. When registration for military service was introduced for them in 1917, 31,500, aged between 18 and 41, registered; again, just under two-thirds were in the Metropolitan Police district. Probably some 2,000 were non-Jews, mostly Polish miners in south-west Scotland.[18] For obvious reasons they did not wish to serve in the Czarist army. At first they were not, as foreign nationals, allowed to join the British army. But with the introduction of compulsory military service for British subjects - the Bill was introduced in January 1916 and became law in May 1916 - the situation became unacceptable to much of public opinion, especially in the localities where young Russian Jews of military age were able to work remuneratively in safety, or merely congregate in the streets, when British young men of the same age were serving. The communal establishment feared a popular backlash and much of the pressure for measures to deal with the Russian Jews of military age came from it, or from the police who feared disturbances, especially in view of hostile comments in much, though not all, of the press. *Herbert Samuel, who was then Home Secretary, told the House of Commons on 29 June 1916 that Russians of military age would be enabled to volunteer, and would be expected to do so - or 'to return to Russia to perform their military obligations there', which many thought a threat of deportation. Herbert Samuel saw a deputation of Jewish trade unionists (London Jewish Bakers; National Union of Boot and Shoe Operatives; Mantlemakers; Amalgamated Society of Tailors; Barbers' Assistants; Furnishing Trades' Association) on 14 August 1916 and told them 'speaking within these four walls, as a member of the Jewish race, speaking to members of the Jewish race, of the shame of the situation'.[19] On 30 August 1916 Samuel wrote to Lucien Wolf: 'If the mass of the Russian Jews in this country refuse to lift a finger to help, when this country is making immeasurable sacrifices in a war with which the cause of liberty all over the world is bound up, the effect on the reputation of the Jewish name everywhere will be disastrous'.[20] Lucien Wolf helped in the framing of a scheme for voluntary enlistment of Russian Jews, with naturalization for those enlisting, but by 10 October only 400 had enlisted voluntarily.[21]

The statement made by Herbert Samuel as Home Secretary on 29 June 1916 was welcomed by the *Jewish Chronicle* and the Board of Deputies, expressing 'the cordial assent of the overwhelming majority of the Jews in Britain'.[22] But it did not necessarily look the same viewed from the East End of London, and possibly from the other immigrant quarters with large concentrations of as yet unnaturalized Russian Jews. Lucien Wolf, in a note of an interview with Balfour on 30 January 1917, wrote that the Conjoint Committee of the Board of Deputies and the Anglo-Jewish Association represented 'a very considerable section of the foreign Jewish community established in this country', who were members of the East End synagogues and the 40,000 members of friendly societies;

> we did not pretend to represent the whole or even the larger part of the foreign Jewish community in this country which, owing to the persecution in Eastern Europe had very largely increased of late years, and which in sentiment and aim were still part and parcel of the communities of their origin.[23]

On 30 November 1916 *Leopold de Rothschild, one of the triumvirate, with *Claude G. Montefiore and D.L. Alexander, who ran the Conjoint Committee, told Lord Robert Cecil, deputy Foreign Secretary, that there was very great unrest in the Jewish quarter in Whitechapel; 'a violent paper, the *Jewish Voice*' had been started and the government must press on with the scheme to enlist Russian Jews.[24] In addition to the objection to serving in the Czarist army – and some no doubt who objected to serving in any army – there is evidence of left-wing activitists encouraging resistance to service in a capitalist war.[25] A Foreign Jews Protection Committee against Conscription, Deportation to Russia and Compulsory Military Service (FJPC) was formed by Abraham Bezalel (also known as Solly Abrahams), Y.M. Zalkind (who edited the *Jewish Voice*) and others. It included representatives of the Capmakers' Union, the International Workers of the World, Jewish members of the British Socialist Party (the predecessor of the Communist Party of Great Britain) and anarchists associated with the Yiddish periodical, *Arbeter Fraynt*.[26] The committee organized mass public meetings, attended by thousands, one on 24 July 1917 reported by the police to have been attended by 6,000.[27] The committee had the active support of Lord Sheffield, who presided over their public meetings, and a group of Liberal MPs, notably Joseph King, who was active in parliament on their behalf. Labour MPs like Ramsay Macdonald and Philip Snowden also supported them, as did the *Nation* and the *Manchester Guardian*, which regarded the pressure on the Russian Jews to serve a breach of the right of asylum. Within the Jewish Community practically their only prominent supporter was *Israel Zangwill, although Zangwill, who supported the idea of a Jewish unit in the British army had earlier written privately that

> no man of fighting age, even though an alien, ought to shelter himself behind the bodies of his fellow-inhabitants. In the case of Jewish aliens, the fact that they have been given hospitality and sympathy for a number of years should evoke gratitude which ought to make them feel that it is a privilege to share the burden of English citizenship.[28]

Zangwill, however, sent a message of support to the meeting on 25 March

1917, although he refused to come and speak, and congratulated Joseph King on his 'good and patriotic work'.[29] Zangwill's line developed into opposition to compulsory service and sending Russian Jews back to Russia, although he welcomed voluntary enlistment.[30] But FJPC opposed Russian Jews even doing essential civilian work of 'national importance', on the ground that this would recognize the right of the 'capitalist state' to 'assign individuals the work they have to do' and mark the 'abandonment of the Right of Asylum'.[31] This attitude of the FJPC persisted after the Russian Revolution of March 1917.

The British government had negotiated conventions with allied powers, such as Belgium, about military service for their nationals resident in Britain. An attempt to negotiate such an agreement with the Czarist government failed; it did not want an arrangement under which Russian Jews, whom it thought would not make good soldiers and might spread disaffection, might be sent back to serve in Russia.[32] The Provisional government after March 1917 however wanted a right for Russian nationals to return to Russia, otherwise it might look as if it was abandoning its citizens to the British army.[33] A convention on Anglo-Russian military service was negotiated and implemented by Order in Council in August 1917. Russians were placed under the provisions of the Military Service (Conventions with Allied States) Order. They would either be conscripted into the British army or could return to their country of origin for military service, unless exempted by that country. They had the same provisions for application for exemption to British tribunals as British subjects. There was provision for naturalization without charge of those enlisted after three months' satisfactory service provided they satisfied the statutory conditions.[34]

The *Jewish Chronicle* and the Jewish establishment welcomed the Convention, although they would have liked to see naturalization on enlistment and Lucien Wolf argued against sending men back to Russia on the ground that Britain would lose manpower if the majority opted for it and it would strain Britain's shipping resources. The FJPC still protested: 'We are not citizens of this country and neither Russia nor Rumania is our home'.[35]

Bezalel was in Leeds at the time of the disturbances there and sent a telegram to Petrograd, which was intercepted, denouncing the Leeds 'pogrom' as evidence that the oppression of the British government was as bad as that of the Czars and therefore Jews should not have to serve in the British army. In August 1917 the British government eventually lost patience with Bezalel, raided the offices of the FJPC, and arrested him along with Israel Bloomfield, secretary of the Russian Anti-Conscription League, for conspiring to defeat the Military Service Act as applied to aliens. Bezalel was deported to Sweden and made his way to Russia.[36] After Bezalel was deported, Moses Margolin took over the secretaryship of the FJPC, taking a more moderate line, co-operating with the repatriation of those who wanted to return to Russia and arguing that, if Jews had to serve in the British army, it should be in ordinary, not special Jewish, units.[37]

Those who wanted to opt under the Convention for repatriation to Russia had to do so by 9 August 1917. Some 7,500 registered, of whom about 1,500 were non-Jews. There were sailings from 15 August to the beginning of October (after which the Bolshevik revolution brought sailings to a halt). Of the 7,500 who had registered, 2,900 actually sailed, including 900 non-Jewish miners. About 3,000 who had been given notice of the boat in which they should sail failed to turn up.[38] One can therefore say that some 2,000 Jews actually sailed to Russia. Of those who remained, a number were exempted by either the Russian representatives in London, who were generous with exemption certificates, as they opposed the Convention, or by appeal tribunals.

The British government did not implement a suggestion to open internment camps for those who had neither returned to Russia nor served in the British army.[39] At the end of January 1918 the Cabinet decided not to recruit any more Russian Jews but not to release those who had joined;[40] after the High Court had decided in a case challenging the Convention that it was still valid, the Cabinet decided on 25 March 1918 to resume recruiting, but only for labour battalions, who were not combatant troups.[41] Some 5,000 Jews joined the labour battalions but not all were Russians. In addition, some 1,500 Russians joined the Jewish battalions of the Royal Fusiliers. Accordingly, it would seem that of the 30,000 Russian Jews of military age, 2,000 returned to Russia, about 8,000 served in the British army in the Jewish units, other ordinary units and labour battalions; the other 20,000 were either exempted or not called for service.[42]

The Conventionists, as those who returned to Russia in 1917 were called, gave rise to two other problems. First, they left behind some 3,000 dependants. Of these, 622 wives and 1,138 children were receiving inadequate support from the government, and the others were supported from other sources. A United Russian Committee, led by Dr David Jochelman, campaigned for their support, and the Board of Deputies pressed unsuccessfully for increases in the allowances paid to them.[43] The question of sending them to Russia to join their husbands and fathers was discussed - difficulties over shipping and the uncertainty of the position in Russia being obstacles to this course - but 200 did sail.[44] In London the Jewish Board of Guardians were unwilling to supplement the dependants' allowances but the Manchester Board did so.[45]

What happened to the Conventionists after they arrived in Russia is not clear. The Bolsheviks were opposed to continuing the war against Germany and concluded an armistice on 4 December 1917, which led to the peace negotiations at Brest Litovsk. So the Conventionists who arrived in Russia in September or October 1917 would have had little, if any, chance of combatant service against the Germans. Some no doubt settled in Russia under the Bolshevik regime but others tried to get back to Britain. The government line was that they had no right of readmission and a number who were found to have entered without permission were arrested. The Board of Deputies asked that at least those with dependants in Britain should be readmitted but the government would concede readmission only to those who could show that they had at least done their best to serve in the war.[46] In June 1920 the Board learned that about eighty of the Conventionists had returned and forty had been deported. The Board sent a deputation on 18 June 1923 to the Home Secretary to discuss deportation; they asked for this to be done not administratively but after some form of judicial action, and feared that deportation might affect the position of the settled alien population, not yet naturalized. The Home Office reply was that those deported had broken the rules by entering the country illegally or had committed some offence, or were undesirable 'in certain cases, such as aliens engaged in revolutionary propaganda or in white slave traffic, whose activities, though well known to the police, cannot be made the subject of prosecution'.[47] The Home Office noted that the cases submitted by the Board did not include any examples of 'old' residents being deported and the deputation was assured there was no threat to the Jewish population generally, even if still aliens; in fact, the number deported was infinitesimal compared with the number of Russo-Jewish immigrants in the Anglo-Jewish community.[48]

The Conventionist episode produced bitterness between the communal establishment and the immigrants, each side feeling it had been let down by the other; it resulted in friction between the community and the government departments concerned; and, because of resentment against those who were thought to have failed in their duty to the country which had given them hospitality, it may have influenced the Home Office in its subsequent attitude to Jewish aliens and refugees.[49]

A way out of the problem of military service for Russian Jews was offered by the proposal for a Jewish regiment or legion, which would fight on the side of the Allies, it was hoped in a campaign for the conquest of Palestine. This was proposed by Vladimir Jabotinsky (1880–1940) at the beginning of the war in the Middle East where he was a correspondent of a leading Russian newspaper.[50] The initial step was the formation in Egypt in March 1915 of the Zion Mule Corps, 600 strong, mainly from Russian Jews deported from Palestine by the Turks; they served as a transport unit in Gallipoli under Colonel J.H. Patterson, whose second-in-command was Jabotinsky's associate, Joseph Trumpeldor, decorated for gallantry in the Russian army during the Russo-Japanese War and one of the very few Jews commissioned in the Czar's forces. The corps was disbanded in May 1916 after the end of the Gallipoli campaign but Jabotinsky continued to agitate for a Jewish unit. This was despite the opposition of the Zionist General Council in Copenhagen in 1915, since it considered that to fight for Britain, especially in Palestine, would mean fighting against Turkey, Germany's ally – half the council were Germans, the rest being Russians.[51] Jabotinsky was in London early in 1916 and saw the problem of the Russian Jews and military service, especially as conscription was now being introduced, as an opportunity to forward his idea. The Zionist leadership in London, with the emphatic exception of *Weizmann, were against him, many because they distrusted his dramatic and impulsive personality. Most Anglo-Jewish establishment opinion was also hostile to the idea of a specifically Jewish unit in the British army. They asked why there should be a special unit for Jews, since they regarded Jews merely as a religious denomination, when there were no special units for Roman Catholics or Free Churchmen. They feared the reputation of all Jews would depend on how this unit happened to behave. Jews born in Britain would not want to be drafted to this unit from their existing units, especially if the language, to accommodate the Russians, was Yiddish; and would not public opinion think that the unit was the sole contribution of Jews to the war effort? There was probably more opposition to the idea of a Jewish unit than to Zionism: the new president of the Board of Deputies, *Sir Stuart Samuel, said he had never known the community so unanimous. Jabotinsky and Weizmann had however managed to convince the War Office, who wanted a solution to the problem of military service for Russian Jews, to announce on 28 July 1917 that such a unit would be formed. This was tied up with the announcement of the action to be taken under the Anglo-Russian Military Convention: the War Office offered those Russians who enlisted in the British army the opportunity of forming groups of at least 200, who could then be allowed to stay together in separate units. In spite of this, Jabotinsky's efforts to hold meetings among the Russian Jews in east London either failed or provoked disorder; only 300 undertook to join such a unit, if formed, to serve for home defence or on the Palestine front.

Lucien Wolf, probably because he thought this a solution to the Russian enlistment problem, broke ranks with the communal leadership and supported the proposal, helping Jabotinsky's associate, Meir Grossman, to come to London.[52] Once the announcement about a Jewish unit was made, there was a deputation against it, which included Dr Hertz, the Chief Rabbi, to Lord Derby, the Secretary of State for War; and the government eventually decided that the new unit should not have a Jewish name or insignia, although these might be granted later in the light of its record of service – a compromise which seemed to satisfy Jewish opinion for the time being. The unit was designated the 38th Battalion of the Royal Fusiliers, the regiment traditionally associated with the City of London. About half the men were British subjects, most of the other half being Russian subjects. In April 1918 the 39th Battalion was formed, half of the men being American or Canadian Jews. The 40th Battalion was formed in Egypt for Jews from Palestine, much of which was by that time under British occupation. After their participation in the Palestine campaign, the units were considered to have earned the title of the Judean Regiment and the badge was changed from the Royal Fusiliers' grenade to a *menorah* (the seven-branched candlestick).[53]

It was not only over Jewish units that Lucien Wolf developed views which seemed inconsistent with his previous opposition to treating Jews as a nationality, rather that a religious denomination. As secratary of the Conjoint, and later the Joint, Foreign Committee, Wolf was the executant, and to a considerable extent the formulator, of an Anglo-Jewish 'foreign policy'. He wanted 'all sections of the Jewish community to unite in pressing forward a liberal solution of the Russo-Jewish question'. To mobilize wider support for this aim, he founded, and became president of, a National Union for Jewish Rights in January 1916, to watch over Jewish interests at a future peace conference. He hoped this would be 'a very big affair', bringing in the friendly societies and Zionist bodies, on the basis of his supporting a moderate amount of Zionist aims and they supporting equal rights for Eastern European Jewry. 'The Union has very loyally accepted my programme, which is a programme of essentials, without any party attachments. We are not going to be Nationalists or Zionists or Territorials [*sic*: the reference was to Zangwill's Jewish Territorial Organization].'[54] In spite of renewed Jewish suffering during the war in Czarist Russia - from mass deportations from the war zone, shooting of Jews accused of sympathy with the Germans, the prohibition on the use of Hebrew letters which ended the Hebrew and Yiddish press - the Conjoint Committee was unable to make effective protests to the Foreign Office, which was irritated by criticism of an ally. Lucien Wolf's line in October 1916, as shown in the Conjoint Committee's memorandum on the desiderata of the Jews in connection with a future peace settlement, was still based on equal citizenship rights for the Jews as individuals in Eastern Europe.[55] Only six months later he wrote an essay in the *Edinburgh Review* (April 1917), recognizing a new 'Jewish Nationality' which had developed in Eastern Europe in the last thirty-five years.

> The Jews of Russia constitute a nationality only third in rank among the peoples which will claim emancipation ..... This Jewish Secular Nationality in the East, admirable though it be in many ways, is a new and utterly revolutionary departure in Jewish life. It is not essentially bound up with Judaism ....[56]

Wolf was, of course, writing after the Russian March Revolution, which was welcomed by Anglo-Jewry. 'Russia Free' was the *Jewish Chronicle* headline and the Provisional government seemed exactly the sort of liberal, democratic regime that Wolf and others who had strenuously opposed the Czarist system had hoped for. But Wolf had been influenced by Diaspora nationalists with whom he had previously been in touch for information about the Jews of Russia, such as the historian Simon Dubnow; and by David Mowshowitch, who became his secretary and later chief assistant at the Joint Foreign Committee. The idea of a national minority status for Jews in Eastern Europe, but with membership on a personal, not geographical, basis, had been adopted by the Bund and other Jewish socialist parties in Eastern Europe; it was however opposed by the Zionists, for whom continued Jewish life in Eastern Europe had no future and the orthodox, such as the Agudas Israel, who objected to the secularism of the concept and preferred individual equal rights.[57]

A further factor helped Lucien Wolf to opt for Jewish minority rights. This was the effect of President Wilson's call for the restoration of Poland in January 1917 and in his Fourteen Points (January 1918) for self-determination for nationalities. In Eastern Europe, the future was uncertain and territory would be transferred from one state to another, according to the decision on which nationality should have it. Jews might have to choose if they opted for individual rights and integration in the dominant nationality, whether to be Russians or Poles: it would be safer and simpler to be, and remain, Jews. Wolf was sufficiently influenced by his anti-nationalist past to resist the use of the term '*national* minority rights' but he included autonomy for the Jewish communities and the right to use Yiddish and work on Sunday, instead of Saturday, with citizen rights for the Jews of the future Polish state.[58] 'Examining all the options, Wolf was persuaded by Mowshowitch to give full support to the national autonomy concept and, ironically, the assimilated Jew championed Yiddish'.[59] This was to have its impact on the Jewish representations to the Versailles Peace Conference. While Wolf and the Joint Foreign Committee would not join the representatives of Eastern Europe, America and other Jewries (except France) in the Comité des Delegations Juives at the Versailles conference, because of their claim to 'national' minority status for Jews in Eastern Europe, Wolf did ask for ethnic, cultural and linguistic minority rights; and he was largely responsible for the inclusion of these collective rights for Jews in the minority treaties which the newly created or extended states had to accept.

While the March 1917 Revolution had been welcomed by Anglo-Jewry, the Bolshevik Revolution (the 'October' Revolution – 7 November in the western calendar) was responsible for an outbreak of anti-Semitism, not merely on the margins of western society but in mainstream and official circles: it was probably the worst expression of anti-Jewish feeling the community had experienced since emancipation. It must, however, be viewed in the context of world reactions to Bolshevism, especially the 'Red Scare' in the United States in 1919. World Communism was seen as a threat to the life, liberty and property of the western democracies and the simultaneous outbreak of communist revolutions in Central European countries in 1918 was regarded as evidence of a deeper conspiracy. The involvement of Jews, albeit Jews who had left Judaism, in the leadership of the Russian Bolshevik party (above all Trotsky), their association with the brutal assassination of the Russian imperial family (so far as details of this still mysterious episode were known in the West), and the part played by persons of Jewish origin in Central European revolutions (Rosa

Luxemburg in Berlin, Bela Kun in Hungary, Kurt Eisner in Bavaria) all led to a perception of a link between Jews and revolution. Nearer home, certain Jews received publicity as communists or left-wing radicals: Maxim Litvinov, who had been in England since 1908, became in January 1918 the Bolshevik government's representative in Britain (he was deported in September 1918); Theodore Rothstein, who had been in Britain since 1891 and active as a radical journalist, succeeded Litvinov as Bolshevik representative until he returned to Russia in August 1920; and there were other Jews associated with the British Socialist Party, which was the predecessor of the Communist Party of Great Britain, and in the Marxist Socialist Party of Great Britain, as well as in the anarcho-syndicalist International Workers of the World and Sylvia Pankhurst's Workers' Suffrage Federation. No matter that, as indeed in Russia, 'those Jews who were active in the general socialist and anarchist movement were unrepresentative of the Jewish community as a whole', because these movements ran counter to Jewish tradition and the developing Zionist movement; although, faced with the anti-Semitic terrorism of the White Russian forces, even the Bolsheviks would seem the preferable alternative.[61]

However, the identification made by publicists of Jews with revolutionaries – what one might call the Trotsky legend – provided material for those already hostile to Jews: this was true of the right-wing group who had been so hostile during the Marconi case to 'rich' Jews: now they could attack 'poor' Jews as well. Hilaire Belloc commented on the previous neutrality or friendship of capitalists towards Jews, now turned, he thought, by fear towards hostility, and he dated the appearance of *open* anti-Semitism in Britain to the Russian Revolution.[62] The theory of a world Jewish conspiracy was fostered by the circulation in 1919 of the *Protocols of the Learned Elders of Zion*, a vivid account of a world Jewish conspiracy, in fact adapted by an agent of the Czarist secret police from a French pamphlet aimed at Napoleon III, and which did not convince even Czar Nicholas II.[63] The *Protocols* were first given publicity in Britain by a series of articles based on them which appeared in the summer of 1920 in the *Morning Post*, a mainstream newspaper, although they had appeared under the title of *The Jewish Peril* in book form, published by Eyre and Spottiswoode, His Majesty's Printers (and also the printers of every edition of Singer's Authorized Daily Prayerbook!); and they were also taken up by *The Times*. The identification of Jews with Bolshevism and world conspiracy quickly became widespread. For instance, Winston Churchill, in an article entitled 'Zionism versus Bolshevism: the struggle for the soul of the Jewish people', divided Jews into three classes: loyal citizens of Britain; those who wanted to rebuild their homeland in Palestine; and international Jews or Jewish terrorists. In his view, Trotsky could only be combated effectively by Weizmann: Zionism was the answer to Bolshevism.[64]

The *Morning Post* had been taking an anti-Jewish line for about three years but the underlying motive for publication of the articles on the

Protocols was sensationalism; the paper had lost readership, was down to 52,000 copies a day from 60,000 in 1918 and badly needed to secure another 10,000 readers – which the publication of the series of articles on the *Protocols*, entitled 'The causes of world unrest', succeeded in getting. Admittedly, the editor, H.A. Gwynne, was a convinced anti-Semite and persuaded himself of the truth of the *Protocols* in spite of warnings of their doubtful authenticity from Sir William Tyrrell of the Foreign Office and Sir Basil Thomson, head of Scotland Yard's Special Branch, and most powerfully from the *Post's* own business manager, Henry Peacock. Peacock, although no friend of the Jews, could not believe in the *Protocols* or that men like Lord Rothschild, *Sir Marcus Samuel (the first Viscount Bearsted) or Lord Burnham (Edward Levy-Lawson, 1833–1916) (owner of the rival *Daily Telegraph*, which in 1937 absorbed the *Post*) were anything but anti-Bolshevik.[65]

Perhaps even more alarming for the Jewish community than the line of the *Morning Post* was that of *The Times*. This, after earlier hostile articles, published on 8 May 1920 an article entitled 'The Jewish peril'. It argued against Lloyd George, as Prime Minister, opening negotiations with the Russian government on the ground that he would be negotiating with the representatives of a world Jewish conspiracy, citing in support that recent events had shown that the forecasts in the *Protocols* were being fulfilled.[66]

The accusations in these and similar articles caused immense anxiety within Anglo-Jewry and a division of opinion on the correct response. This was brought to a head in April 1919 when ten leading members of the Anglo-Jewish establishment wrote to the *Morning Post* to dissociate themselves from the views on Bolshevism which had been expressed in the *Jewish Chronicle* and the *Jewish World* (which was owned by the *Chronicle*). Dissension had already arisen in the community about the line to be taken on the pogroms being carried out by the White Russians in 1919. Some communal leaders wanted a low-key response, so as not to damage the campaign the government was carrying on against Bolshevism, which involved support for the Whites. Others, notably Zangwill, wanted maximum publicity and protest, along the lines of what had been done against Czarist oppression before the Revolution. *L.J. Greenberg, editor of the *Jewish Chronicle*, writing in it in the regular column he contributed under the pseudonym, 'Mentor', developed an extremely subtle argument to explain the undeniable fact that many Jews had joined the Bolsheviks: Bolshevism was a protest against the old social order in Russia but also a terrible warning; while it was a disaster, its ideals were in many respects congruent with the ideals of Judaism and Christianity. The *Jewish World* had a leading article on similar lines. The ten wrote to the *Post* to welcome a call by that paper for British Jews to dissociate themselves from a cause which was doing harm to the Jewish people in all parts of the world. As British Jews they did dissociate themselves from the views of those Jewish newspapers and the statement that Bolshevism had ideals, and that these ideals were consonant with Judaism. They took the opportunity to draw attention to the League of British Jews, founded in 1917 to combat Zionism. The ten were *Lionel de Rothschild (president of the United Synagogue), the *second Lord Swaythling (still uneasily president of the Federation of Synagogues), *Sir Philip Magnus (president of the Reform Synagogue), Sir Marcus Samuel (soon to become Viscount Bearsted), (Sir) Harry S. Samuel (1853–1934), *Leonard L. Cohen (president of the Board of Guardians), Sir Israel Gollancz (1863–1930), Sir Isidore Spielmann (1854–1925), *Claude G. Montefiore (president of the Anglo-Jewish Association) and Sir John Monash (1865–1931), the former General Officer Commanding the Australian forces in France.

The results of the letter were predictable. The *Morning Post* said it showed the *Post* was not anti-Semitic in calling on Jews to dissociate themselves from Bolshevism (although in the light of the papers of Lady Bathurst, the *Post's* proprietor, this seems disingenuous). L.J. Greenberg wrote to the *Post* that he had never advocated Bolshevism and within the community attacked the '*minyan* of *mosserim*' (prayer quorum of ten informers), who denounced their own people; and Morris Myer, editor of the Yiddish daily *Die Tsayt*, condemned the *Yahudim* (assimilated Jews) for denouncing the *Yidn* ('real' Jews), in order to curry favour with non-Jews. On 29 April 1919, the Board of Deputies deprecated the letter of the ten as making a distinction between 'British' and 'foreign' Jews, but repudiated Bolshevism. The Jewish socialists regarded the letter as a blow in the class struggle. The whole incident shows the anxieties of the community in face of the accusations of Bolshevism and their division on how to respond, with parties forming up on lines similar, though not identical, to those adopted in the struggle over Zionism in 1917.[67]

In August 1921 *The Times* published three articles by its Constantinople correspondent, Philip Graves, revealing the true story of the forgery of the *Protocols* and completely demolishing any claim to authenticity for their contents.[68] After that the *Protocols* and the world Jewish conspiracy theory were not put forward by any serious newspaper in Britain. Though the anti-Jewish attacks did not cease after *The Times* exposed the *Protocols* as a forgery in August 1921, they became almost insignificant'.[69] But the period from 1917 to 1921 was one particularly traumatic for Anglo-Jewry. Whereas in the time of the aliens question, the attack was ostensibly on 'aliens', and not on British Jews as such, in the years between the Russian Revolution and the exposure of the *Protocols*, the attacks were on Jews as such, and often no exception was made for 'loyal' or 'British' Jews. It was probably the time of greatest anxiety for the Anglo-Jewish leadership since emancipation.

Notes

1. C.C. Aronsfeld, 'Jewish enemy aliens in England during the First World War', *Jewish Social Studies* XVIII, 1956, 275–83.
2. Kurt Grunwald, 'Windsor-Cassel', *Leo Baeck Year Book* XIV, pp. 149–57.
3. For the position of the Conjoint Foreign Committee at the outbreak of war, see Mark Levene, 'Lucien Wolf, the Conjoint Committee and the War, 1914–18', *TJHSE*, XXX, especially pp. 185–6.
4. Wickham Steed, *Through Thirty Years*, 1924, II, p. 9.
5. *Jewish Chronicle*, 31 July 1914.
6. Ibid. 7 August 1914; (Cecil Roth), *The Jewish Chronicle 1841–1941*, 1949, p. 142. (the phrase was coined by 'Mentor', who, it was revealed much later, was the editor, L.J. Greenberg, p. 136).
7. M. Adler (ed.) *The British Jewry Book of Honour*, 1922; Barry A. Kosmin and Nigel Grizzard, 'Jewish war deaths in the Great War', *Immigrants and Minorities* 5, pp. 181-92.
8. V.D. Lipman, *A Century of Social Services: The History of the Jewish Board of Guardians*, 1959, p. 284.
9. *National Review*, September 1914.
10. Colin Holmes, *Anti-Semitism in British Society*, 1979, p. 123.
11. Stuart Cohen, *English Zionists and British Jews*, Princeton, NJ, 1982, p. 217; C. Abramsky, 'Lucien Wolf and Eastern Europe', *TJHSE* XXIX, 1988, p. 283 about the view of Wolf as a very pro-German journalist. See also Mark Levene, 'Lucien Wolf, the Conjoint Committee and the War', p. 186.
12. Cohen, *English Zionists*, p. 266.
13. *JC*, 18 June 1915.
14. *Jewish World*, 19 May 1915; *JC*, 16 March 1917, both cited in L. Paliakov, *A History of Antisemitism*, Oxford, 1985, IV p. 191.
15. Bill Williams, *Manchester Jewry 1788–1988*, 1988, p. 25.
16. Holmes, *Anti-Semitism*, p. 131; A. Gilam, 'The Leeds and anti-Jewish riots of 1917', *Jewish Quarterly* 29 (1).
17. Holmes, *Anti-Semitism*, p. 131.
18. In addition to the published works mentioned in the following notes, there is an as yet unpublished London University MA dissertation by Professor A. Tropp, 'Russian Jews in Britain during the First World War', which has made intensive use of the Home Office papers in the Public Record Office. I am grateful to Professor Tropp for giving me a copy of the dissertation, which has provided references additional to those I have myself consulted in the PRO. For the 45,000 figure the source is PRO HO 45/10821/318095/410; for the number of those registering, HO 45/10819/318095/127.
19. PRO HO 45/10818/318095.
20. Leonard Stein, *Balfour Declaration*, 1961, p. 489.
21. Hansard, House of Commons Official Report, 10 October 1916.
22. Holmes, *Anti-Semitism*, p. 127.
23. CZA Lucien Wolf papers A 77/3/57.
24. Lord Robert Cecil to Herbert Samuel, 30 November 1916 (HO 45/10819/318095).
25. George Chicherin (1872-1936), then a Russian revolutionary in exile, was

secretary of the Committee of Delegates of the Russian Socialist Groups in London, which campaigned against military service for Russian Jews (*The Call*, 20 May 1917); he subsequently became, after expulsion from Britain, Vice-Commissar for Foreign Affairs in the USSR. According to the Special Branch, he was active in stirring up opposition among Jews to military service (HO 45/10820/318095). *The Call*, which regarded the Foreign Jews Protection Committee as 'the most representative body of Jewish working class opinion that has ever been brought together' (24 August 1916), was the organ of the British Socialist Party.

26. Holmes, *Anti-Semitism*, p. 128; Cohen, *English Zionists*, p. 253; Board of Deputies archives C11/29. Bezalel was said by the Special Branch to have been a corporal in the French army (HO 45/10820/318095).
27. HO 45/10821/318095.
28. CZA Zangwill papers: Zangwill to Joseph Cowen, 22 June 1916, A/120/60/5.
29. Ibid., A/120/16,60/5 (letter to J. King MP, 10 July 1916).
30. For example his letter to Dr Rappaport in CZA A 120/60/5.
31. *JC*, 27 October 1916.
32. HO 45/10810/318095/4.
33. HO 45/10810/311932/268.
34. Holmes, *Anti-Semitism*, p. 128, citing HO 45/10821/318095/367; 10823/318095/623,623,633.
35. Article in *Daily Chronicle*, 13 July 1917. It seems that the British government would have preferred the men to stay but the Russian Provisional government wanted them back. See telegram of 5 April 1917 to Buchanan, British ambassador in Moscow, on HO 45/10820/318095.
36. Holmes, *Anti-Semitism*, p. 132.
37. Ibid., pp. 132–3; Hansard, House of Commons Official Report, 1 August 1917.
38. HO 45/10821/318035. In addition to the Leeds riot, there were some disturbances in Bethnal Green on 23 and 24 September 1917 but the story of a riot at Euston station, when some of the Conventionists were entraining for the boat, seems an exaggeration from a very small incident (HO 45/10822/318095/468,473).
39. HO 45/10821/318095 and 10822/318095.
40. PRO CAB 23/5/239 War Cabinet meeting, 22 January 1918.
41. HO 45/10822/318095/574,579.
42. I am indebted to Professor Tropp (see note 18) for these estimates which represent the findings so far reached in his researches at the Public Record Office.
43. *JC*, 27 December 1918; 31 January 1919; 28 March 1919.
44. HO 45/10822/318095/584.
45. *JC*, 21 March 1919; 4 April 1919.
46. *JC*, 2 May 1919.
47. This last point was made by officials at the briefing meeting for the Home Secretary before the deputation was received: 'it would be difficult to say much about this to the deputation' (HO 45/24765).
48. See minute by Sir John Pedder of 18 July 1923 on HO 45/24765.
49. This point was suggested by Professor Tropp (see note 18) from his study of official files.
50. Stein, *Balfour Declaration*, pp. 486–7.

51. Ibid., p. 487.
52. Ibid., pp. 488–93; Josef Fraenkel, 'Lucien Wolf and Theodor Herzl', *TJHSE* XX, 187–8. When Grossman landed, the immigration officer was very suspicious of a Russian Jew coming from Denmark to raise a Jewish army. J.F. Henderson of the Home Office wrote to E.M. Lafone at Scotland Yard that, while 'Jabotinsky seems to be an entirely reliable person', the police should keep an eye on Grossman (Ho 44/10819/318095).
53. For the Jewish units, see (among others), Cohen, *English Zionists*, p. 258; *EJ* 10, 67–76; Stein, *Balfour Declaration*, pp. 486–94; Cyril Silvertown, *Jewish Quarterly* 32 (2), 37–40.
54. Lucien Wolf's memorandum of his meeting with Weizmann on 17 August 1916: CZA Wolf papers A 77/3/2. For the National Union, see Cohen, *English Zionists*, pp. 254–7.
55. CZA Zangwill papers A 120/60/5; Lucien Wolf to Israel Zangwill, 17 January 1916.
56. David Mowshowitch, 'Lucien Wolf as diplomatist', in Cecil Roth (ed.) Lucien Wolf, *Essays in Jewish History*, 1934, p. 21.
57. Chimen Abramsky, 'Lucien Wolf and Eastern Europe', *TJHSE* XXIX. 289–91.
58. Ibid., pp. 289,291; Mowshowitch, 'Wolf as diplomatist', p. 22.
59. Abramsky, 'Wolf and Eastern Europe', p. 291.
60. Mowshowitch, 'Wolf as diplomatist', pp. 22–3. The whole story of Wolf's diplomacy in the First World War and Peace Conference is the subject of a major new work by Dr Mark Levene, to be published by Oxford University Press, which I have been fortunate to read in typescript. His preliminary study 'Anglo-Jewish foreign policy in crisis – Lucien Wolf, the Conjoint Committee and the war, 1914–18, is in *TJHSE* XXX, 179–98.
61. Sharman Kadish, 'Jewish Bolshevism and the Red scare in Britain', *Jewish Quarterly* 34 (4), 1987, 13–19. I have drawn on this valuable article for much of the preceding paragraph.
62. L. Paliakov, *History of Antisemitism*, IV, Oxford, 1985, p. 201.
63. Norman Cohn, *Warrant for Genocide*, 1967.
64. Poliakov, *History* IV, pp. 207–8.
65. See the analysis of the private correspondence of Lady Bathurst, who owned the *Morning Post*, in Keith M. Wilson, 'The *Protocols of Zion* and the *Morning Post*', *Patterns of Prejudice* 19 (3), July 1985, 5–14.
66. Poliakov, *History*, IV, p. 210.
67. For this incident see the essay by Dr Sharman Kadish in Jonathan Frankel (ed.) *Studies in Contemporary Jewry IV: The Jews and the European Crisis, 1919–21*, New York and Oxford, 1988.
68. Poliakov, *History*, IV, p. 215.
69. S. Almog, 'Anti-Semitism as a dynamic phenomenon: the 'Jewish Question' in England at the end of the First World War', *Patterns of Prejudice* 21 (4), 3–18.

Rev Dr N. M. Adler,
Chief Rabbi 1845–1890

Rev Dr H. Adler,
Chief Rabbi 1890–1912

Rev Dr M. Gaster, Haham,
Sephardi Congregation

Chief Rabbi Joseph Hertz

The Revd S. Singer

Ecclesiastical leaders of the Community

Lionel L. Cohen, M.P.

First Lord Rothschild, 1910

Sir Samuel Montagu,
later 1st Lord Swaythling

Second Lord Rothschild

Israel Zangwill

Some notables before 1920

Selig Brodetsky

Edwin Montagu

Sir Herbert Samuel, later Lord Samuel

Sir Robert Waley Cohen (and the author) in London, 1946

Chaim (Charles) Weizman

Some notables of the twentieth century

Foreign Jewish Beth Hamedrash (House of Learning)
in the East End of London, 1889

Interior, Machzike Hadath (Springboard)

The Spitalfield Great Syngogue, Machzike Hadath.
This was successively a place of worship for
Huguenots, Wesleyans, Jews, and now Moslems

The Society wedding of Maria Perugia and Leopold de Rothschild

Tailoring workshop, *c.* 1914 (Barbara Marks)

BALANCE SHEET

OF THE

GREAT STRIKE OF EAST LONDON TAILORS,

For 10½ hours per day.

EXTENDING FROM AUGUST 27th, to OCTOBER 2nd, 1889.

Introductory Note by the Secretary on behalf of the Strike Committee.

In presenting this Sheet before the attention of the public, we beg to take the opportunity of offering our heartiest thanks to all sympathisers who so readily and freely responded to our appeal for help, and more so to those who did not even wait for our appeal. And while, considering the importance of monetary assistance in such critical times to save the struggling soldiers from bending before the whip of starvation, we express our utmost appreciation at the way in which sympathisers of all grades, rich and poor, laborers and manufacturers, subscribed to our funds, we cannot refrain from emphasizing with great pleasure the fact that the readiness and fraternal spirit shown to us by the various Trade Organizations and other English Working Men's Bodies armed us with a most effective weapon to carry the fight to victory. We only hope that our brethren all over the Globe will not fail to take a grand lesson of solidarity from the Dock Labourers' Strike, as well as from this of the Tailors and of others, which will mark a new and splendid epoch in the history of Labour; a lesson that will lead the workers of all countries to their complete emancipation and real happiness.

INCOME.

	£	s.	d.
Half Balance from Joint Fund of Tailors and Cabinet Makers ...	6	5	8¼
Collections in the Streets ...	47	18	4¾
Do. in West London Shops, by West London District, A.S.T. ...	44	3	10
Do. by the Machinists' Society ...	0	10	0
Do. do. Pressers' Society ...	0	10	0
Executive Council Amalgamated Society of Tailors ...	25	0	0
Collection by Mantel Makers' Co-operative Society ...	0	7	2
Per Mr. Rabin, List No. 9 ...	0	5	6
,, L. Diemshitz ,, 5 ...	0	8	5
,, W. Wess ,, 8, 14, 20, 43 & 48 ...	3	0	10
,, W. Rosenthal ,, 12 ...	0	4	0
,, Stargatt ,, 52 ...	1	14	6
,, Connor, Jun. ,, 2 ...	0	2	6
,, Cohen ,, 44 ...	0	2	0
,, Moses Frankel ,, 24 & 25 ...	1	0	0
,, S. Goldberg ,, 2 ...	0	2	3
,, Goldstein ...	0	3	0
,, Goldberg ...	0	4	3
Per "Jewish Standard" ...	4	13	6
Per Mr. Fisher ...	0	9	1
Employès of Messrs. Hunter, Wiltshire & Co. Cigar Manufacturers ...	0	11	0
Do. of Mr. Van Oestren, Cigar Manufacturer ...	0	8	4
Do. of Mr. Charles Baker ...	0	12	6
Amalgamated Society of Boot and Shoe Makers ...	10	0	0
Cigar Makers Provident Society ...	2	0	0
London Society of Compositors ...	10	0	0
Cigar Makers Mutual Association ...	5	0	0
Dock Labourers Strike Committee ...	100	0	0
Mr. Jacob Hershman ...	1	0	0
City Clothing Manufacturer ...	10	0	0
Mr. S. Montagu, M.P. ...	30	10	0
Mr. Goodman ...	1	1	0
Mr. John Piggott ...	1	1	0
Anonymous Friend, per Mr. Montagu, M.P. ...	5	0	0
Lord Rothschild ...	73	0	0
Mr. N. L. Cohen, per Mr. Montagu, M.P. ...	5	5	0
Per "Star" Office, from Finsbury R.F., and others ...	4	3	0
Manchester International Working Men's Club, per "Worker's Friend" ...	1	18	8
Total ...	£398	15	5

EXPENDITURE.

	£	s.	d.
ORGANISING.			
Printing ...	10	2	0
Postage and Telegrams ...	1	17	3
Stationery ...	0	16	7
Banners ...	1	4	0
Bands ...	29	0	0
Vans for Demonstrations ...	2	3	0
Caretakers and Porters of Meeting Places ...	2	4	6
Fares of Deputations ...	2	4	11
Bill Posting ...	0	17	9
Pickets ...	1	14	4
Collection Box and Banner Bearers ...	2	10	2
RELIEF.			
In Cash ...	54	17	6
In Tickets ...	212	9	6
In Cash taken home to sick cases ...	1	19	0
Bread and Cheese to Strikers at Demonstrations ...	3	18	7
Refreshment to Box and Banner Bearers ...	2	10	10½
DEFENCE.			
Towards legal expenses of Asher Cohen ...	3	0	0
Police Court Expenses to Lewis Winter ...	0	4	6
RENT AND DAMAGES.			
Proprietor "White Hart" ...	5	0	0
GENERAL.			
Committeemen and Chairman ...	39	2	6
Treasurer for time lost and travelling ...	0	13	2
Secretary's Salary ...	6	10	0
Sundry Expenses, (including Collecting Boxes) ...	6	18	1½
Granted to Secretary in recognition of good services rendered ...	5	0	0
Audit Expenses ...	0	15	0
	397	13	3
* Balance in hand ...	1	2	2
	£398	15	5

* This Balance, or whatever may come in, will be handed over to the Silvertown Strike Fund, in accordance with the decision of the Committee.

Audited and found correct,

H. COOMBE, West End Branch, Amalgamated Society of Tailors.

J. T. JEWELL, Dragon Branch, Amalgamated Society of Tailors.

H. J. CLARKE, Dock, Wharf, Riverside & General Labourers' Union.

W. PARISH, Treasurer.

WILLIAM WESS, Secretary,

October 22nd, 1889. 40, Berner Street, Commercial Road, London, E.

Presented to Dr V. D. Lipman by A.R. Rollin

Balance Sheet of the Great Strike of East London Tailors, 1889. (Presented to the author by A.R. Rollin.)

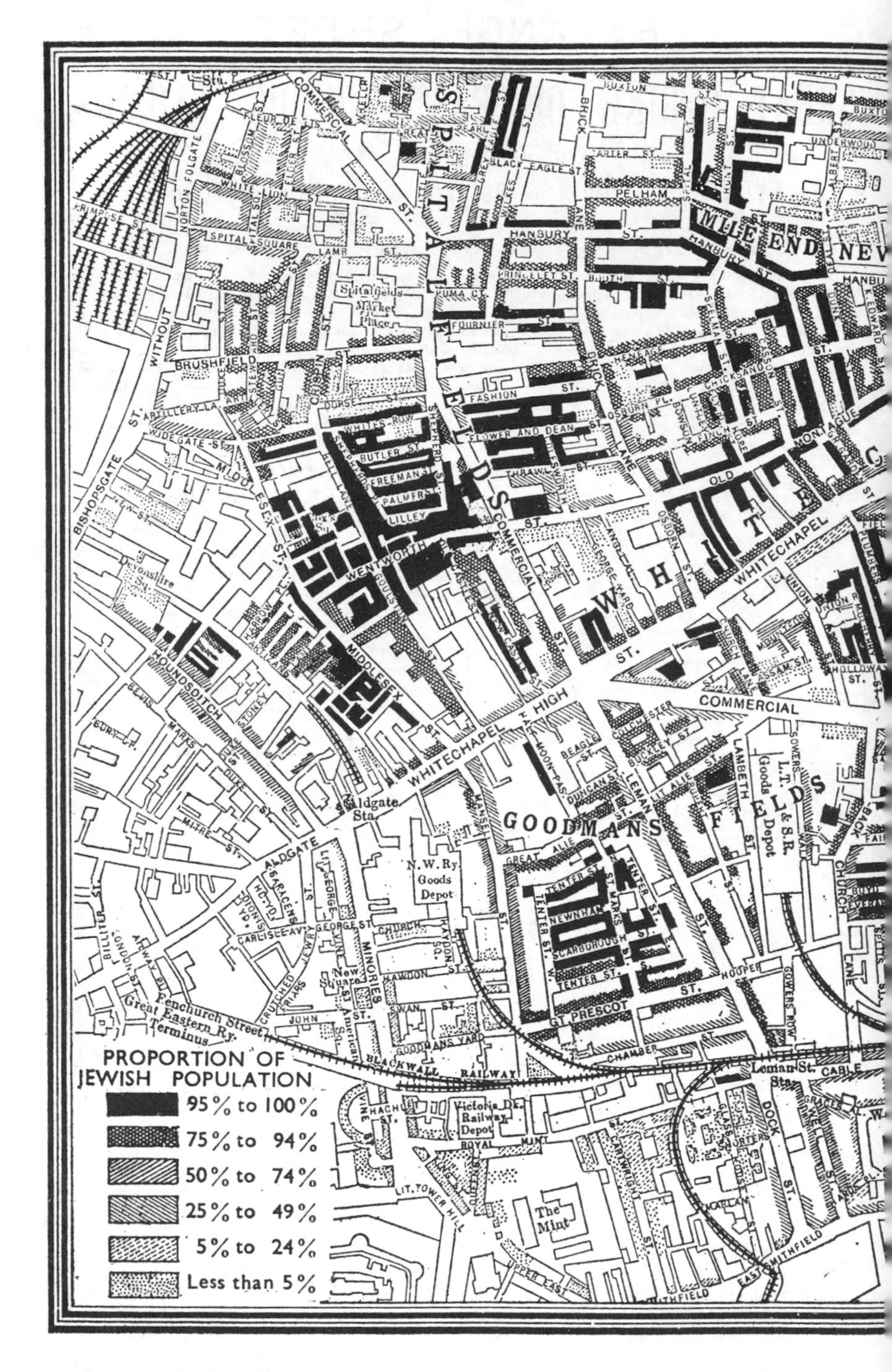

The East End of London *c.* 1900 showing Jewish residents in proportion to the total population. (Adapted from Russell and Lewis, *The Jew in London.*)

Jews Burial Ground
MILE END ROAD
WHITECHAPEL ROAD
Whitechapel Sta.
London Hospital
MILE END
OXFORD ST.
NEWARK ST.
RUTLAND ST.
CLARK ST.
WALDEN ST.
VARDEN ST.
NELSON ST.
COMMERCIAL ROAD EAST
Bedford Square
Sidney Square
Arbour Square
JUBILEE ST.
EXMOUTH ST.
JAMAICA ST.
DEMPSEY ST.
CHARLES ST.
SMITH ST.
REDMAN'S ROAD
BLAKESLEY ST.
TARLING ST.
SHERIDAN ST.
SPENCER ST.
MARTHA ST.
BLACKWALL RAILWAY
Shadwell Sta.
CABLE ST.
CANNON ST. ROAD
ST. GEORGES IN THE EAST
SHADWELL
HIGH ST.
CARRIAGE WAY
ELM ROW
LOVE LANE
NEW GRAVEL LANE

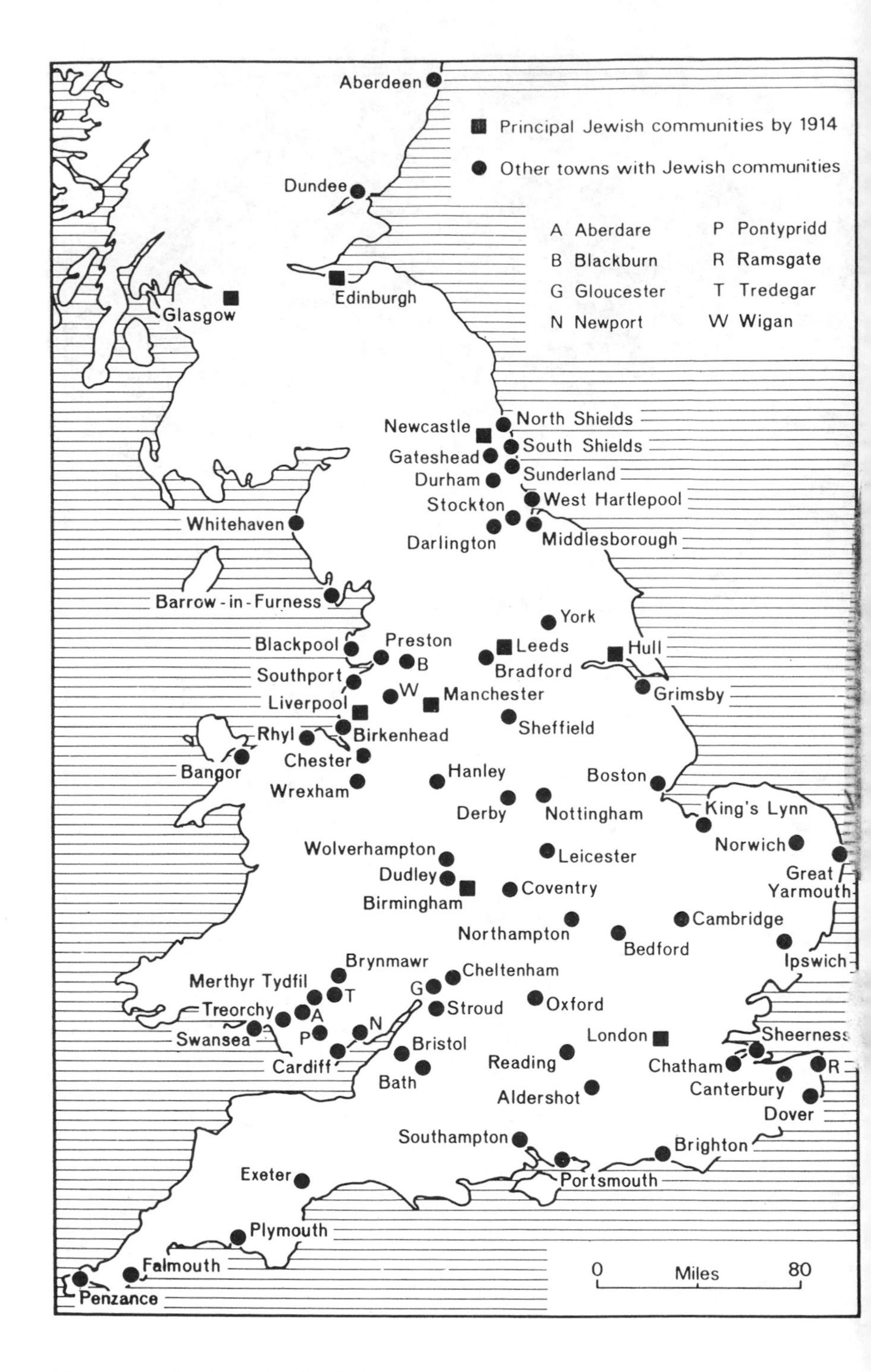

Map of Anglo-Jewry in the 19th century

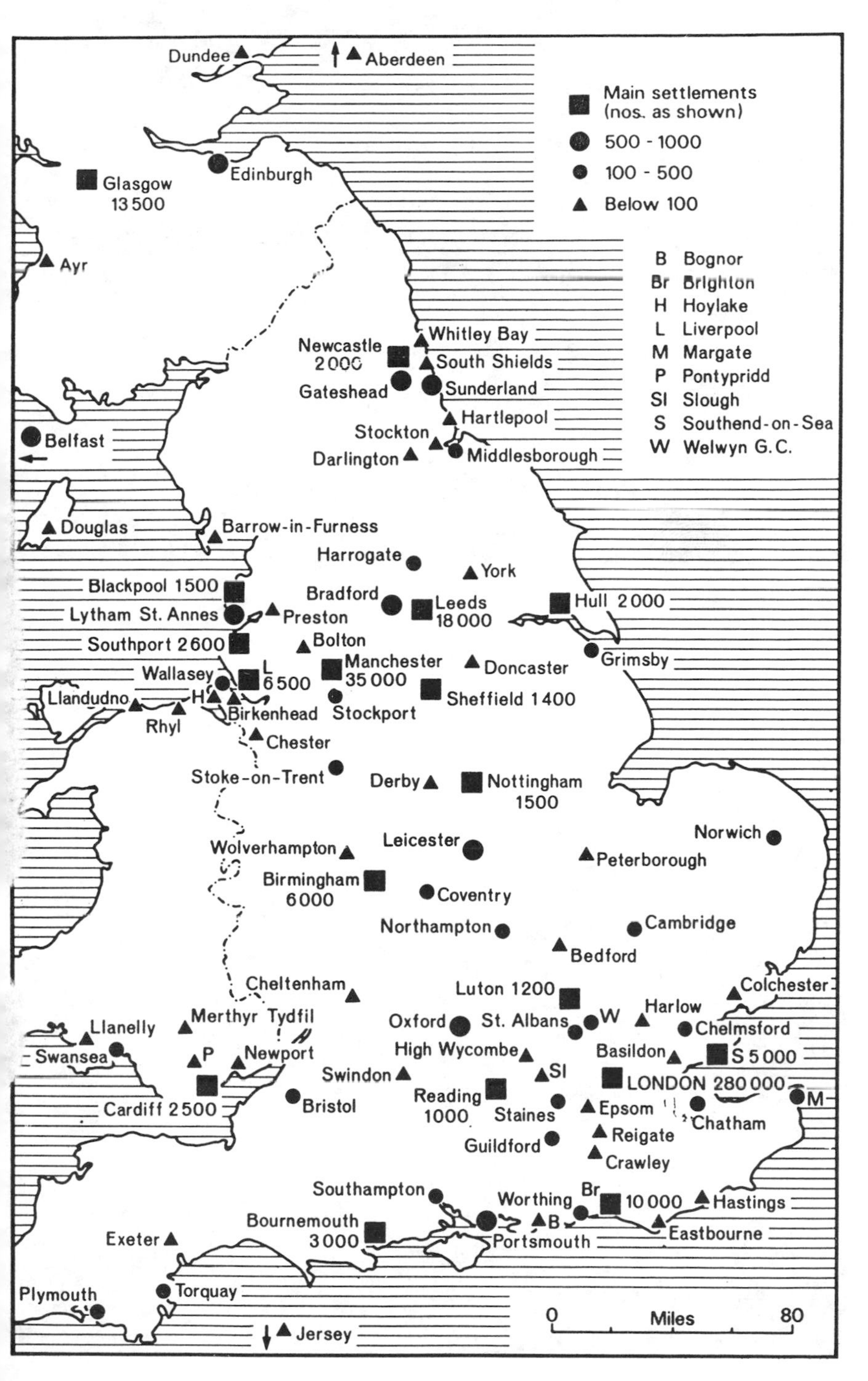

Map of Anglo-Jewry, 1978

Girls at Myrdle Street School, 1908 (Springboard)

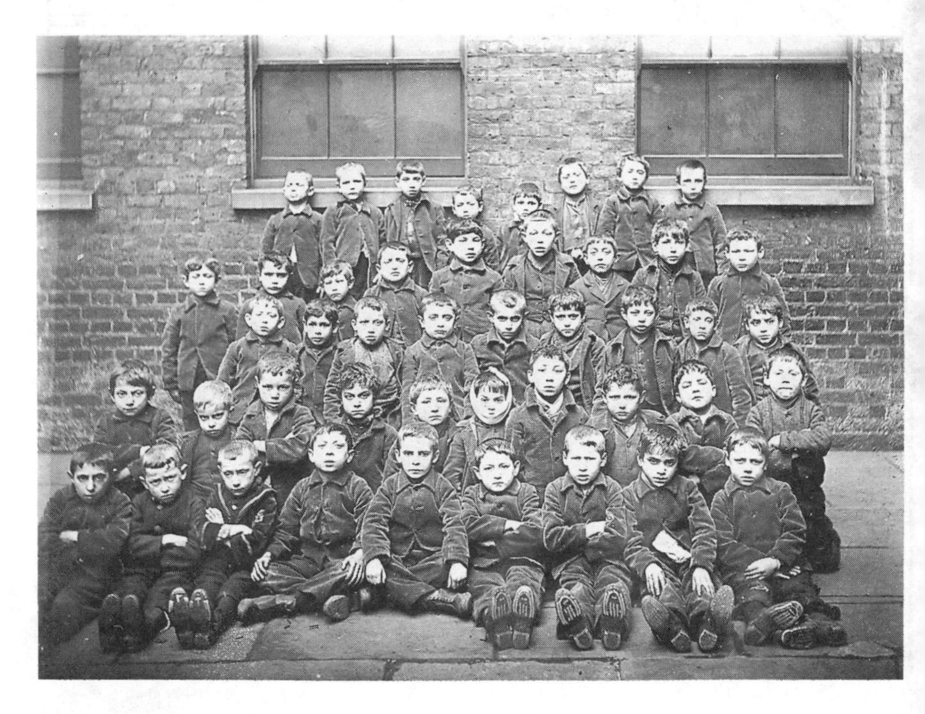

Boys at the Jewish Free School, pre-1914 (Springboard)

Jewish Legion 'Fixed Bayonet' March-past, East End
(Jabotinsky Institute)

Jewish Lads' Brigade/Territorials (Springboard)

The Jews' Temporary Shelter, Leman Street, London E.1., 1893

A Jewish Court (Beth Din), including the Chief Rabbi and (far left) Revd N. Lipman, grandfather of the author

Chapter 8

External Challenges 1918–39

Between the two world wars, the communal leadership of British Jewry had to meet three challenges, all arising from factors outside the community. The first was how to react to the development of Zionism and the Jewish national home, in the special circumstances of the assumption by the British government of responsibility for Palestine under the League of Nations mandate. The development of British policy towards Palestine was bound to produce problems. In the first instance, reaction to these was a matter for the Zionist leadership: this, while based in London and including leading members, like *Weizmann, who were British citizens, was quite separate from the Anglo-Jewish leadership. But the latter could not be isolated from the relationship between the Zionist organization and the British government, and there were consequent tensions within the community on what the attitude should be towards government policy. Second, there was a continuation of some of the anti-Jewish pronouncements that had been seen in the aftermath of the First World War. This was transformed by the rise of Fascism in Europe, especially after the coming to power of the Nazis in Germany in 1933. The growth of Fascism in Britain after 1933 presented the community with the problem of finding the right reaction to a new kind of problem. Previously, British Jews had encountered discrimination or experiences of anti-Semitism but not a political party, an essential part of whose policy was action against Jews as such, not merely against 'aliens'.

Third, with the influx of refugees from Central Europe between 1933 and 1939, the community had to find the appropriate way of influencing government policy not only on the admission of refugees, while doing what they could to help the refugees settle, but also on the government's relationship with the Nazi and Fascist powers in Europe. This, like Palestine, gave Jews as citizens a direct interest in government policy but there was no unanimity on whether this should be pursued as an interest different from that of other citizens.

On all these issues, there was divergence within the community. On the one hand, the communal leadership adopted what it regarded as a moderate line, a low public profile, arguing it was better to persuade government through the means it claimed to have of influence behind the scenes. On the other hand were radicals who advocated a more aggressive and public stance. To some extent, on each of these three areas, the moderates and radicals tended to be the same individuals. Throughout the period up to the outbreak of war in 1939 the advocates of the traditional policies remained in control of most, if not all, of the communal institutions.[1]

Zionism and Palestine

On 24 April 1920 the Supreme Council of the Peace Conference at San Remo resolved that the Balfour Declaration should be incorporated in the Treaty of Peace with Turkey and that the Mandate for Palestine should be allotted to Great Britain. In consequence the British government appointed *Herbert Samuel to be the first high commissioner of Palestine, which he reached on 1 July 1920. In the meanwhile, the Zionist movement decided to locate its central office in London; Dr Chaim Weizmann was elected president of the World Zionist Organization at a conference in London in July 1920 and the political department was put under his direct control.[2]

The first major development in the Mandate came in 1922. In the previous year Palestine east of the Jordan had been invaded by Abdulla, who was subsequently recognized as emir by Winston Churchill, then Colonial Secretary responsible for Palestine. In 1922, after visiting Palestine, Churchill issued a White Paper which clarified the Balfour Declaration as meaning not that 'Palestine as a whole should be converted into a Jewish national home but that such a home should be founded in Palestine', which for this purpose excluded Transjordan. It also included the principle of adapting the scope of Jewish immigration to the 'absorptive capacity' of the country. This doctrine was interpreted flexibly in the 1920s and, while immigration was temporarily stopped from time to time, after local disturbances, it continued. The Arabs rejected the Churchill White Paper; the World Zionist Executive reluctantly accepted it.

During the 1920s, the response to government policy on Palestine was mainly a matter for the World Zionist Organization, centred in London. The attitude of the Board of Deputies as the representative body of British Jewry was characterized by the Zionist historian, Dr S. Levenberg, in the 1920s as 'acting really as a non-Zionist body . . . it gave general support to the Mandate but was not deeply involved in furthering the advance of the Jewish national home'.[3]

The Board was composed then almost entirely of representatives of synagogues; those elected might, as individuals, be Zionists but they did not stand for election as such. Representatives were normally elected on personal grounds, although many of the smaller synagogues or congregations in the provinces were represented by people without other connections with their 'constituency'.

After the issue of the Balfour Declaration, the anti-Zionist elements, while still opposing the concept of a Jewish state and nationality which would include all Jews, sought a *modus vivendi* with the Zionists. This trend continued in the 1920s and up to the mid-1930s, transforming anti-Zionists into non-Zionists.[4] There were three factors which facilitated this process. First, the issue between the Zionists and the others was that of a Jewish nationality, if it included Jews in Diaspora communities like Britain as members of that single nationality, rather than as members of their own current nationality. But the issue need not arise, or could be postponed *sine die*, if the Jewish national home, which the Balfour Declaration postulated *in* Palestine, did not imply a separate Jewish state or nationality. Second, the anti- or non-Zionists conceived of the developing Jewish settlement in Palestine as Palestinian: this was essential to exclude the idea of a *Jewish* state. Hence they opposed the granting of privileges to Jews as such in Palestine. But this was not a live issue between Zionists and the anti- or non-Zionists in the 1920s and early 1930s because all Palestinian subjects were to be equal before the law administered by the British mandatory government. Third, since the development of a Jewish national home in Palestine was an obligation accepted – until the 1939 White Paper – by the British government, it was incumbent on British Jews as patriotic British citizens to help in this work and contribute to the economic development of the country; and, since what they would be building was Palestine, not Israel, a Palestinian state was an acceptable objective for them. Even if this might eventually have a Jewish majority, such a state was acceptable provided it was limited to Palestine and did not seek to include Diaspora Jews in its nationality.[5] As *Sir Robert Waley Cohen put it in 1923, British Jews had 'a double obligation to help in the restoration of Palestine (1) as Jews whom England is helping (2) as Englishmen who are helping the Jews'.[6]

The Churchill White Paper of 1922 had specifically rejected the idea that Palestine should become 'as Jewish as England is English' and denied that the development of the Jewish national home meant 'the imposition of a Jewish nationality upon the inhabitants of Palestine' and this again made it easier for those previously regarded as anti-Zionists to co-operate in the upbuilding of Palestine. The League of British Jews, founded to oppose Zionism after the issue of the Balfour Declaration, regarded the Churchill White Paper as a vindication that they had been right all along about the meaning of a national home and in opposing the idea of a Jewish nationality embracing all Jews.[7]

A way was available to give institutional expression to this newly found unity in the Anglo-Jewish community. The Palestine Mandate, as confirmed by the League of Nations in 1922, provided in Article 7 for the establishment of a 'Jewish Agency for the purposes of advising and co-operating with the Administration of Palestine' in promoting Jewish immigration, land settlement and acquisition by Jews of Palestine citizenship. Initially, the Zionist Organization was recognized as the agency but the aim was to establish a separate Jewish Agency, in which the non-Zionists could co-operate, especially in providing finance, with the Zionist Organization. This aim was reinforced by the economic difficulties of Palestine, which began in spring 1926, produced serious unemployment and a net outflow of Jews in 1927 and 1928, and lasted into 1929 – a major setback for Zionism.[8] The financial aid of non-Zionists was urgently needed, both to respond to appeals and loans, and for direct investment. In 1927 Weizmann offered to expand the Agency to include the non-Zionists and, although there were difficulties in the negotiations on the scale of representation, the Agency was enlarged in August 1929. Britain, with a national Jewish representative body in place in the Board of Deputies, was the country in which non-Zionist participation could most readily be organized. Some leading non-Zionists had already shown willingness to co-operate. Sir Robert Waley Cohen was ideologically a non-Zionist and opponent of the concept of Jewish nationality. But as effective second-in-command of the giant Shell-Royal Dutch Petroleum group and a dominant figure in Jewish communal life, particularly in the United Synagogue, his co-operation would be very valuable. In 1918 and 1919 he had sought to achieve some sort of compromise between Zionists and non-Zionists and refused therefore a leading role in the League of British Jews. Weizmann defined Waley Cohen's position, in a letter to him of 19 December 1920 as 'a supporter of, let me say, Palestinian Zionism', and he invited Waley Cohen first to be a member of the Zionist executive, with chairmanship of a financial committee, and then to be one of three trustees of the Zionist Organization.[9] In the event, Waley Cohen did not join the Zionist Organization for reasons unconnected with ideology but he involved himself in the Economic Board for Palestine, founded in 1921, and created the Palestine Corporation, which developed a variety of enterprises, from Nesher Cement to the King David Hotel.[10] Other very prominent Jews became associated with Palestine's economic development; for instance, *Rufus Isaacs, Marquess of Reading, after his viceroyalty of India, became in 1926 chairman of the Palestine Electric Corporation; in 1927, even *Sir Philip Magnus, a founder of the League of British Jews, announced a contribution to the Jewish National Fund's Balfour Forest in Palestine.[11] In these circumstances it was not surprising that in April 1929 the president of the Board of Deputies, *Mr (later Sir) Osmond d'Avigdor-Goldsmid convened a representative communal conference of over 200 delegates from every major Jewish organization in Britain. D'Avigdor-Goldsmid had also been a founder of the League of British Jews but he declared at the conference: 'As an Englishman I feel that so long as the British

Government holds the Mandate for Palestine, it is our bounden duty to assist in the development of the country'. The conference resolved that the Board should appoint the non-Zionist members from Britain of the Agency and itself should form a Palestine Committee.[12]

The new partnership of the Zionists and non-Zionists in the Agency was soon to be tested by the outbreak of Arab violence in August 1929 and the reaction of the British government to it – the Passfield White Paper. In the riots 133 Jews were killed and 116 Arabs – most of the latter by the police in trying to repress the Arab disturbances. A commission under Sir Walter Shaw (a retired colonial chief justice) was sent to report on the causes of the riots. While the riots followed a dispute over the erection of a partition between men and women at the Western Wall in Jerusalem (and therefore over the Jews' right to pray there), the commission found that the real cause was Arab hostility to the Jews 'consequent upon the disappointment of their political and national aspirations and fears for their economic future'. Going beyond their terms of reference, in March 1930 the commission recommended restriction of Jewish immigration and land purchase. Harry (later Lord) Snell, a Labour MP, disagreed with his colleagues on the commission in criticizing both the government and the Arabs.

A follow-up technical report by Sir John Hope Simpson, an Indian Civil Service expert on land settlement, concluded in August 1930 that, given current methods of Arab cultivation, there was 'no margin of land available for agricultural settlement by the immigrants'. On the basis of these two reports, in October 1930 the Labour Colonial Secretary, Lord Passfield (Sidney Webb), issued a White Paper which put on the same level the British government's commitments to Jews and Arabs, stating that the former related only to Palestine Jews,' that Jewish immigration must depend on the absorptive capacity of the Arab majority and that accordingly there was no scope for mass Jewish immigration.[13]

The bitter Jewish reactions to the White Paper included the resignation of Weizmann as president of the Jewish Agency; and there were similar resignations by leading non-Zionists, including *the first Lord Melchett from the joint chairmanship of the Agency Council. Immediately after the issue of the White Paper there was a by-election in Whitechapel, previously a Labour-held seat, and the main contestants were James Hall (the future Viscount Hall) for Labour and *Barnett Janner, a Zionist and at that time a Liberal. The Liberals sought to exploit the unpopularity of the White Paper in a constituency where Jews were estimated to be a third of the voters (12,000 out of 37,000), and the *Jewish Chronicle*, under its strongly Zionist editor, *L.J. Greenberg, called for Jews to vote for Janner against Labour. The young Zionists in east London campaigned for Janner; the English Zionist Federation maintained neutrality as a body although leading members also campaigned for him. The Zionist Labour Party, Poale Zion, hesitated. The Palestine Labour Party's representative in London, Dov Hos, was in close touch with Ernest Bevin, leader of the Transport and

General Workers' Union, and then regarded as a friend of Zionism. Other Palestine Labour leaders then in London, like Dov Hos, urged support for the Labour candidate, especially as he promised, if elected, to fight the White Paper. Poale Zion supported Hall, who won but with a majority reduced from 9,180 to 1,099.[14]

Intervention with government leaders, including a visit by *Professor Harold Laski, not previously identified with Zionism, to the Prime Minister, Ramsay MacDonald, led to reconsideration of the White Paper. A Cabinet committee, chaired by the Foreign Secretary, Arthur Henderson (Passfield effectively being excluded), which consulted Zionist representatives, recommended revision of the White Paper. On 13 February 1931, the Prime Minister issued a letter revoking the White Paper and restoring the policy set out in the Churchill White Paper of 1922.[15]

In the years following the 1929–30 Passfield White Paper crisis, partnership in Anglo-Jewry between Zionists and anti- or non-Zionists increasingly came under strain, and collapsed before 1939. The original founders of the partnership were no longer in place. Weizmann, because of his pragmatic, gradualist approach, was not re-elected president of the World Zionist Organization, and was out of office until 1935; leading non-Zionists in the Agency, such as the American Louis Marshall or the first Lord Melchett, died.[16] The non-Zionists, other than in Britain, had difficulty in organizing themselves and in filling their places in the Agency. The question of parity on the Agency between Zionists and non-Zionists became an issue, with the rising Ben-Gurion opposed to parity. In Britain, however, Zionists and non-Zionists initially continued to work together and the Board of Deputies provided a unique structure for representing the non-Zionists, which other Jewish communities did not have. There was however a change in the leadership of the Board in January 1933 when d'Avigdor-Goldsmid was succeeded by *Neville Laski.

Laski, at that time a barrister of 42, was the son of the Manchester Jewish communal leader, Nathan Laski (1863–1941, born in Eastern Europe but brought up in Britain), and the son-in-law of the Zionist rabbi, *Moses Gaster, Haham of the Spanish and Portuguese Jews' community. At first Neville Laski was thought to be favourable to Zionists, attending the 1933 World Zionist conference. As a non-Zionist, he was elected vice-chairman in 1933 (chairman, 1934) of the Administrative Committee of the Jewish Agency; he was invited, but refused, to take office in the Zionist Federation of Great Britain. Once in office at the Board as president, Laski identified himself with the non-Zionists and was a hardliner on opposition to any suggestion of Jewish nationality or state.[17]

Laski soon found himself in conflict with Ben-Gurion on the issue of parity for non-Zionists on the Agency and in 1936 Laski blocked the proposal that the Board of Deputies should affiliate to the recently founded World Jewish Congress, not only because its inspiration was Zionist but because it implied that all Diaspora Jews were members of a single Jewish nation. Laski urged that the Jews in each country had their own outlook and should continue to make representations for themselves to their own governments. The Congress was however joined by other organizations like the Federation of Synagogues, friendly societies and trade union groups; and this provided another dichotomy of attitudes.[18]

In the 1920s the numbers and intensity of Zionist membership had declined.[19] But this trend was reversed: the number of societies affiliated to the English Zionist Federation, which had been over 200 at the beginning of the 1920s and had fallen to 144, increased to 250 by 1939. Membership of the World Zionist Organization, and the right to vote at its elections, was marked by the purchase of a *shekel* (which then cost 2 shillings, or 10p.); the number of *shekalim* sold increased from 9,291 in 1928–9 to 23,513 in 1938–9, in a total population then estimated at 350,000.[20] Further, the figures of societies affiliated to the Zionist Federation did not represent the whole picture, because of the change in the character of the Federation. Originally, as the English Zionist Federation, it had sought to include all Zionists in the Anglo-Jewish community. But, with the development of the party system in Zionism, the Federation (which was renamed the Zionist Federation of Great Britain in 1930) increasingly came to represent the General Zionist party and those not identified with any particular political group. The other parties included the Poalei Zion (Workers of Zion, who combined Zionism with socialism), who had about 100 members before 1914 and 1,000 between the wars;[21] the Religious Zionists or Mizrachi, founded in 1918; and the Revisionists, the followers of Vladimir Jabotinsky, who opposed the leadership of Weizmann and demanded a political solution, with a Jewish majority on both sides of the Jordan. The Revisionists mainly seceded from the Zionist Organization in 1932 to form the New Zionist Organization, those remaining within the Zionist Organization forming the Jewish State Party. Some idea of the relative strengths of the Zionist factions within Anglo-Jewry can perhaps be gained from the representation at the 1939 World Zionist Congress, which reflected the numbers of *shekalim* brought by each section – eight representatives for the Zionist Federation, three Poalei Zion, three Mizrachi, one Jewish State Party – the New Zionists were not, of course, included.[22]

The Zionist Federation had, from the time an Arab delegation came to London in 1921–2 to campaign against the Mandate, developed an efficient technique for briefing and organizing their local membership to lobby members of parliament (not least ministers who were lobbied by their constituents). This gave the Zionist Federation a political role, while reserving the major policy negotiations to the World Zionist Organization. This technique was deployed by the Federation in subsequent crises such as that of 1929–30 over the Passfield White Paper. Even so, the Federation was not primarily an ideologically oriented body on the lines of continental Zionist organizations but it had a social base in the religious and cultural life of the Anglo-Jewish community, especially in the suburban communities which were developing during the 1930s. Fund-raising was a primary objective, and this gave those capable of giving large sums, or of persuading others to do so, a very influential role in the organization.[23]

But what the senior organization may have lacked in ideological commitment was compensated for by the developing youth movements associated with Zionism; by the 1930s their active, indeed in some cases militant, leaders (who included Aubrey Eban, the future Israeli foreign minister) influenced the policies of the Federation. The Association of Young Zionist Societies, a mainly social and educational movement, merged in 1935 with the University students' University Zionist Council to form the Federation of Zionist Youth, with 2,500 members and an activist policy. The *Habonim* ('builders') youth movement began in 1929 as a Jewish scouting movement (for 10 to 18-year-olds) and had 4,000 members in 1939; it acted as a 'feeder' to the Federation of Zionist Youth; although the initial group of Habonim was formed in 1929 in a *heder* (religious classroom), they developed into a secularized and socialist movement.[24] The Habonim and the arrival of young people from Central Europe in and after 1933, who had come from the European Zionist movements with their positive attitude towards personal settlement and agricultural work in Palestine, resulted in a small but qualitatively important British contribution to the *Halutz*, or pioneer movement, for agricultural settlement in Palestine. Training farms, like that at Harrietsham in Kent or that loaned by the Balfour family at Whittingehame in Scotland, sent some hundreds of young people as agricultural settlers to Palestine between 1933 and 1939.[25] With this enhancement of Zionist feeling and effort in the 1930s, it is not surprising that steps should be taken to organize Zionists as a voting bloc in the communal institutions, notably the Board of Deputies. This had been suggested in 1918 by Harry Sacher in a letter to *Simon Marks, suggesting the organization of 'all Zionist forces on the Board of Deputies .... We must form a Zionist party with Whips and endeavour to fill every vacancy with Zionists'.[26] But this was not followed up and there was no Zionist organization of deputies until the 1930s.[27] Then the initiative was taken by the general secretary of the Zionist Federation, *Lavy Bakstansky. In 1934 he became a member of the Board (in the usual way, as representative of a small synagogue, although personally not a very religiously observant Jew). He became very active on the Board, especially on the Palestine Committee, and worked steadily to build up a committed Zionist party able to elect its own nominees to the Board's key positions.

The scene was thus set for a confrontation between the Zionists and the others. What brought matters to a head was the reappearance of the issue of a Jewish state in the report of the Peel Royal Commission in 1937, which recommended the partition of Palestine. After the coming to power of the Nazis in 1933, Jewish numbers in Palestine had increased to some 400,000 by 1936, and the slump of the late 1920s was reversed by the influx of population. But the Arab opposition grew, leading to a three-year period of disorder, beginning with riots in Jaffa in April 1936, a six-week strike the same year, and developed into a campaign of attacks by armed bands on Jews and on British soldiers and police, which major use of the British army and aircraft was needed to suppress. A Royal Commission under Lord Peel, sent out to enquire and report on the problem, recommended the partition of Palestine into two states, Jewish and Arab, with a Jerusalem–Jaffa corridor remaining under British rule, with responsibility for the Holy Places.[29] The commission's report was accompanied by a statement of policy of the British government that they were 'in general agreement with the arguments and conclusions of the Commission' and would take the necessary steps to implement the scheme of partition.[30] On 21 July 1937 the House of Commons, after debate, resolved to bring the proposals before the League of Nations to enable the government, 'after adequate enquiry, to present to Parliament a definite scheme'.

The Zionists were acutely divided in their response to the proposals. Weizmann, Ben-Gurion, the General Zionists (the party with whom the Zionist Federation of Great Britain was associated) and the Poale Zion or Labour Zionists were in favour, because partition gave the prospect of a Jewish state and therefore an assured haven for Jews from Germany or from Eastern Europe, who were increasingly finding life intolerable. The partition proposals were opposed by other Zionist groups for different reasons: the veteran Zionist leader Menahem Ussishkin (1869–1941), president of the Zionist Congress, and the Revisionists because partition denied Jews the whole of the historic land on both sides of the Jordan; the Mizrachi, or religious Zionists, because it truncated the Biblical land even west of the Jordan and by excluding Jerusalem meant Zionism without Zion; the Hashomer Hatzair or left-wing Labour Zionists because it negated their aim of a bi-national state with the Arabs; and it was similarly opposed by others (such as Norman Bentwich) who sought an agreement with the Arabs, even at the expense of a Jewish state. The Zionist Congress which met in Geneva in mid-August 1937 eventually voted in favour of a resolution rejecting the partition proposals as formulated in the Peel Report but empowering the executive to negotiate with the British government on the precise terms for a Jewish state.[31]

Opinion within British Jewry was also divided. Even within the Zionist Federation, not all followed the Weizmann line. The editor of the *Jewish Chronicle,* Ivan Greenberg, (son of L.J. Greenberg), who tended to Revisionism, campaigned against the proposals and Ussishkin came to London to urge opposition to partition. Outside the Zionist movement, Neville Laski, as president of the Board of Deputies, Sir Robert Waley Cohen (now a vice-president of the Board) and other non-Zionists met on 19 July 1937 to plan opposition to partition and to try to persuade Weizmann against the proposals. They even made direct representations to the Colonial Office against the establishment of a Jewish state.[32]

The issue eventually came before the Board of Deputies in January 1938 on a motion submitted by the Board's Palestine committee (on which there was a Zionist majority) welcoming 'a solution for the future of Palestine which will provide for the establishment of a Jewish Dominion within the British Commonwealth of Nations'. The inclusion of a reference to the Jewish state becoming a British dominion was intended to conciliate the non-Zionists who prided themselves on their status as patriotic Britons and as a means of reconciling a Jewish and a British nationality. The leading non-Zionists on the board – Laski, Waley Cohen, Sir Osmond d'Avigdor-Goldsmid, and *Lionel (later Lord) Cohen – resisted the idea of a Jewish state on the same grounds as their predecessors in 1917: denial of the existence of a Jewish nationality and prejudice to the position of Jews in the Diaspora as citizens of their own countries; and they were not deflected by the reference to a British dominion. However, the resolution was passed by an overwhelming majority, with only 7 votes against. This showed a split between the majority of the board and those who considered themselves its natural leadership. This situation had already emerged the previous year when the majority of the Board wished radically to alter the composition of the Joint Foreign Committee, which gave parity to the Board and to the numerically limited and self-appointed Anglo-Jewish Association; but their wishes were frustrated by Laski, as president of the Board.[33]

In the meanwhile the government, taking into account Arab opposition to the Peel proposals, had appointed a technical commission under Sir John Woodhead to report on the boundaries of the proposed partition. The commission reported in October 1938 that it was impossible to find acceptable boundaries for partition. After an abortive conference of Arabs and Jews, at St James's Palace at which the former refused to talk to the latter, Malcolm Macdonald, as Colonial Secretary, issued a White Paper in May 1939, in which completely abandoned the Peel proposals. The White Paper looked to independence in ten years for a Palestinian state with a two-thirds Arab majority, limiting Jewish immigration for the next five years to 75,000, and thereafter subject to Arab consent. Zionists and non-Zionists alike denounced the White Paper as a denial of the Mandate; speaking at the Board of Deputies, Sir Robert Waley Cohen described the White Paper as 'a proposal which is as unworthy of the history of the British Empire as it is false to its high place in the vanguard of civilization'.[34] But the hypothetical prospect of a Jewish state, evoked by the Peel proposals even though they came to nothing, had revealed the dichotomy in Anglo-Jewish opinion. The Board could no longer continue with a Zionist majority and a non-Zionist leadership. The real balance of opinion in the community was shown when at the end of 1939 Neville Laski unexpectedly resigned the presidency of the Board of Deputies for personal reasons. In spite of Laski's opposition and his attempts to secure a non-Zionist successor, the Zionist, *Professor Selig Brodetsky, was elected unopposed as president. The Zionist voting bloc, organized by Bakstansky, was dominant, yet this was not a new victory but a recognition of a transfer of power which had occurred perhaps two years before; and Brodetsky, the senior wrangler of 1908, had achieved leadership in the Anglo-Jewish community through his leadership in British Zionism.[35]

Anti-Semitism

Anti-Semitism was a second general issue to which the Anglo-Jewish community had to respond and on which there was division as to the correct response, especially after the rise of a British version of Fascism in the 1930s. The press coverage of Jews as part of a world Bolshevik conspiracy eased off after the exposure of the *Protocols* by Philip Graves in *The Times* in 1921. It was then more difficult for respectable opinion to profess belief in the charges: that was left to marginal groups.[36] To some extent, however, the unfavourable image of the Jews was continued in the press and political campaign against the cost to the taxpayer caused by the British government's commitment to the Jewish national home under the Palestine Mandate. This campaign, from 1921 to 1924, was taken up by several national newspapers – the *Morning Post, Daily Mail* and the *Daily* and *Sunday Express.* In addition to cost, the campaign represented Zionism as the forcing of an alien, Eastern European, régime on the native Arab inhabitants of Palestine, a line of argument begun when the Palestine Arab delegation came to London in 1921–2 to protest against the Balfour Declaration. Their propaganda enlisted a supporting group of members of parliament, mainly right-wing politicians, who raised the issue several times in debate in 1921 and 1922. A leading politician involved, whose anti-Zionist speeches included remarks with anti-Semitic implications, was Sir William Joynson-Hicks (later Lord Brentford), who as Home Secretary from 1924 to 1929 would have to deal with representations from the Board of Deputies about the treatment and naturalization of aliens.[37]

The Board of Deputies had approached the Home Office on the question of the deportation of Russian Jews, particularly those who had gone back to Russia as 'Conventionists' in 1917 and returned without consent to land. The power of deportation was exercised without appeal to a tribunal and the Board was unsuccessful in its attempt to get this changed. In 1924 it turned to the question of delays in naturalization which seemed to show – the Board did not know how well grounded its suspicions were – discrimination against Eastern European Jews tantamount to anti-Semitism. On 8 May 1924 a deputation from the Board was seen by Arthur Henderson, Home Secretary in the 1924 Labour government. Because of the suspension of naturalization during and after the First World War, there was a backlog by 1920 of some 7,500 applications; and, in dealing with these, the Russian and other Eastern European applications were put at the bottom of the pile, as being the largest and least assimilable category. The minimum statutory period of residence for naturalization was five years but, as Sir John Pedder, the responsible Assistant Secretary, minuted on 1 May 1924 in briefing the Home Secretary: 'The period of residence currently demanded of applicants from the disturbed parts of Europe, Russians, Poles, Lithuanians, etc., is now 15 years. This figure cannot be stated in public or to the Deputation'.[38] The period had in fact been reduced from twenty-two years in 1922 to fifteen years in 1924, when 55 per cent of the applicants were Russians. They probably formed about the same percentage of the successful applicants,[39] but a small proportion of the Jews wanting and eligible for naturalization. The Home Office policy at this period was to adhere to

> the practice which experience has thrown up of not entertaining applications from a certain class of aliens unless and until the applicants have resided in this country for a considerable period, far longer than the minimum statutory period of five years... Slavs, Jews and other races from central and Eastern Europe... do not want to be assimilated in the same way [as Latins, Teutons, Scandinavians] and do not identify themselves with this country.... Even the British-born Jews, for instance, always speak of themselves as a 'community' separate to a considerable degree and different from the British people.[40]

Against this policy, of which it could have been aware only in general terms, the Board of Deputies could make no headway, certainly not with Joynson-Hicks as Home Secretary. Even in 1930, when it deputed to his Labour successor, J.R. Clynes, it was unable to get the fee for naturalization reduced from £10, although administrative simplification was made to reduce the overall cost to applicants. Mr J.M. Ross, who has examined the files (HO 45/14736) found no trace of anti-Semitism as such but concluded that 'the effect of the policy followed throughout the 1920s with Ministerial approval was to delay or deny naturalization to a very large number of Jews of Russian or Polish origin'. By 1932, however, the backlog had been worked through and all cases were dealt with on receipt if the statutory minimum residence of five years was completed.[41]

In general, the Board of Deputies felt by 1926 that the tide of anti-Semitism of the immediate postwar years had abated. The Board's press committee, set up to deal with 'objectionable' references to Jews in the press, found it had practically nothing to deal with. 'It is rare now to find anything to which exception can be taken in newspapers and periodicals which a short time ago contained diatribes and innuendoes... there exists only one avowedly anti-Semitic journal, a weekly concerned with a so-called patriotic society, and there are many indications that its influence is negligible.[42] This was the Britons, an extreme nationalist group, focusing on anti-Semitism, which virtually ceased to exist as a political movement in 1925.[43] Another group, the Imperial Fascist League, was founded by

Arnold Leese in 1928.[44] Both of these marginal groups were far less worrying to British Jewry than the British Union of Fascists (BUF), founded by Sir Oswald Mosley in October 1932.

Even so, the alarm bells did not begin to ring all at once. Mosley maintained initially that his party was not anti-Semitic, although its anti-Jewish line was implicit in the references to 'alien' power. Open allegations against Jews appeared in the party organ, the *Blackshirt,* in November 1933. Anti-Semitism was toned down between January and July 1934 when the party was supported by Lord Rothermere and the *Daily Mail*: one of the reasons Lord Rothermere gave for breaking with Mosley in July 1934 was the latter's anti-Semitism. From 1934 on, anti-Semitism was an established part of BUF policy and propaganda – indeed from 1936, when it concentrated agitation on East London, with its still large Jewish population, perhaps the dominant part.[45]

From 1932 on there had been sporadic incidents of physical violence against Jews, vandalism against synagogues, bricks through Jewish windows, perhaps stimulated by discontent arising from the economic depression of 1929–31. From 1934 the Fascists sought to capitalize on this discontent and concentrated their campaign of anti-Jewish street meetings, Jew-baiting and hooliganism on the East End of London (including the adjacent area of Dalston at the junction with north London), and to a lesser extent in Leeds and Manchester.[46] Violence culminated in 1936, when left-wing groups joined to challenge the Fascists and thus came to be provoked into retaliation and confrontation with the police. A major incident took place at a BUF meeting of 12,000 at Olympia on 7 June 1934 when interrupters were thrown out by uniformed stewards, with what the police outside the hall recorded as horrific violence.[47] The organization by the BUF of uniformed columns, with bands and flags, copied from the Nazi storm-troopers and Italian *fascisti,* with the black shirt as a symbolic dress, produced a feeling of fear among the Jewish population, who knew what these phenomena meant in Nazi Germany. The organization of marches through Jewish and working-class areas intensified this fear and stimulated resistance from left-wing groups, who mobilized to resist. The culmination was the BUF march through east London on 4 October 1936 when a crowd estimated at 100,000 turned out to block the march; the march was diverted by the police, 5,000 of whom were on duty. When trying to remove barriers to clear the street, the police came into violent confrontation with the crowd in the so-called 'Battle of Cable Street'; a march by the BUF a week later led to window-smashing and violence in Mile End.[48]

The government had before them the example of uniformed political parties on the continent and, after the Olympia meeting in 1934, the then Commissioner of Metropolitan Police, Lord Trenchard, asked for legislation to prohibit 'political' armies or at least to ban uniforms for political purposes. No action was taken by the government on this suggestion but on 16 July 1936 the Home Secretary asked the commissioner to take decisive action to suppress the anti-Semitic activities of Fascist groups by concentrating police in Jewish areas, keeping notes of all speeches at public meetings and intervening in the event of provocation or violence; and the Commissioner repeated the instruction to all ranks of the Metropolitan Police.[49]

After Cable Street, legislation was introduced to ban the use of uniforms for political purposes and to enable marches and processions to be banned by order in specified areas for up to three months at a time. The Public Order Act came into force on 1 January 1937 and, on the recommendation of the Metropolitan Police Commissioner, now Sir Philip Game, all public processions through east London areas with a large Jewish population were banned, to prevent a BUF march from the East End to Trafalgar Square. This ban was renewed by successive extensions until 1940.[50]

The ban on uniforms and marches removed only one cause of anxiety and fear from the Jewish population – the ban on marches also inhibited counter-action by anti-Fascists on the left – but meetings, with associated insults and violence, continued. Meetings by the Fascists concentrated on the London County Council elections in March 1937 and the Borough Council Elections later that year. The Fascists put up candidates in Bethnal Green, Shoreditch and Limehouse. The choice of east London as an area for political campaigning by the BUF in the 1930s reflected not only its still large Jewish population but its social deprivation and potential discontent. There were also local pockets of working-class anti-Semitism which dated back to the tensions of the period of mass immigration, and this was influenced by local factors such as the character of the population in the core of Bethnal Green (described by Arthur Morrison in his novel *A Child of the Jago*, 1896).[51] The London County Council election campaign continued the feeling of tension among the local Jewish population but the results, in seats held and retained by Labour, were disappointing for the BUF, whose candidates polled 23 per cent in Bethnal Green, 19 per cent in Limehouse and 14 per cent in Shoreditch. None of these had a high proportion of Jewish voters and the results in these areas selected by the BUF after long campaigning suggested that their political chances on a wider scale were small.

The Jewish response to the first nationally based party for whom anti-Semitism was a main policy was at first hesitant and then divided. Initially, there was a readiness to accept that the BUF was not anti-Semitic in principle, not like the Nazis but like the Italian Fascists who at that time were not anti-Jewish and had Jewish members. The Board of Deputies in its 1932 annual report printed a reassurance from Mosley to Lord Melchett: 'It is quite in accord with my definition of the BUF's attitude on this question to say that anti-Semitism forms no part of the policy of this organization, and that anti-Semitic propaganda is forbidden.'[52] On 13 January 1933 the *Jewish Chronicle* wrote: 'Sir Oswald Mosley has definitely arrived at the safe haven of tolerance and common sense'. Later in 1933, the Board, while noting 'some evidence of anti-Semitic activities in Great Britain', stated they were 'conducted by agents under direct instructions from abroad' and proposed to counter them by the formation, with the B'nai B'rith of a Central Jewish Lecture Committee to supply speakers to address non-Jewish audiences on the true facts about Jews in Britain.[53] This belief that the British were a rational people open to conviction by argument, and therefore anti-Semitism could be fought by appeals to reason, was characteristic of the Board's approach to the problem in the following years.

There were two distinct kinds of reaction within the Jewish community. The first, which may be termed radical, was to regard the fight against anti-Semitism as part of a general fight against Fascism that must be conducted militantly, and to seek allies from any other like-minded group, which in practice generally meant the political left. The other was to adopt a non-political stance, to rely on the forces of law and order to deal with breaches of the peace, and to concentrate on propaganda against anti-Semitism rather than Fascism in general. But organized reaction from the Jewish community of either kind was not undertaken till 1936.

In that year, the Board organized its defence activities and the Jewish People's Council, a much more radical body, associated with the National Council for Civil Liberties, was formed. Within the Board the initiative was taken by Sir Robert Waley Cohen, who became a vice-president in February 1936. In May he suggested the formation of a Jewish Defence Committee but was opposed by the president, Neville Laski, on the ground that this would exaggerate the crisis and cause panic.[54] On 22 June 1936, Waley Cohen wrote to the *Jewish Chronicle,* acknowledging 'the growing and justified anxiety of the Jewish community as they see . . . the campaign of calumny and falsehood . . . whilst they see no sign of any steps being taken to give equally prominent expression to the truth by an exposure of the malignant falsehood of these attacks'; he begged Jews, however, to continue to refrain from violent reaction and assured them that Anglo-Jewry's leaders were 'fully alive to the poisonous seriousness of the attack and determined to concert measures . . . of defences'. Eventually in July 1936 the Board agreed to set up a Co-ordinating Committee of the Law and Parliamentary and the Press and Information Committees 'to have one body responsible to the community to unify and direct the work of anti-defamation'. This committee, which included the president of the Board (Neville Laski) and the two vice-presidents (Waley Cohen and Lionel Cohen), was renamed the Jewish Defence Committee in November 1938. Sidney Salomon, a barrister who had been chief sub-editor of the *Yorkshire Post* since 1925, was appointed secretary and press officer of the committee.[55] In the next year, 1937, a London Area Council was established with offices and staff in east London, which bore the brunt of the Fascist attack. It supervised all defence meetings in east London, which had previously been organized mainly by the Association of Jewish Friendly Societies[56] – the friendly societies were associated with the Board's rival, the Jewish People's Council. Finally, a secret defence fund, raised by Waley Cohen, paid 'a very substantial annual sum' to Neville Laski, the president of the board, to enable him to suspend his legal practice and devote himself whole-time to co-ordinate Jewish defence.[57]

Laski busied himself with meetings with the Home Secretary, Metropolitan Police Commissioner, leaders of the main political parties, the TUC and others, although with the reticence characteristic of the traditional Anglo-Jewish leadership, no detail of his activities was conveyed to the Board or the community. He seems however to have had access to leading politicians and officials and to have been trusted by them.[58] At any rate, F.A. (later Sir Frank) Newsam of the Home Office advised the Home Secretary in June 1937 not to see the National Council for Civil Liberties (NCCL) because, *inter alia,* 'it might give rise to serious embarrassment to the Board of Deputies of British Jews who have hitherto refused to lend countenance or support to the Jewish People's Council'[59] (which was associated with the NCCL). But efforts to influence the authorities were only part of what was a comprehensive public relations campaign by the Board. The second, and largest, aspect was the production or subsidization of literature – books pamphlets, leaflets – and the organization of 200 or more lectures a year to non-Jews about Jews and Judaism.[60] Contact was maintained with the press to answer criticism by letters to the editor, and supplying press and radio with material. A third aspect was the attempt to improve the conduct of Jews in trade and industry, to meet complaints about price-cutting or unreasonable conditions of employment: this was the origin of the Trades Advisory Council subsequently formed under the auspices of the Board.[61]

This attitude of self-criticism – that Jews must always be on their best behaviour or they would cause anti-Semitism – was characteristic of the Board's approach. It was well intentioned but it considered the symptoms rather than the underlying causes of anti-Semitism. Finally, the Board continued to appeal to the Jewish community to stay away from Fascist meetings and not to become involved in violence. But even *Basil Henriques, no left-wing radical, defined the dilemma in a letter to *The Times* on 10 October 1936: if Jews kept away from Fascist meetings, lies about them went unanswered; if they went, confrontation followed; and, anyway, it was un-English to leave it to others to defend you, if attacked.[62] The Board's policy, while moderate and rational, and law-abiding – in that it recommended that measures against Fascists be left to the authorities and the police – reflected 'the incredulity of both Gentiles and Jews that anti-Semitism really existed in Britain and was a real physical menace to the safety of British Jews in the streets where they lived'.[63] The Jews of east London may or may not have been aware of the declaration of the Home Secretary that anti-Semitic violence must be put down: they could not have known of the Police Commissioner's instructions. But they did see cases where police on the ground – either because they could not or would not act – allowed Fascist provocation and even violence to go unchecked, and Jews to be arrested for responding to provocation. Of 1,075 arrests in the East End between January 1936 and December 1938 for disturbances arising out of meetings and processions, 352 were of Fascists and 723 of anti-Fascists.[64] *Colonel Robert Henriques, hardly a biased critic of the police, wrote that he refused to believe such reports until he went down to the East End and personally saw the police standing by and watching savage attacks on elderly Jews by gangs of 'blackshirts'.[65] It was not surprising therefore that many East End Jews should seek a more active response and accept the initiative of left-wing organizations which aimed to fight Fascism as a whole and combat anti-Semitism as part of that struggle. The Jewish Labour Council (representing Jewish trade unionists, socialist societies and branches of the originally anarchist Workers' Circle) took the initiative,[66] in founding the Jewish People's Council against Fascism and Anti-Semitism (JPC). This was at a conference in 1936, called by the Jewish Labour Committee and attended by delegates representing eighty-seven Jewish organizations – synagogues, friendly societies, trade unions and Zionist bodies. Its declared objects were to 'unite the Jewish People in their own defence against Fascist attacks; to co-operate with anti-fascist organizations; to point out to the British people the dangers of anti-Semitism, since through Jew-baiting the Fascists intend to destroy the liberties of the people'.[67] It was characteristic of the JPC's radical approach, and the attraction it had for younger and more militant elements wanting to challenge the communal leadership, that it was joined by the Association of Young Zionists; this was in spite of the opposition of the executive of the Zionist Federation who objected to the communist influence on the JPC.[68]

The JPC evoked the immediate opposition of the Board of Deputies. This was not only for its policy of alliance with 'other anti-fascist organizations' and active combating of Fascism as political party rather than merely anti-Semitism. The Board regarded the JPC's approaches to government and local authorities to ban Fascist meetings as impermissible trespassing on its own preserves.[69]

Dr Colin Holmes has characterized the JPC as 'a Communist front organization'.[70] It certainly co-operated with left-wing bodies, like the NCCL, which was involved in monitoring police activities as well as fascist attacks, and with the Communist Party. The latter sought to build a united front of Jews and non-Jews against Fascism, and by taking the lead thus to attract support from Jews who might otherwise not have had any sympathy with them but felt deserted by their own communal leadership. The Communists and the JPC, supported by members of other parties and organizations, were responsible for the turnout of 100,000 against the BUF on 4 October 1936 which resulted in the 'Battle of Cable Street'. The

Communists saw the struggle as primarily a working-class rather than pro-Jewish one, and organized tenants against Jewish landlords accused of unfair practices in Stepney: thus deflecting a protest movement which might have turned to the Fascists.[71] The Communists' tactics of militant confrontation attracted a violent or hooligan element, whose conduct alienated the police and enabled the Fascists to claim they were being denied free speech.[72] But the role of the communists was a factor which may have helped them to return Phil Piratin as MP for Mile End from 1945 to 1950.[73]

In the latter part of 1938 the Board sought a *modus vivendi* with the JPC on the basis of a non-political platform. But the events of 1936 to 1938 revealed yet another cause of dichotomy of attitude between the official leadership of the community and an appreciable part of its constituency; by providing an immediate common enemy, the leadership gave an enhanced feeling of communal identity which ran counter to the process of acculturation and integration in the wider society. Because they were attacked as Jews, the Jews felt separate again. Not even the adjurations of Neville Laski that Jews' duties as British citizens must override their sentiments as Jews could convince most Anglo-Jews that they were not being singled out for attacks which other British citizens did not have to suffer.[74]

Nazism and the Refugees

The third external challenge to the community was the impact of Nazism and its two consequences: what British Jews could do to combat it and how to influence British opinion favourably towards the arrival of refugees from Central Europe. Indeed, the two were inter-linked because the communal leadership saw the ending of persecution in Central Europe as the effective solution of the refugee problem.

Hitler took office as chancellor on 30 January 1933; this was followed by an initial wave of terror; a national boycott of Jewish business, and the first anti-Jewish legislation, relating to Jews in the civil service, law, medicine and dentistry and in education, began in April 1933.[75] There followed arrests of political opponents and their internment in concentration camps. The Nuremberg Laws of 15 September 1935 defined Jews by origin, religion and family ties and deprived them of citizenship; they prohibited intermarriage and forbade the employment of 'Aryan' maids. While between 1935 and 1937 some Jews continued in business, there were increasing confiscations and forced sales of Jewish enterprises. In March 1938 Germany occupied Austria (the *Anschluss*), and this was followed by anti-Jewish excesses even worse than in Germany, and immediate emigration of Jews from Austria. This also happened to the Jews when Germany entered Czechoslovakia in March 1939. The most horrific single incident before 1939 was the burning or destruction of 267 synagogues, and over 1,000 shops and dwellings on 9 November 1938, with over 30,000 arrests and a collective fine of one billion marks (the *Kristallnacht*). By 1939 thousands of Jews were in concentration camps and only 15.6 per cent (compared with 48.12 per cent in 1933) had regular employment.[76] There was a consequent flow of refugees from Germany, Austria and Czechoslovakia - well over 300,000.[77] By 1940, about 73,000 refugees had been admitted to Britain from Germany and Austria: not all of these were Jews and not all were to settle permanently.[78] Most came between March 1938 and the outbreak of war,[79] so until March 1938 the number of refugees in Britain was noticeable but manageable; the major problems arose in the last months before the outbreak of war in 1939.

British Jewry was quick to recognize the implications of what was happening in Germany. 'The work of the Board [of Deputies] during 1933 was dominated by the tragedy which overwhelmed the Jews in Germany' was how the Board's annual report for 1933 put it.[80] The Board set up a comprehensive committee structure to respond to various aspects of the challenge. The Joint Foreign Committee of the Board and the Anglo-Jewish Association, under the chairmanship of the two presidents, Neville Laski and *Leonard G. Montefiore, was meeting weekly during the spring and summer of 1933, even twice a week. An elaborate structure of sub-committees was set up to deal with refugees, information, parliamentary affairs, (public) meetings, finance and co-ordination with the grassroots Jewish movements in east London.[81] The board's leadership, realizing that the composition of the Board, based mainly on representation of synagogues, could not be completely representative of the community as a whole, brought into the sub-committees co-opted members who were the relevant experts and also the activists within each area of operations. The Joint Foreign Committee co-opted the Chief Rabbi, *Dr Hertz; Lionel Cohen, who was vice-president of the Board of Guardians as well as of the Deputies (from 1936; before then chairman of the Law and Parliamentary Committee); Professor Selig Brodetsky, as the leading British Zionist; Sir Robert Waley Cohen; the Revd J.K. Goldbloom (1872-1961), chairman of the Zionist Federation and pioneer of Hebrew education; H.A. Goodman of the strictly orthodox Agudas Israel; *Sir Philip Hartog; Simon Marks (of Marks and Spencer and a leading Zionist associate of Weizmann); *the second Lord Melchett; *Otto Schiff; H.L. Nathan MP (later Lord Nathan of Churt); and Nahum Sokolow, then president of the World Zionist Organization.[82]

Initially the number of refugees coming to Britain was only a few thousand and so the primary concern of the communal leadership was with what could be done for German Jewry as a whole. A Central British Fund for German Jewry (CBF) was formed and it launched its first appeal in May 1933, which raised over £100,000. In accord with the aim of securing communal unity, especially between Zionists and non-Zionists, the CBF had five joint presidents: the Chief Rabbi, *Lord Reading, Chaim Weizmann, Nahum Sokolow and Lionel de Rothschild; *Lionel de Rothschild was the conciliator who worked out the details of the agreement. The governing council of the CBF had equal representation of Zionists and non-Zionists and the vital Allocations Committee had a mutually agreed chairman, Sir Osmond d'Avigdor-Goldsmid. There were joint secretaries: Myer Stephany of Jews' College and Lavy Bakstansky of the Zionist Federation. In 1936 the Council for German Jewry was formed, to represent the American, British and other major Jewish communities, to fund the settlement of refugees, especially of young people in Palestine, thus bringing together both philanthropic and Zionist interests. It was a delicate task to reconcile the divergence between the 'philanthropic' approach, advocated by the non-Zionists, for funding refugees in diaspora communities or other havens, and the 'Zionist' claim that the only sure solution was to fund the reception and settlement of the refugees in the Jewish national home in Palestine. In 1938 an appeal was made by Earl Baldwin, who was Prime Minister until 1937, for what became known as the Baldwin Fund; the main ultimate beneficiary of this was the Movement for Refugee Children from Germany. Since the Baldwin Fund's objects were non-denominational, as the victims of Nazism included many non-Jews, it had an Allocations Committee which distributed funds to the Council for Germany Jewry, the Christian Council for Refugees, and the Scottish Council for Refugees, who then sub-allocated to their respective relief bodies.[83]

With the increasing number of non-Jewish refugees, whether religious like the Quakers and non-Aryan Christians or the political refugees, as well as refugees from other countries like Czechoslovakia, it became necessary in 1938 to form a Co-ordinating Council for Refugees, whose chairman was the former Indian governor, Lord Hailey. The main case-working organizations – the German Jews' Aid Committee, Friends (Quakers') Germany Emergency Committee, Movement for Care of Children from Germany, International Students' Service, Catholic Committee for Refugees from Germany – together with the specialized functional agencies (such as the Domestic Bureau, placing refugees as domestic servants), were accommodated together from 1938 in a Central Office for Refugees, in Bloomsbury Street, London WC1, known as Bloomsbury House.

In the last months before the outbreak of war in 1939, the Chief Rabbi, Dr Hertz, set up an Emergency Committee for the Relief of European Jewry, of which Dr Solomon Schonfeld, soon to become his son-in-law, was appointed director. Rabbi Schonfeld acted with initiative, resource and courage: 'when others petitioned and prayed, he demanded and got. He chartered ships and planes and travelled to the Continent himself to rescue whole families from the Nazis and bring them back to Britain'.[84] Between 1933 and 1939, over £2m was raised by Jewish organizations from voluntary contributions, from or through the efforts of British Jewry.[85]

If there was a measure of unity in fund-raising and in trying to co-ordinate the proliferating bodies dealing with the refugees, there were acute divisions over other policy issues. One of the first was the question of a boycott of German goods. Immediately after the Nazi victory in the elections of 5 March 1933, Jews throughout the world held protests and started spontaneous boycotts of German goods. As part of this movement, a mass boycott began among Jews in east London on 24 March 1933 which brought the Anglo-German fur trade practically to a halt.[86] Captain Walter Webber formed a committee to promote the boycott and was initially supported by the *Jewish Chronicle* with the slogan 'Jewry Awake'.[87] Other boycott groups sprang up and the principle of the boycott received support from many non-Jewish personalities including Winston Churchill. In November 1933 this led to a Jewish Representative Council for the Boycott of German Goods and Services.[88] The Board of Deputies, on 18 November 1934 passed a resolution that 'no self-respecting Jew will handle German goods or utilize German services'.[89]

But the Board continually refused to organize an 'official' boycott of German goods as likely to be prejudicial to the interests of Germany Jewry themselves; the Chief Rabbi, Dr Hertz, quoted a letter to him from Jacob Rosenheim, president of the strictly orthodox World Agudas Israel to this effect.[90] The Board's policy therefore was for the boycott to be a matter for individual, not collective, action. When the second Lord Melchett, a supporter of the boycott, was co-opted to the Joint Foreign Committee, he had to renounce public support for the boycott.[91] The Board's policy on this was that of analogous bodies like the Alliance Israelite Universelle and the American Jewish Committee, although the more democratically representative American Jewish Congress supported the boycott.[92]

In fact, the boycott as a world Jewish movement was doomed to failure. The ground was cut from beneath the feet of the boycotters by the World Zionist Organization's 1933 'transfer agreement' with Nazi Germany, under which German Jews emigrating to Palestine could take at least part of their capital with them provided it was used to purchase German goods. In Britain Captain Webber, the original initiator, had used up by 1935 a considerable part of his personal assets in the campaign;[93] and even the *Jewish Chronicle* toned down its support for the boycott from August 1933.[94] Ironically, there is 'now evidence that the Nazis, at least during the first two years of their regime', did fear 'that a tight boycott would cripple their economy'.[95] There was a similar difference of view about public protests against Nazi treatment of the Jews. There was a protest march of Jews through London on 20 July 1933, with which some Zionist leaders were associated,[96] but the Board of Deputies' policy was opposed to demonstrations if organized mainly by Jews; they favoured large public meetings only if addressed mainly by non-Jews. Thus they supported a protest meeting at Queen's Hall in 1933 because it was addressed by the leaders of the British political parties. The Joint Foreign Committee tried to prevent Jewish demonstrations: a mass demonstration called by the United Jewish Protest Committee evoked 'strong disapproval'.[97] This attitude was maintained by the official leadership until after the Anschluss in 1938 when Israel Cohen and Morris Myer, as members of the Joint Foreign Committee, pleaded for public protests to be organized by the Jewish community: had this been done earlier, they argued, the persecution of Austrian Jews might not have been so severe and protests would be a deterrent to countries like Rumania and Hungary. The issue was discussed at the Joint Foreign Committee on 24 May 1938. Neville Laski thought it impossible to get 'persons of prominence and standing' outside the community for protest meetings but he had discussed with the Chief Rabbi simultaneous intercession services – 'a mass movement of prayer' – since this would not be 'political'. Although Barnett Janner MP thought non-Jewish opinion was expecting Jewish protest meetings, the Committee backed Laski.[98]

However, following pressure at the Board meeting on 19 June 1938, Laski and Louis (later Sir Louis) Gluckstein saw the chaplain to the Archbishop of Canterbury, Cosmo Lang, and were told that the Archbishop would not associate himself with any platform that might be deemed 'political' and might embarrass the government in the 'present delicate international situation'. It is clear that the attitude of the Chamberlain government and its hopes of rapprochement with Germany influenced non-Jewish, and thus indirectly Jewish, responses. But after the *Kristallnacht* Laski organized a protest meeting on 1 December 1938 at the Albert Hall, attended by the Archbishop of York (William Temple), the Cardinal Archbishop of Westminster, the Moderator of the Free Church Federal Council, and the Chief Rabbi, with the former Lord Chancellor, Lord Sankey, in the chair.[99] This low profile on protests caused dissatisfaction in the community and even Laski's father, Nathan, the leader of Manchester Jewry, protested bitterly in a letter to his son on 22 July 1935: if the Church of England would not come to a protest meeting, then the Roman Catholics and Free Churches would 'stand on platforms all over the country to protest against the persecution of religion in Germany and to intervene against the Nazi tyranny'. In his reply his son condemned the 'usual frothy' discussions at the Board of Deputies and asserted that the government would not be influenced by meetings addressed by Jews; only 'respectable persons, the higher the better who are national figures would do – the Prime Minister, Foreign Secretary, Minister for League of Nations Affairs, Archbishop of Canterbury .... Not [Sir Herbert] Samuel as a Jew or [Lord] Reading'.[100]

The use of non-Jewish publicists to enlighten the British public about the Nazis was undertaken by the British Non-Sectarian Anti-Nazi Council to Champion Human Rights, reorganized in 1935 as Focus for the Defence of Freedom and Peace. Winston Churchill took a leading role and among others associated with it was Wickham Steed, the former Vienna correspondent and editor of *The Times* (see Chapter 6). The group issued a series of pamphlets on Nazism and a journal *Focus*, with a number of minor activities, co-ordinated by H.T. Montague Bell; they also provided briefing for letters to the press from eminent people attacking Nazism. All this activity was financed from a fund, initially £50,000. The raising of this fund was planned by a small group meeting regularly at New Court (the Rothschild banking headquarters in the City of London) and the money was raised and supervised by Sir Robert Waley Cohen – an example of the low profile, 'behind the scenes' activity which the communal leadership regarded as the effective way of action.[101]

Waley Cohen was also closely involved in bringing order into the raising of funds for the care of German refugees coming to Britain.[102] The first report of such arrivals appeared in the *Jewish Chronicle* on 14 April 1933. They were being accommodated at the Jews' Temporary Shelter and the lead in dealing with refugees was taken by the Shelter's president, Otto M. Schiff. His work for Belgian refugees in the First World War had given him close contacts, which he maintained, with officials in the Home Office and other government departments. He organized and chaired a German Jewish Refugees Committee: this was renamed in 1938 the German Jewish Aid Committee because it was wished to avoid the implication that Jews from Germany would be permanent refugees, even if they needed temporary aid, because it was hoped they would establish themselves economically, or go elsewhere, as many did.[103] This Committee was the executive body concerned with admission, hospitality, accommodation, financial help, training and emigration for refugees. It dealt with adults from Germany and their children, but only if children were under 16 and accompanying their parents; other children were the concern of the Movement for Refugee Children from Germany. Both aspects were funded by the CBF and, after 1938, from the Baldwin Fund. Under the regulations then in force, refugees were allowed to stay in Britain for only a month and the communal leadership therefore had immediately in 1933 to negotiate with the government for a right of asylum.

A memorandum, undated but presumably drafted in March 1933 (as it is annexed to a Home Office document dated 7 April 1933) set out 'Proposals of the Jewish Community as regards Jewish Refugees from Germany'. These were signed by Neville Laski, as president of the Board of Deputies, Leonard Montefiore (president of the Anglo-Jewish Association, the other partner on the Joint Foreign Committee), Otto Schiff (as president of the Shelter) and Lionel Cohen (as chairman of the Board's Law and Parliamentary Committee). The document details arrangements for receiving refugees, including accommodation for 160 at the Shelter and 340 in other temporary accommodation, and the provision of 'more permanent homes among the Jewish community', with a view to the 'ultimate transmigration of the refugees to countries other than England'. The Home Office stated that the 'British Jewish authorities' estimated the number of refugees entering the United Kingdom at not more than 3-4,000, most members of the professional classes. A Cabinet Committee on Aliens Restrictions was appointed 'as a matter of urgency, to consider the Jewish community's proposals; they doubted whether it was possible to form any correct estimate, 'as much must depend on events in Germany'.[104] The document contained the pledge: 'All expense, whether in respect of temporary or permanent accommodation or maintenance will be borne by the Jewish community, without ultimate charge to the State'.[105] The report of the 1933 Cabinet Committee on Aliens Restrictions makes clear that it was only 'provided that the Jewish community were prepared to guarantee so far as may be necessary, adequate means of maintenance for the refugees concerned', that those refugees given temporary permission to land would have it extended.[106] It was established policy under the 1920 Aliens Order to refuse leave to land to those who could not show that means were available for their maintenance; and the committee rejected the option of granting permission to land without guaranteed means of maintenance. So the pledge, which in many cases took the form of personal guarantees, was an essential factor in allowing entry to refugees. The German Jewish Aid Committee worked with the Home Office in selecting refugees for admission; and in 1938-9 when the need to rescue Jews from Europe was overwhelming, temporary asylum, which was offered generously, was linked with the prospect of re-emigration. It was not till December 1939, when the voluntary organizations could no longer cope in the economic conditions of wartime, that the government authorized a grant for maintenance; and the effort the Jewish community had made till then to support the refugees was an important consideration in the decision to make the grant.[107]

Once the refugees had arrived, there was a certain ambivalence in the attitude of the communal leadership towards them. On the one hand, at the end of 1938, by which time there were probably around 30,000 Jewish refugees in the country, the Board of Deputies issued a booklet for general consumption, *The Refugees: The Plain Facts,* which defended and praised them. They were making a substantial contribution to the British economy and far from taking away jobs from Britons they were increasing employment.[108] This was a measure in the Board's Jewish defence campaign. At this time, the press were making precisely these allegations against the refugees, for example the *Sunday Pictorial* headline 'Refugees get jobs - Britons get dole';[109] and the medical and dental professions resisted the entry into practice of refugee doctors and dentists qualified abroad. In a period of Jewish anxiety in the fact of anti-Semitic attacks on British Jews, it is understandable that a booklet should have been issued at the beginning of 1939, entitled *Helpful Information and Guidance for Every Refugee.* This told refugees to be loyal to Britain, not to criticize British institutions and ways, and to refrain from speaking German in public or being conspicuous in manner or dress. The advice also not to tell

British Jews 'it's bound to happen in your country' implies some irritation on the part of native Jews with some of the refugees. This was certainly true of Laski, who in a letter to Otto Schiff on 8 December 1938 wrote: '... from my own personal experience, which is confirmed by the experience of a large number of my friends, the refugees are pestilential in the matter of derogatory remarks about various things in this country.'[110] Similar remarks about the need for tactful conduct were included in a note of guidance for refugee dentists, in which they were told *inter alia* not to seek to attract other dentists' patients.[111]

While many individuals laboured selflessly with personal service and money to help the refugees to settle and adjust to British life, there is evidence from provincial communities of some friction between the refugees and the existing Jewish community. The refugees who still had to learn the English language naturally kept together for social purposes, preferring the company of others with similar experiences and problems. The existing community sometimes resented this as aloofness on the part of the refugees, and there may possibly have been memories on the part of those British Jews whose origins were in Eastern Europe of the former superiority felt by Central towards Eastern European Jews.[112]

Responses to Zionism, anti-Semitism and Nazism and the refugees have been analysed separately but they are all interlinked. The same people were in at least two, if not all three, of these areas. The 'activists' and the 'moderates' in each line-up were usually, though not always, the same. Attitudes in one area were influenced by considerations applying in others. For instance, consciousness of the urgency of the problems caused by Nazism influenced attitudes to the national home: if Jews desperately needed a haven then that enhanced the attractions of even a small state, which would have control of its own immigration policy. Again, Zionists who advocated the expression of Jewish nationality and deprecated assimilation were more likely to take an activist line in demonstrating against Fascism; or those concerned to keep a low profile against Fascism did not want the conduct of refugees to arouse criticsm of Jews. Those who stressed the importance of integration of Jews in British society and resisted the concept of Jews as a separate nationality were more likely, in dealing with anti-Semitism at home, to urge restraint and reliance on the government and the assumed tolerance of British society.

The 1930s were marked by the beginning of a transfer of communal authority from the older, anglicized *haute bourgeoisie* to a newer group of middle-class first and second generation immigrants. The older leadership was weakened by the loss of young men in the First World War and by the comparative reduction in its wealth, which placed it at a disadvantage in a society which placed a high value on charitable giving and financial support for institutions. This was a need which some of those associated with the newer group, who had built up fortunes in retailing and light industry, could meet. Zionism provided an ideology on which the transfer of authority could be based, although not to the extent of actually leaving Britain to settle in Palestine. It also filled an ideological vacuum which traditional religion was no longer able to fill and which the Anglo-Jewish middle-class was unwilling to fill with a more radical ideology of the left.[113]

Notes

1. For a recent general survey, see David Cesarani, 'The Transformation of Communal Authority in Anglo-Jewry 1914-1940' in David Cesarani (ed.), *The Making of Modern Anglo-Jewry*, Oxford, 1990, pp. 115-140.
2. Israel Cohen, *The Zionist Movement*, London, 1945, p. 121. The Central Office was at 75-77 Great Russell Street, next to the British Museum, with the main entrance at 77, which became synonymous with the Zionist Organization in British Jewry in this period (ibid., pp. 123-5).
3. The Churchill White Paper was published in Cmd. 1700; S. Levenberg, *The Board and Zion*, 185, p. 59.
4. See especially the two articles by Dr Gideon Shimoni, 'From Anti-Zionism to Non-Zionism in Anglo-Jewry', *JJS* XXVIII (1), June 1986, 19-48 and 'The Non-Zionists in Anglo-Jewry 1937-48', *JJS* XXVIII (2), December 1986, 89-116. The only full-length study is the as yet unpublished 1986 Oxford D.Phil. thesis by Dr David Cesarani, 'Zionism in Anglo-Jewry 1918-39'.
5. Shimoni, 'From Anti-Zionism', p. 24.
6. Ibid., p. 28.
7. Ibid., pp. 27-8.
8. *EJ* 9, pp. 340-2.
9. Robert Henriques, *Sir Robert Waley Cohen*, 1966, p. 264.
10. Ibid., pp. 273-4.
11. Shimoni, 'From Anti-Zionism', pp. 28-9.
12. S. Levenberg, *The Board and Zion*, 1985, pp. 59-60; Shimoni, 'From Anti-Zionism', pp. 30-1.
13. Shaw Report, Cmd. 3530; Hope Simpson Report, Cmd. 3686; Passfield White Paper, Cmd. 3692.
14. Geoffrey Alderman, *Jewish Community in British Politics*, Oxford, 1987, pp. 112-13; Joseph Gorny, *The British Labour Movement and Zionism 1917-1948*, 1983, pp. 91-3.
15. An analysis of the crisis and the pressures upon and within the Labour Party, which provided the government then in power, is given in Gorny, *British Labour Movement*, pp. 51-108.
16. During Weizmann's absence from the presidency of the World Zionist Organization, Nahum Sokolow was president until 1935.
17. Neville Laski in 1934 made a private apprach to the Colonial Office, offering to keep them informed on events at the Jewish Agency Administrative Committee meeting at Lausanne, which he was about to chair, and seeking a direct line to the Colonial Office, because he disapproved of the political, rather than economic, approach of the Agency. British officials were reluctant to get involved behind the back of the Agency leaders, although the Colonial

Secretary, Sir Philip Cunliffe Lister (later Lord Swinton), thought 'we want English Jews like Laski with us; and they have the right to come and talk to us'. See Gabriel Rey, 'Laski's offer', *JC* 17, August 1984; Shimoni, 'From Anti-Zionism', p. 35.

18. G. Shimoni, 'Selig Brodetsky and the ascendancy of Zionism in Anglo-Jewry', XXII, 1980, pp. 128–9.
19. This is attributed by Dr Cesarani in his as yet unpublished 'Zionism in Anglo-Jewry 1918–39', to decline in membership in the East End societies and others in the areas of first settlement, which was not made up until the 1930s by the development of Zionist societies in the growing suburban communities.
20. Shimoni, 'Non-Zionists', p. 91 and p. 111, note 6.
21. *EJ* 13, p. 661.
22. *EJ* 16, p. 1117.
23. The only detailed study of the Federation during this period so far is Dr Cesarani's 'Zionism in Anglo-Jewry'.
24. Shimoni, 'Non-Zionists', pp. 92–3; *EJ* 8, p. 1243. I am very grateful to Mr Matthew Kalman for lending me his Cambridge University history tripos (1983) dissertation on 'Young Zionism' and Jewish youth in London between the Wars', a pioneer study.
25. For the Halutz movement generally, see *EJ* 8, pp. 247–54, and for Britain in the 1930s, Cesarani, 'Zionism in Anglo-Jewry', pp. 383–8.
26. Stuart Cohen, 'The conquest of a community? Zionists and the Board of Deputies in 1917', *JJS* XIX (2), 1977, 163.
27. Gideon, 'Selig Brodetsky.
28. Ibid., p. 131.
29. Cmd. 5479.
30. Cmd. 5513.
31. Israel Cohen, *The Zionist Movement*, 1945, pp. 214–15.
32. David Cesarani, 'Patriots against partition', *JC*, 29 April 1988, 28.
33. Shimoni, 'Selig Brodetsky', pp. 126–9, 155 n. 11; Shimoni, 'Non-Zionists', p. 94.
34. Henriques, *Waley Cohen*, pp. 369–70.
35. Shimoni, 'Selig Brodetsky', 132–3; Selig Brodetsky, *Memoirs*, 1960, p. 194.
36. Colin Holmes, *Anti-Semitism in British Society*, 1979, p. 159.
37. See David Cesarani, 'Anti-Zionist politics and political Anti-Semitism in Britain 1920–4', *Patterns of Prejudice* 23 (1), Spring 1989, 28–43, a pioneer study drawing attention to the importance of this campaign against Zionism.
38. PRO HO 45/24765/13.
39. See Table 2, Appendix II, J.M. Ross, 'The naturalization of Jews in England', *TJHSE* XXIV, p. 72, which however gives figures for 1921 and 1931 only.
40. PRO HO 45/24765/17.
41. Ross 'Naturalization', pp. 68–9. Mr Ross estimates, from a sample of names, that the number of Jews naturalized went up from 536 in 1921 to 922 in 1931.
42. Board of Deputies Annual Report, 1926, p. 40.
43. G. Lebzelter, *Political Anti-Semitism in England 1918–39*, Oxford, 1978, pp. 49–67, especially p. 66.
44. Ibid., pp. 68–85.
45. For the BUF see ibid., pp. 86–109; Holmes, *Anti-Semitism*, pp. 176–98.

46. Holmes, *Anti-Semitism*, p. 191.
47. Lebzelter, *Political Anti-Semitism*, pp. 105-6.
48. Ibid., p. 39.
49. Ibid., pp. 115, 118, 119, 120.
50. Ibid., pp. 130, 134.
51. Holmes, *Anti-Semitism*, pp. 191-3. For a description of Bethnal Green anti-Semitism, see J.H. Robb, *Working Class Anti-Semite: A Psychological Study in a London Borough*, 1954.
52. Board of Deputies Annual Report, 1932, pp. 43-4.
53. Ibid., 1938, pp. 47-8.
54. Henriques, *Waley Cohen*, p. 244, 353.
55. Board of Deputies annual Report, 1936, pp. 57-8.
56. Ibid., 1937, p. 68.
57. Henriques, *Waley Cohen*, p. 364.
58. Lebzelter, *Political Anti-Semitism*, pp. 144-5.
59. Ibid., p. 167, quoting HO 45/502735/265.
60. Nearly 600,000 copies of leaflets and 11 sets of 'Speakers' Notes' were distributed between July and December 1936 (Board of Deputies Annual Report, 1936, p. 58).
61. This was originally a committee advisory to the Board of Deputies. When reconstituted in 1940 as the Trades Advisory Council 'under the auspices of the Board of Deputies' its objects were: 'The strengthening of goodwill amongst traders of all creeds and classes; the elimination of friction between Jew and non-Jew in trade and industry; the maintenance of the highest standards of commercial conduct amongst Jewish traders'.
62. *The Times*, 10 October 1936.
63. Henriques, *Waley Cohen*, p. 361.
64. Holmes, *Anti-Semitism*, p. 193.
65. Henriques, *Waley Cohen*, p. 361, n. 1.
66. Shimoni, 'Non-Zionists', p. 93.
67. *Jewish Year Book*, 1939, p. 65. The chairman was J.W. Bentley; Treasurer, A.R. Rollin (a respected Jewish trade unionist and later council member of the Jewish Historical Society and contributor to their *Transactions*); secretary, J. Jacobs.
68. Shimoni, 'Non-Zionists', p. 93.
69. Lebzelter, *Political Anti-Semitism*, pp. 141-2.
70. Holmes, *Anti-Semitism*, p. 193.
71. Ibid., p. 199.
72. Lebzelter, *Political Anti-Semitism*, pp. 161-4.
73. Alderman, *Jewish Community*, pp. 117-18, 161-2.
74. Neville Laski, *Jewish Rights and Jewish Wrongs*, 1939, p. 132.
75. Louise London, 'Jewish Refugees, Anglo-Jewry and British Government Policy 1930-1940' in David Cesarani (ed.), *The Making of Modern Anglo-Jewry*, Oxford, 1990, p. 168; A.J. Sherman, *Island Refuge*, 1973, pp. 19-22.
76. *EJ* 7, 489-90, 494.
77. *EJ* 16, 1524.
78. Jules Isaac, *British Post-War Migration*, Cambridge, 1954, pp. 5-6.
79. Sherman, *Island Refuge*, Appendix I. The British government responded to *Kristallnacht* by allowing Jewish children from Germany and Austria to enter

Britain without their parents and without visas. By the end of December some 300 had arrived at Harwich and thereafter an average of 1,000 arrived each month, so that by September 1939, 10,000 of these so-called *Kindertransporte* children (90 per cent of them Jewish) had arrived in Britain.

80. Board of Deputies Annual Report, 1933, p. 29.
81. Board of Deputies Joint Foreign Committee Minutes, April 1933, p. 204.
82. Joint Foreign Committee, minutes 12 July, 14 July 1933; Board of Deputies Annual Report, 1934. The existing members of the board on the Joint Foreign Committee included the Zionist administrator and writer, Israel Cohen and the editor of the Yiddish newspaper, *Die Tsayt,* Morris Myer.
83. Joan Stiebel, 'The Central British Fund', *TJHSE* XXVIII, 51–4.
84. *The Times,* 8 February 1984. Rabbi Dr Solomon Schonfeld (1912–84) succeeded his father, Rabbi Dr Victor Schonfeld, as presiding rabbi, Adath Yisroel Synagogue and of the Union of Orthodox Hebrew Congregations; founder and principal of the Jewish Secondary Schools Movement (Avigdor and Hasmonean Schools).
85. Norman Bentwich, *The Refugees from Germany,* 1936; p. 121 gives figures for 1933–5; for 1936–9, see letter from Sir A. Maxwell of 8 November 1939 on PRO HO 213/294.
86. *EJ* 4, 1281.
87. *JC,* 24 March 1933.
88. Shimoni, 'Non-Zionists', p. 92.
89. Lebzelter, *Political Anti-Semitism,* p. 137.
90. Joint Foreign Committee, Minutes of 14 June 1933, p. 227.
91. Ibid.,20 July 1933.
92. *EJ* 4, 1281.
93. Lebzelter, *Political Anti-Semitism,* p. 197, no. 3.
94. Bernard Krikler, 'Boycotting Nazi Germany', *Weiner Library Bulletin* XXIII (4) new series no. 17, 1969, 30.
95. *EJ* 4, 1282.
96. Shimoni, 'Non-Zionists', p. 92.
97. Joint Foreign Committee minutes, 7 June, 15 June 1933.
98. Ibid., 24 May 1933, p. 169.
99. Ibid., 21 June 1938, 16 November 1938; Report to Board, 14 December 1938.
100. Correspondence in Board of Deputies C11/12/14 pt. 2.
101. Lebzelter, *Political Anti-Semitism,* pp. 137–8; Henriques, *Waley Cohen,* pp. 361–4.
102. Henriques, *Waley Cohen,* pp. 337–9.
103. Board of Deputies Aliens Committee minutes, 6 January 1938.
104. PRO CP 96/33, para. 5.
105. Appendix I, para. 4 to Home Secretary's memorandum, CP 96/33. In the archives of the Board of Deputies there seems to be no reference to this pledge, or to the whole memorandum being reported to the joint Foreign Committee or to the board, although it is hinted at in *JC* 14 April 1933, and it became generally known.
106. PRO CP 96/33 para. 18.
107. Louise London, 'Jewish Refugees, 1930–40', pp. 173–183; letter of Sir Alexander Maxwell, Home Office, to G.T. Reid, Unemployment Assistance Board, 8 November 1939 on HO 213/294.

108. Board of Deputies G/6/26.
109. Note by A.G. Brotman, secretary of the Board, of the meeting which Laski and he had with the Home Secretary, Sir Samuel Hoare on Board of Deputies E6/286/26/2.
110. Board of Deputies G/6/26.
111. Ibid., E3/280.
112. Rayner Kölmel, 'German Jewish Refugees in Scotland' in Kenneth Collins (ed.) *Aspects of Scottish Jewry*, Glasgow, 1987, pp. 73–7; Zoe Josephs, *Survivors: Jewish Refugees in Birmingham 1933–45*, Birmingham, 1988. p. 80.
113. David Cesarani, 'The Transformation of Communal Authority', pp. 137–140.

Chapter 9

Social Change in British Jewry 1918–39

The period between the two world wars was one of social consolidation within the community. It completed the process, which began even before 1914, of integrating the Eastern European immigrants of the 1881–1914 period and their children with the descendants of the pre-1881 community. The immigrants of the previous generation, and even more so their children, were improving their social and economic status within British society. This was a process which can be charted in patterns of family structure, occupations, social class, areas of residence, education and religious attitudes. All the indicators point to a continuing process of upward social mobility and at the same time fusion with the pre-1881 community.[1] To some extent this process was caused by the relative stoppage of immigration during the First World War, and the reduced rate at which immigration was possible after it. When Jewish immigration began again in appreciable numbers between 1933 and 1939 with the arrival of refugees from Central Europe, these immigrants were numerically only a fraction of the size of Anglo-Jewry of the 1930s, and they were predominantly middle-class in character, therefore socially more akin to the Anglo-Jewry of the 1930s to which they came.[2]

These developments between the two world wars were set against the background of wider changes in British society. The First World War caused severe economic dislocation, and the late 1920s and early 1930s saw severe and prolonged economic depression, followed by recovery in the later 1930s. Nevertheless, Britain still experienced overall economic growth which raised the living standards of the majority of the population of Britain during the 1930s. It is true that the slower growth in world trade in the 1920s, and the 1929 stock market crash, reduced demand and output in Britain's staple industries such as coal, iron, steel, shipbuilding and textiles; and that, in contracting world markets, Britain's competitiveness was reduced and export markets were lost. But the First World War had stimulated growth in new industries like chemicals, electrical goods, automobiles, aircraft, precision engineering and the products of the science-based industries generally.

Recovery began in 1933 although even by 1939 world trade had regained only its 1929 level.[3] But a number of factors, which are very relevant to the social and economic life of British Jews in the 1930s, produced increases in the British gross domestic product, in industrial output and in real living standards, compared with the situation before 1914. These factors included the growth of industries producing artificial fibres and plastics, and electrical goods from cookers to radios. These were encouraged by the boom in private housebuilding in the 1930s, itself stimulated by the increase in the number of households needing accommodation and the fact that smaller families and increased earning capacity provided the resources available to pay for it. Technical advances and rationalization of production, for instance through mergers, increased output per head.[4] Employment in distribution rose by 50 per cent during the 1930s compared with 1920: ordering by mail, the development of chains of retail stores and of department stores, and of hire purchase (which by 1938 accounted for two-thirds of all larger retail purchases) contributed to the expansion of consumer-oriented activity in the 1930s.[5]

The total population of Britain, which was 40.8 million in 1911 increased to 42.7 million in 1921, 44.7 in 1931 and 44.8 (estimated) in 1940. The Jewish population was under 1 per cent of the total population of Britain. But, whereas the general population grew by natural increase, with (apart from 1931–40) a net loss by emigration over immigration, the Jewish population increased appreciably, especially between 1933 and 1940, by immigration. The actual size and growth of the Jewish population of Britain in this period can only be roughly estimated. The *Jewish Year Book,* which was published more or less annually, gave an increase in the Jewish population from 276,000 in 1919 to 297,000 in 1934. This was followed by a jump to 333,000 in 1936–8. This dramatic increase was based, not on a real major change, but on a new estimate. Figures of 370,000 published for 1939 and 385,000 for 1940. These last increases were attributable, it must be assumed, to the coming of refugees from Central Europe but otherwise the figures were based mainly on an aggregation of estimates of local communities and represented more British Jewry's perception of its own size than any scientific estimate for the whole country.[6] There were only two major calculations in this period based on Jewish burial and cremation figures, and both make certain debatable assumptions about the relationship of Jewish to general mortality rates. However, one of these estimates put the Jewish population of inner London and nine adjacent boroughs (East Ham, West Ham, Barking, Leyton, Walthamstow, Tottenham, Hornsey, Willesden, Acton) in 1929 at 190,000 to 205,000.[7] Subsequently, another estimate gave 234,000 as the Jewish population of a rather wider area of Greater London as an average for the years 1931–3; 184,000 for inner London (the then County of London)

19,000 for the nine boroughs mentioned and 29,000 for the remainder of the outer areas of Greater London.[8]

Since the London Jewish community has fairly consistently appeared to be about two-thirds of British Jewry, it would not be unreasonable to assume that Anglo-Jewry was just over 300,000 at the beginning of the 1920s and increased to around 335,000 by the mid-1930s as a result of natural increase (which was rather below the national average) and a modest amount of immigration; and then increased to around 370,000 in 1939, mainly as a result of the Central European immigration of the later 1930s. The official figure for refugees admitted up to October 1939 to settle was 49,000 (including 9,000 children) from Germany and Austria, and 6,000 from Czechslovakia.[9] The majority of the refugees came in 1938-9, so the impact was mainly at the end of the period.[10] The total number of refugees in the country by 1940 was larger because of those admitted on temporary permits while awaiting admission elsewhere: one estimate of the total is about 73,000 (55,000 adults) from Germany and Austria, 4-5,000 from Poland and about 2,000 from Italy and other places.[11] Not all of these were Jewish but the figures exclude a number of Jews from Central Europe who came under private arrangements, including those who left just before the Nazis came to power in 1933. All in all, whereas the 1881-1914 immigrants were almost three times as numerous as the pre-existing Jewish community in Britain, the 1933-9 Central European immigrants were about a sixth or seventh of the 1933 Anglo-Jewish community. An estimate of this order is supported by the fact that of a very carefully selected sample of London Jews in 1970 just under a seventh were from Central Europe.[12]

The reduction in the rate of East European immigration after the Aliens Act of 1905, and its virtual cessation after 1914, produced an increasingly British-born Jewish population in the 1920s and 1930s which the Central European immigration was insufficiently numerous to do more than modify. Whereas in 1891 it had been estimated that half the Jewish population of east London (which held the vast majority then of London's Jewish population) had been born abroad,[13] in 1929 less than 30 per cent of the Jewish population of the same area were born outside the United Kingdom. Taking together the Jewish population of east and north London in 1929, the sample survey in the *New Survey of London Life and Labour* of the Jewish population showed that none of those in the sample born between 1915 and 1929 were born abroad and less than 5 per cent of those born between 1909 and 1915.[14] An equally striking contrast is shown in the places of birth of those married in orthodox synagogues in 1904 and 1934 respectively. In 1904, only 26 per cent of those married were born in Great Britain and 71 per cent abroad; in 1934, 82 per cent had been born in Britain and only 17 per cent abroad.[15]

Thus in a generation British Jewry, instead of being born predominantly in Eastern Europe, had become predominantly British-born. This was reflected, as Dr Kosmin has shown,[16] in a demographic revolution in

British Jewry. The Eastern European immigrants had brought with them a more traditional Jewish pattern of early marriage, a high marriage rate per thousand population, and a tendency to large families: these had obscured the earlier Anglo-Jewish pattern of rapid acculturation to a western European model of later age at marriage, a lower marriage rate, and fewer children per family. The immigrant pattern in its turn was reversed within a generation: the children of the immigrants adopted the demographic pattern of the older Anglo-Jewry. By 1929 the age of marriage for Jewish bridegrooms was 29.2 years, almost the same as the general England and Wales average of 29.1; the figure for Jewish brides was 25.8, which compared with the England and Wales figure of 26.6.[17] The increase in age at marriage, together with an unquantifiable amount of out-marriage, produced a small fall in the synagogue marriage rate, relative to the general marriage rate for the population as a whole.[18] Such evidence as there is – the sample in the 1929–30 *New Survey* and material from post-1945 social surveys of Jewish communities – all suggests that Jewish women between the wars who had children had fewer children than their mothers had and also than their non-Jewish neighbours. There is also evidence that 83 per cent of Jewish women married in the 1920s practised birth control compared with an average of 62 per cent for the general population in the same period.[19] In 1977 in the London suburb of Redbridge, where 93.4 per cent of the sample were British-born (57.3 per cent were born in east or north London, the area of the *New Survey* Jewish sample of 1929), there is a clear division between Jewish women married before and after 1922. Those married before 1922 had on average 4 children, those between 1923 and 1932 2.0, and those between 1938 and 1942, 1.8. The corresponding figures for the national average of births per married woman for those married in this period were 2.5 up to 1927, 2.2 for those married between 1928 and 1932 and 2.1 for those married between 1933 and 1942.[20] Thus, whereas before 1922 the average number of births per Jewish married woman was above the national average, by 1933–7 it was below it. The evidence from the much smaller (and more affluent) Jewish community of Sheffield showed a similar pattern but with even lower figures of births per married woman (averaging 1.76 for women married between 1925 and 1975).[21] On the other hand, while Jewish women between the wars seem to have had fewer children per marriage, fewer Jewish women seem to have been childless than in the general population: in Redbridge, there were no childless couples among those married before 1938, compared with about 12 per cent for the general population.[22] These demographic patterns may also have been influenced by the increasingly middle-class character of the community, which will be described later.

So by the inter-war years there was no longer any substantial difference between the demographic patterns of an older and an immigrant Anglo-Jewry. This may have been due to the relatively high proportion of males among the 1881–1914 Eastern European immigrants. This led to their often marrying British-born Jewish women, with the result that the young Jews of the inter-war period were more likely to have British-born mothers than British-born fathers.[23] On the other hand, the situation was one of transition. In 1929 the *New Survey* sample of Jews in east and north London showed an average of 3.82 persons per family (3.98 for those with earners in the family) compared with 3.68 for all families in the area (3.83 for those with earners). This was in spite of the fact that the Jewish sample included middle-class families, who might be thought to have had fewer children, and the general sample was limited to working-class families.[24] The explanation is that the great majority of married couples in 1929 would have been married before 1922 when, as the other evidence shows, larger families were the rule. But by the 1930s the influence of Eastern European demographic patterns was fading, due to the biological fusion of the older and immigrant sections of the community and the adoption by the latter of the demographic patterns of the former.

The process of fusion in the community can also be seen in the increasing tendency to move from the Jewish quarter, or area of first settlement of the immigrants, into suburban areas. This was a process noticeable in the older Anglo-Jewry from the mid-nineteenth century on and continued, so far as the middle classes were concerned, throughout the period of mass immigration. That immigration, however, by building up Jewish quarters, densely packed and of Jewish character, in London and half a dozen other large cities, obscured the fact that this process of movement to the surburbs was continuing. In fact, the immigrants themselves often moved out of their area of first settlement within a generation, although up to 1914 they were replaced by fresh immigrants just off the boat. By 1914, the largest Jewish immigrant quarter – east London – was probably below its peak Jewish population of 125,000, although still containing about two-thirds of London Jewry.[25] By 1929, the Jewish population of east London was down to about 85,000, which was 40 per cent or less of the total Jewish population of Greater London. This was in line with the decline in the total population of the east London borough of Stepney, from 280,000 in 1911 to 225,000 in 1931, due to clearance and relocation of overcrowded and substandard housing and conversion of residential property into offices, warehouses and industrial uses.[26] The Jews showed an even greater tendency to move than their neighbours, even if only into the area of second settlement in north London. North London had about 25–30,000 Jews in 1914, about a fifth of the total London Jewish population.[27] By 1929 this was about 35,000 – 28,000 in Hackney, 6,000 in Stoke Newington – though this was now only one-sixth of the total London Jewish population.[28] This relative decline of north London's share of London's Jewish population was due to the spread of population to suburban areas further out – areas of third settlement – especially in north west London. This area, which had about 10,000 Jews, or 7.5 per cent, of the Jewish population of London in 1914, had about 20,000, or 10 per cent by 1930; and then grew rapidly in the 1930s.[29]

This movement was part of a general trend outwards to the suburbs in line with the development of public transport and the increase in automobile ownership, which grew notably in the 1930s. This was partly owing to population pressures - the increase in the number of households - and greater real incomes which made it possible to seek healthier accommodation - a house with a garden - outside the congested inner areas. But it was also caused by the boom in private housebuilding in the middle and late 1930s when 350,000 houses a year were being built in Britain for sale. These were available on easy terms, with a small house offered for sale at £450, which could be borrowed at 4½ per cent interest. New houses were thus within the financial reach of the clerk, skilled artisan or small shopkeeper, as well as the professional middle class and small employers.[30]

It is not easy to quantify the move of the Jewish middle class and skilled working class to the suburbs in the 1930s. One indication is that seven suburban synagogues (two in north-west London) were admitted to the United Synagogue, the main London synagogal organization, in the 1920s and nineteen (fourteen in north-west London) in the 1930s:[31] admission to the United Synagogue usually took place some time, often about ten years, after the initial settlement of a Jewish group and the holding of services had begun. Thus this supports the thesis of a mass spread of settlements in the suburbs in the late 1920s and the 1930s.

There were two main areas of development for London Jewry between the wars. One followed the commuter lines of the main line railway to East and West Ham, Leyton and Ilford - largely a working-class and lower middle-class movement.[32] Synagogues were founded in Ilford and Barking in 1927, with another in Ilford (later the most numerous synagogal congregation in the country in the 1950s) in 1936.[33] The other axis was predominantly middle class, marked by the successive foundation of synagogues in Golders Green (which the underground railway had reached in 1907), Edgware, Hendon and Finchley. By 1939 the four synagogues in the United Synagogue with the largest male membership were Hampstead, the New Synagogue in north London, Cricklewood,[34] and Golders Green, with Hendon sixth. When the 1933-9 Central European immigrants, a middle-class immigration, came, they settled in Hampstead (which in 1951 still had 6,727 German and Austrian-born residents), Golders Green and Hendon.[35] Similar outward movement was found in the provincial communities. The trend to settle in developing middle-class suburbs, to relocate synagogues and other communal institutions, and to abandon the original area of settlement to all but a relatively few and elderly people can be documented for both the larger communities such as Leeds and smaller, like Sheffield.[36]

In Leeds, the city with probably the largest proportion of Jewish to general population (between 3.5 and 4 per cent), the area of first settlement - the Leylands - reached its numerical peak in the 1910s. In the

1920s two areas of second settlement (Camp Road and Chapeltown) grew fast. In the 1930s the area of first settlement (the Leylands) declined and one of the areas of second settlement (Camp Road) reached its peak. In his study of Leeds Dr Ernest Krausz noted the time lag between movement of population and relocation of synagogues and later still of communal institutions.[37] This time lag was not so marked in Greater London, which had a central synagogal organization - the United Synagogue - which could plan and provide for the spreading population. Two points are characteristic of all these movements. First, that the Jewish population continued to move along the same geographical axis as before 1914 - or in the case of a community of the size of Manchester, two axes, or in London, at least three. The second point is the persistence, in spite of economic and social acculturation, of specifically Jewish areas in which Jews voluntarily clustered. They moved from the area of first settlement as part of a general trend towards the suburbs but when there they retained much of their original pattern of settlement.[38]

The period also saw the growth of relatively large communities in seaside resorts - Brighton, Bournemouth, Blackpool, Southend, Southport. This was in line with the general movement of population, since in England and Wales all the areas - 131 out of about 1,450 - which increased their population by more than 30 per cent between 1921 and 1931 were either suburbs of large cities or seaside resorts.[39]

Movement of Jews to suburbs and seaside resorts in accordance with general trends was accompanied also by a movement towards the south-east and midlands. These were the areas of growth industries and of the developing office and service sectors of the economy, whereas the north and Wales were affected by depression and association with the older, contracting industries.[40] It is noticeable that the northern Jewish communities did not increase so much as those of Greater London and the southern towns. The Jewish population of Greater London increased by about 40 per cent between 1918 and 1939. This is based on reasonable population estimates but for other cities, one has to rely in most cases on statistics given annually in the *Jewish Year Book*. These were often estimates, rarely changed, and give mainly what was locally perceived as the size, and change in the size, of the local Jewish community. The figure given for Leeds during the whole period (25,000) shows no change at all; for Manchester, there is an increase from 32,000 in 1920 to 37,500 in 1939, including Salford; for Glasgow, a slight increase from 14,000 to 15,000 and for Liverpool from 7,000 to 7,500 are reported between 1920 and 1939. For the neighbouring north-eastern communities of Newcastle and Sunderland, in depressed Wearside and Tyneside, sharp decreases from 4,000 to 2,500 and 2,000 to 950 are reported between 1920 and 1939; Hull similarly is reported as declining from 2,500 to 2,000. In South Wales, the smaller communities like Swansea decline from 1,000 to 565 or disappear but the central community, Cardiff, increases from 2,025 to 2,300 - well below the

London rate of increase and probably due to absorption of residents from smaller communities in the area; this may also explain part of the growth in Manchester and Salford. But by contrast with this perceived decline in communities in the north and Wales, which had grown swiftly by immigration in the previous generation, seaside resorts are recorded as growing, although here too the growth is greater in the south than in the north. Whereas Southport is reported as increasing from 375 to only 500, Brighton (with Hove) is shown as increasing from 675 to 2,500 and Bournemouth from about 200 (40 families in 1920) to 700. While these figures are estimates, they are probably near the truth for the smaller communities where the details were readily ascertainable and in any case they reflect a perception of the movement from north to south which is explicable in terms of general economic and social trends.

Geographical movement of Jews from city centres to suburbs was part of the pattern of fusion of immigrants with the older community. So too was the change in occupational patterns of the Eastern European immigrants and their children from the so-called immigrant trades, their adoption of new occupations – particularly those which were expanding in this period – and their steady rise to middle-class status. Tailoring, in which 40 per cent of the gainfully employed male Russians and Poles in London had been engaged in 1901, remained an important trade for Jews, probably by far the largest single trade; but its relative importance declined. In east and north London in 1929 it accounted for 20,000 Jewish males – a quarter of the occupied Jewish males in the area. But some idea of the change in trends can be gained from the statistics, given in the *New Survey of London Life and Labour*, of the 14–20-year-old entrants to the Jewish friendly or benefit societies. Since these societies after 1911 were the agencies for national insurance, they probably picked up the vast majority of the young Jewish employees. In 1913, 46 per cent of the 14–20-year-old male entrants to employment were tailors, in 1921 34 per cent and in 1930 23 per cent.[41] In 1930 the London Jewish Board of Guardians reported the decline in the number of Jews entering the tailoring trade, which the Board attributed to the increasing trend towards factories, while the preference of Jewish operatives was for work in small workshops, with opportunities of becoming master tailors, rather than as factory operatives.[42] Tailoring still remained very important in the provincial communities. In Leeds possibly a higher proportion of the total Jewish workforce was still in tailoring than in London since the city was the 'home of large model factories and multiple tailoring concerns'.[43] In Manchester, it was regarded as the principal Jewish employment and in Liverpool in the late 1930s half the parents of the children at the Liverpool Jewish (day) School were tailors or cabinetmakers.[44]

The boot and shoe trade, which even before 1914 had been in decline and depression because the Jewish workshops could not meet factory competition, continue to decline. In London in 1929 it accounted for only 3 per cent of the Jewish male workers in east and north London, and its proportion of young entrants went down to 2.5 per cent in 1921 and 0.3 per cent in 1930. Even among clients of the London Jewish Board of Guardians, the number of those in the boot and shoe trade declined from under 9 per cent in 1921 to 6 per cent in 1932.[45]

On the other hand, numbers in the furniture manufacturing trades rose to about 8 per cent of Jewish employed males in north and east London in 1929 (about 6–8,000 persons) and 12½ per cent of the new entrants in 1930. According to the *New Survey*, however, apart from tailoring and furniture (cabinetmaking), no industry or craft had more than 4 per cent of the occupied Jewish males in north and east London in 1929, which shows an increasing tendency to diversity of occupations after the concentration of the vast majority of the immigrants before 1914 in a few trades. Even the percentage of hawkers – the calling immigrants had perforce to adopt if they had no skills or other means of employment – was down to 4.7 per cent of the Jewish male employed labour force in 1929, in north and east London.

Among women, according to the *New Survey*, tailoring employed 23 per cent, about the 1901 percentage, but here too the figures of young women joining the Jewish friendly societies showed a decline from nearly 40 per cent of the entrants in 1913 to 9 per cent in 1930. Dressmaking and embroidery employed 15 per cent of the women and seemed to be increasing with the percentage of young female entrants to friendly societies going up from 8 per cent in 1913 to 28 per cent in 1930. Millinery had 12 per cent of the young female entrants in 1930. The women's fashion industry also developed in the 1930s. There was a marked increase in the 'white-collar' occupations. The percentage of young friendly society entrants becoming clerks increased from 6.5 in 1913 to 9.2 in 1930 for males, and from 5.6 to 11.9 for females; and in 1930 another 12.1 per cent of the girls became typists. 'Salesmen and shop assistants' formed almost 20 per cent of the young male entrants to friendly societies in 1930, and 17 per cent of the young females. This was in line with the increase in the distributive trades generally in Britain in the period, from 10 per cent to 13 per cent of total employment, as employment in distribution was growing faster than in any other sector.[46] Young Jews were thus, in a period of high unemployment, entering those occupations where there was still growth. But the tendency was more marked among young Jewish employees, to judge by the statistics of young London entrants to the Jewish friendly societies, since in 1930 30 per cent of them became clerks, shop assistants or salesmen and among girls also 30 per cent plus 12 per cent typists; thus between a third and nearly a half of the young entrants were going into the office or distributive sectors.

Similarly, movement of Jews in the 1930s into hairdressing, taxi-driving and entertainment, even the Jewish boxers, can be regarded as a response to unemployment in the staple trades and the prospects in consumer-oriented occupations which were improving in the 1930s with more money available to spend and rises in real living standards. Hairdressing, which in 1929 was the occupation of 2.5 per cent of the Jewish males in north and east London, saw its percentage of the young friendly society entrants increase from 5.5 in 1913 to 9.3 in 1930.[47] These occupations were usually also those which gave scope for the observed tendency of British Jews towards self-employment; in 1929 in north and east London 20 per cent of the occupied males were described as 'owners and managers'. Evidence from the early 1950s suggests that the proportion of Jews engaged in business on their own account was well above the national average.[48]

For much of economic and social change, education was the key. Young Jews, not least those of recent immigrant stock, took advantage of the improved facilities for education available between the wars. First, although the statutory school-leaving age remained at 14, an increasing number of pupils who did not go to grammar school were in reorganized 'modern schools' offering higher courses more suitable for those over 11, instead of merely staying on in the upper classes of elementary schools. Second, while the grammar schools provided for only a minority of the pupils in the 11–14 age group, the percentage of their places which were free and available by examination at 11 rose from under a third in 1920 to almost half by 1938.[49] There is evidence that Jewish children in elementary schools took advantage in the 1920s of the growing facilities for higher courses,[50] as well as increasingly competing for free places in the grammar schools; although, because the grammar school places were limited, only a minority of Jewish children of the relevant age group were in grammar schools, even if this minority was a higher percentage than for the general population.[51] The majority, who left school at 14, had to find a way upward by application, ingenuity and willingness to find new openings, as those who went into consumer-oriented trades did in the 1930s.

Movement of Jews into the professions, which before 1914 had been more or less limited to the older Anglo-Jewish community, spread after 1920 to the whole of the British Jewry as the children of the immigrants sought higher education. The proportion of Jews at the universities was bound to be low when as late as 1938 only 2 per cent of the 19-year-olds in the population of Britain were receiving full-time education. About 2 per cent of the 50,000 university students in 1936–7 were Jewish, about three times their proportion of the population but probably not disproportionate, bearing in mind the increased proportion of the middle class in the Jewish population. Of the Jewish students in a 1936–7 sample, 53.1 per cent were studying medicine or dentistry, and 10.9 per cent law.[52] Even allowing for the fact that many solicitors qualified by articles without going to the university, it still appears that medicine was a more favoured profession than law.

Accountancy and estate agency were professions into which young Jews steadily entered in the 1930s. 'For lower to middle-class Jewish families, estate agency became a favourite half-way house between trade and the professions like law and accounting'.[53]

In the absence of contemporary social survey material (other than in the *New Survey of London Life and Labour* of 1929-30), it is impossible to measure the pace of mobility between skilled occupations and the professional and employer classes among British Jews in this period. But that this process was taking place appears clear from later surveys indicating upward mobility.[54] This is indicated by information about occupations and social class of those born before and after certain dates. For instance, in Sheffield in 1975 there was a marked difference between those born before 1900 and those born between 1900 and 1930. Thus, of those born before 1900 33.7 per cent were skilled manual workers (social and economic group [SEG] 9 in the registrar-general's classification) but only 5.4 per cent of those born between 1900 and 1930; conversely 5.5 per cent of those born before 1900 were in the professions (SEGs 3 and 4) but 24.3 per cent of those born between 1900 and 1930.[55]

The *New Survey* of 1929 gave information about the social class structure of a sample of Jewish households in north and east London; the total Jewish population of these areas, 120,000, was about 60 per cent of the Jewish population of London or 40 per cent of that of Britain. The *Survey* distinguished between 'middle' and 'working' class roughly according to whether household income was above or below £250 a year. On this criterion, the 84,000 Jews of east London (Stepney, Bethnal Green, Poplar, Shoreditch) were 78 per cent working class and 22 per cent middle class. Jews formed 42.8 per cent of the Borough of Stepney's population, according to the samples; by comparison, only about 7 per cent of the non-Jewish population of Stepney was middle class. On the other hand, the 35,000 Jews estimated to live in north London (Hackney and Stoke Newington) were divided into 65 per cent middle class and 35 per cent working class. The move from east to north London was clearly economic and social as well as geographical.[56]

On these samples, 45,000 (37.5 per cent) of the Jews of the 120,000 in north and east London in 1929 were ranked as middle class. Since east and north London did not include the obviously middle-class suburbs of north-west London or the still thriving and affluent Jewish groups in west and central London, it is likely that the middle-class element of London Jewry was between 40 and 50 per cent by 1930, and that it would rise even higher, with increasing living standards and the immigration of the socially bourgeois Central Europeans, by the end of the 1930s.

How, in a period of depression, did the Anglo-Jewish community, in spite of acknowledged areas of poverty,[57] show such signs of upward mobility and a picture different from that of the Jewish quarters before 1914? The answer is first that after 1931 the depression affected primarily the industrial north, Wales and Scotland. Unemployment, apart from the depths of the depression of 1929-30, was largely a regional problem. In the 1930s the south-east and midlands were growth areas with much lower levels of unemployment. Because two-thirds of British Jews lived in the Greater London area and others in the rest of the south-east and in the midlands, the great majority of Jews lived in areas which recovered in the 1930s. Second, even in the 1920s average annual earnings in real terms were above the pre-1914 level and rose steadily almost throughout the 1930s: there was a rise of about 10 per cent from 96.7 (1930 = 100) in 1929 to 105.1 in 1931. The Jews were not generally in the coal, steel or shipbuilding industries or even still in textile manufacture, which all bore the brunt of the depression. The rise in real earnings increased demand for employment in the service and distributive trades and in consumer-oriented industries. It was precisely in these that the Jewish hairdressers, taxi-drivers, newsagents and tobacconists or confectioners were able to start their own businesses as self-employed workers. In retail shopping, Jews were involved in two main innovations of the period, which spread during the 1930s: multiple chains of shops and hire purchase. Both were often combined in the retail selling of furniture. In Birmingham between the wars 'the cheaper end of the trade was in Jewish hands.... We didn't compete with Maples [the famous London furniture store] but we aimed to supply the working classes. It was known as the "one shilling a week" trade; 95 per cent of our business was on the "never-never" (hire purchase).'[58] Of the 1,000 new retail chain stores opened between the wars, Marks and Spencer opened 129 between 1931 and 1935 and extended 670 previously opened stores.[59] Jewish entrepreneurs also developed a wide range of electrical goods, including radios, lamps and cookers. These were to meet the increasing demand in the 1930s for electrical equipment to go in the new private houses going up in the building boom of that decade. Increases in standards of living also resulted in more expenditure on leisure activities and entertainment, which led to Jewish involvement in films - both production and cinema ownership; and the 1930s were also the era of dance halls and many famous Jewish dance band leaders and musicians.[60] Thus the Birmingham Jewish community, with a population of about 6,000, could show a family of Jewish theatre owners; several owners of cinemas (some, like Oscar Deutsch, of national importance); and a remarkable number of professional musicians playing to popular audiences.[61]

A distinctive contribution was made by the Central European refugees of 1933-9. They could make their impact almost from the time of arrival because they were mainly middle-class professionals. In November 1939, *Otto Schiff, at the request of the Home Office, made an estimate that of 55,000 adult refugees 15 per cent were professionals, 50-60 per cent commercial, 15-20 per cent technicians, agricultural or domestic workers and only 5-10 manual workers. So, unlike many of the earlier Eastern European immigrants, they required no interval to adjust to the conditions of western life in large cities. Their integration in British economic life was, apart from any delay in learning English, limited only by restrictions on their use of their previous professional qualifications. Lawyers (apart from international lawyers) were faced with a very different legal system; doctors, whose skills were more readily transferable, were met by restrictions imposed largely, if not solely, by fear of competition. But by 1938 in commerce and industry refugees had started about 250 firms, which provided 15–20,000 jobs. These included clothing, textiles, furs (some 80 firms, transferred from the fur trade based on Leipzig). Before November 1938, when the earner refugees came, they could still bring some capital with them; the more numerous refugees who came in 1938 and 1939 could not, and therefore, their ability to open their own firms was more limited. However, refugees took advantage of the government's efforts to introduce new industry into the areas of high unemployment ('special areas'). Up to 200 businesses were opened by refugees in south Wales, the north-east and west Cumberland. These included businesses in clothing, textiles, chemicals and engineering.[62]

One aspect of the arrival of the Central Europeans between 1933 and 1939 was its effect in increasing the number of academics and scientists in the Jewish community. Before 1914, Jewish academics and scientists were comparatively rare and almost limited to members of pre-1881 families. Between the wars the new generation of East European origin began to enter the universities but the arrival of the Central Europeans had a dramatic effect. One index for measuring scientific achievement is the number of Jewish Fellows of the Royal Society; the Fellows as a whole remained more or less at the figure of 450 between 1900 and 1947, 15 being elected annually till 1930 and 17 annually between 1931 and 1938, an objective test of scientific achievement. In 1901 1.0 per cent of the Fellows (other than foreign Fellows resident abroad) were Jewish, in 1910 0.6 per cent, in 1920 2 per cent, in 1930 3 per cent, in 1940 3.7 per cent and in 1947 5.3 per cent. The rise in the percentage between 1910 and 1940 was due to the children of the 1881–1914 immigrants, since of the 20 Jewish Fellows elected between 1900 and 1940 over three-quarters came from families which settled in Britain after 1850. The even more remarkable rise between 1940 and 1947 was caused by the Central European immigration, which took less time to make itself felt in British science and professional life.[63]

While in terms of demographic, occupational and social class patterns there was thus a progressive fusion between the pre-1881 and recent immigrant sections of the community, this was true only to a limited extent of the communal leadership. The Board of Deputies, the main representative body, the United Synagogue, the largest religious body, and the Jewish Board of Guardians, the leading social welfare organization may be regarded as typical; although the last two were concerned with London alone, the London community was two-thirds of the British Jewish population. Between 1918 and 1939 fourteen people held leading office (president, vice-president) in the Board of Deputies: of these at least nine were members of families (Rothschild, Henriques, Cohen, Samuel) which had led the community before 1881; the remainder were all British-born of families settled before 1881. The four presidents of the Deputies were *Sir Stuart Samuel; H.S.Q. Henriques (1865-1925); *Sir Osmond d'Avigdor-Goldsmid; and *Neville Laski. The first three were all members of pre-1881 leading families. Only Laski was of Eastern European origin and his father, Nathan Laski, the leader of Manchester Jewry and a former treasurer of the board, had been born in England in 1863; Neville Laski himself had served as an officer in the First World War, was educated at Oxford and became a King's Counsel before 1939. Of the twenty leading officers of the United Synagogue during the period, at least twelve were members of pre-1881 leading families, none was a member of an 1881-1914 immigrant family and possibly none were even of Eastern European origin. Symbolically, throughout the period *Lionel de Rothschild was president and *Sir Robert Waley-Cohen one of the two vice-presidents. In the Board of Guardians, nine at least out of fifteen holders of high office were members of pre-1881 leading families and none were of 1881-1914 immigrant families. Two of the presidents were first cousins, *Sir Leonard and Hannah Cohen (1875-1946).

Thus at the highest level of communal institutions there was little, if any, change compared with 1881. At a slightly lower level of the process a change was beginning to appear. The Joint Foreign Committee of the Board of Deputies and the Anglo-Jewish Association was about as near as Anglo-Jewry came to having a central policy-making body. It had seventeen members in 1925 and eighteen in 1935. In 1925 half were members of pre-1881 leading families, in 1935 a third. Already figures unlikely to have been found in the pre-1881 equivalent, the Conjoint Foreign Committee were appearing. In both years, Rabbi Samuel Daiches (1878-1949), lecturer at Jews' College, born in Vilna and educated in Germany, was a member, as was Morris Myer (1876-1944), born in Rumania and a Yiddish writer and editor of the Yiddish daily, *Die Zeit*. In 1935 the membership also included *Israel Cohen, born in Manchester of Eastern European immigrant parents, secretary of the Zionist Organization, and H.A. Goodman, the political secretary of the right-wing orthodox Agudas Israel World Organization. By 1935 the Board and even the Anglo-Jewish Association were beginning to reflect the rise of the East Europeans,[64] even if the leadership was still firmly in the hands of the pre-1881 leading families and their co-opted associates.

For spiritual leadership, however, British Jewry continued to look outside its own native ranks. The Chief Rabbinate was held from 1913 to 1946 by the Slovakian-born, American-educated *Dr Joseph Hermann Hertz; the principalship of Jews' College from 1907 to 1939 by the Hungarian-born Adolph Büchler (1862-1939); and from the 1930s the dominant influence on the London Beth Din (the Chief Rabbi's court) and thence on the standards of religious observance in the United Synagogue was that of the Eastern European Talmudist, Rabbi Yehazkel Abramsky

(1886–1976). Even among the non-orthodox religious movements, while *Claude G. Montefiore, the patrician theologian, had virtually founded Liberal Judaism, he had called in from America in 1911 the East European-born Israel Mattuck (1883–1954) as minister; and the latter was probably the outstanding cleric in progressive Judaism in Britain between the wars. There were however a growing number of rabbis and ministers of either British or European origin but of British education who served the United Synagogue and analogous provincial congregations. These continued to try to combine adherence to traditional Judaism (as defined by the Chief Rabbi) with an English approach to congregational organization and conduct. This pattern, which had been characteristic of British Jewry for at least half a century before the mass immigration began in 1881, increasingly became acceptable to the immigrants and their children, to judge by the extent to which they joined and thereby expanded the United Synagogue and its provincial analogues. This process was assisted, in London at least, by the fact that the centrally organized United Synagogue was able to offer help to those founding new congregations in the suburban areas. Thus, when the East Europeans or their children moved to a suburb, they would normally find a congregation under the authority of the Chief Rabbinate already in existence but not usually a reform or liberal congregation at this period. Hence, if they wished to continue to identify with Judaism by joining a synagogue, the traditional synagogue was the readily available option.

Throughout this period J.H. Hertz was Chief Rabbi, a dominant, controversial figure: it was said of him in the *Dictionary of National Biography* that he never despaired of finding a peaceful solution to a problem when all other possibilities had failed. His outspoken Zionism, notably in his letter to *The Times* of 28 May 1917, refuting the views of the presidents of the Board of Deputies and the AJA, brought him into conflict with a communal leadership which was then substantially anti- or non-Zionist. His quarrels with Sir Robert Waley Cohen, who was the leading lay force in the United Synagogue throughout nearly all of his chief rabbinate, were legendary. These were not entirely due to the clash of two overpowering temperaments. While they co-operated on a number of questions, there was an increasing divergence of religious philosophy. Waley Cohen, personally non-observant, believed passionately in an Anglo-Jewish religious tradition which he held to be officially orthodox; Hertz felt that this was irretrievably diluted unless reinforced by full traditional observance. Hertz defined his own position in 1919 as 'Traditional Judaism – the teachings and practices which have come down to the House of Israel through the ages... and the life consecrated by Jewish observances – all of these in indissoluble union with the best thought and culture of our times'; or in 1931 as 'Progressive Conservatism: religious advance without loss of traditional Jewish values and without estrangement from the collective consciousness of the House of Israel'. He was a fierce opponent of reform, and even more of Liberal Judaism, which he described as a 'moving staircase out of Judaism' and as having 'fatal consequences to Jewry and Judaism'. Towards the end of his life he seems increasingly to have appreciated the virtues of the exclusive orthodoxy represented by his son-in-law, Dr Solomon Schonfeld, presiding rabbi of the Union of Orthodox Hebrew Congregations (a body which did not recognize the authority of his Chief Rabbinate). He was, however, no obscurantist; a magnificent popularizer, his commentary on the Pentateuch drew freely on non-Jewish as well as Jewish sources; and, while regarding higher criticism as 'a perversion of history', he included references to archaeology and ancient history not to be found in later orthodox Jewish commentaries in English.[65]

Some idea of the relative strengths of the different religious trends can be gained from the statistics of synagogue marriages. In 1929 there were 2,380 synagogue marriages of which all were 'orthodox' except 31 reform and 8 liberal; in 1938, 2,723 of which 71 were reform and 64 liberal.[66] While there was thus a considerable proportionate increase in reform and liberal marriage during the 1930s, these still were only 5 per cent of the total. The United Synagogue gives some idea of how far the pre-1881 Anglo-Jewish pattern of synagogal organization replaced the pattern of small *hebroth* which the Eastern European immigrants had brought with them. Between 1870 and 1920 twenty-one individual congregations had joined the United Synagogue, including the five original constituents; between 1920 and 1940, thirty-one joined and the male membership nearly doubled in those twenty years. In 1926 the Federation of Synagogues had 12,565 families; in 1937, 13,000 families in 68 synagogues (compared with 51 in 1912).[67] There was also an increase in the total number of synagogues in England and Wales from around 150 in 1901 and 250 in 1921 to about 300 in 1931 and 350 in 1940.[68] These increases were more than the estimated increase in the Jewish population and seem to represent a general trend towards increased synagogue membership, which it has been estimated was held by about a third of all Jewish households in Britain in 1933.[69]

Another indication of the change in pattern from life in concentrated quarters of recent immigrants to middle-class suburbia can be seen in the changes in the figures for attendance at different types of part-time Jewish education in London:

	1919–20	1938
Jewish Religious Education Board (JREB)	4,801	2,893
Talmud Torah Trust	3,845	2,636
Synagogue classes	3,544	4,931

These figures, however, represented only about half the total number of

Jewish children in the 7-13 age group for which these classes catered. In 1938-9, the Director of Jewish Education, Herbert M. Adler, estimated that 'just half our children are being taught in the Provinces, and a little more in London'.[70]

The Jewish Religious Education Board classes met after school hours in local authority schools with a considerable proportion of Jewish pupils; they were characteristic of the previous generation, when Jews were crowded in the immigrant quarters and overflowed from the Jewish day schools into the local authority schools. During the inter-war period in less than twenty years their numbers declined by nearly a third. Even more marked was the fall in the number of those attending the Talmud Torahs which provided a fairly intensive Jewish education, on most evenings after school as well as Sunday mornings, in east and north London. On the other hand, the synagogue classes, meeting mainly on Sunday mornings, with some pupils attending one or two evenings a week, were characteristic of the suburban synagogues; and their numbers increased significantly, although in their more restricted hours, and with a different and less traditional curriculum, they gave a more modest Jewish education than the Talmud Torahs.

An attempt to raise a Jewish War Memorial Fund to reorganize Jewish education, including the transfer of Jews' College to either Oxford or Cambridge, had only limited success. It resulted in the establishment of a Central Council of Jewish Education in 1920 to co-ordinate and monitor Jewish education. No new voluntary day schools, assisted by the local authority, were founded although the Jews' Free School still had some 3,000 pupils in east London. The main educational thrust of the communal establishment was in part-time education. But new initiatives were taken by groups peripheral to the main communal bodies. This was done under the inspiration of continental patterns of Judaism and therefore ran counter to the pattern of anglicization so marked in other aspects of communal development in this period.[71] For instance, there were important developments in the field of the *Yeshivot* (Talmudical colleges). In addition to the *Yeshivot* already founded in London (Etz Hyyim, Tree of Life College, 1903) and Manchester (1911) and smaller provincial *Yeshivot*, the small community of Gateshead, of about 2-300 members, which had maintained a strict standard of Eastern European orthodoxy - exclusive in that only strict sabbath observers were eligible for full synagogue membership - founded in 1929 a *Yeshiva*, with some help from neighbouring communities, notably Sunderland. Central European immigration in the 1930s brought both distinguished scholars from German orthodox institutions and many students. Over 600 young men studied at the *Yeshivah* between 1933 and 1939, making Gateshead a centre of learning of international significance in the Jewish world. The arrival of orthodox Jewish businessmen who opened firms in the Development Area added to the financial support for Gateshead institutions.[72]

While the East European immigrants, after they had settled, tended broadly to enter and strengthen the central or establishment form of traditional Judaism, the Central European refugees of 1933-9 tended to reinforce the outer wings of religious adherents. On the other hand, the German tradition of moderate reform, and of official communities which included varying religious elements, brought new recruits to the British ranks of reform Judaism. On the other hand, the tradition begun in Frankfurt, and continued elsewhere in Germany such as in Berlin and Koenigsberg, of congregations whose membership was limited to those of strict orthodox observance and who therefore opted out of the local general community, led to the strengthening of similar groups of exclusive orthodoxy in Britain. This was particularly true in north London where the strictly orthodox congregation Adath Yisroel (Congregation of Israel) had grown out of the north London Beth Hamedrash in 1909, after its former partner, the Machzike Hadath, had joined the established community in 1905.[73] The Hungarian-born Rabbi Victor Schonfeld who came to the Adath Yisroel in 1909 made it the nucleus of the Union of Orthodox Hebrew Congregations, which he formed in 1927. In 1927 he formed the Jewish Secondary Schools Movement, which aimed at combining secular with orthodox religious education, on Samson Raphael Hirsch's Frankfurt model.[74]

By 1938 it had 300 pupils in north London.[75] The Central European immigration led to the foundation of new orthodox communities in north-west London, Manchester and elsewhere. Rabbi Dr Eli Munk (1900-1978), who came to London in 1930 as temporary successor to Rabbi Victor Schonfeld, founded in 1934 his own community in Golders Green, which was joined by increasing numbers of orthodox refugees and won a reputation for meticulous orthodoxy combined with appreciation of western culture.[76] A vital contribution was made by the refugee rabbis who came from Central Europe in the later 1930s. There were more than thirty orthodox rabbis, who were appointed to congregations throughout the country. In addition to the right-wing orthodox congregations already mentioned, several took key positions in mainstream orthodoxy including three *dayanim* of the London Beth Din (Rabbis Grunfeld, Julius Jakobovits and Steinberg) and Rabbi Dr Alexander Altmann as communal rabbi of Manchester. In general, the influence of these orthodox rabbis from Central Europe was to replace the latitudinarian attitudes of Anglo-Jewish orthodoxy with a stricter continental approach, emphasizing the importance of day schools and various forms of religious study. Similarly, the arrival of thirty-five reform refugee rabbis, used to a strong reform movement in Germany, developed new congregations and transformed 'a motley group of scattered synagogues' into a coherent movement.[77]

A new religious element that was built up in the inter-war period, especially in north London, was that of the Hasidim. There had been Hasidic groups among the Eastern European immigrants before 1914 but no really major Hasidic figures, and the number of Hasidim was limited by the fact that the immigrants came mainly from areas in Eastern Europe, such as Lithuania, which were not distinctively Hasidic, with relatively few from Hasidic areas like Galicia. There were Hasidic groups in east London, which generally worked with the established community through membership of the Federation of Synagogues in London (which after 1905 included the Machzike Hadath Synagogue, some of whose prominent members were of Hasidic origin).[78] Rabbi Moses Avigdor Chaikin (1852-1928), a Habad Hasid, served as minister in Sheffield, chief minister of the Federation of Synagogues and a member of the London Beth Din or court of the Chief Rabbi. There were also Hasidic groups from before 1914 in Manchester, Glasgow, Leeds and Liverpool. In the 1920s a number of Hasidic rabbis settled in London, among them Rabbi A.L. Twersky (the 'Trisker Rebbe'), who was associated with Rabbi Victor Schonfeld in setting up the Jewish Secondary Schools movement and remained in north London till his departure for Israel in 1964; and the rabbi of Biala, Rabbi N.D. Rabbinowicz, whose home in Dalston became a centre of Hasidism in north London.[79]

Overall, however, so long as British Jews identified with the community, they tended to do so through the institutions which recognized the authority of the Chief Rabbinate, or the analogous authorities of the Spanish and Portuguese congregations; and control of these institutions still remained ultimately in the hands of the same elements who had controlled the community even before 1881. But, as the children of the immigrants grew up and the descendants of earlier generations of British Jewry became further integrated in British life, there was an inevitable trend in a free society towards assimilation (i.e. merging in the wider community) as distinct from acculturation (i.e. adopting its social habits). The growing number of mixed marriages and their effect on the integrity of the community resulted in a pronouncement by the London Beth Din in 1945, banning those who had married wives not converted to Judaism according to the *Halakha* (Jewish Law) from congregational membership or, if already admitted to it, from holding office. It is difficult, however, to find firm evidence of any high rate of intermarriage between the wars. Between 1921 and 1940 synagogue marriages averaged 2,565 a year and increased during the period; they averaged 8.2 per 1,000 of the estimated Jewish population. This is below the 9 per 1,000 of the 1901-20 period, when the recent immigrants brought a high marriage rate with them from Eastern Europe. But 8.2 per 1,000 is only marginally below the 8.3 per 1,000 marriage rate for England and Wales in the same period.[80] This suggests that there was not a substantial amount of intermarriage outside the synagogue with any substantial impact on the size of the community.[81]

The process of communal integration may have been assisted by the apparent tendency of the immigrant males to marry British-born Jewish brides.[82] This resulted in households in which one parent was foreign-born, one English. In such families,

> despite their foreign sounding surnames, a surprising proportion of Jewish children grew up in an English-speaking home environment during their formative years and thus were able to take full advantage of the educational system.... Children [born between 1900 and 1930] were able to enter the general social milieu with comparative ease for first-generation British.... They did not initially regard themselves as temporary residents in Britain. They were therefore highly motivated to adapt and succeed from the outset and they threw themselves into becoming British in every sense of the word, from playing cricket to wearing bowler hats.

Aided by the established Jewish population the newcomers wanted to adapt to the surrounding British society. 'The most dramatic result was that Yiddish as a spoken language almost died out in a generation.'[83] Whereas Britain has since 1867 had some 160 Yiddish newspapers and periodicals, only about 30 remained active between 1920 and 1940. On the other hand, the continuity and continued growth of a weekly in English like the *Jewish Chronicle* (which in 1934 absorbed the *Jewish World*, founded in 1873) provided a unifying link for the Jewish population, moulding opinion and keeping families informed about personal and communal events.[84]

The process of integration between 1918 and 1939, which resulted in the fusion of the 1881-1914 immigrants and their descendants with the pre-1881 community, was no doubt helped by the longstanding policy of the communal leadership to further anglicization through the Jewish voluntary schools, clubs, youth organizations like the Jewish Lads' Brigade and even friendly societies;[85] the continuation of this policy after 1914 was made possible by the grip that the pre-1881 leading families continued to have on the machinery of communal government. But it was assisted by other factors. Jews joined the general trade unions after trade boards set up in 1909 regulated wages and conditions even in the former immigrant trades like tailoring.[86] The Amalgamated Society of Tailors joined the union which became the National Union of Tailors and Garment Workers, and in 1938 the United Ladies Tailors Trade Union joined the National Union as well. By 1939 the only specifically Jewish trade unions were the Bakers, and a branch of the general Furniture Trades Union.[87]

With the rise of the Labour Party, the Jewish working class in east London and other cities transferred its allegiance from Jewish political movements or the Liberal Party to Labour and sometimes the Communists. By the mid-1930s most working-class Jews in Britain, and probably a significant number of the middle class, voted Labour. In so far as Jews began to make a political career on the left, they did so as members of a British political party, not of a specifically Jewish one.[88]

Thus by 1939 one could regard the Anglo-Jewish community as one in which the descendants of the Eastern European immigrants of 1881–1939 had been fully integrated, indeed might be said to have taken over the community; and the Anglo-Jewish community itself had increasingly become integrated in British society. While both these developments had been objectives of the communal leadership, they also happened because they were what the overwhelming majority of the people concerned, in their different ways, wanted.

Notes

1. See Chapter 5.
2. Morris Ginsberg, *The British People Today*, London, 1956, p. 18. Apart from the post-1933 Central European refugees, the 'typical emigrant of the 1930s was from Poland and saw Britain only as a staging post'. This is based on records of over 25,000 emigrants annually at the Jews' Temporary Shelter during the 1930s (Louise London, 'Jewish Refugees, Anglo-Jewry and British Government Policy' in David Cesarani (ed.), *The Making of Modern Anglo-Jewry*, Oxford, 1990 pp. 167–8).
3. World trade grew by 25 per cent a decade before 1914 and by only 8.5 per cent in the 1920s. For a recent general survey of the economy of the inter-war period, see John Stevenson, *British Society 1914–45*, London, 1984, pp. 103–15.
4. Average annual real earnings were 82.8 (1930 = 100) in 1913 and 107.7 in 1938 (D.H. Aldcroft, *The Inter-War Economy: Britain 1919–39*, London, 1970, pp. 352, 364).
5. The number of workers in the distributive trades increased from 1.6m in 1920–2 to 2.4m in 1937–8 (Stevenson, *British Society*, p. 113).
6. The *Jewish Year Book* figures are given in S.J. Prais and M. Schmool, 'Statistics of Jewish marriages in Great Britain 1901–65', *JJS* IX (2), 1967, Appendix, Table I.
7. H.L. Trachtenberg, 'Estimate of the Jewish population of London, 1929', *Journal of the Royal Statistical Society* 96, Part I, 1933.
8. M. Kantorowitsch, 'Estimate of the Jewish population of London, 1929–33', *Journal of the Royal Statistical Society* 99, Part II, 1936. A critique of Kantorowitsch is given by Hannah Neustatter, 'Demographic and other statistical aspects', in Maurice Freedman (ed.) *A Minority in Britain*, London, 1955, pp. 66–8, who also discusses Redcliffe N. Salaman, 'Anglo-Jewish vital statistics', *Jewish Chronicle Supplement* 1921, 4–8, Salaman gave an estimate of 300,000 for Anglo-Jewry but this was for 1914 and based on extrapolation from the calculation of S. Rosenbaum of 240,000 for 1901. See S.J. Prais and M. Schmool, 'Size and structure of the Anglo-Jewish population', *JJS* X (1), 8.
9. Figures given by the Home Secretary, House of Commons Official Report, 12 October 1939, c. 539.
10. A.J. Sherman, *Island Refuge*, 1973, Appendix I.
11. Julius Isaac, *British Post-War Migration*, Cambridge, 1954, pp. 5–6.
12. Julius Gould, *Jewish Commitment: A Study in London*, London, 1984, p. 11.

13. Charles Booth, *Life and Labour of the People of London,* 1900 edn, First Series, I, p. 577.
14. Henrietta F. Adler in *New Survey of London Life and Labour,* London, 1934, VI, p. 273 and p. 293, Table I.
15. Prais and Schmool, 'Jewish marriages', Table 4.
16. Barry A. Kosmin, 'Nuptiality and fertility patterns of British Jewry 1850–1980', in D.A. Coleman (ed.) *Demography of Immigrants and Minority Groups in the United Kingdom,* London, 1982, pp. 245–61.
17. Ibid., p. 255, Table VII(d).
18. Kantorowitsch, 'Jewish population of London', pp. 75–83; Kosmin, 'Nuptiality', p. 256.
19. E. Lewis-Fanning, 'Family limitation and its influence on human fertility', *Papers of the Royal Commission on Population,* London, 1949, I, quoted in Kosmin, 'Nuptiality', p. 258.
20. Barry A. Kosmin, Caren Levy and Peter Wigodsky, *The Social Demography of Redbridge Jewry,* 1979, pp. 14–16, 18.
21. Barry A. Kosmin, Varzy Bauer and Nigel Grizzard, *Steel City Jews,* 1976, p. 18.
22. Kosmin *et al., Redbridge Jewry,* p. 18.
23. Kosmin, 'Nuptiality', p. 257.
24. Adler, *New Survey,* VI, p. 294.
25. V.D. Lipman, 'The rise of Jewish suburbia', *TJHSE* XXI, 91–2.
26. V.D. Lipman, *Social History of the Jews in England,* London, 1954, pp. 168–9.
27. Lipman, 'Suburbia', p. 92.
28. Adler, *New Survey,* VI, p. 297.
29. The *New Survey* (VI, p. 298) gives for 1930 5.3 per cent of London synagogue membership to synagogues in Hampstead and Willesden, and 3.6 per cent in Southgate, Hendon, Finchley and Wembley. These percentages probably underrepresent the percentage of Jewish residents in those areas because of the number of residents who still retained membership of synagogues in the City of London, Westminster, St. Marylebone, or elsewhere.
30. Stevenson, *British Society,* p. 129. In 1935 the average annual salary for a railway clerk was £224, for a bank clerk £368 (John Burnett, *A History of The Cost of Living,* London, 1969, p. 299).
31. Aubrey Newman, *The United Synagogue 1870–1970,* 1976, pp. 216. 218.
32. Geoffrey Alderman, *History of the Hendon Synagogue,* London, 1978, p. 1.
33. Deborah J. de Lange and Barry A. Kosmin, *Community Resources for a Community Survey* (Redbridge) London, 1979, p. 7.
34. For a description of the Cricklewood congregation, which then had a relatively large number of observant and scholarly members, see the account by the then rabbi, L.I. Rabinowitz, in *JC,* 29 May 1981.
35. Lipman, *Social History,* p. 178; Alderman, *Hendon Synagogue,* p. 1. For Finchley, where settlement began in the mid-1920s but grew slightly later in the 1930s because the underground railways did not come to East Finchley till 1940, see Hilary and Salmond S. Levin, *Jubilee at Finchley,* London, 1976.
36. Ernest Krausz, *Leeds Jewry,* Cambridge, 1964; Kosmin *et al., Steel City Jews,* p. 5.
37. Krausz, *Leeds Jewry,* pp. vii, 22–6.
38. For a general account of the pattern of Jewish urban settlement in America and the meaning of the terms, 'areas of first, second and third settlement', see

Marshall Sklare, *Conservative Judaism*, Glencoe, IL, 1952; for the process in London, see Lipman, 'Suburbia'.

39. D.H. Aldcroft, *British Economy between the Wars*, Oxford, 1983, p. 25.
40. Stevenson, *British Society*, p. 144.
41. Lipman, *Social History*, p. 107 (for 1901 figures); Adler, *New Survey*, VI, p. 295.
42. V.D. Lipman, *A Century of Social Service*, London, 1959, p. 150 n.2.
43. J. Thomas, 'Leeds and its industrial growth', *Leeds Journal*, September 1954 (quoted in Krausz, *Leeds Jewry*, p. 29).
44. Harold Pollins, *Economic History of the Jews in England*, London and Toronto 1982, pp. 186–7.
45. Lipman, *Social Service*, p. 151 n.1.
46. Aldcroft, *British Economy*, p. 66. See also Anne J. Kershen, *Off the Peg*, London Museum of Jewish Life, 1988, for the Jewish contribution to the women's wholesale clothing industry.
47. Adler, *New Survey*, VI, p. 295.
48. For a discussion of the figures, see V.D. Lipman, 'Anglo-Jewish occupations', *JJS* II, 212–13.
49. Stevenson, *British Society*, pp. 250, 252.
50. For instance in a school where Jews formed 30 per cent of the roll, 66 per cent of those taking higher courses were Jewish; in another, where Jews were 90 per cent of the roll, the number taking higher courses rose from 2 per cent to 11 per cent between 1923 and 1929 (Adler, *New Survey*, p. 283).
51. Pollins, *Economic History*, p. 189. As late as 1950 only a quarter of Manchester Jewish children were in grammar schools.
52. Stevenson, *British Society*, p. 252; G.D.V. Block, 'Jewish Students at the Universities, 1936–9', *Sociological Review* XXIV (3–4), 183–97.
53. Oliver Marriot, *The Property Boom*, 1967, p. 15. This book also gives a list of 110 developers who owned at least £1m worth of property shares in 1967; 70 or 63.5 per cent of them appear to be Jewish and, out of these 70, twenty-four are listed as having estate agency as their original profession.
54. See e.g. S.J. Prais and M. Schmool, 'The social class structure of Anglo-Jewry 1961', *JJS* XV (1), 1975, especially pp. 9–11 (comparison of older and younger age groups).
55. Kosmin *et al.*, *Steel City Jews*, p. 24. Sheffield, though a small community of 1,100 in 1975 is cited because it was a mixed-class community without undue movement from it of the more successful.
56. The details, in so far as not printed in Adler, *New Survey*, VI, are available in a folder (6/1) containing the original draft and statistics of Miss Adler's chapter on the Jews of London, in the Manuscript Room of the British Library of Political and Economic Sciences. The definition of middle class is given in *New Survey*, III, p. 416. It includes professional and clerical (including commercial travellers, insurance agents, etc.); publicans; shopkeepers; self-employed if their earnings exceed £250 a year; but shop assistants are treated as working class, unless they are managers or supervisors or earn over £250 a year, and hawkers and street traders are similarly regarded as working class. In the printed analyses the middle class is generally excluded but retained in the Jewish statistics because of the relatively small number in the Jewish house sample.

57. For the causes of poverty among London Jews between the wars, see Lipman, *Social Service*, pp. 145-52. While in Stepney in 1929 Jews comprised over two-thirds of the total middle-class households in the borough, when Jews in the borough were working class, they tended to be poorer than their neighbours. The house sample of east London showed 13.7 per cent of working-class Jews below the poverty line as defined in Adler's *New Survey* (£2 per week for a 'moderate-sized' family, corresponding to 18/- to £1 per week in the Booth survey over forty years earlier), compared with 12.7 per cent of the working class as a whole in the same area (*New Survey*, VI, p. 287).
58. Zoe Josephs, 'The furniture trade', in Z. Josephs (ed.) *Birmingham Jewry II: More Aspects 1740-1930*, Birmingham Jewish History Group, 1984, p. 53.
59. Gornowy Rees, *St. Michael: A History of Marks and Spencer*, 1969.
60. For details, see Pollins, *Economic History*, pp. 203-4.
61. Josephs, *Birmingham Jewry II*, pp. 103-21.
62. Pollins, *Economic History*, pp. 205-8. For Otto Schiff's estimate, ms. addition to letter of 17 November 1939 from J.N. Beckett, Ministry of Health to Miss J. Williams, Home Office, PRO HO 213/294.
63. Redcliffe N. Salaman, 'The Jewish Fellows of the Royal Society', *M* V, 146-75. Salaman included as Jewish all persons of Jewish parentage on both sides, even if they were not themselves Jewish by religion, which he thought (p. 149) to be the case with a third of the Fellows listed between 1723 and 1947.
64. The composition of these organizations and details of their leading members can be found in the annual *Jewish Year Book*. See also Newman, *United Synagogue* and Lipman, *Social Service* which have lists of officers in their respective appendices.
65. For Hertz, *EJ* 8, pp. 397-8; *DNB* 1940-50, s.v.; Robert Henriques, *Sir Robert Waley Cohen*, 1966, pp. 339-48; Newman, *United Synagogue*, pp. 125, 136-7; J.H. Hertz, *The New Paths: Whither Do They Lead?*, 1946, pp. 4, 5, 20. For Büchler, see Bruno Marmarstein, 'Adolph Büchler, Principal of Jews' College, 1906-1939', *TJHSE*, XXX, pp. 219-234. For Abramsky, *DNB*, 1970-80 s.v.
66. Prais and Schmool 'Jewish Marriages', Appendix I, Table 1.
67. Newman, *United Synagogue*, pp. 214-16; Geoffrey Alderman, *Federation of Synagogues*, 1987, p. 58.
68. The figures are based on the slightly different totals published by the registrar-general and in the *Jewish Year Book*; these are given in S.J. Prais, 'Synagogue statistics in Great Britain', *JJS* XIV (2), 1972, 225.
69. Prais and Schmool, 'Size and Structure', p. 12, based on analysis of figures of those buried or cremated under any kind of Jewish auspices.
70. Figures in *Jewish Year Book*, 1920; and 1938-9. Report of Central Committee for Jewish Education, p. 39; ibid, p. 24.
71. A.M. Hyamson, *Jews' College 1855-1955*, 1954, pp. 98-102; *EJ* VI, p. 448; S.J. Gould and Shaul Esh, *Jewish Life in Modern Britain*, 1964, p. 67.
72. Lewis Olsover, *The Jewish Communities of North East England*, Newcastle, 1981, pp. 221-50.
73. A. Carlebach in *EJ* 2, pp. 254-5.
74. *EJ* 14, p. 994.
75. *Jewish Year Book*, 1939.
76. See *The Blessing of Eliyahu*, 1982, pp. 28, 31, 92. This states that Rabbi

Munk's Marburg University Ph.D. was on the religious poetry of Wordsworth.

77. Jonathan Magonet, 'Refugee rabbis who changed Anglo-Jewry', *JC*, 1 September 1989.
78. Examples of Hasidic groups in east London before 1914 were the 'Jerusalem Shul' (Union Street); *Hevrat Agudat Ahim Nusach Ari* (Hanbury Street, later New Court, Fashion Street), which were original constituents of the Federation of Synagogues in 1887; the Austrian (ie Galician) Dzikower Synagogue (Fieldgate, later Dunk Street) from 1896; the Hasidim of Rizhyn at Buxton Street; and the 'Kahal Hasidim' for Hasidim in general from 1892 (Old Montagu Street, later Black Lion Yard). See H. Rabinowicz, *The World of Hasidism*, 1970, pp. 229–31, 234.
79. *JC*, 24 July 1964; Rabinowicz, *World of Hasidism*, pp. 231–2.
80. S.J. Prais in V.D. and S.L. Lipman (eds.) *Jewish Life in Britain 1962–77*, New York, 1981, pp. 5, 6.
81. This is the conclusion of Moshe Davis, *Mixed Marriages in Western Jewry*, Jerusalem, 1969, p. 185. Appendix III of this perceptive study gives the London Beth Din pronouncement of 1945.
82. Prais and Schmool, 'Jewish marriages', p. 157; B.A. Kosmin and N. Grizzard, *Jews in an Inner London Borough*, n.d. (c. 1975), p. 22.
83. Kosmin *et al.*, *Steel City Jews*, pp. 25–6.
84. Josef Fraenkel, *The Jewish Press in Great Britain 1826–1963*, 1963, pp. 7, 47–62.
85. Lipman, *Social History*, pp. 144–9.
86. Pollins, *Economic History*, p. 146.
87. *Jewish Year Book*, 1939; for the end of the separate tailoring and mantlemaking unions, see Kershen *Off the Peg*, p. 19.
88. Geoffrey Alderman, *The Jewish Community in British Politics*, Oxford, 1983, p. 115. Emanuel (later Lord) Shinwell was the first Jewish Labour member of parliament, elected in 1922. By 1931, when there were seventeen Jewish MPs (2.8 per cent of the House of Commons) six were Labour, five Liberal and six Conservatives, but this was a bad year for Labour (Alderman, *Jewish Community*, pp. 106, 174).

Chapter 10

Prospect: 1939–89

Background

The past half century has included in its first decade two of the most important events of modern Jewish history: the holocaust and the creation of the State of Israel. Even after half a century one cannot be certain in evaluating the long-term effects of these events on British Jewry. The holocaust of European Jewry was especially poignant in its impact on those more recent immigrants whose relations perished but it had a traumatic effect on the community as a whole, as shown by a continuing, indeed increasing, preoccupation with the spiritual and historical significance of the unique tragedy. The losses of European Jewry also meant that British Jewry for a time became not only the leading but the largest Jewish community in Europe (until by the 1960s the immigrants from north Africa began to arrive in France and made that community by 1989 more than twice the size of British Jewry).

The conflicts which preceded the creation of the State of Israel created tensions with the British government and, to a lesser extent, with the British people: this was the very situation that the opponents of a Jewish national entity had feared. These tensions continued in the first years after the creation of the state but eased after the establishment of normal diplomatic relations between Britain and Israel in 1949. British Jews, virtually without exception, identified passionately with Israel during that country's major crises in 1956, 1967 and 1973. They enjoyed the wide popularity that Israel's unexpected victory in the Six Day War of 1967 evoked in Britain. But in the 1980s they were acutely sensitive when Israel was subjected to increasing criticism during the Lebanon war and the Palestinian *intifada* (uprising). Nor during the 1980s was British Jewry unanimous in its support for Israel government policy. The spectre of dual loyalties, however, which haunted the anti-Zionists in the first half of the century did not appear; but, in the absence of any life and death confrontation between the two countries, it could not be said that it had been laid permanently to rest or had never existed at all.

A third factor, which affected the status of Anglo-Jewry and its relations with other sections of the population, was the considerable immigration from the New Commonwealth in the 1960s and subsequently. This and what has been termed a multicultural society have put the question of Jewish identity in a new perspective. With so many ethnic groups proclaiming their separate identity, in the 1980s Jews, especially the younger generation, have felt freer to display their own religious and cultural identity, instead of, as in the past, always trying to acculturate to a uniform British norm of appearance and behaviour. Hence, towards the end of the period, *kippot* (skull-caps, worn to comply with the religious injunction to cover the head) and varieties of Hasidic dress were worn without embarrassment in several areas. On the other hand, some of the new ethnic minorities displayed a hostility to Israel and to Zionism, which could only too easily become indistinguishable from anti-Semitism; and, numerically, Jews were a far smaller minority than several of the recent immigrant ethnic communities.

The outbreak of war in 1939 had caused a disruption of Jewish life in Britain, although nothing like that inflicted on European Jewry. At the outbreak of war children and some mothers were evacuated from London and other large towns in which the Jewish population was concentrated. The heavy bombing which began in the autumn of 1940 brought a more general dispersal, including the foundation of quite large communities in towns like Oxford which had previously had no, or only small, Jewish communities. The general effect of evacuation was to plunge Jewish children, used to the routine of life in a more or less traditional Jewish environment, into a non-Jewish home life. In spite of the efforts of communal organizations, Jewish education of children was reduced to a minimum. A similar disruption was caused by the call-up of both men and women into the armed forces. A third cause of disruption was the internment of enemy aliens for some months, and the deporation of some overseas to the commonwealth. After internment, some 4,000 refugees from Central Europe joined the Pioneer Corps and other units. The effects of wartime conditions, however, were not wholly negative. The need to deal with education under evacuation conditions led to a reappraisal of the aims and structures of Jewish education, with results after the war; and dispersal of the pre-1933 community probably helped the Central European refugees to integrate more quickly into the main community at the end of the war.

Zionism and Israel

The election in December 1939 of Professor Selig Brodetsky as president of the Board of Deputies meant that Zionists were in a majority on the Board, and probably in the community as a whole. There was widespread opposition to the 1939 White Paper on Palestine. But the adoption by an Extraordinary Zionist Conference in New York in May 1942 of the 'Biltmore Programme', calling for a Jewish commonwealth in Palestine after the war, gave rise to further divisions. A carefully planned campaign to return Zionist deputies to the Board of Deputies led in July 1943 to a decision to disband the Joint Foreign Committee, in which the non-Zionist Anglo-Jewish Association had been in partnership with the Board since 1878. In November 1944 the Board adopted as its policy that Palestine should become a 'commonwealth' within the British Commonwealth. In the meanwhile, however, tensions were heightened by a conflict between the Mandatory government and the Jewish *yishuv* in Palestine, beginning with the assassination of Lord Moyne in 1944 and culminating in Britain's giving up of the Mandate in 1947. The events leading up to the end of the Mandate brought out the divergence between the Zionist majority and the non-Zionist, or even moderate Zionist, Anglo-Jewish Association, whose president, Leonard Stein, was the former political secretary of the World Zionist Organization. A Jewish Fellowship, active during these years, took on the anti-Zionist role of the League of British Jews after the First World War. However, once the State of Israel was formed, the Anglo-Jewish Associaton welcomed it and the Fellowship was dissolved.

The British government, with Ernest Bevin as Foreign Secretary, refused to recognize the State of Israel when it was proclaimed and did not do so until the end of January 1949. After the establishment of diplomatic relations, better, although still reserved, relations followed between the two governments. The conflict of 1956 between Israel and Egypt, and the takeover by Egypt of the Suez Canal found Britain and Israel in unpredictable and undeclared military association against Egypt. The Suez crisis produced a crucial test of attitudes for Anglo-Jewish leadership. When on 1 November 1956 the Labour Party challenged the government over Suez, all 17 Jewish Labour MPs, including the president of the Board of Deputies and Zionist Federation, followed the party line. While Jewish MPs were forthright in speaking up for Israel, when it came to a vital vote they opted for their party and for what they considered their constituents' interests, rather than their more strictly Jewish interests.

Mobilizing political and financial support for Israel became the main communal and social activity, the one cause that transcended all divisions within the community. An estimate in 1984 put at 60 per cent, or £23.7m, the sums raised for the annual Joint Israel Appeal and other Israel causes out of the £40m raised a year for all Jewish causes in Britain; and 1984 was not a crisis year like 1967 when contributions reached exceptional levels. The Six Day War of 1967 involved the whole Anglo-Jewish community for Israel more than ever before. The initial perception of extreme danger for Israel and the subsequent appreciation of victory produced an unprecendented emotional reaction, even among many previously estranged from any Jewish identification. This together with an earlier sense of having survived the holocaust, produced a feeling of solidarity in a Jewish peoplehood which included Anglo-Jewry. Personal links with Israel took the form of the settlement of some 500 to 1,000 immigrants every year, mostly young or early middle-aged people; plus an unquantifiable number of older people spending all or part of their year in Israel on retirement. Tourism from Britain to Israel was intensively promoted; even so, a survey of the middle-income Jewish suburban community of Redbridge in 1977 showed that only 26 per of cent the sample questioned had visited Israel: only 1.5 per cent of the adults had made preparations or had decided to settle and 26 per cent had considered it (1.3 per cent had been but returned). Among teenagers the attitude was less negative: 25 per cent contemplated settlement in Israel and 35 per cent might possibly go.

Population Trend

Increased by a net addition of some 55,000 refugees from Central Europe, Anglo-Jewry probably reached its highest numbers in the early 1950s. An estimate made then put the total at 450,000, although later research suggested this was an over estimate and that 410,000 would be nearer the correct figure. In 1977 an estimate of 353,720 was made on the basis of the annual death rate, taking account of the social composition and age structure of the Jewish population. A later estimate, for the Jewish population for 1980–3, was 330,000. These figures applied to what may be termed the affiliated community: those who identified sufficiently with Judaism to want to be buried (or in some cases cremated) with some form of Jewish religious ceremony. Such a calculation would omit those who regarded themselves as Jews in a secular sense but did not wish to identify themselves in death by any form of religious ceremony.

What is demonstrable however is that the overall size of the community as defined by some form of religious identification has been falling since the 1950s. Indeed, the decline may have begun earlier but been concealed by the additions due to immigration. But after 1945 the amount of immigration was limited and there was a regular, although small, outflow, especially to Israel. Admittedly in the 1970s and 1980s there was a considerable inflow of Israelis. To some extent these did not identify themselves with Anglo-Jewry; and, even where they did, they were unlikely so soon to have influenced the death figures. But the basic cause for the fall in population was the decline in the number of children born in relation to the number of those dying. The number of deaths remained between 4,400 and 4,900 a year between the 1960s and 1988, although in the 1980s the number tended to fall to the lower end of the range because of the overall decline in the Jewish population. In the 1960s over 5,000 Jewish children were born each year; in the 1970s an average of 4,300 and in the 1980s an average of fewer than 3,500. After the 1960s therefore the Jewish community was not reproducing itself. It was not that the number of children per marriage fell. On the contrary, the number of children born per Jewish marriage was estimated to have increased from an average of 2.4 in 1965–9 to 2.9 in 1980–3. The basic factor seems to have been the absolute decline in the number of Jewish marriages from a peak of 3,768 in 1947 (a figure probably abnormally high because of marriages deferred due to the war) to 2,000 in 1958 and then 1,100 in 1988; these figures include second and subsequent marriages, an important consideration in the later years because of the increase in Jewish divorces and remarriages. On the basis of the 1988 figure, the Board of Deputies Community Research Unit estimated that as many as two-thirds of the young single Jews of marriageable age were not marrying in a synagogue. The reasons for this have not been researched – whether Jews are marrying by civil ceremony or living together without marriage, or remaining single, or marrying or living with non-Jews.

The population was also ageing at a faster rate than the general population of England and Wales: in 1975–9, 18.1 per cent of the Jewish population was estimated to be over 64, compared with 14.5 per cent for the total population of England and Wales. As a result, the Jewish community had to devote a high proportion of its communal expenditure to the care of the aged: in 1984 this was calculated to amount to over 70 per cent (£14.25m out of £19.6m) of communal expenditure on welfare.

Geographical Distribution

From 1945 to 1989, after the temporary disruption of wartime, London continued to have about two-thirds of the Anglo-Jewish population; but, because of the decline in the overall Jewish population, London's Jewish population declined from around 300,000 to about 200,000. Of the other main centres only Greater Manchester with about 30,000 Jews remained static or even tended to increase; this was partly due to Jews in smaller communities, which had declined below the point of viability for sustaining a communal life, moving to Manchester, and perhaps also to the development in Manchester of a vigorous, strictly orthodox community where large families were the rule. Of the other main centres, Leeds saw its Jewish population decline from 25,000 to 14,000, Glasgow from 13,400 (1959 estimate) to 11,000, Birmingham from 6,300 to 6,000, Liverpool from 7,500 to 5,000, Sheffield from 1,850 to 1,000. These falls in size produced problems in communal provision of services. For instance, while Liverpool and Birmingham retained their Jewish day schools, these had a high proportion of non-Jewish pupils by the late 1980s.

On the other hand, the trend, already noted between the wars, to increase in the Jewish populations of certain seaside resorts continued: Brighton from 4,500 to 10,000, Bournemouth from 1,500 to 3,000. By contrast Jews by the 1980s were few in most medium-sized cities and towns, in the midlands and in Scotland and Wales. Within the major centres, the trend to the suburbs continued; Jews increasingly became a suburban population. Within Greater London, the traditional Jewish quarter of the East End emptied of Jews until by 1984 the whole London borough of Tower Hamlets (which included the former Jewish areas of Stepney, Bethnal Green and Poplar) had only 7,500 Jews. On the other hand, it was estimated in 1984 that the London borough of Barnet (Hendon, Finchley etc.) had some 50,000 Jews, a sixth of the entire population of Anglo-Jewry. The north-west sector of Greater London (the boroughs of Barnet, Harrow, Brent, Camden and Westminster), stretching from St John's Wood to Edgware and Stanmore, with the adjacent areas of Hertfordshire, had over 100,000 Jews, a third of Anglo-Jewry. Elsewhere in London, the London borough of Hackney, which included the ultra-orthodox groups of the N.16 postal district, had about 20,000 Jews; and the north-eastern borough of Redbridge another 20,000.

The centrifugal thrust to the suburbs was paralleled in other major urban areas. In Greater Manchester, the community spread two ways, to the north into the metropolitan borough of Bury (Prestwich, Whitefield) and to the south towards, and over the border into, Cheshire.

Anti-Semitism

There was some understandable manifestation of anti-Semitism between the end of the war and 1948, when British soldiers were in conflict with Jews in Palestine, especially at the time of the hanging of two army sergeants in August 1947. This incident was followed by some disorders in provincial cities and some attacks on Jewish property. These were anxious times for British Jews, and they continued when there was immense publicity over the activities of Sidney Stanley, who claimed to be able to obtain favours for clients from the government through his influence with ministers and others in positions of power. His activities were investigated by a tribunal of inquiry under Mr Justice Lynskey; no great corruption was found and no one was prosecuted but a junior minister and a member of the board of directors of the Bank of England, who was also chairman of a nationalized industry, resigned.

However in the 1950s and 1960s there was an apparent lull in anti-Semitic activity. Israel even gained popular admiration, especially for her achievements in the 1967 war, and the memories of what anti-Semitism had effected in the holocaust seemed to act as a deterrent to its recrudescence;

anti-Semitism was now regarded as unacceptable. In 1976 the extreme right-wing National Front began disseminating overtly anti-Semitic material. In the county council elections in May 1977 they received 205,000 votes (of which 119,000 were in Greater London, 5 per cent of those voting). But, owing to the 'first past the post' principle of British elections, the party failed to win a seat. In the 1979 general election, however, with a much higher turnout of voters, over 300 National Front candidates polled 191,000 votes between them, none receiving more than 2,000 votes. This was 1.3 per cent of the total votes cast, and in the 1983 general election the extreme right-wing share of the vote fell to 0.7 per cent. The rise and fall of National Front fortunes may have been influenced less by the Jewish issue than by concern among some who were normally Labour voters about the Labour Party's policy on coloured immigration; this was deflected when the 1979 Conservative government adopted a more restrictive line on immigration. The United Nations resolution of November 1975 equating Zionism with racism provided a text on which the extreme left, such as the Socialist Workers' Party, and Arab students, of whom there were 12,000 in British universities and institutions of higher education, could attack Israel. The continuing campaign, especially among students, resulted in discrimination against Jewish students and their organizations, which was, in its effects, anti-Jewish. University Jewish societies were denied facilities and at Salford University a visiting rabbi was banned from giving a religious talk on campus. These actions were usually taken by activists at poorly attended and unrepresentative meetings. University authorities were uneven in their reactions; some however, such as the York vice-chancellor, took effective action and the National Union of Students later acted to proscribe anti-Jewish discrimination as such. In 1980 Exeter University, which had received considerable donations from Arab sources, excluded Israeli scholars from a colloquium; this was widely criticized as an infraction of academic freedom. Jewish students at universities and colleges continued in the 1980s to be in the front line against anti-Israel propaganda.

The plight of Soviet Jewry became a major issue for British Jewry, particularly after the harsh sentences imposed on Jews in the Leningrad trial of December 1970. This led to the formation of the National Council for Soviet Jewry and a continuing campaign for human rights for Soviet Jews. Students and women were especially involved, notably in demonstrations outside Soviet buildings in London and on the occasion of visits by Soviet leaders, and persuading British ministers, including Mrs Thatcher, to make representations when visiting Russia.

Politics

The 1945 election, which brought Labour to power for the first time with an absolute majority in the House of Commons, returned an unprecedented number of Jewish MPs, all Labour except for an Independent Conservative and a Communist. There were several Jewish Cabinet ministers in the 1945–51 and 1964–70 Labour governments. The vast majority of Jewish MPs before 1979 were Labour, although they were fewer when Labour was in opposition and fewer Labour MPs were elected. Official Conservative Jewish MPs were absent until the 1955 parliament in which there were two, both baronets. After 1970 there was an increasing number of Jewish Conservative MPs and the number of Labour Jewish MPs declined, until in the 1983 elections seventeen Conservative and eleven Labour MPs were elected. For a short time during the Conservative administration in 1986 there were five Jews in the Cabinet of twenty-two, although this number was soon reduced by resignation and retirement to three and by 1989 to two and then one.

Estimates of the precentage of Jewish voters voting for a particular party is generally unverifiable but the number of Jewish MPs for each party gives some idea of the relative strength of the support for the party even though most Jewish MPs sat for constituencies with few or no Jewish voters. The increase in the number of Conservative Jewish MPs supports the hypothesis that between the 1950s and 1959 there was a substantial shift of Jewish voting allegiance from Labour to Conservative. This can be explained by changes in the attitudes of the two major parties: the Conservatives became far more willing to adopt Jewish candidates and to accept Jewish leaders of Conservative groups on local councils. Conversely, Jews may have been influenced against Labour by the left-wing opponents of Israel, and in September 1982 the annual conference of the Labour Party adopted resolutions recognizing the PLO as the legitimate representative of the Palestinian people and called for the establishment of a secular democratic state of Palestine – although these did not become official party policy.

Social Class

But probably the underlying cause for the change in party allegiances was social change in the Anglo-Jewish community. The census identifies five social classes: I professional; II managerial and intermediate occupations; III skilled occupations; IV partly skilled; V unskilled. I and II have been found to tend to vote Conservative, IV and V Labour. The composition of the older, pre-1945, Anglo-Jewry can be seen from a study of the Jewish population of Hackney, based on the 1971 census. This showed a substantially older population, with nearly 20 per cent aged over 65. Even so, only 15 per cent were in classes IV and V. A study of a sample of Jewish death records for 1961 on a national basis showed for males aged 45–74 at death 3 per cent in Class 1, 13 per cent in Class II, 48 per cent in Class III, 20 per cent in IV and 12 per cent in V. By contrast, the same analysis applied to those aged 15–44 in 1961 showed 7 per cent in Class I, 32 per cent in II, 41 percent in III, 16 per cent in IV and none in V. This is evidence of upward social mobility as the younger sample showed higher social class composition than the older sample; the national figures for the general population in 1961 for the five classes were 4, 15, 49, 19 and 8 respectively. Even higher percentages in Classes I and II and lower in IV and V were found in later surveys of particular Jewish communities. For instance, the 1977 study of the 20,000 Jews in the north-east London borough of Redbridge, which was perhaps not untypical of Anglo-Jewry as a whole, showed 40 per cent in the 'middle class' with the rest mainly in skilled occupations.

Occupations

These figures indicate the increasingly middle-class composition of Anglo-Jewry, at least after 1960. The figures reflect the occupations and economic structure of the community. Since 1945, the 1881–1914 picture of a largely proletarian community of manual workers in a limited range of trades has virtually disappeared. Geographical dispersal was matched by occupational diversification. While predictably groups of Jews in middle-class suburbs showed high proportions in middle-class occupations, a study in the 1970s of the relatively small provincial community of Sheffield, some 1,100 Jews, showed them to be overwhelmingly professionals or in business; even in the older, much less middle-class, Jewish population of Hackney 26 per cent of the occupied men were self-employed: self-employment was a mark of Jewish economic activity during the period. Only a very general idea of a complex situation can be gained from the limited statistics available. Soon after 1945 the main Jewish trades were still textiles (including drapery and the fashion trade as well as tailoring), furniture, jewellery, furs, cosmetics, and the then newly developing radio and electrical industries. In the 1950s, some evidence of the changes taking place was provided by information about apprenticeships by the London Jewish Board of Guardians from 1952 to 1957: of over 400 boys, 20 per cent were apprenticed to jewellery (including the diamond trade), 13 per cent to hairdressing, only 9 per cent to tailoring and 8 per cent as electrical, radio and television engineers and mechanics. Of the minority articled to professions, accountants outnumberd solicitors.

In the 1970s the board (renamed the Jewish Welfare Board) continued to find jewellery the most popular trade for apprenticeship, followed by furs, printing, watchmaking, electrical engineering and management careers. The JFS Secondary (later Comprehensive) School in the fifteen years to

1975 noted among school-leavers a decline of interest in hairdressing, continuance of interest in secretarial and clerical jobs (about 15 per cent of school-leavers) and an increasing number going on to further education. thus causing an increase in those entering the professions. In the professions, Jews had a higher representation than average in medicine, accountancy and university teaching; other professions with above average Jewish representation were law, dentistry, pharmacy, estate agency and property. On the other hand, Jewish representation in shopkeeping seems to have declined. As distinct from the great retail chains founded by Jewish entrepreneurs, the small Jewish family shop seems to have declined, replaced no doubt by the growth of the Asian retail shopkeepers.

The fullest study of Jewish occupations and businesses during the period is in Harold Pollins' *Economic History of the Jews in England*, which cites many individual case histories. There is space here to mention only two general points. First, certain callings continued to be popular among Jews but probably also there was no occupation in which some Jew would not be found: an article in 1975 cited school-leavers going into occupations ranging from Post Office engineering to radiography, from motor mechanics to stable work, from poodle parlours to the Merchant Navy. Second, there was a similar contrast among entrepreneurs between concentration on certain trades and diversity. Refugees from Central Europe were given government help to open businesses in what were called the distressed, later special and then development areas; other Jews took advantage of technical training and experience gained during the war to open new industrial enterprises; businesses which expanded and took over other firms acquired these businesses because of their availability or financial attractiveness rather than because of the kind of articles they made or sold. With the development of conglomerates in the 1970s and 1980s, it became difficult to particularize the nature of groups of firms; and there was always the problem of what was a 'Jewish' firm: how long does a complex enterprise remain a 'Jewish' firm merely because the business was originally begun by a Jew?

The importance of property and estate agency for Jewish entrepreneurs can be illustrated by the fact that a list compiled in 1967 of 110 property developers estimated to have made £1m since 1945, 70 seemed to be Jewish and 25 of these had estate agency as their original profession.

Yet, in spite of this evidence of concentration, Jews were found in every profession and by the end of the 1980s every position in a profession was open. Whereas in 1939 it was rare for a Jew to be a full Fellow of an Oxford or Cambridge college, several Jews had become heads of such colleges by 1989; and even the most exclusive medical schools and London teaching hospitals had appointed Jews as consultants by 1989.

Education

This trend towards more complete economic and social integration in British society was accompanied in the last two decades of the period by an intensification of Jewish consciousness on the part of appreciable sections of the community. One expression of this trend towards self-identification was the development of Jewish day school education.

The need to provide for the Jewish education of children evacuated during the Second World War led to a joint emergency organization. This developed after the war into new structures for part-time education, with a central council to co-ordinate education over the whole country. The outstanding feature was the growth of full-time education. In 1967, 35,000 children received some form of Jewish education, 25 per cent of them in day schools; by 1982 the total had gone down to 30,000 because of the overall fall in the Jewish population but the number receiving full-time education had increased from 9,000 to 14,000, or nearly half the total. There was a variety of provision of full-time Jewish schools, the largest being the Jews' Free School refounded after the war on a new site as a secondary school for 1,500 pupils. The Jewish Secondary Schools Movement, founded in 1929 by Rabbi Victor Schonfeld, developed under his son, Solomon, into a network of schools in north and north west London, for boys and girls, and primary as well as secondary; intended originally for the right-wing orthodox, with the movement to the right of the mainstream United Synagogue, it began to attract pupils from the United Synagogue as well.

Other day schools were organized in the 1950s under Zionist inspiration but subject to the religious supervision of the Chief Rabbi. There were independent right-wing orthodox schools, with maximum emphasis on traditional religious studies and minimum secular instruction, often with much of the teaching in Yiddish; the reform movement founded its own day school; and in 1948 Rabbi Kopul Rosen founded Carmel College on the model of an English public boarding school, combining traditional religious atmosphere with modern secular instruction. Altogether, by the 1980s over 20 per cent of the relevant age group were at Jewish full-time schools, although this may have owed something to the perception by parents of deficiencies in the ordinary local authority schools and the intense competition, especially in London, for the relatively few good independent schools.

In the last decade of the period there was an upsurge of interest in adult education, although with varying degrees of academic quality and commitment. Many synagogues provided adult education lectures and small, though regular, groups for studying Talmud and Bible. Examples on a wider scale were the Spiro Institute, originally founded to provide courses in Jewish history in non-Jewish schools, which developed wide cultural programmes for adults, and the 'Seed' project for individual tuition for Talmud study.

In higher education, the former professorship of Hebrew at University College London was developed by Professor Siegfried Stein into a comprehensive department of Hebrew and Jewish History; associated with it was the Institute of Jewish Studies originally founded by the rabbi and philosopher, Alexander Altmann. At Oxford the Centre for Postgraduate Hebrew Studies developed a range of research and teaching far beyond its normal title, including a remarkable awakening of interest in Yiddish. But Jewish Studies remained essentially a specialist discipline; apart from individual courses it did not, as in the United States, become an option that non-specialist Jewish undergraduates would take for general university education.

Synagogue Membership

Synagogue membership remained the most widespread means of Jewish self-identification and there was some evidence that proportionately it increased. Before 1977 statistics of synagogue membership were usually collected on the basis of male membership, to give a standard basis of comparison since the extent of female membership varied between congregations. Female membership did increase, partly because some congregations encouraged wives to become members in their own right and, because of the increase in families with female heads (widows, single parents etc.). From 1977 statistics were collected of households affiliated to synagogues. While, with the decline in the Jewish population, male membership decreased from 88,438 in 1970 to 78,899 in 1983, it was estimated that the number of Jewish households affiliated to a synagogue had declined little betwen 1977 and 1983. With an estimated 109,426 households affiliated to a synagogue in 1983, this must represent a high percentage of synagogue affiliation (88 per cent) for a community estimated to total 330,000; but is may also reflect the increasing number of one-parent households, mainly widows, a mark of a declining population.

Among synagogue groupings, the right-wing orthodox have tended to increase; the reform and liberals to increase (the former much more than the latter); the Sephardim and the Central Orthodox (United Synagogue and Federation of Synagogues in London, and most congregations outside London) to decrease. Thus counting male membership in Greater London, the right-wing orthodox increased from 2.6 per cent to 5.3 per cent, the Central Orthodox and Sephardim declined from 76.8 per cent to 69 per cent and the reform and liberals increased from 20.6 per cent to 25.4 per cent. The 1983 figures are slightly different if the whole country is considered because of the predominance of the Central Orthodox outside London – most provincial communities, being smaller, had only one or two congregations, mostly under the authority of the Chief Rabbinate. Thus for the country as a whole in 1983 the right-wing orthodox had 4.4 per cent of the male membership, the Central Orthodox 70.5 per cent, Sephardim 2.7 per cent and reform and liberals 22.4 per cent. The figures probably underestimate the strength of the right-wing orthodox: their proportion of the total of marriages (9 per cent in 1983) was so much higher than their percentage of male membership that it suggests they were a fast-growing sector, founding many new households which also had a higher than average number of children per family. By 1988 the right-wing orthodox had 10 per cent of the total of synagogue marriages in Britain.

Religious Life

*Dr Hertz died in January 1946 and was succeeded in May 1948 by Rabbi (later Sir) Israel Brodie (1895–1979). The first Chief Rabbi to be both born and educated in Britain (at Jew' College and University College London, with postgraduate study at Oxford), Brodie had served as rabbi for many years in Melbourne and as chaplain in both world wars. A quiet, gentlemanly and conciliatory person, Brodie was appointed at a time of strain between Jewry and the British government over the Palestine conflict but his main problems proved to be within the community. The reform and liberal congregations were reinforced by former refugees from Central Europe; German Jewry had been highly educated and, for the most part, moderate in its reform Judaism. While the liberal and reform movements failed to unite, in spite of many points of similarity, they joined to found Leo Baeck College to train ministers for both. Within the United Synagogue, and elsewhere among the mainstream orthodox, the children of the East European immigrants brought a new, more traditionalist, spirit. The influence of the London Beth Din, led by the great authority on Jewish law, Yehezkel Abramsky (1886–1976), provided a parallel force to the Chief Rabbinate; *shechita* and *kashrut* controls were tightened and a very strict line was taken to exclude converts of dubious sincerity, whose reason for conversion was matrimonial; and the religious stance of the United Synagogue as an institution was kept firmly to the right. A new generation of rabbis, qualified as such, including graduates of Jews' College, remodelled by its principal, Isidore Epstein, gradually replaced the former Anglo-Jewish 'ministers'. In 1962 Sir Isaac Wolfson became the first president of the United Synagogue from outside the old patrician Anglo-Jewish families. From then on the leadership of the United Synagogue (as distinct from its rabbinical authorities) was no longer patrician, but unlike their predecessors, generally religiously observant.

Sir Israel Brodie was happy to go along with this trend, indeed to foster it but in the 1960s he had to face a crisis. Religious tension within the community crystallized in the 'Jacobs Affair', which attracted extensive coverage in the British media. Rabbi Dr Louis Jacobs, widely respected as a scholar, had questioned the literal inspiration of scripture and argued that there was a human element in its composition. A minister of the New West End Synagogue, he became a tutor at Jews' College but his appointment as principal in 1962 and his subsequent reappointment to his former congregation (which required the express certification of the Chief Rabbi) were both vetoed by Israel Brodie. The cause of Jacobs was championed by those within the United Synagogue and elsewhere who resented what they considered the trend to the right. Jacobs became minister of an independent New London Synagogue but, contrary to some predictions, this did not give rise to a widespread movement in Britain on the lines of American Conservative Judaism.

Brodie retired in 1965, the first Chief Rabbi to retire at 70, and was succeeded in 1966 by Rabbi (later Sir and Lord) Jakobovits. Born in 1921 in Koenigsberg, he was educated at Jews' College and had served as chief rabbi of Ireland and as rabbi of the Fifth Avenue Synagogue in New York. He set himself to extend Jewish education, especially through day schools, for whose support he founded in 1971 the Jewish Educational Development Trust; this supported education in all sections of the community (including the reform Akiva day school). He offered a conciliatory approach to non-orthodox Jews but firmly opposed any watering down of orthodox standards, for instance on marriages and conversions. A specialist in medical ethics, he increasingly became recognised by the British public as the exponent of traditional Jewish religious values and the contribution which Judaism could thereby make to British life. This role, appreciated by the Conservative government, which came to power under Mrs Thatcher in 1979, was enhanced by his creation as a life peer in 1988, the first rabbi to sit in the House of Lords.

Polarization and Decline

A perceptive contributor to the 1962 conference on 'Jewish Life in Modern Britain' noted the trend in what he estimated to be then 20 per cent of the community towards increased orthodoxy: Sabbath observance amongst lay leaders, Jewish day schools, orthodox youth movements, the increasing replacement of 'ministers' by rabbis. He quoted the 'quite a few grandparents' who boasted of an orthodox grandchild. But he noted that orthodoxy was then without any missionary feeling.

By the time of the analogous conference in 1977, this last lack had been met by the arrival in Britain of the Lubavitch Hasidic movement, based in Brooklyn, which sought to encourage all Jews to perform their ritual precepts and worked especially among the young and students. Chief Rabbi Jakobovits, addressing the same 1977 conference, emphasised the strongly traditional character of Anglo-Jewry, its likely overall decline in numbers but the intensity of religious commitment on the part of a minority, which was increasing in numbers because of a relatively high birth rate (to which could be added in the 1980s an appreciable number of young recruits from less orthodox backgrounds). By the 1980s in north London, Hendon and Manchester there were whole communities, amounting to a few thousand men, women and children, of Hasidic sects, whose dress, mores and way of life (although not necessarily their occupations) were characteristic of Eastern Europe in the nineteenth century. Much of their leadership and membership had come to Britain in the years after 1945 and in their attitude to western culture and university education were very different from the religiously equally orthodox congregations of Central European origin.

Within the mainstream orthodox congregations, which proclaimed and enforced orthodox standards of communal observance irrespective of the personal habits of their individual members, there was a perceptible tightening of standards and even some evidence of increased personal commitment. Whereas before 1939 parents within this mainstream speculated about the possibility of their children, let alone their grandchildren, remaining Jews, by the 1980s the spectacle of children more observant than their parents became commonplace. Within the reform and liberal movements the movement was also to the right, with increased stress on traditional observances and ceremonies, on the use and knowledge of Hebrew and the complete disappearance of the old anti-Zionism.

Yet overall these trends could have affected only a minority; for the vast majority the situation was represented by the decline of Jewish marriages by 80 per cent and the calculation that by 1989 only one-third of young Jews were marrying by any form of Jewish religious ceremony. Contrasting these two opposing trends, the process of the period of 1939 to 1989 in Anglo-Jewish history can be defined only as one of polarization, with the minority becoming more Jewish and the majority less so, and the overall total continuing to decline in numbers for the foreseeable future. There is some mitigation in the increasing tendency towards Jewish self-identification on ethnic lines and the growth in the 1980s of groups identifying themselves as Jews on a secular basis. But the religious would ask how these can perpetuate their identity in future generations.

As the half century ended in 1989, the outlook for the Anglo-Jewish community seemed to be polarization and decline. But, reflecting on how unpredictable the situation of 1989 would have appeared in 1939, to refrain from prediction might seem the wisest counsel of the historian.

Note on Sources

Summaries relating to British Jewry from 1939 to 1970 are given in *EJ* 6: 763–72, and for subsequent years under 'England' in the annual or biennial volumes of the *Encyclopaedia Judaica*. Relevant articles are in the *Jewish Chronicle* colour magazines: 'The changing face of Anglo-Jewry 1945–1975', 28 November 1975 (the information about apprentices and school-leavers is taken from p. 76) and 'The Jews of Britain', 24 November 1978. The papers of the 1962 and 1977 conferences were published in Julius Gould and Shaul Esh (eds) *Jewish Life in Modern Britain,* 1964 (the quotations about religious trends in 1962 come from the paper by Norman Cohen, pp. 41–54) and Sonia and V.D. Lipman (eds) *Jewish Life in Britain 1962–77,* New York etc, 1981 (Lord Jakobovits' paper which is quoted is on pp. 33–48). The Board of Deputies Research Unit, which has, with very limited resources, produced so much statistical and sociological information about Anglo-Jewry since 1965, published *British Jewry in the Eighties,* 1986, a comprehensive guide to the relevant knowledge then available. It includes a bibliography of nearly a hundred items. These include papers by Professor S.J. Prais and Mrs M. Schmool and by Dr B.A. Kosmin: among these no. 31 in the *British Jewry in the Eighties* bibliography has been used for Jewish marriages 1901–65, no. 74 for information on social class, nos. 52 and 53 for synagogue membership, among other sources. The bibliography also contains details of the published accounts of the Edgware (pp. 69–71), Hackney (p. 67), Sheffield (p. 66) and Redbridge (pp. 76–9) surveys. Details about Sir Israel Brodie and Dayan Y. Abramsky are based on the relevant entries in the *Dictionary of National Biography* 1970–80 volume by Professor R. Loewe. For information about Jews as consultants in London teaching hospitals, see Claire Hilton, 'St Bartholomew's Hospital and its Jewish connections', *TJHSE* XXX, 33–7. Information on communal expenditure in 1984 is taken from the Anglo-Jewry Research Project report (I am grateful to Mr Bernard Garbacz for sending me a copy of this). For Jewish education, see two articles by Professor Bernard Steinberg, 'Jewish Education in Great Britain during World War II, *JSS*, XXIX, pp. 27–63; 'Anglo-Jewry and the 1944 Education Act', *JJS*, XXXI, 1989, pp. 81–108. The crisis at the Board of Deputies in 1943 is dealt with in G. Shimoni, Selig Brodetsky and the Ascendancy of Zionism in Anglo-Jewry, *JJS*, XXII, pp. 125–161, and Stuart Cohen, 'Selig Brodetsky: Another View of his Achievements', *JJS* XXIV, pp. 25–38.

Glossary

Agudas Israel: political movement of strictly orthodox Jews.
Ashkenzai (pl. Ashkenzaim): Jews of Central and East European origin whose rite is the commonest in Britain.
Ba'ale Batim (lit. householders): The term was used to indicate full or 'privileged' membership of synagogues to the mid-nineteenth century.
Bar Mitzvah: A boy on attaining his religious majority or confirmation on reaching 13 years of age.
Beth Din: A court, of at least three members, administering Jewish law; in modern times, a Jewish ecclesiastical court.
Beth Hamedrash: House of study.
Cheder: See HEDER.
Chevra: See HEBRA.
Dayan: Judge (ecclesiastical), member of Beth Din (q.v.).
Gemara: Part of the Talmud, being the commentary on the Mishnah, (q.v.).
Haham (lit. sage): Chief Rabbi of a community of Sephardim (q.v.).
Halacha (adj. Halachic): The whole of Jewish law or a specific rule.
Hasidim, Hasidism: Jewish religious movement, originating in Eastern Europe in second half of eighteenth century, in which fervent piety is based on mysticism. Its adherents are divided into sects, led by hereditary spiritual leaders, and wear distinctive old-fashioned dress.
Hebra (pl. Hebrot): Social or voluntary association for religious purposes, often forming the congregation of a small synagogue. (Often spelled 'Chevra', e.g., Chevra Shass - Society for studying the Talmud.)
Heder (pl. Hedarim) (lit. room): old-fashioned religious school.
Herem: Ban or excommunication.
Ivrit B'ivrit: Method of teaching Hebrew, using only Hebrew in instruction.
Kasher (Kashrut): Applied to food, fit (or fitness) according to Jewish law.
Kehilla: Jewish community.
Landsmannschaft (German): Organization of persons from a particular town or district.
Ma'ariv: Evening service.
Maggid: Preacher.
Ma(c)hzikei Hadath: Name of strictly orthodox synagogue.
Matzo (pl. Matzot): Unleavened bread eaten at Passover.
Mikvah: Ritual bath.
Mincha: Afternoon service.
Minhag: Religious rite or custom.
Minyan: Quorum of ten adult males for divine service; small group meeting for divine service.
Mishnah: The basic text of the TALMUD (q.v.).
Mitzvah(h) (pl. Mitzvot): Religious commandment; religious obligation or observance.

Rav: Rabbi.

Rebbe: Spiritual leader of HASIDIM (q.v.).

Rosh Hashana: Jewish New Year.

Sephardi (pl. Sephardim): Jews originating from Spain and Portugal, having a distinctive rite and pronunciation of Hebrew.

Sepher Torah: Scroll of the Law.

Shechita: Slaughter of animals for food according to Jewish Law, carried out by Shochet (pl. Shochetim).

Shiva: Week of confined mourning.

Shomer (pl. Shomerim): Ritual superviser.

Succah: Tabernacle or booth used during festival of Tabernacles (Succoth).

Talmud: The classic collection of rabbinic law and commentary, recording legal decisions and discussions from about 200 B.C.E. to 450 C.E.

Talmud Torah (lit. Study of the Law): Religious school.

Torah: Jewish Law; Pentateuch.

Trefa: (of food) forbidden by Jewish Law.

Yeshiva(h) (pl. Yeshivot): College for Jewish religious studies, especially studying TALMUD (q.v.).

Yom Kippur: Day of Atonement.

Biographical Appendix of Anglo-Jewish Personalities

NB. Inclusion in, or exclusion from, this list is not intended as a criterion of relative importance.

Abrahams, Israel (1858–1924): joint editor, *Jewish Quarterly Review*, 1888–1908; reader in rabbinic, Cambridge from 1902; associated with Jewish Religious Union and Liberal Synagogue; works include *Jewish Life in the Middle Ages*, 1896; president, Jewish Historical Society, 1904–5.

Abrahams, Sir Lionel (1869–1919): entered India Office, 1892; on secretariat of Indian Currency Committee, 1898; assistant financial secretary, India Office, 1901; financial secretary, 1902; assistant under-secretary of state, 1911; president, Jewish Historical Society, 1916–18; honorary secretary then vice-chairman then chairman, Visiting Committee, Board of Guardians, 1893–1901; KCB.

Adler, Hermann (1839–1911): born Hanover and brought to London as child; educated University College London and Leipzig (Ph.D.); rabbinical ordination from S.J. Rapaport, Prague; minister of Bayswater Synagogue, 1864; delegate Chief Rabbi from 1879, and succeeded his father as Chief Rabbi 1891; CVO.

Adler, Nathan Marcus (1803–90): born Hanover then under British rule; Ph.D. Erlangen; rabbi, Oldenburg, 1829; Hanover, 1830–45; Chief Rabbi, British empire, 1845–90; author of *Netinah lager* (on Targum Onkelos), 1875.

Alex, Ephraim (1800–82): born Cheltenham; overseer of poor of Great Synagogue; president of Board of Guardians, 1859–69; dentist.

Ascher, Benjamin Henry (1812–93); born Peisern (Posen); came to England, 1840; burial society preacher, Great Synagogue, 1843; published translations of *Ibn Gabirol* and *Benjamin of Tudela*.

Asher, Asher (1837–89): born Glasgow; educated Glasgow University; medical officer, Board of Guardians, 1862; secretary of Great Synagogue, 1866 and of United Synagogue, 1871; physician, almoner and friend of Rothschild family; contributor to Jewish press as 'Aliquis'.

Bakstansky, Lavy (1904–71): born Slonim, Lithuania; taken to Palestine as child; educated Herzlia Gymnasium and London School of Economics; assistant secretary, 1928–30, general secretary 1930–71, Zionist Federation of Great Britain Director Joint Palestine Appeal.

Benisch, Abraham (1811–78): born Drosau, Bohemia; studied surgery, Vienna, 1836; came to London, 1841; editor, *Jewish Chronicle*, 1854–69, 1875–8; a founder of

Anglo-Jewish Association, 1871; author of works on Bible, biography, travel and defence of Judaism.

Brodetsky, Selig (1888–1954): born Olviopol, south Russia; brought to London as child; professor, applied mathematics, Leeds, 1924–48; member of executive, World Zionist Executive and Jewish Agency for Palestine; president, Zionist Federation of Great Britain; president, Board of Deputies, 1940–9; president, Hebrew University of Jerusalem, 1949–51.

Cohen, Arthur (1830–1914): fifth wrangler, Cambridge, 1853 (but unable to take degree until Cambridge University Reform Act, 1871); called to bar, 1857; specialized in shipping and insurance cases; QC, 1874; MP 1880–7; judge of Cinque Ports; privy councillor, chairman of Bar Council; president of Board of Deputies, 1874–94, succeeding his uncle, Sir Moses Montefiore; vice-president, Jews' College.

Cohen, Sir Benjamin Louis, Bt (1844–1909): brother of Lionel Louis Cohen; representative of City on LCC, 1888–1901; Conservative MP, East Islington, 1892–1906; member of Stock Exchange; vice-president, United Synagogue; president, Board of Guardians, 1887–1900; president, Jews' Orphan Asylum, Jews' Hospital, London Orphan Asylum; created baronet, 1906.

Cohen, Israel (1879–1961): secretary, Zionist Central Office in Cologne and Berlin, 1910–14; interned Ruhleben, 1914–16; general secretary, Zionist Organization; member of Joint Foreign Committee from 1931; prolific author on Zionism and Jewish affairs.

Cohen, Sir Leonard Lionel KCVO (1858–1938): son of Lionel Louis Cohen, stockbroker; president, Board of Guardians, 1900–20; warden, Central Synagogue, 1899–1903; president, ICA.

Cohen, Rt Hon Sir Lionel Leonard, Lord Cohen of Walmer (1888–1973): British judge and Anglo-Jewish communal leader; Judge of High Court, 1943–6; Lord Justice of Appeal, 1946–51; Lord of Appeal, 1951–60; chairman of Company Law Amendment committee and responsible for Companies Act, 1948; chairman of Royal Commission on Awards to Inventors, 1946–56; chairman of Prices, Productivity and Incomes Council (the 'Cohen Committee' or 'Three Wise Men'), 1956–9; president, Board of Guardians, 1940–7, Jewish Historical Society, 1947–9, Union of Liberal and Progressive Synagogues; vice-president, Board of Deputies, 1934–8.

Cohen, Lionel Louis (1832–87): son of Louis Cohen and later senior partner in family firm of Louis Cohen and Sons, foreign bankers and members of Stock Exchange; manager and subsequently trustee of Stock Exchange; authority on Indian railways and Turkish finance; member, Royal Commission on Depression of Trade and of Select Committee on Endowed Schools; Conservative MP, North Paddington (1885–7); founder and vice-president, United Synagogue, 1870–87; honorary secretary, 1859–79, president, 1869–87, Board of Guardians.

Cohen, Sir Robert Waley (1877–1952): British industrialist and Anglo-Jewish communal leader; joined Shell petroleum company, 1901; represented company in negotiations leading to amalgamation with Royal Dutch Petroleum Company; played key role in ensuring oil supplies for allies in First World War and knighted

(KBE) for services, 1920; subsequently, second-in-command of Shell Group; vice-president, 1918–42, president, 1942–52, United Synagogue; vice-president, Board of Deputies, 1936–43.

D'Avigdor-Goldsmid, Sir Osmond (1877–1940): Anglo-Jewish communal leader; son of Elim d'Avigdor, and added the name Goldsmid on inheriting the estate of cousin, Sir Julian Goldsmid; high sheriff of Kent, 1912; baronetcy originally created for Sir Isaac Lyon Goldsmid revived for him, 1934; president, Anglo-Jewish Association, 1921–6; president, Board of Deputies, 1926–33; chairman, Jewish Colonization Association (ICA).

Deutsch, Emanuel (1831–73): born Neisse, Silesia; trained in Hebrew by uncle, David Deutsch, and in classics at Berlin University; appointed to British Museum, 1855; famous for article on Talmud in *Quarterly Review*, correspondent of Dean Stanley and friend of Sir George Grove and George Eliot (who based the character of 'Moredecai' in *Daniel Deronda* on him).

Dukes, Leopold (1810–91): born Pressburg, Slovakia; studied under Rabbi Moses Sofer and at Wurzburg Yeshiva; wandered over Europe, spending about twenty years in London; writer on rabbinics, Jewish literature, ethics and history.

Filipowski, Hirsch (Philip) (1819–72): born Wirballen, Russia; came to London, 1839; after teaching and publishing works on Hebrew literature, calendar and mathematics, worked as actuary in Edinburgh, publishing works on logarithms; designed Hebrew type; published *Hebrew National* for six months, 1867.

Friedlander, Michael (1833–1910): born Jutrosin (Posen); head of Talmud Torah school, Berlin, 1862–5; principal, Jews' College, 1865–1910; translator of Maimonides, *Guide for the Perplexed*; expert on calendar; father-in-law of Haham Moses Gaster.

Gaster, Moses (1856–1939): born Bucharest; studied Breslau University and Seminary; taught Rumanian language and literature and published works on Rumanian literature at Bucharest University, 1881–5; expelled because of denunciation of Rumanian treatment of Jews, 1885; appointed to teach Slavonic literature, Oxford, 1886; Haham of Spanish and Portuguese Jews' Community, from 1887; principal, Judith Montefiore College, Ramsgate, 1891–6; retired from office of Haham, 1918; authority on folklore and Samaritan literature; vice-president, first four World Zionist Congresses.

Goldsmid, Albert Edward Williamson (1846–1904): born Poona; entered British army, 1866; entered Judaism, 1870; brigade major, Belfast, 1879; colonel on staff, 1894; assistant adjutant-general, 1897; served in Boer War as chief of staff, 6th Division; retired from army and appointed MVO, 1903; mission for Baron de Hirsch in Argentina, 1892; founder, Jewish Lads' Brigade; chief of Hovevei Zion in Britain and Ireland.

Goldsmid, Sir Francis (1808–78): first Jew to be called to English bar, 1833; QC, 1858; Liberal MP 1860–78; campaigner for Jewish emancipation; president of council of founders, Reform Synagogue; vice-president, Anglo-Jewish Association; DL; succeeded to father's baronetcy and Portuguese barony, 1859.

Goldsmid, Sir Isaac Lyon Bt (1778–1859): banker and financier of railway construction; a founder of University College London and of Reform Congregation; prominent in campaign for emancipation; created baronet, 1841 and Baron de Palmeira by King of Portugal.

Goldsmid, Sir Julian (1838–96): graduated University College London and called to bar; Liberal MP, Honiton, 1866–7, Rochester, 1870–80, St Pancras South, 1885–96; chairman of committees, House of Commons, 1894; vice-president, 1871–86, president, 1886–95, Anglo-Jewish Association; chairman, Russo-Jewish Committee, 1882–94; president, Jews' Infant School, 1883–95; chairman of council and occasional preacher, Reform Synagogue; vice-chancellor, University of London; treasurer, University College London; succeeded uncle, Sir Francis, as baronet, 1878; colonel, 1 Sussex Rifle Volunteers and hon. colonel 1 Sussex Artillery Volunteers; chairman, Submarine Telegraph Company, and Imperial Continental Gas Association.

Green, Revd Aaron Levy (1821–83): minister, Bristol, 1831–51; second reader, Great Synagogue, 1851–5; minister, Central Synagogue, 1855–83; joint honorary secretary, Jews' College, 1852–83; regular anonymous contributor, as 'Nemo', to *Jewish Chronicle*.

Greenberg, Leopold Jacob (1861–1931): journalist and leader of Zionist Federation; friend of Herzl; editor-in-chief, *Jewish Chronicle*, 1907–32.

Hartog, Sir Philip Joseph (1864–1927): lecturer in chemistry, Manchester, 1891–1903; academic registrar, University of London, 1903–20; vice-chancellor, University of Dacca, 1920–5; chairman, committee of inquiry into Hebrew University, 1933; chairman, Jewish Professional Committee to assist refugees from Germany; chairman, Liberal Jewish Synagogue; knighted, 1930.

Henriques, Sir Basil Lucas Quixano (1890–1961): social worker and authority on juvenile delinquency; after serving as officer in First World War, founded in 1920 the Bernhard Baron St George's Jewish Settlement and lived there in east London; magistrate and chairman of East London Juvenile court; vice-president, National Association of Boys' Clubs and of World Union for Progressive Judaism; leader of anti-Zionist Jewish Fellowship; appointed CBE and knighted in 1955 for services as magistrate and social worker.

Henriques, Robert David Quixano (1905–67): British soldier and author; regular army officer, 1926–33; colonel, general staff (combined operations staff of General Montgomery), 1943–5; Territorial army officer, 1933–9 and 1947–50; novelist (author of *No Arms, No Armour*, which won several prizes) and biographer; originally anti-Zionist; after 1956 built cottage in Kibutz Kfar HaNasi and visited Israel annually; president of The Bridge (organization promoting friendship between Britain and Israel).

Hertz, Very Revd Joseph Herman (1872–1946): born Slovakia; taken to USA, 1884, where he was first graduate, Jewish Theological Seminary, 1894; rabbi, Syracuse, NY, 1894–6; rabbi, Johannesburg, where his denunciation of Boer opression of *uitlanders* led to deportation, but returned after Boer War, 1899–1911; rabbi, Orah Hayyim congregation, New York, 1911–13; Chief Rabbi, United Hebrew Congregations of British Empire, 1913–46; Companion of Honour, 1943; works include *Book of Jewish Thoughts* (1917) and commentaries on Pentateuch (1929-36) and Prayerbook (1942-5).

Hirsch, Baron Maurice de (1831-96): entered banking house of Bischoffsheim and Goldschmidt of Brussels, London and Paris; financed and built railways in Austria, Balkans and Russia; supported Alliance Israelite Universelle; founded Jewish Colonization Association (ICA); founded Baron de Hirsch Fund for relief of Jewish immigrants in USA; supported London hospitals and gave the winnings of his racehorses to charity; left over £20m to charity.

Hirschell, Solomon (1762-1842): born London, son of Hirsch Levin, rabbi of Great Synagogue; taken as child to continent and educated there; rabbi, Prenzlau (Prussia); rabbi, Great Synagogue, 1802-42 and recognized as presiding rabbi and later Chief Rabbi of Ashkenazim, first in London and then in Britain and overseas colonies.

Hurwitz, Hyman (1770-1844): born Posen; came to England, C.1800; ran Jewish Academy at Highgate from about 1800 to 1821; professor of Hebrew, University College London from 1828; friend of Coleridge.

Isaac, Saul (1823-1903): associate of his brother, Samuel (promoter of the Mersey Tunnel) as army contractor; MP for Nottingham, 1874-80.

Isaacs, Sir Rufus Daniel, 1st Marquess of Reading (1860-1935): MP 1904-13; solicitor-general, 1910; attorney-general, 1910-13; Lord Chief Justice, 1913-21; special ambassador to USA, 1918-19; Viceroy of India, 1921-6; Foreign Secretary, 1931.

Jacobs, Joseph (1854-1916): born Australia, graduated Cambridge and studied in Berlin; author and journalist; editor, *Folklore*; organized Anglo-Jewish Historical Exhibition, 1887; editor, *Darkest Russia*; editor, *Jewish Year Book*, 1896-99; president, Jewish Historical Society of England, 1897-9 and pioneer of archival research in medieval Anglo-Jewry; went to America, 1900 as editor, *Jewish Encyclopaedia*.

Janner, Sir Barnett, Lord Janner (1892-1982): Anglo-Jewish leader and British politician; Liberal MP (Whitechapel), 1931-5; Labour MP (Leicester), 1945-70; president, Zionist Federation; president, Board of Deputies, 1955-64; knighted, 1965; created life peer, 1970.

Jessel, Sir George (1824-83): called to bar, 1847; Queen's Counsel, 1865; Liberal MP, 1868-73; solicitor-general, 1871-3; Master of the Rolls, 1873-83; member of council, Jews' College, 1855-63, whose constitution he drafted; vice-president, Anglo-Jewish Association.

Joseph, Nathan Solomon (1834-1909): architect, for Guinness and Iveagh Trusts, Four Per Cent Industrial Dwellings (all providing housing for poor) and of Central and Bayswater Synagogues; chairman of executive, Russo-Jewish Committee and conjoint committee of Russo-Jewish Committee and Board of Guardians, 1893-1909; chairman, Visiting Committee, Board of Guardians, 1895-1900 and of Sanitary Committee, 1892-1904; joint honorary secretary, Jews' College, 1861-9; chairman, Visitation Committee, United Synagogue; author of many tracts on

Jewish religion and of *Religion Natural and Revealed*; a founder of Jewish Religious Union.

Landau, Hermann (1849-1921): born Constantinov, Poland; settled, England, 1864; originally schoolmaster and Hebrew teacher, then stockbroker, specializing in Western Australian mines; founder, Jews 'Temporary Shelter', 1885; vice-president, Federation of Synagogues; founder and president, Talmud Torah Trust, 1907; OBE (work for Belgian Refugees in First World War).

Laski, Harold Joseph (1893-1950): British socialist and political theorist; lecturer in political science at McGill, 1914-16 and Harvard Universities, 1916-20; lecturer, London School of Economics, 1920-6; professor of political science, 1926-50; member of government committees and from 1936 of National Executive of Labour Party (chairman, 1945); author of many works on political science.

Laski, Neville Jonas (1890-1969): British lawyer and Anglo-Jewish leader; successively recorder of Burnley, judge of appeal for the Isle of Man and recorder and judge of the Crown Court in Liverpool; servied in First World War as officer in Lancashire Fusiliers; president of Board of Deputies, 1933-9; as son-in-law of Haham Gaster, active in Spanish and Portuguese Jews' community.

Lewis, Harry S. (1863-1940): resident, Toynbee Hall (1889-1909); Stepney borough councillor, 1900-6; honorary secretary, Sanitary Committee, Board of Guardians, 1905-9; associated with Jewish Religious Union, 1903-8 and minister, Manchester Reform Synagogue; went to America and became teacher and chaplain at Jewish Institute of Religion, New York; joint author, *The Jew in London*, 1900.

Liebermann, Aaron Samuel (1845-80): born Lunna, Lithuania; secretary of community and teacher, Suwalk; member of revolutionary group, Vilna, 1872-5; Berlin, then London, 1875-6; Vienna, 1877-9, where he published *Ha-Emet* and contributed to Hebrew and German press; expelled to Germany, 1879 and came to London, 1879-80; to New York, where he committed suicide, 1880.

Loewe, Louis (1809-88): born Zülz, Silesia; after study at Yeshivot and Berlin University, oriental secretary to Duke of Sussex, 1839; after travel in Near East, accompanied Montefiore to Damascus, 1840 and on nine subsequent journeys; principal, Jews' College and of Montefiore College, Ramsgate; wrote on origins of Egyptian, a Circassian dictionary and Nubian grammar.

Löwy, Albert (1816-1908): born Aussee, Moravia; after study in Vienna, became a reform minister in London under D.W. Marks until 1892; founder and secretary of Anglo-Jewish Association, 1871-89; catalogued Samaritan manuscripts in collection of Earl of Crawford and Balcarres, and the City of London Library's Hebraica and Judaica.

Magnus, Sir Philip, Bt (1842-1933): minister of reform synagogue, 1866-80; director of City and Guilds Institute, pioneer of technical education and MP for University of London, 1906-22; chairman of Council, Reform Synagogue, vice-president, Board of Deputies and Anglo-Jewish Association.

Marks, David Woolf (1811-1909): assistant reader, Western Synagogue and in Liverpool; professor of belles-lettres, Wigan College, Liverpool; minister of reform synagogue, London, 1840, where he remained for over sixty years; professor of Hebrew, University College London, 1848–98.

Marks, Simon, 1st Baron Marks of Broughton (1888–1964): chairman of board, Marks and Spencer, 1917–64; secretary, Zionist delegation to Versailles Peace Conference, 1919; chairman, Keren Hayesod Committee; vice-president, Zionist Federation; member, Zionist Executive; president, Joint Palestine Appeal; knighted, 1944; created peer, 1961.

Melchett, 1st Lord. See *Mond.*

Melchett, Henry Mond, 2nd Baron (1898–1949): MP, 1923–4, 1929–30; succeeded father as chairman, Jewish Agency council; president, World Maccabi Union; member, Joint Foreign Committee.

Meldola, Raphael (1849–1915): chemist and naturalist; grandson of Haham Meldola; professor of chemistry, Finsbury Technical College, 1885–1915; discoverer of dyestuffs (Meldola's blue and first alkali green); president, Chemical Society and Institute of Chemistry; FRS (vice-president of Royal Society); president, Maccabeans.

Mocatta, Frederick David (1828–1905): partner in Mocatta and Goldsmid, bullion brokers; vice-president, Charity Organization Society; vice-president, Board of Guardians; president, Home for Aged Jews; vice-president, Anglo-Jewish Association; president, Anglo-Jewish Historical Exhibition, 1887; traveller, patron of learning and author of *The Jews and Inquisition* and *Jews at the Present Time*; bequeathed his library to University College London and Jewish Historical Society.

Mond, Sir Alfred, 1st Baron Melchett (1868–1930): British industrialist and politician; younger son of Ludwig Mond, founder of Brunner Mond chemical firm; chairman, Brunner Mond and Mond Nickel companies; responsible for expansion of Brunner Mond, which, after merger with other companies, became Imperial Chemical Industries (1926) of which he became first chairman; Liberal MP, 1906–28; First Commissioner of Works, 1916–21; Minister of Health, 1921–2; joined Conservatives, 1928; after 1917 became committed Zionist and chairman of enlarged Jewish Agency Council, 1929–30; created peer, 1928; FRS, 1930.

Montagu, Hon. (later Rt. Hon.) Edwin Samuel (1879–1924): Liberal MP (1906–22); parliamentary under-secretary, India Office, 1910–14; financial secretary, Treasury, 1914–15, 1915–16; chancellor, Duchy of Lancaster, 1915, 1916; Minister of Munitions, 1916; resigned with fall of Asquith but rejoined Lloyd George government as Secretary of State for India, 1917–22; married Venetia Stanley, daughter of Lord Sheffield, with Jewish rites after her conversion to Judaism, 1915.

Montagu, Sir Samuel, Bt, 1st Baron Swaythling (1832–1911): born Liverpool, son of Louis Samuel; married sister of Lionel Louis Cohen; founded Samuel Montagu & Co., foreign exchange bankers; Liberal MP for Whitechapel, 1885–1900; bimetalist and member of Gold and Silver Commission, 1887–90 and president, Decimal Association; founder and acting-president, Federation of Synagogues; member of Board of Guardians, 1865–83 and chairman of Loan Committee, 1873–82; president, Shechita Board; warden, New West End Synagogue, created baron, 1902.

Montefiore, Claude Joseph Goldsmid (1858–1938): pupil of Jowett at Balliol College, Oxford, then at Berlin Hochschule für Wissenschaft des Judenthums, and under Solomon Schechter, whom he brought to England as tutor; founder and editor, *Jewish Quarterly Review*, 1888–1908; founder, Jewish Religious Union, 1902 and Liberal Jewish Synagogue, 1911; president, World Union for Progressive Judaism, 1926–38; president, Anglo-Jewish Association, 1895–1921, and joint chairman, Joint Foreign Committee to 1917; president Jewish Historical Society, 1899–1900; author of many theological works, including *The Synoptic Gospels*; Hibbert Lecturer, 1892.

Montefiore, Leonard Nathaniel Goldsmid (1889–1961): president, Anglo-Jewish Association, 1926–39; member of council, later chairman, Jewish Colonization Association; OBE.

Montefiore, Sir Moses, Bt (1784–1885): born Leghorn, during visit by parents Moses Vita and Esther Racah; stockbroker; director of Alliance Assurance, Provincial Bank of Ireland, Imperial Continental Gas; married Judith, daughter of Levi Barent Cohen, 1812 and thus brother-in-law of Nathan Mayer Rothschild; sheriff of London, 1837 and knighted; created baronet, 1846; High Sheriff, Kent, 1843–4; DL; FRS.

Neubauer, Adolf (1831–1907): born Hungary; after reporting on Karaite mss in St Petersburg and writing *La Géographie du Talmud*, joined Bodleian Library, where he became sub-librarian and published catalogue of Hebrew mss, 1886; reader in rabbinic Hebrew, Oxford, 1884–1900.

Neumegen, Leopold (1787–1875): born Posen; came to England c.1816; took over Highgate Jewish Academy, 1821; moved it to Kew, 1842.

Phillips, Sir Benjamin Samuel (1811–89): common councilman, City of London, 1846; sheriff, 1859; alderman, 1857–88; Lord Mayor of London, 1865; life member of council of United Synagogue, 1880; member of Board of Deputies for thirty years; vice-president, Anglo-Jewish Association; father of Sir George Faudel-Phillips, also Lord Mayor.

Pirbright, Lord. See *Worms Baron Henry de*.

Reading. See *Isaacs*.

Rothschild, Sir Anthony de, Bt (1810–76): second son of Nathan Mayer Rothschild; banker in family firm and country gentleman; president, Jews' Free School; president, United Synagogue, 1870–6; created baronet, 1846; Austrian baron and consul-general.

Rothschild, Leopold de (1845–1917): third son of Baron Lionel and brother of 1st Lord; partner in N.M. Rothschild and Sons; won Derby, 1904; president Jews' Free School and United Synagogue, 1915–17; treasurer, Board of Guardians, 1879–1917; vice-president, Anglo-Jewish Association, Board of Deputies and Jews' Temporary Shelter; CVO.

Rothschild, Baron Lionel de (1806–79): eldest son of Nathan Mayer Rothschild; studied Goettingen; became head of firm, 1836; provided funds for Irish Famine Loan, 1847, Crimean War, 1854, purchase of Suez Canal shares, etc.; president,

Great Synagogue; elected MP for City of London from 1847 until finally admitted, 1858; MP, City of London, 1858-74.

Rothschild, Lionel Nathan de (1882-1942): son of Lepold and nephew of 1st Lord and cousin of 2nd Lord Rothschild; president, United Synagogue, 1918-42; MP, 1910-23.

Rothschild, Lionel Walter, 2nd Baron (1869-1937): MP, 1899-1910; succeeded to peerage, 1915; honorary president, English Zionist Federation from 1917; distinguished naturalist with private zoo.

Rothschild, Sir Nathaniel Meyer, Bt, 1st Baron Rothschild (1840-1915): partner, N.M. Rothschild and Sons; son of Baron Lionel Nathan de Rothschild; succeeded to baronetcy of uncle, Sir Anthony de Rothschild, 1879; MP, Aylesbury, 1865-85; created peer, 1885; lord-lieutenant, Buckinghamshire, 1889-1915; privy councillor, GCVO, 1902; director of bank of England; member of Royal Commission on Alien Immigration, 1902-3; president, United synagogue, 1879-1915.

Salomons, Sir David, Bt (1797-1873): a founder of London and Westminster Bank, 1832; Lloyds underwriter, 1834; admitted to Coopers' Company and City of London livery, 1831; sheriff of London and Middlesex, 1835; high sheriff of Kent, 1839-40; elected City of London alderman, 1835, 1844, 1847 but not admitted till 1847; Lord Mayor of London, 1855; elected MP for Greenwich from 1851 but unable to take seat until 1859; created baronet, 1869; president, Board of Deputies, 1838-40, 1846.

Samuel, Herbert Louis, 1st Viscount (1870-1963): Liberal MP, Cleveland, 1902-18, Darwen, 1929-35; parliamentary under-secretary, Home Office, 1905-9; chancellor, Duchy of Lancaster, 1909-10 and 1915-16; postmaster-general, 1910-14 and 1915-16; president, Local Government Board, 1914-15; Home Secretary, 1916 1931-2; high commissioner, Palestine, 1920-5; created GBE, 1920 GCB, 1926 and viscount 1932; OM, 1958; president, British Institute of Philosophy and author of works on philosophy.

Samuel, Sir Marcus, 1st Viscount Bearsted (1853-1927): entered father's ornamental shell business; formed partnership with brother, Sam (1855-1934), trading in Far East and as banker in London to Japanese government; entered oil trade, 1892; founded Shell Transport and Trading Company, 1897; merged with Royal Dutch Petroleum Company, 1907; Lord Mayor of London, 1902-3; created baron, 1921, viscount, 1925; financed Bearsted (Jewish maternity) hospital; benefactor of Jewish and non-Jewish charities.

Samuel, Sir Stuart Montagu, Bt (1856-1926): brother of 1st Viscount; Liberal MP, Whitechapel, 1900-16; president of Deputies, 1917-22.

Schechter, Solomon (1847-1915): born Focsani, Rumania; studied at Berlin Hochschule where he met C.G. Montefiore, who brought him to England as tutor, 1882; lecturer in Talmud, 1890; reader in rabbinis, 1892, Cambridge; professor of Hebrew, University College London, 1899; won fame for work on Cairo Genizah fragments; president, Jewish Theological Seminary, 1901; a founder of United Synagogue of America, 1913; works include *Studies in Judaism* (3 vols, 1896-1924).

Schiff, Otto Moritz (c.1874-1952): banker and Jewish communal leader; born Frankfurt, nephew of banker Jacob H. Schiff; after coming to England, took up charitable work under influence of Hermann Landau, whom he succeeded as president of the Jews' Temporary Shelter, 1922–48; appointed OBE for work for 12,000 Belgian refugees in First World War; treasurer, Jews' College; overseer of poor, United Synagogue; chairman, Jewish Ecclesiastical Advisory Committee (on admission of rabbis and ministers from abroad); appointed CBE for work for refugees after 1933.

Schiller-Szinessy, Solomon (1820–90): born Alt-Often, Hungary; Ph.D., Jena, and rabbinate; assistant professor, Lutheran College, Eperles, Hungary; fought in 1848 Hungarian rising but escaped to Ireland; minister of Manchester community subsequently of reform congregation, taught at Cambridge from 1863, where he became reader in rabbinics; catalogued Hebrew mss in Cambridge University Library, 1876.

Sieff, Israel Moses, Baron (1889–1972): born Manchester; associated with brothers-in-law Simon Marks and Harry Sacher in help to Weizmann; vice-chairman and joint managing director, later president, Marks and Spencer; founder of Political and Economic Planning (PEP); vice-chairman, Royal Archaeological Institute; hon. president, Zionist Federation of Great Britain; chairman, Joint Palestine Appeal; created life peer, 1966.

Simon, Sir John (1818–97): born Jamaica (on mother's side descended from Orobio de Castro family); graduated London, 1841; first Jew to practise at common law bar; first Jew to sit as English judge; one of last serjeants-at-law, 1864; QC, 1868; MP 1868–88; regarded as 'member for Jewry' (*JE* XI, 369); knighted, 1886; organized Mansion House protest meeting, 1882; a founder of Anglo-Jewish Association, 1871; associated with reform Synagogue from 1842.

Singer, Simeon (1848–1906): headmaster, Jews' College School, then minister, Borough (south London) Synagogue; minister, New West End Synagogue, 1879–1906 obtained rabbinical diploma, 1890; editor and translator, Authorized Daily Prayerbook, 1890; described as 'the ideal Anglo-Jewish minister'.

Solomon, Henry Naphtali (1796–1881): started school in Queen Square, then Hammersmith, finally Edmonton, 1836.

Stern, Sidney. See *Wandsworth*.

Swaythling, 1st Lord. See *Montagu, Sir Samuel*.

Swaythling, Louis Samuel Montagu, 2nd Baron (1869–1927): president, Federation of Synagogues, 1911–25; an anti-Zionist, he married the daughter of Col. Albert E.W. Goldsmid.

Sylvester, James Joseph (1814–97): mathematician; FRS, 1839; second wrangler, Cambridge, 1837, but as Jew unable to take degree; professor, University of Virginia, 1841; professor, Royal Military Academy, Woolwhich, 1855–70, then at Johns Hopkins, 1877–83, Oxford, 1883; Royal Society Sylvester Medal named for him.

Waley, Jacob (1818–73): barrister; professor of political economy, University College London, 1853–65; expert on conveyancing; a founder of United Synagogue; first president, Anglo-Jewish Association, 1871; president, Jews' Hospital and Orphan Asylum.

Wandsworth, Sidney, Stern, Baron (1845-1912): son of David de Stern (Portuguese) viscount; senior partner, Stern Brothers, bankers; MP, Stowmarket, 1891-5; created peer, 1895; hon. colonel, 4th Volunteer Battalion, East Surrey Regiment; gave estate to Home for Aged Jews (Nightingale House).

Weizmann, Chaim (1874-1952): born Motol, near Pinsk; studied in Germany, 1892-8; lecturer in chemistry, Geneva, 1901-6; came to England, 1906; lecturer, then reader, in biochemistry, Manchester University from 1907; developed new process for making acetone in First World War; active in Zionist movement from 1898; chairman, Zionist Federation and obtained Balfour Declaration, 1917; president, World Zionist Organization, 1920-30, 1935-46; president, State of Israel, 1949-52.

Wolf, Lucien (1857-1930): journalist from 1874; editor, *Jewish World*, 1905-8; foreign editor, *Daily Graphic*, 1890-1914; editor, *Darkest Russia*, 1912-14; secretary, Conjoint Foreign Committee; 1915-17 and Joint Foreign Committee, from 1917 and attended Versailles Peace Conference; organizer of Anglo-Jewish Historical Exhibition, 1887; founder and frequent president, Jewish Historical Society; prolific writer on Anglo-Jewish history, on the Marranos and anti-Seminitism; biographer of Lord Ripon, 1921.

Worms, Baron Henry de, 1st Baron Pirbright (1840-1903): in family retailing business; Conservative MP, 1880-95; parliamentary secretary, Board of Trade, 1885-8; under-secretary of state, Colonies, 1888-1892; created peer, 1895; vice-president, United synagogue, 1880-2; president, Anglo-Jewish Association, 1872-86, when forced to resign after attending his daughter's wedding in church; FRS.

Zangwill, Israel (1864-1926): novelist and dramatist; began as teacher at Jews' Free School; *Children of the Ghetto*, 1892; *King of Schnorrers*, 1894; *The Melting Pot*, 1909; Zionist until 1905, when he founded Jewish Territorial Organization.

Zedner, Joseph (1804-71): born Glogau, Silesia; taught and tutored in Germany; librarian, Hebrew department, British Museum, 1846-69; catalogue of Hebrew books in British Museum library published, 1867.

Epilogue

If it was a poignant experience for Vivian Lipman to find his wife's corrections on the early chapters of his manuscript it was even more so for me to see his own handwritten emendments all the way through this manuscript. His death on 10th March 1990 came just before the arrival in the Leicester University Press Offices of the page proofs of what has now become his last completed book. I was invited to see it through its last stages, and the process has proved to be very humbling. It may seem an easy cliché to describe the book as being based upon a lifetime of research, but that is precisely what it has proved itself to be. The references and footnotes show a lifetime's labour in bringing together thoughts and facts, all carefully filed and indexed in what must always have been intended by him for the writing of the definitive history of modern Anglo-Jewry. But at the same time the original typescript shows how closely he had paid attention to lectures he had just heard or books and articles he had just read, and those who knew him will remember the notebooks in which he avidly took down points brought up in lectures and discussions: his text shows clearly how many of these very recent references he had already absorbed.

It is the more impressive because the bulk of his working career had been as a civil servant, and in the course of his thirty-one years he had been deeply involved in the conservation of historic towns and buildings. His historic writings had to fit into these other activities, but both in those years and in the years after his retirement he created a body of writing within the field of Anglo-Jewish historiography which will remain unequalled for years to come. The first of these works had been the pioneering *Social History of the Jews in England, 1850–1950*, published in 1954, and it is perhaps fitting that in this last work he returned to the same theme. But in doing so he illustrated very clearly how far he himself had carried forward the ways in which these years should be understood and interpreted.

Aubrey Newman

Index